Business as Usual

BUSINESS AS USUAL

The Germans and Their Law, 1943 to 1948

Benjamin Lahusen

Translated by Randi Goring

berghahn
NEW YORK • OXFORD
www.berghahnbooks.com

First published in 2026 by
Berghahn Books
www.berghahnbooks.com

Translated from German. Published under the title:
'Der Dienstbetrieb ist nicht gestört': Die Deutschen und ihre Justiz, 1943–1948.
C. H. Beck, 2022

Library of Congress Cataloging-in-Publication Data

Names: Lahusen, Benjamin author | Goring, Randi translator
Title: Business as usual : the Germans and their law, 1943 to 1948 / Benjamin Lahusen ; Translated by Randi Goring.
Other titles: 'Dienstbetrieb ist nicht gestört' : Die Deutschen und ihre Justiz, 1943–1948 English
Description: First edition. | New York : Berghahn Books, 2026. | Includes bibliographical references and index.
Identifiers: LCCN 2026009635 (print) | LCCN 2026009636 (ebook) | ISBN 9781836956266 hardback | ISBN 9781836956297 epub | ISBN 9781836956303 adobe pdf
Subjects: LCSH: Courts--Germany--History--20th century | Justice, Administration of--Germany--History--20th century | National socialism and justice | Germany--History--1933-1945 | Germany--History--1945-1955
Classification: LCC KK595 .L3413 2026 (print) | LCC KK595 (ebook)
LC record available at https://lccn.loc.gov/2026009635
LC ebook record available at https://lccn.loc.gov/2026009636

British Library Cataloguing in Publication Data
A catalogue record for this book is available from the British Library

EU GPSR Authorized Representative
LOGOS EUROPE, 9 rue Nicolas Poussin, 17000, LA ROCHELLE, France
Email: Contact@logoseurope.eu

ISBN 978-1-83695-626-6 hardback
ISBN 978-1-83695-629-7 epub
ISBN 978-1-83695-630-3 web pdf

https://doi.org/10.3167/9781836956266

CONTENTS

PREFACE

This book is about the self-deception of normality. It began with the question of why the German justice system functioned in 1945 and was also vividly used. The proceedings I found in the archives were disturbing—neighbors stubbornly suing each other for the punctual cleaning of stairwells seemed incompatible with the cruel reality of the rest of the world. After more than ten years of research, I have come to the conclusion that the contradiction I initially perceived is not actually a contradiction at all. Violence needs the ordinary; the state of emergency depends on the normal state. Evil can be banal, but the banal can also be evil. That is what this book is about.

When I began my work on it in 2009, the world was different than it is today. The temptation to flee to small islands of normality and decouple them from the rest of the world is now even greater than it was then—the West is collapsing, war is raging again in Europe, and even established democracies are sliding into authoritarianism and corruption. The world is in turmoil. If my book helps to understand that insisting on a supposed normality does not solve problems but usually perpetuates them, then it will have achieved much more than I originally hoped for.

The German edition of this study was published in 2022. It was made possible by a generous grant from the Volkswagen Foundation. Of the many people who supported me during my work, I would like to mention Diethelm Kaiser, Miriam Lahusen, Regina Ogorek, and Dieter Simon, who all encouraged and affirmed me in different but ultimately decisive ways. When putting my thoughts into a book, Rebekka Göpfert (Agentur Göpfert) and Ulrich Nolte (C. H. Beck) were of great help.

For the English version, I tried to avoid overly detailed descriptions of German law and German bureaucracy or, where necessary, to provide explanations. In this respect, too, I was able to rely on the support of many kind readers. I would like to thank Stephanie Ireland and Bridget Atkin from Berghahn Books for their conceptual and technical support. Robin

Lickefett (Frankfurt/Oder) provided me with valuable assistance with the literature and footnotes. I am indebted to Nike Haerdle and Niklas Schäufele for the index. Without Benjamin Ziemann (Sheffield), I would not have dared to undertake the project of an English-language edition. Randi Goring (Paris/New York) has translated the text with the empathy and sensitivity of a true friend; it was a pleasure of sharing yet another part of the journey.

Berlin, November 2025

Introduction

Paper World

It starts with paper. Its surface is rough and porous, the color a dirty beige. The smell emanating from the bundles situates them somewhere in the basement of history. The edges are frayed, the folds cracked, the covers barely managing to contain the folders' inner contents. The files unabashedly abide in the past. They have had their time: they have passed through hands and over desks, circulated among authorities, been submitted and resubmitted, requested, read, considered and implemented, until their normative glow first dimmed by the passage of time finally completely extinguished. A curt "Filed" sealed their end. Measured against its original purpose, the paper was now useless; it remained on site for a decent period of time, but at some point, it was inevitably handed over to the official depository for old paper: the archive. There it met with new signs of wear (signatures, stamps, stickers), was re-sorted (in bundles, drawers, crates), and normatively reconfigured (archival value, data protection, personal rights), before the next utilization cycle could start again. The paper now describes the time in which it was once itself described, history bubbles out of the files. The files compress time: time of creation, time of use, time of remembrance, time of history, a papery thicket of time that moves effortlessly between today and yesterday and easily leads astray any view to the past. It begins with paper. But when?

Justice in Total War

On 26 August 1944, the Reich Ministry of Justice relayed to the higher regional courts a communication entitled "Lifestyle in Total War," a collection of thoughts from Joseph Goebbels, the fanatic Propaganda Minster who had just received new powers to organize the "Total War Effort." The "style of public life," Goebbels complained, still had "in some places a strongly peacetime character"; theater performances tried to shine through "the most magnificent staging possible," as did exhibitions "through the refreshments served at their opening." This had to come to an end. In the future, all forms of socializing—receptions, inaugurations, festivals, music festivals, family celebrations—not directly related to the war effort were to be avoided. From now on, cultivating a visibly abstinent lifestyle would be an honor and demonstrate to foreign countries that Germany could not be expected to compromise.[1] The needs of the war became the guiding principle for all of life. With consequences at all levels: a few days later, Reich Justice Minister Otto Thierack announced, with immediate effect, that he would refrain from sending "all kinds of congratulatory letters" and "only sign letters of condolence to relatives of the fallen."[2] The following week, the consequences came for the toilets, which were also expected to provide resources for the war; it was angrily noted that timed flushers were still being used on a regular basis, causing water consumption that was "objectively unjustified."[3]

Then it was the turn of the court staff themselves. To minimize the impact on the workforce, in the late summer of 1944 the courts' hours of operations were increased to 60 hours a week including Sundays,[4] which, however, had to be reversed the following winter due to the lack of heating and electricity.[5] On 1 November, the accountants at the Ministry noted that, percentage-wise, the judiciary now had more casualties than in the First World War.[6] In Danzig, the guillotine and the gallows were packed in crates to keep them safe in view of the expected Soviet offensive,[7] and in Stettin, the judicial authorities received a Christmas card at the end of 1944 with an encouraging quote from the war metaphysician Heinrich von Treitschke: "Therein lies the majesty of war, that the small man disappears completely before the great thought of the state; the sacrifice of one's compatriots (*Volksgenossen*) for each other is nowhere so glorious."[8]

State, *Volk*, sacrifice, glory: the judiciary was happy to make a contribution to these words of historical gravitas. The judiciary was well prepared for the war. As early as 1937, the Ministry had begun preparations in strict confidence, gratefully drawing on the wealth of experience from the First World War. At the beginning of the war, no fewer than 31 laws and ordinances were in place to transform the judiciary for its wartime operations. Two considerations were decisive. Firstly, to the greatest extent possible, the administration of justice should not get in the way of the war. Personnel had to be saved for the front, and those who were deployed were to receive comprehensive legal protection against legal objections at home. On the other hand, the civilian population should not have to do without legal services. The law was not allowed to disrupt the war, but, conversely, the war was not allowed to disrupt the law excessively. Justus Wilhelm Hedemann, the grand seigneur of National Socialist legal renewal, issued the shibboleth that a state could not renounce its legal system "even in the most bitter and consummate war"; it was known from the last war that "civil legal life continues unabated despite the most severe war events," which is why the courts of civil and criminal jurisdictions, i.e., the ordinary courts, "must remain the palladium of the administration of justice in civil life."[9]

And so they remained. A first major wave of closures was announced in February 1943 after the defeat at Stalingrad, but their implementation caused so many concerns that of the 2,000 or so local courts, in the end only 98 were shut down.[10] Shortly afterwards, an order was issued to postpone all legal disputes that were "not war urgent."[11] This measure also had no major impact. Nobody knew what "war urgent" meant, especially with regard to civil proceedings. The judiciary therefore translated "war urgency" as "procedural efficiency" and used this as an instrument to emphasize its own importance for the home front and at the same time control the daily workload. Complex proceedings were postponed—affecting 2–4 percent of all cases received—while the rest continued as before.[12]

Of course, this "rest" was still not comparable to the workload in peacetime. The political, economic, and ideological conditions of the war greatly changed the judicial statistics at all levels. The last call-ups to the *Volkssturm* (the German territorial army) reduced the workforce to around 30 percent of what it had been in 1939, and of the almost 14,000 judgeships, only a good 6,000 remained occupied in 1944.[13] There were also fewer and fewer trials. In criminal law, more and more responsibilities were initially transferred to the *Sondergerichte* or "special courts" (as opposed to ordinary courts); attempts at streamlining this process dated from 1943. Ordinary crime was to be dealt with through administrative channels wherever possible or brought before the ordinary courts. The criminal justice system had therefore declined noticeably but was still kept busy. In civil law, on the other hand, there had been deeper cuts. Property disputes fell by around three quarters; a formal explosion of divorces and child support cases and the continued existence of tenancy disputes only partially compensated for the decline.

In the fall of 1944, the traditional court system faced a further blow when Goebbels wanted to remove the final peacetime veneer from public life. The legal process was abolished in principle on 27 September. The higher regional courts were to disappear completely and the *Reichsgericht* ("Supreme Court of the Reich") to handle only a few meager residual responsibilities; the timing: six weeks. But even this radical cost-cutting measure came to a halt halfway through. The timeline that was set for the courts to wind up their affairs had to be extended several times and was finally scrapped at the end of the war.[14] Even Goebbels had to be instructed that abolishing the judiciary would jeopardize the preservation of state order, give the population "a feeling of lawlessness," and generally trigger "chaotic conditions."[15]

And then there was legal obstinacy. It had retained its traditional stubbornness even during the total war. In November 1944, the judges were informed in a detailed circular that in the future the cumbersome calculation of court costs according to the value in dispute and the scale of fees was to be replaced by a "free estimate" by the judge.[16] Such an accusation drove the judiciary into resistance. The Nordhausen Regional Court President brought out the last guns of dogmatic differentiation in order to demonstrate the full extent of the legislative failure: if the defendant loses and is ordered to reimburse the opposing party's lawyer's fees and advances, but the latter is less than the actual costs, then the plaintiff must obtain a title against the defendant for these actual costs. This is only possible through a cost assessment procedure, which in this case—unlike in the past—can also be carried out without an explicit application. In the Nordhausen district, the report summarized, the new costs law is therefore rejected without exception; it is "unreasonable and outdated."[17]

Who could disagree? The accusation of failing to meet the demands of the time referred to what state propaganda described as the "vital hour of fate for our people."[18] In September 1944, the Red Army was on the borders of East Prussia, the population was working on the defensive walls and assembling themselves for the *Volkssturm*, and in the west, US troops were crossing the Reich border for the first time. The regulation of court fees was really not suited to making a measurable contribution in this crisis, regardless of whether it was with or without a free estimate. Nevertheless, it was difficult to conceal the fact that the judiciary, in their glorious sacrifice for State and People, not only maintained the usual biotopes of legal know-it-allism, but also further cultivated their already existing tendency to agnosia. The jurists clung to the few problems they could still solve themselves. In November 1944, the Aachen Local Court President, who had already lost his judicial district by this time and was therefore sitting in Düren, detailed regulations on how to prepare now for future relocations. By the time his ingenious plan reached his superiors in Berlin, the new office in Düren had also been destroyed by a bombing raid, which is why the Reich Ministry of Justice limited itself to the terse remark: "Overtaken by developments."[19]

One administered one's own downfall, objectively, soberly, unrealistically. The deeper the Allies advanced into the interior of the country, the greater the void in the German justice system became. At the end of 1944, the Zweibrücken Higher Regional Court President had to admit to the Reich Ministry of Justice "that the vast majority of the Lorraine courts are no longer accessible to me."[20] On 5 February 1945, the Breslau Higher Regional Court President went on record with the sheer insanity that the situation in his district could "currently be regarded as substantially relaxed," an almost schizoid assertion—two regional courts were already occupied by the Red Army, and the Higher Regional Court itself had left Breslau due to an acute enemy threat.[21] The chain of command had to take ever more tortuous byways to pave a path for service through the shrinking Reich. On 10 April 1945, the Rostock General Prosecutor, who had been residing in Schwerin for three years following his office's destruction, inquired about the fate of his colleagues at the Reich Ministry of Justice, which itself was sitting in Berlin with only a tiny emergency staff. He was informed by telephone that "for the authorities of the Higher Regional Courts of Cologne, Düsseldorf, Frankfurt/M., Darmstadt, Zweibrücken, and Kassel, neither alternative offices nor administrative staff had been set up";[22] Königsberg, Danzig, Breslau, Stettin, and Kattowitz were already lost anyway. German law had lost its area of application. A good week later, the *Reichsgericht* disappeared with the occupation of Leipzig by US troops, and shortly afterwards dissolved the last remnants of the Ministry. With the capitulation of the German Reich, the administration of justice had come to an end. The law was suspended.

Justitium: A Brief Digression on the Emergence of Legal Theology

At the very back of the legal cabinet of curiosities, we can attribute a legal consequence to this peculiar case. The law stands still—*ius stat*, murmurs the educated jurist, which is why the suspension of law is also called "*Justitium*," a peculiar remnant from antiquity, originating somewhere in the depths of the Roman Republic, where all pending court hearings were interrupted when the troops had to be mustered.[23] It soon became a general symbol for major events in public life. Wherever a temple was to be inaugurated, an imperial descendant was to be admired, or the death of a ruler was to be mourned, a *Justitium* could be proclaimed, and the repertoire of conceivable measures correspondingly varied: closure of the treasury, exchange offices, markets and stores, suspension of auctions, senate meetings, and court hearings, supplemented by, depending on the occasion, the renunciation of jewelry, festive garments, marriages, or offerings. The *Justitium* paralyzed public life in an almost proverbial sense; Livius speaks of an "*iustitio simile otium*," a calm similar to the *Justitium*.[24]

The modern era rediscovered the *Justitium* in a more technical sense. "*Tempore hostilitatis non currit praescriptio*" belonged to the canon law since the twelfth century,[25] the statute of limitations does not apply in the event of a force majeure. This idea appeared in secular legislation from the early modern period, for example in the Prussian Land Law of 1620, which stipulated that the statute of limitations could be interrupted in the event of war, plague, flood or "other emergencies."[26] Half a century later, the first expressly so-called *Justitium* of modern times was issued. In 1671, the Great Elector of Brandenburg retroactively imposed a *Justitium* for the years 1626 to 1648 so that "the passage of these years should not be detrimental to anyone's rights."[27] The order of the law was not to be disturbed by the disorder of the world. The *Justitium* ultimately made it possible to operationalize every state of emergency in legal terms—by simply declaring it irrelevant when nothing else worked.

This is a very typical process for modern law. As soon as the functioning of the law came under threat, more law was simply enacted. In 1780, the *Justitium* officially found its way into the new Prussian Code of Procedure, was subsequently adopted in all reforms, and finally in 1877 ended up in the Code of Civil Procedure for the German Reich.[28] The government draft was succinctly worded: "Should, as the consequence of war or another event, the court cease its activities, the proceedings shall be interrupted for the duration of this situation." The proposal contained no justification, was adopted without debate in both the first and second readings and, apart from spelling adjustments, has not been amended once since.[29] No big words: the suspension of the law is self-evident.

What can you say to that? If the courts no longer work, then they no longer work. This carefree tautology has hardly left a trace beyond its own tracks. Even 200 years of dedicated military history has only produced a handful of footnotes.[30] But for all its pointlessness, the regulation certainly had a deeper meaning. With the suspension of legal services, the law was given an instrument to legally avert the danger of lawlessness, a kind of legal threshold that decides between the existence and non-existence of law—and pretends that this question also is a question of law. An encapsulated myth remained in the *Justitium*, which carried within it the memory of a milestone in legal phylogeny, the transition to the omnipresence of law. In the middle of the nineteenth century, Philipp Eduard Huschke, a biblically faithful Romanist, cloaked this tireless progression of law in particularly devotional imagery: "The expression *iustitium* itself, compared with for example *solstitium*, also apparently expresses the idea that the *iuris dictio* itself runs through all the working days like the sun in the sky."[31]

The very suspension of law is linked to an almost messianic expectation of salvation. In the *Justitium*, the law anticipates itself. At some point things will move on; and if then completely different than before, then it is still normal. Law distributes the grace of its normativity to all places and at all times. This legal theology is not a question of faith. Legal reality rests on an opulently institutionalized compendium of rules that can, if necessary, authenticate itself in its enforcement. In law, nothing comes from nothing. The normativity of programs compels us to seek points of reference in our own system's history—laws, regulations, precedents, academic authorities—even in radical new beginnings. Anyone who doubts the law therefore has access to a large number of law journals, libraries and law firms; if this is not enough to boost one's fundamental trust in the law, then the marshal threatens and, for persistent sinners, prison. The law is always there, whether one likes it or not. And so it is only logical that in the legal literature of the twentieth century, unclouded by any irony, the disconcerting assessment prevailed that "a purely actual obstruction of the court"—whatever that may be in contrast to war or flooding—would no more lead to a suspension of law than the "death of all judges."[32] This idea was introduced by Adolf Baumbach's standard commentary, in the eleventh edition of 1936. If the judges are alive, the law proceeds as usual; once they are dead, so too. And then? "The determination of a suspension of law," Baumbach continues with astonishing ease, "is for the judge to decide."[33] Somewhere, someone will be found to replace the lethally incapacitated colleague: another judge, a new judge, an instant judge, a pseudo-judge who rises to the status of a normal judge through self-appointment. Whatever. A brief flicker in the engine room, and then the law works again as calmly and reliably as usual. Whether the law still exists is a question—of the law.

Interface 1945

The suspension of law in Germany at end of the Second World War, described by contemporaries as a "comical product of theorizing conceptual speculation"[34] and later stylized as a "legal disaster,"[35] was certainly not beyond reach of the legal imagination. Since the judiciary itself was supposed to decide whether it was still operational or not, even its non-existence remained dependent on its existence. This was also the case in 1945. The Allies closed all the courts under their control, committed the apparatus to democracy and the rule of law, denazified the staff, and eventually allowed the courts to continue operating, usually after a few weeks. They brought many new ideas with them. But no new paper. "We didn't even have paper, but started on the back of former NSDAP calendars," Werner Baerns, the second post-war president of the Düsseldorf Higher Regional

Court, later recalled.[36] The old waste became the basis for the new judicial administration.

Emergency paper provided the ingredients for legal work, thin and brittle, soaked with time; judgments, orders, decrees, court fee stamps, delivery certificates from the German *Reichspost*, all covered with the emblems of the defunct regime. After the occupation, they were crossed out, pasted over, cut out. "Crossing out the swastika emblem with pen strokes is not enough," the Stuttgart Ministry of Justice instructed its authorities—the forbidden symbol had to be completely obscured.[37] Until the end of the 1940s, lawyers' letterheads, often only thinly concealed, announced former membership of the *Nationalsozialistischer Rechtswahrerbund* ("National Socialist Association of Legal Professionals"). Even the courts occasionally required reminders. In 1949, the Berlin-Mitte Local Court complained that National Socialist emblems had recently been used on official letters and further noted: "This has offended recipients and given rise to misinterpretations."[38]

Misinterpretations: the new era was no longer the old. But it was not yet the new one either. Pinpointing its location in this in-between time was impossible. It was rarely even attempted, and when it was, it was well hidden somewhere in the logbooks of the bureaucratic machinery. In the diary for judicial administration matters of the regional court in Freiberg, Saxony, a last entry on 5 May 1945 documents the "occupation of offices by the Wehrmacht"; at the end of June it continues with the "startup of the judiciary" and the "report of members of the judiciary on leave for political reasons."[39] In between was a small, crooked double line—later reinforced by a sharply drawn red line—with which someone has illustrated the upheaval. At the Hanover Local Court, an unnamed court clerk drew a coy little red line in the criminal proceedings register, marking off the dates of 6 April 1945 (three cases of receiving stolen goods, punishable by between two and eight months in prison) from the first theft, which was sentenced on 13 June under the new system (fine: 50 Reichsmarks).[40] At the Plauen Regional Court, the clerk allowed himself a particularly striking ornament. He initially gave his line in the civil proceedings register a pithy title—"New entries since the occupation by the Allied troops"—then, in a second step, introduced new file numbers, which postponed the start of the ongoing proceedings until after the capitulation.[41]

Such an act of historical-political self-empowerment was, of course, an isolated case. Interventions in the statistical recording of annual business or in the numbering of files were otherwise not even considered. The judicial proceedings had emancipated themselves from current events; they followed a legal choreography that was not necessarily dictated by the dramas of world history. An inconspicuous line remained the boldest measure. In court, the mass murder, the destruction, the end of the war, the subsequent denazification and the new political framework were circumstances whose legal relevance had to be proven on a case-by-case basis. Just one example: on 27 March 1945, a lawyer responded to a lawsuit that had just been filed at the Stuttgart Regional Court, stating that he would "only be able to respond in some time in view of the circumstances and my involvement as a member of the *Volkssturm*." The next page in the file documents the plaintiff's lawyer's response dated 1 December 1945. The entire letter: "In the Kuhn/Müller case, the legal dispute could not be continued at the time due to enemy occupation. I hereby call again and request that a new trial date be set. I immediately request the defendant to submit the still outstanding defense."[42] In the logic of legal action, war and peace are, to borrow a phrase from Niklas Luhmann, a noise in the environment. "We lived in a fiction of the continued existence of the service," recalled a contemporary witness in retrospect.[43] Not even the validity of the business distribution plans was questioned but merely readjusted "for the remainder of the financial year."[44] The year 1945 was a temporal continuum, like all previous years.

Balance Sheet

This was long suppressed. Even decades after the end of the war, 8 May continued to be used as a caesura to mark an epochal transition from a National Socialist before to a forced democratization after. Things were bleak until 8 May, after which the arduous reconstruction began, with much more success in the West than in the East. In reference to military terminology, this turning point was called "zero hour." It has long been known that this "zero hour" never happened. Nevertheless, 8 May still exerts something of a long-range narrative effect.

Judicial history also readily uses this before- and after- lens.[45] Those who study National Socialism are looking for National Socialism, especially in the judiciary, and those who study the post-war period are looking for a fragile constitutional state, sustained by the continuity of National Socialist careers. The descriptions revolve around obedience, opportunism and rare examples of resistance, and extend to an almost comical cliometrics that claims to have calculated that in civil law, "0.58 percent of judgments ... were influenced by National Socialist legal thinking."[46] Routine legal work thus comes close to resistance; what function the remaining 99 percent had, whether judgments were also influenced in this sense after 1945 and, in general, why only the political should be political, remains unclear.

Anyone who argues in this manner marginalizes the role of the judiciary. The massive restrictions imposed by the National Socialist justice system must be taken into account; criminal law became increasingly brutalized, civil law lost procedural steps, and many issues could not be heard for official or informal reasons. But where the judiciary still had a say, its authority to make final, binding decisions on right and wrong was not seriously contested. Criticism of judgments were limited to a tiny fraction of the decisions rendered.[47] In July 1943, Reich Justice Minister Otto Thierack issued a circular complaining that even within the same special court, similar cases were being decided very differently.[48] As late as May 1944, the minister promised his judges a new law that would finally adequately reflect their special position in the state apparatus, as they were representatives of the Führer himself and—unlike the other officials—independent in their decisions.[49]

Who emerges victorious from a tenancy dispute and for what reasons was, legally speaking, as contingent in 1945 as it is today. Some cases went one way, others another. The judiciary was entirely at peace with itself: its social composition linked it, as usual, to the upper middle class. The war caused an increase in the average age of those in office, which at the same time weakened any revolutionary tendencies, as the generation born before 1900 had still experienced the stability of the bourgeois age. The administrators of the law were free to transfer whatever conflicts brought to their attention elsewhere and to treat them dogmatically until the political content was diluted into homeopathic doses. It was precisely in this way that they performed their intended function, namely to increase the utility value, efficiency, and resilience of social structures; and this very function remained in demand even after 1945.

In other words, the politics of National Socialist law is not to be found solely in the political.[50] Quite the opposite: the search for National Socialism within National Socialism promises little return. In the history of justice, there are no longer any legends to be refuted, no crimes still to be proven—just as, conversely, the discovery of previously unknown pockets of resistance is not to be expected. The tone of indignation with which the Nazi era was explained after 1968 now seems out of date. Today's enlightenment no longer hurts anyone. The German judiciary has recently been pursuing with holy seriousness the last surviving craftsmen of the death machine, subjecting them to an act of symbolic justice before their predictably imminent death. The files can be closed. National Socialism has been relegated to the realm of general history.

The consequences are, as always, ambivalent. On the plus side, there is an alignment with the usual professional practices, which at times seems almost liberating. No one has to fear restrictive archival policies and collusive networks anymore. National Socialism is undergoing a kind of secularization. The tone is becoming more serene. The narrative helplessness, however, stands out all the more clearly as a result. The emphatic "Never again!"

that has accompanied research in the background for decades has become unmistakably tired. At the same time, the political decency that has long provided distance to right-wing excesses is rapidly dissolving. The guiding principle that "Auschwitz" must not be repeated is trite if it is not supported by a consensus on what "Auschwitz" actually was and where its causes lie. The way we deal with the "Third Reich" has now reached the stage of systematic othering; National Socialism is what we are not. There is something quite paradoxical about the situation. The evidence of the regime's crimes is simultaneously proof of its categorical otherness and therefore also of why we no longer have to deal with it today. "Right-wing perversion," "unspeakable suffering," "monstrous crimes" are then both exculpatory and incriminating terms: it is always the others who are perverse. National Socialism is receding into a comfortably distant place.

Shared Normality

This is one of the reasons why the perspective has been shifted here. The focus is not on what separates us from National Socialism, but on what we share with it: the normal. The link between present and past experience is formed by the problems of everyday life as they are dealt with by the judicial system, then as now: tenancy law, marital law, insults, minor bodily harm, cases that can count on a routine objectivity in court. The reproduction of this objectivity through constant repetition is what is referred to here as the administration of "normality." At its core is the question of why, even under the conditions of 1945, it was still attractive for anyone to settle their disputes through the legal system. Violence was omnipresent, and yet, time and again, people stubbornly referred to the tenuous power of paper. The normal did not lose its appeal even under completely abnormal circumstances. Why?

The discourse surrounding "normality" makes use of decidedly unspecific semantics. In the words of the German writer Hans Magnus Enzensberger, it feeds on a "terminological pudding."[51] Its fields of activity can initially be characterized primarily negatively, namely by the fact that hardly anyone perceives them as spectacular or extraordinary. The only positive characterizations available are clumsy synonyms such as everyday life, average, or banal. This relatively loose use of the term has a certain tradition in research on National Socialism, beginning with Hannah Arendt's characterization of Adolf Eichmann, but reached the historiographical mainstream in 1993 at the latest, when Christopher Browning's study on the *Ordinary Men* exposed the view of the "ordinary" German as a potential Nazi perpetrator behind the legend of the proletarian perpetrator of violence, excess, and riot.[52]

If this soft rhetoric of the average is applied to the law, then sources that have so far played a rather marginal role in research into National Socialism become relevant: the files of the ordinary courts. This research collected as many of these as possible to be able to trace the functioning of the judiciary during the final battle and reconstruction period. They were supplemented where available by administrative and general files, general decrees, file regulations, and service instructions from the institutions involved, as well as personnel files of the most important actors.

The capitulation of the German Reich also provides a temporal orientation here but does not establish a sharp narrative boundary. The aftermath of the war lasted for years in many places—in some areas, decades—while, conversely, the clean-up efforts did not only begin after the capitulation but, depending on the military situation, long before. The external circumstances—personnel, premises, inventory, provisions—were generally less favorable after 8 May 1945 than before. The periodization was therefore designed to trace the overlapping effects of legal obstinacy. Ruptures and disruptions are also possible in this system, but they are not structurally prescribed by limiting the cases dealt with to the years of National Socialism or to the historical period of reconstruction.

The study therefore takes its sources from the entire period between Stalingrad and the currency reform.[53] At the turn of the year 1942–43, the lost battle of Stalingrad marked the beginning of the long end of the war, and 1948—the Trizone, currency reform, Berlin blockade—marked the end of the all-German occupation period. Afterward, the West indulged in the pipe dream of the continued existence of the German Reich, while the East saw itself as the true, new Germany. Until then, there was more to unite than to divide, which is why the sources are taken from all the occupation zones. Until 1947, there was a lively exchange between the zones. Legal assistance was provided to one another for arrests, literature and jurisprudence from the West was studied in the East, and authors and jurisprudence from the Soviet zone were published in the West.

In the first years after the war, "East" and "West" did not confront each other as monolithic blocs. In the French occupation zone, for example, a well-liked separatism had no support in the other zones. The Americans initially pursued a rigorous denazification policy that bore more resemblance to Soviet practice than to that of their Western allies. Within the Soviet zone, on the other hand, there were considerable differences, as Thuringia and Saxony in particular initially clung stubbornly to a bourgeois concept of the rule of law. Under the aegis of Eugen Schiffer, the veteran Reich Minister of Justice, the bourgeois jurist remained the ideal of the state administrative official in the East, which was able to keep the new *Volksrichter* (people's judges) at bay for a few more years.[54] Accordingly, "positivism" was found to be the suitable culprit in all occupation zones, which could only be combated in future with the help of the higher powers of natural law. The later so-called "natural law renaissance" received its decisive impetus from the East in this first phase.[55]

From Brute Force to Court Records

As this research only begins when the systematic disenfranchisement of entire population groups had already been completed, the focus on the normal is sufficient. It has been known for decades that the judiciary played a significant role in these processes of exclusion.[56] The macabre juxtaposition of welfare and murder was clear to see in the *Volksgemeinschaft* ("national community") at the end of the Second World War. Carl Schmitt's dark fantasies of true democracy, which thrived on homogeneity and the destruction of heterogeneity,[57] had long since established themselves as maxims of state action. "Within the community, peace, order, and justice prevail. Outside the community, power, struggle, and destruction prevail," was Ernst Fraenkel's famous analysis in 1941.[58] The loyal *Volksgenossen* could, if necessary, settle their disputes in court without being confronted with the unpleasant questions of politics; other forums had long been available for these issues.

If the activities of ordinary jurisdiction are brought into focus here, this serves to supplement the already familiar depictions of violence, not to replace them. One cannot exist without the other. Only the normal gave form and meaning to the state of emergency; without order, the extraordinary could not unfold. The fact that this legal everyday normality can actually be documented is already an initial result of this work. Public memory, but also the apologetic writings of the first post-war decades, have condensed the post-Stalingrad period into a single, uninterrupted night of bombing, during which there were neither the conditions nor the need for normal legal life. All that remained of the justice system was criminal justice, albeit in such a perverted form that it could no longer be described as justice at all.[59] This assessment is wrong in several respects. Even the special courts produced far more mass-produced legal goods than their name suggests, and even at the *Volksgerichtshof* ("People's Court"), one repeatedly encounters peculiar residues of normality.[60] Admittedly, the overall source situation is not favorable. Complete court records below the *Reichsgericht* are rare, especially from the final months of the war. They have survived more often on the periphery than in the centers, are not always filed where they belong, and their titles create expectations that often have to be corrected after reading them—in both positive and negative respects. But they can be found.

Another source problem that usually indicates "normality" does not arise here either. Memory is mostly interested in the abnormal, in storms, wars, disasters, and other deviations from the usual course of events. Everyday life, on the other hand, is accorded little space in cultural memory. Court records are different. Modern law is under a constant pressure to keep records, which particularly values the inconspicuous and formal. Unlike general history, working with court records therefore does not suffer from a lack of normality. Even in their outward form—the sentencing formula, date of the main hearing, the court composition, the structure of the facts and arguments, alternation of perfect and imperfect tense, etc.—the judgments of the time are structured in such a way that a jurist today can easily recognize himself in them, in other words: normal.

Rather, the operational mode of law harbors the opposite danger of succumbing to a—possibly only imaginary—overdose of normality. Since the dawn of the modern era, law has predominantly been played out in files. However, files are a highly indifferent medium. They document disputes between neighbors as well as Freisler's tirades of hatred before the *Volksgerichtshof.* Paper creates distance, and legal paper is particularly thick in this respect. The written record obeys an order that turns the color of the file covers into signifiers and assigns each position of the file number—conveyed by the general file plan—its own meaning. The files are based on the ideal of an identical structure; the highest possible degree of formalization is intended to make official paper processing as efficient and rational as possible.

The workings of law therefore consist primarily of two steps: first, the brute force that occurs in so-called reality is translated into the cool words of technical jargon, then these words are captured on paper. The resulting paper world absorbs the legal world.[61] This lends legal disputes a strangely civilized character, even where life and death are at stake, especially in retrospect. Sounds and smells, dust and sweat, but also drama, comedy, and boredom evaporate without a trace; even an execution only survives in the form of a prefabricated protocol that offers the attending judicial officer the columns "time of presentation," "time of handover," and "time of execution" for a second-by-second accounting. There is a great danger of mistaking the normality of the law for the normality of the world, of confusing the elegant words with real life, and of inferring a clean reality from the neat order of the files. The law shows too much rather than too little normality, a danger that can only be countered with the tried and tested historical remedies of contextualization and relativization.

Between Chaos and Cosmos

Court files record the events at the heart of the law. Nevertheless, they are used here for predominantly non-legal purposes. The aim is to shed light on a society's history through the form of institutionalized conflict resolution. The path via the normality of law is not necessarily required. In other areas of government and society—administration, science, art and culture, religion, or sport—a tenacious defense of one's own normality can also be observed right up to the point of collapse. From the book production of German legal scholarship: In 1945, the staunchly National Socialist Hanseatische Publishing House presented its loose-leaf collection *Kriegssachschädenrecht* ("War Damages Law") for the last time. Gustav von Schmoller gave the interested public a final overview of *Das Wirtschaftsrecht in Böhmen und Mähren* ("Commercial Law in Bohemia and Moravia"). Leo Raape updated his outline of *Deutsches internationales Privatrecht* ("German International Private Law"). The final sign of life of National Socialist jurisprudence—quite meaningful for self-absorbed German *Rechtswissenschaft*—was a commemorative publication: *Festschrift für Leopold Wenger. Presented by friends, colleagues and students on his 70th birthday. Second volume*, with foreword by Mariano San Nicolò and Artur Steinwenter in Munich and Graz, April 1945.[62] Examples from the rest of the world: on 20 April 1945, the German Reichspost in Vienna issued its last stamps ("Party formations SA and SS"), on 21 April, Lufthansa operated the Berlin-Munich route for the last time, and on 29 April, a last friendly match took place in Hamburg between the Hamburger Sportverein and Altona 93.

The fact that law, of all things, is examined here as a normality operation is not a random choice. Normality and law are closely interlinked. Both are omnipresent and generally inconspicuous, yet both fulfil fundamental functions of human socialization. Normality provides a projection surface for the longing for peace and order. It guarantees reliable procedures and promises calculable results; it ensures the correspondence of experience and expectation and stands for a predictable future. It marks the transition from chaos to cosmos. The "normal" is the backdrop to the fragility of the world.

Key components of this backdrop are of legal provenance. Law, too, lies between chaos and cosmos. Anyone who wants to end the state of nature and transform the army of lone warriors into a society must pass through the gate of law. This essential function is reflected in the fact that since the beginning of the modern era, a professionalized staff has been in place for the administration of law, whose sole task is the rational, unbiased, and reliable maintenance of the state's stock of norms. In practice, as we know, these requirements are not always met. Nevertheless, the law is perceived as a repository of the expected. Outliers are not excluded, but they also emerge as such. Law promises neutrality, objectivity, stability, composure, procedures for de-escalation and linguistic containment.

Law is therefore, at least to a certain extent, always "normal." Every disruption, every defect, every confusion has its place on the legal map. The dogmatics of the *Justitium* demonstrate this: for the legal self-conception, mapping the legal vacuum is also a legal operation. The *Justitium* bridges the abysses of existence. What happens in life is abstracted, conceptually dissected, and formalized in law in a way that guarantees that even the most outrageous impositions remain legally manageable. Legal constructs create a second level of reality, a paper world that is not only separate from the world of life, but also hierarchically superior to it. Paper governs life. Even the death of all judges is no obstacle to the proper administration of law. And therein lies a difference from other areas of society: the law assumes almost religious omnipresence. A legal capitulation to the afflictions of the world is out of the question.

The analysis of normality therefore contains no stylistic device of moral relativization—on the contrary. The law described here is neither politically nor even morally normal, but it is based on structural and organizational principles that would still be considered "normal" today. The label of "normality" reduces distance. It does not exonerate the past but rather describes the burdens of the present. The usual reflexes such as "legal perversion" or "darkest chapter" are then no longer enough to protect us from National Socialism. In the fabric of normality, National Socialism is moving closer to us than we would like. The stage is open.

Notes

1. A *Rundverfügung* or "RV," i.e., a circular issued by a ministry, in this case the Reich Ministry of Justice or "RJM," to subordinate authorities such as the Higher Regional Courts, dated 26 August 1944, in: BA, R 3001 No. 8463/22 (unpaginated). On the context: Evans, *The Third Reich at War*; Kershaw, *The End*; Ullrich, *Acht Tage im Mai*; Keller, *Volksgemeinschaft am Ende*; Blatman, *Die Todesmärsche 1944/45*; Müller (ed.), *Der Zusammenbruch des Deutschen Reiches*; Arendes/Wolfrum/Zedler (eds.), *Terror nach Innen*; Henke, *Die amerikanische Besetzung Deutschlands*.
2. RV RJM, 31 August 1944, in: BA, R 3001 No. 8463/22 (unpaginated). The quote comes from the preparatory meeting of department heads, 8 August 1944, in: BA, R 3001 No. 24688, p. 33.
3. RV RJM, 5 September 1944, in: BA, R 3001 No. 8463/22 (unpaginated).
4. AV (*Allgemeinverfügung*, defined as a "general order" addressed to a larger audience), RJM, 14 August 1944, in: ibid.

5. For example, the RV from the winter of 1944/45 OLGP Stettin, in: LAG, Rep. 75 No. 258 and Rep. 76 No. 836, p. 95.
6. See the statistics in BA, R 3001 No. 25043 and No. 25113, which, however, mainly rely on Prussian figures.
7. Becker, *Mitstreiter im Volkstumskampf*, 253.
8. LAG, Rep. 76 Stettin (new) No. 330 (unpaginated).
9. Hedemann, "Der Krieg und das bürgerliche Rechtsleben," 1516–1523, quotations from 1516 and 1518. Ready-to-use information in Staud, "Bürgerliche Rechtspflege," 1481–1484; Fechner, "Gerichtsverfassung," 1732–1738; Freiherr von Stackelberg, *Das bürgerliche Kriegsrecht*; Jonas, *Zivilprozeßordnung*; overview in Thompson, *Krieg ohne Schaden*, 38–59.
10. RJM to all Higher Regional Court Presidents, 11 February 1943, in: BA, R 3001 No. 20284, pp. 15–17.
11. War Measures Ordinance of 12 May 1943, in: Reichsgesetzblatt I, p. 290.
12. Statistics in BA, R 3001 No. 22796, pp. 165–211, pp. 287–329 and 332–378; see also note to Dept. VI, 4 August 1944, in: BA, R 3001 No. 24301, pp. 1–28.
13. On the personnel situation, see the letter from the RJM to the Reich Plenipotentiary for the Total War Effort, 1 August 1944, in: BA, R 3001 No. 25113 (unpaginated). The probably last Reich statistics as of January 1944 can be found in: BA, R 3001 No. 24514, pp. 38 et seq. See also von Gruenewaldt, *Die Richterschaft des Oberlandesgerichts Frankfurt am Main*, 72–79; Rottleuthner, *Karrieren und Kontinuitäten*, 216–219.
14. Second War Measures Ordinance, Reichsgesetzblatt I, 229–237, in force from 15 October 1944, see Altstötter, "Rechtspflege," 253–262. The guidelines on the urgency of war were also tightened once again (Deutsche Justiz 1944, 265–267). Last deadline extension: RJM summary letter to all Higher Regional Court Presidents, 1 March 1945, in: BA, R 3001 No. 8463/23 (unpaginated).
15. RJM to Reich Plenipotentiary for the Total War Effort, 1 August 1944, in: BA, R 3001 No. 25113 (unpaginated).
16. RV RJM, 10 November 1944, in: BA, R 3001 No. 8463/22 (unpaginated).
17. Regional Court President of Nordhausen to the Higher Regional Court President of Jena, 9 December 1944, in: the HStAW), Thüringisches Oberlandesgericht Jena No. 909, p. 25; Higher Regional Court President of Jena, 2 December 1944, in: BA, R 3001 No. 23369, p. 123.
18. Thierack, "Deutsche Rechtswahrer!," 1.
19. Regional Court President of Aachen to RJM, 8 November 1944, and reply, both in: LAV NRW-R, Ger. Rep. 255 No. 151.
20. Situation report of the Higher Regional Court President of Zweibrücken, 28 November 1944, in: BA, R 3001 No. 23389, Bl. 119. Overview in Kermann, "Das Oberlandesgericht Zweibrücken," 207–226.
21. AV of the Higher Regional Court President of Breslau (currently Görlitz), 5 February 1945, in: BA, R 3001 No. 22730, p. 2.
22. Memorandum of conversation from the General Prosecutor's Office in Rostock, 10 April 1945, in: LHAS, 5.12-6/4 No. 854 (unpaginated).
23. On the etymology: van Huyssen, *De Justitio*, Caput I, §§ 1–3; somewhat differently: Salmasius, *De modo usurarum liber*, 810 et seq. and Sextus Pompeius Festus, *De verborum significatione* 1, 74. Examples in Cicero, *Philippica* 5, 12; Livy 3, 27, 2; Suetonius, *Vita Galbae*, 10, 2 and *Vita Caligulae*, 5 et seq.; Tacitus, *Annales*, liber 2, 81; Gellius, *noctes atticae*, liber 20, caput 1, 42–43; Cassius Dio, 59, 7. Overview in Mommsen, *Römisches Staatsrecht* 1, 250–253. Kunkel/Wittmann, *Staatsordnung und*

Staatspraxis, 225; Versnel, "Destruction, *devotio* and despair in a situation of anomy," 541–618. For the sake of completeness: Golden, *Crisis Management*, 87–103.
24. Livius 7, 1 was prompted by the political blockade following the introduction of the plebeian consulship in 366 BC.
25. Decretals in the Liber Extra of Gregory IX, 2, 26, 10.
26. From the Land Law of 1620: Book 1, Tit. XXIV, Art. X (personal appearance) and Book 3, Titulus IV, Art. II § 3 (statute of limitations). At this point, the major reforms of 1685 and 1721 were limited to practically identical new proclamations. Similarly in this respect: Project 1766, Part III, Title X § 21 IX.
27. Rescripts dated 28 January 1671, 5 April 1671, and 24 March 1674 (CCM, No. XL, XLI and XLVI).
28. The draft of the *Corpus Iuris Fridericianum* can be found in: GStA PK, I. HA Rep. 84 XVI No. 15, Bd. 5, therein Part I Title 20 § 8, fol. 91–92r. Further: Draft PO Prussia 1864, § 759. Outside Prussia: CPO Transylvania (1852), draft BPO for Saxony (1860, chapter XX, § 855), § 103 CPO for Bosnia and Hercegovina (1883), § 161 Austrian CPO (1895). On the parallel development in constitutional law ("state of emergency"), see the references in Kaiser, *Ausnahmeverfassungsrecht*, 49–52.
29. See Hahn, 252, 584, 962.
30. In 1807, Napoleon led to an almost year-long Justitium at Warsaw (EKO 45 [1861], 97–102) and Posen (EKO 14 [1847], 365–369), in 1814 at Danzig; see the Rescript of 17 May 1814, *Jahrbücher für die preuß. Gesetzgebung* 3 (1814), 262 et seq., and the Allerhöchste Kabinets-Ordre of 5 May 1815, in: ibid. 5 (1815), 8, and also EKO 17 (1849), 314–319; 23 (1852), 1–13. On the cholera outbreak of 1831 *PreußGS* 1831, 156 and 157 et seq.
31. Huschke, *Römische Studien* 1, 281 note 174.
32. Instead of all: Baumbauch, *Zivilprozessordnung*, § 245.
33. Ibid.
34. According to Kesseböhmer, the first General Prosecutor at the Higher Regional Court of Hamm, in his memoirs after the war (1967), in: LAV NRW-R, RWN 139 No. 8, p. 14.
35. Rückert, "Die Beseitigung des Deutschen Reiches," 166–194, 172.
36. Quoted from Wenzlau, *Der Wiederaufbau*, 70 footnote 5.
37. Circular decree from the Ministry of Justice of Württemberg-Baden, 20 September 1946, in: StAL, EL 300 V Bü 192, Vorgang 86.
38. Local Court Berlin-Mitte, 15 March 1949, quoted from Reuß, *Berliner Justizgeschichte*, 99 footnote 328.
39. HStAD, 11031 No. 210.
40. LAH, Nds. 725 Acc. 2004/112 No. 11.
41. Citation in StACh, 30096 No. 8551 (Regional Court Plauen, 1st Civil Senate) and No. 8537 (2nd Civil Senate), new file numbers in ibid., Nos. 2168, 2209, 8505, 8509, 8527, 8537, 8551.
42. Regional Court for Stuttgart, 1 O 11/1945, in: StAL, E 315 Zugang 2007/11 Mappe 6.
43. Memoirs of Kesseböhmer (1967), in: LAV NRW-R, RWN 139 No. 8, p. 17.
44. Here: Distribution of business at the Düsseldorf Regional Court, 7 August 1945, in: LAV NRW-R, Ger. Rep. 142 No. 209, p. 257.
45. Rare exception: Wrobel, *Verurteilt zur Demokratie.*
46. Dreyer, *Die zivilgerichtliche Rechtsprechung*, 330. In Oldenburg, the contamination was five times as high ("approx. 2.5 percent"), according to Bartels, "Zivilrechtsprechung," 253–288, 288.

47. See generally Meinck, "Justiz und Justizfunktion," 28–39; Simon, "NS-Richter," 11–25; Angermund, *Deutsche Richterschaft*, 231–245; Niermann, *Strafjustiz*, 372; Wittreck, *Verwaltung*, 64–66; Rottleuthner, *Karrieren und Kontinuitäten*, 13.
48. RV RJM, 5 July 1943, in: BA, R 3001 No. 22489, p. 152. See Angermund, "Richterkönige," 324 et seq.; Dörner, "Justizterror," 29.
49. Minutes of a meeting of the Higher Regional Court Presidents, the General Prosecutors and the Reich Ministry of Justice in Kochem, 23–25 May 1944, in: HStAW, Thüringisches Oberlandesgericht Jena No. 1166, p. 139 (reprinted in Schubert, 546).
50. This is the fundamental misunderstanding of Weinkauff, *Die deutsche Justiz*, 95. Similarly wrong: Grunsky, "Gesetzesauslegung," 146–162; Markovits, *Diener zweier Herren*, esp. 218.
51. Enzensberger, "Normalität," 209.
52. Browning, *Ordinary Men*; Welzer, *Täter*; Kühl, *Ganz normale Organisationen*.
53. Broszat/Henke/Woller (eds.), *Von Stalingrad zur Währungsreform*; Herbst, *Das nationalsozialistische Deutschland 1933–1945*, 435; Kleßmann, "Kriegsende," 211–218.
54. Schneider, "Der deutsche Einheitsjurist," 235–264.
55. Wagner, *Naturrecht und sozialistische Gesetzlichkeit*.
56. Rüthers, *Die unbegrenzte Auslegung*; Majer, "Fremdvölkische"; Majer, "Grundlagen des nationalsozialistischen Rechtssystems," 117–200; Walk (ed.), *Sonderrecht*.
57. Schmitt, *Parlamentarismus*, 14.
58. Fraenkel, *Doppelstaat*, 193.
59. For example, Wagner, *Gerichtsverfassung*, 313; Erdsiek, "Chronik," 20; Schorn, *Festgabe*, 133; Scholz, Berlin und seine Justiz, 3 et seq.; more recently, Manthe, *Richter in der nationalsozialistischen Kriegsgesellschaft*, 118–126.
60. See the compilation in Marxen/Schlüter, *Terror und "Normalität."*
61. Vismann, *Akten*, 23, 269.
62. Nicolò/Steinwenter (eds.), *Festschrift für Leopold Wenger 2*. For the rest: Kroll/Christiansen (eds.), *Kriegssachschädenrecht*, (as of December 1944); Schmoller, *Wirtschaftsrecht*; Raape, *Deutsches internationales Privatrecht*.

Chapter 1

The Pleasures of Duty

Legal Service and the Final Battle

Justitium in Theory

"Should, as the consequence of war ..., the court cease its activities, the proceedings shall be interrupted for the duration of this situation," states § 245 of the German Code of Civil Procedure, in a loose continuation of emergency rules that originate in the old days of Roman law. However, such interruption was never actually intended: not in the seventeenth century, when in the aftermath of the Thirty Years War, the *Justitium* reappeared on the legal tableau as a legal definition; not in the nineteenth century, when it became firmly established in the German-language codes of procedure; and not in the twentieth century, when war mushroomed from a military matter into a societal condition.[1] Even in the Second World War, the *Justitium* found its place only in the realm of theory. In practice, "suspension" was not an option. The Reich Ministry of Justice was concerned that a large-scale or prolonged *Justitium* would have unforeseeable consequences, both for economic life, which depended on binding conflict resolution, and for the population, which could not do without legal services altogether. They were also concerned about the consequences for those who worked in the legal field themselves, whose position was already threatened by constant hostility from the Nazi Party and Gestapo.

According to the traditional dogmatics of civil procedure, the trial judge was responsible for establishing a *Justitium*. And yet, as it became more apparent to those in power that the Allied air raids might intensify to a point at which a *Justitium* would be unavoidable, they began to question the wisdom of leaving such responsibility in the hands of a trial judge. The Reich Ministry of Justice officially announced that judges might evaluate the impact of an air strike differently and thus, for the same court, different judges might reach conflicting decisions. At the end of 1943, the Reich Ministry of Justice claimed jurisdiction over a *Justitium* before passing it on directly to the presidents of the higher regional courts; it was argued that only they had a reliable overview of conditions on the ground and, as a rule, only smaller courts were affected.[2]

These considerations were certainly correct, though they were probably only half the story. A decision to suspend the law at that time had implications for state policy that could not simply be left to the discretion of the judiciary. To suspend the law would have signaled that the German administration was no match for the enemy attacks, and that the destruction had brought it to its knees. To concede such a thing and to entrust such responsibility to the lowest ranks of the judicial administration was not possible. Judging the impact of the enemy attacks was up to those at the top. However, the fact that even they could not simply proceed at their own discretion resurfaced at the beginning of 1944. On 3 and 4 February, the presidents of the higher regional courts and representatives of the Reich Ministry of Justice gathered for one of their regular meetings, this time in Weimar. The question of the suspension of law was at the end of a long list of items on the agenda.

In this regard, Undersecretary Eberhard Staud explained how the presidents should proceed: first, he explained that the existing legal situation already offered "so many possibilities to help" that it was hardly ever necessary to suspend legal services. If it was only individual courts that were to be affected, and only temporarily, then there would be no need to impose a *Justitium*. Only in the case of a longer suspension would a decision be unavoidable. In this scenario, the press should not be informed, unless other administrative departments initiated this communication. Staud was not comfortable with all this. In his concluding statement, he could hardly put enough distance between himself and the subject matter: "We imagine the practice to be very restrained. One does not like to find that one can go no further."[3] The use of *pluralis auctoris*, the double indefinite pronoun and double negation—something akin to a rhetorical maximum security prison had to be erected around the idea that the law could be suspended.

Staud's audience would have received his comments without any great emotion, not simply due to the fact that they had already internalized the repressed semantics of administrative language. What Staud set out for them in Weimar as a guideline for a supposedly new legal situation corresponded closely to the pre-established practice, which dated to the beginning of the Allied carpet bombings in the spring of 1942. No mere judge would have taken a decision on a *Justitium* without explicit instructions. Such a decision was to be treated as a prerogative of the higher regional court presidents, who in turn had this implicit approval of the Reich Ministry of Justice. One does not like to find that one can go no further: it was clear to all concerned that a *Justitium* could only be considered as an *ultima ratio.*

Ius non stat: Avoiding the Standstill

The beacon for this situation was Rostock. Rostock's city center had been almost completely destroyed in several waves of attacks between 23 and 27 April 1942. The judiciary was also severely affected. All court buildings were "completely burned down to the walls," the president of the Higher Regional Court reported to Berlin and, in addition, "all inventory and all records" were destroyed.[4] Although none of the court employees had lost their lives, it was assumed that a "large number" of them had "become very much in need of rest as a result of the mental and physical exertions during the cataclysmal nights."

Nevertheless, the attacks did not result in a total legal breakdown. The Special Court, a political court with far-reaching powers, passed the first death sentences on the day after the attacks. They ordered that the executions were to be carried out immediately and distributed reports about them throughout the city on the dreaded red posters, which, as the president of the Higher Regional Court proudly announced, "were in part personally pasted up by our judges and prosecutors."[5] Administrative business also resumed immediately, with a motorized courier service replacing the failed postal operations and telephone service. The high court treasury was relocated on the night of the attacks, and resumed operation the next day in Neustrelitz, such that salaries made it "into the hands of the civil servants with only a short delay." Only the courts of civil and criminal jurisdictions, the "ordinary courts," needed a few days to get back on their feet. A few rooms were quickly rented in undamaged houses, whilst courts from the surrounding area contributed typewriters and other inventory. As of 6 May, the president of the Higher Regional Court declared, "the Rostock judicial authorities" orderly legal service is deemed assured"—with that, the *Justitium* was over.[6] The interruption had lasted just seven working days.

The lessons to be learned from this event were simple: even the complete destruction of all buildings and records justified, at best, a short break in the court's activities. If necessary, an undamaged alternative location had to be found. In fact, the Rostock *Justitium* remained an isolated event: there seems to have been no further suspension of law during the entire Second World War.

Following the Rostock *Justitium*, suspension was considered only twice more. The first consideration came in the case of the destruction of Cologne on 30 and 31 May 1942. The destruction did not reach the same scale as it had in Rostock, but it caused a greater psychological blow as this attack targeted a major metropolis and, symbolically, a fleet of over 1,000 aircraft carried out the offensive. Sixty-thousand people lost their shelter; electricity, gas and water supplies were severely disrupted; and public transport was cancelled. The president of the Cologne Higher Regional Court telephoned the ministry to ask for permission to impose a *Justitium*, primarily to allow lawyers to restore their law offices and to give the parties time to sort out their personal affairs.[7] The request was denied. For "military reasons," a *Justitium* was out of the question, since it would "contain valuable clues for enemy propaganda about the effect of the air raids."[8]

Shortly thereafter, the Reich Ministry of Justice reaffirmed this decision. The Duisburg local and regional courts were badly hit by aerial bombs on 21 December 1942. On 24 December, the authorities informed the public, with a notice posted on the doors of the regional court building, that urgent claims could be made to the neighboring courts in Oberhausen and Ruhrort. The first civil cases were processed by the regional court on 31 December; the criminal law colleagues followed suit in the first half of January. Subsequently, the Düsseldorf Higher Regional Court president asked the Reich Ministry of Justice to record the period of closure as a suspension of law. His request was denied. The Ministry informed him that the "temporary *de facto* obstruction in the running of individual courts" was not tantamount to a suspension of law.[9]

For the rest of the war, no further considerations of this sort were transmitted to the Reich Ministry of Justice. Legal practitioners had soon internalized the lessons of the first major air raids; a *Justitium* was neither imposed nor requested. A few further examples of this unflinching business-as-usual approach in the early war years include the Saarbrücken public prosecutor's office and the regional court, which were completely burned down during an attack on the night of 29 July 1942. The next morning, as reported by the Attorney General of Zweibrücken, the office resumed limited operations, a week later it was "again working at full capacity as before."[10] In Kassel, all judicial buildings, all law offices, and all records, forms, stamps, paper supplies and books were destroyed in a bombing raid on 23 October 1943. Four days later, the president of the Higher Regional Court reported succinctly to Berlin that "The judiciary has been given temporary alternative accommodation in three rooms of the Oberfinanzpräsidium."[11] When Leipzig's city center was destroyed on Saturday 4 December 1943, the Dresden Higher Regional Court President complained of a general lethargy among his subordinates. The president himself, however, was all the more pleased with his air of resolve. Of the four court buildings, one was half destroyed and the other three affected, though they had "*brilliantly* survived" the attack overall. Thanks to his own courageous commitment, the criminal justice system was soon "swept clean again, so to speak"; "the court of standing"—a Special Court convened on an ad hoc basis—"'stood' from the very first day" and had already handed down the first death sentence on Sunday 5 December. On Monday morning a marriage was dissolved, whilst on Wednesday "a civil session was held in a judge's chambers that went off without a hitch." Satisfied, the reporter summarized that "there was no interruption whatsoever to legal services."[12]

Air War and Air Protection

The Reich Ministry of Justice also chose this *de facto* ideal of services running as smoothly as possible as the focus of its ever-new administrative circulars. On 7 August 1943, they informed officials of the following principles: it was to be "ensured by all means" that threatened or affected authorities continued to perform their duties. Certainly, those affected by an air raid usually had more important things to do immediately afterward than to simply continue judicial business as before. In particular, the population should not be bothered with hearings and one's own personnel should be made available to other administrations. When it came to the less affected parts of the district, however, it was maintained that care should "always" be taken to ensure that one "shall pursue, as much as possible, the undisturbed continuation of judicial business."[13]

But this did not clarify *how* exactly the required "undisturbed continuation of judicial business" was to be achieved; a large-scale air raid, in which employees died, whilst buildings, records, and inventory were destroyed, had to appear as a "disturbance" even to the most unclouded administrative sensibilities. In order to resolve this contradiction, the Ministry developed a new communications policy. Since the beginning of the war, numerous instructions on air raid protection had been issued. They were mainly concerned with the organization of official self-protection and repeatedly reminded their readers of the continual blackouts, the clearing of attics, and the use of fire retardants. Important records such as land registers and, to a lesser extent, typewriters and office equipment, were to be secured. Telephones and radios were to be placed on the floor after closing time, and pay slips, settlement notes, and assessments were to be taken into the bunker, if possible, to facilitate the making of payments even after an air raid.[14]

From the spring of 1943 onward, the showcasing of such preventive measures was increasingly backed up by empirical evidence. On 30 April, the judicial authorities received an administrative circular in which the Reich Ministry of Justice adopted some of the suggestions of the president of the Hamm Higher Regional Court. A permanent deployment and reporting system was recommended so that suitable members of the judiciary could be called upon immediately to take part in firefighting and cleanup work. Those who could not be notified by telephone were to report to the court at 6 a.m. the morning after the attack.[15] On 27 July, the Reich Ministry of Justice issued a three-page overview of "Air Raid Protection Measures in Government Buildings," with an appended five-page report written by the president of the Essen Regional Court, which summarized his experiences after the last large-scale attacks. No detailed advice was spared: water, sand, and ladders should be kept ready, land registers and other valuable records should be secured or, if possible, photocopied. "Firm, purposeful leadership" and a good organizational overview were declared decisive in the event of an emergency. Even unpleasant details offered useful experience. The Essen authorities stated that seldom does "*one* bomb (especially an incendiary bomb) fall alone," and that, therefore, in the event of a fire, it was necessary to search for other sources of fire, and anyone who found one was emphatically advised that "*Fires must be fought from close up and from below.*" Larger bags were useful for salvaging records, it was noted, and it was a good idea to form a chain in the case of heavy stacks or imminent danger. The cleanup work should be tackled "during the fire," particularly because water damage was usually much greater than fire damage. In Essen, the cleaning ladies were notified during the night and several prisoner squads were called in. They first removed the water used in fighting the fires and then cleaned the building, at least roughly. The reward for these efforts was clear: on the day after the bombardment, legal services could be carried out "without any significant impairments."[16]

These insights, dispiriting in themselves, were soon supplemented by new illustrative material. When the Essen report reached the Reich's judicial authorities, Hamburg was only just becoming the target of "Operation Gomorrah," which destroyed large parts of the city center in the last days of July 1943 and unleashed the infamous firestorm. Three weeks later, the Reich Ministry of Justice passed on this little, Hamburg-harvested nest-egg of experience in the form of a new general order: once again, they called for water and sand, as well as good fire brigades and, prophylactically, "a reserve of boards and roofing tar paper." Uninterrupted salary payments and communal meals for their cohort were also important and, if possible, emergency accommodation should be offered. In terms of operations, the Hamburg synopsis was similar to Essen's: services could be "considerably downsized because of the decrease in clientele that occurs during major disasters," and extra staff could first be made available to other administrative bodies. However, after severe attacks, "experience shows that … individual parties and witnesses come to hearings," which is why "court services" must in any case "continue uninterrupted as an emergency service." It is "decidedly reassuring, if the public notices that the courts did not let themselves get rattled and continued their work." In Hamburg, "all court buildings were [kept] operational" in this way; in particular, it was thanks to the "energetic intervention of the firefighting teams" that court services never came to a halt "not for a single day."[17]

Written Materials

Of course, it was obvious to everyone that housing for the court itself was rather an external problem. The institution could more or less simply be relocated from a destroyed to an intact building. Yet, destroyed records could not be corrected as easily. Oral history is not a legal discipline; the limits of the court records are also the limits of the legal world. Without records, legal service could hardly be maintained, causing judicial work during the war to focus on preserving court records. Records were duplicated, transcribed, carried away, and hidden. Relocations of court archives began as early as 1939, with civil registers, church records, and similar dossiers that did not need to be consulted every day being moved from supposedly endangered locations to safer, remote locations.[18]

In view of the large-scale inner-city bombardments from the summer of 1943, politics developed a systematic claim here as well. The court districts in Düsseldorf, Cologne, and Hamm, considered to be particularly vulnerable to a war fought in the air, were assigned partner districts in which they were to place their especially valuable records for safekeeping. Such records included "land registers, civil registers, criminal records, unopened wills, and lists of persons." The procedure was expressly recommended to all other districts for imitation.[19] Now, railroad loads full of records traveled through the Reich and, at the end of November, Hamburg and Bremen reported that the process had been completed. In Hamburg, "all valuable material was combined in large bunkers," and the Bremen land registers were housed in the Grasleben salt mine near Helmstedt, while the wills were walled up in the basement of the Bremen courthouse.[20] There were no limits to this hive of activity of precautionary measures. From Weimar came the jumbled report that they had 10,000 sheets of typing paper, 1,000 sheets of scratch paper, 1,000 (standard) envelopes, 500 16 x 23 cm-sized envelopes, six stamp pads, one bottle of stamping ink, eight rolls of tacking thread, ½ a gross of pencils, ½ a gross of ink pens, two rolls of adhesive tape, one bottle of black ink, one bottle of fountain pen ink, 3,000 staples in strips, three gross of thumbtacks, five ink ribbons, four red pens, 100 sheets of carbon paper, and four typewriters transported to the quiet Blankenhain Local Court. The Jena Local Court, in addition to office chairs and coat hooks, also brought 11 soap dishes and 16 wash racks to safety at the Camburg Local Court.[21]

At the same time, the duplication of records became a common prevention strategy. Records were copied everywhere in order to minimize the risk of their complete destruction. In Stettin, it was calculated that, with the current paper quality, judgments could be produced in six copies, allowing a copy to be deposited thereafter with the criminal register.[22] From January 1944, judicial employees in Stuttgart were repeatedly delegated to transcribe pages of the land register. The number of these transcribed pages ran into the tens of thousands. In the end, the judicial authorities even took up the fight with the Labor Office, which considered the copying of land registers to be incompatible with total war, an assessment that the president of the Stuttgart Regional Court described as "peculiarly uncomprehending," and in which the president of the Higher Regional Court fully agreed with him.[23] In December 1944, the Reich Ministry of Justice issued a general decree which, under the highest level of urgency—"Urgent!"—for the prospect of photographic imaging of land registers and other important records, it was regretfully added that the machines belonging to the judiciary were not operational at the moment, but that one could fall back on one of the fifty offices of the "Kriegsgemeinschaft Sicherheitsarchiv" (War Community Security Archive), which were to be found all over the Reich.[24]

Even if all this failed, if records could not be evacuated and duplicated, one was not helplessly at the mercy of the air war. After the air raids on Hanover, the Celle Higher Regional Court published a meticulously prepared plan, indicating which records were to be moved to the basement or to fireproof rooms on the ground floor "after closing time and during full alert." The plan also detailed how registers were to be secured, and which parts were to be transcribed as a precautionary measure.[25] The *Kammergericht* (the Higher Regional Court of Berlin) distinguished itself with instructions on how records burned in air raids were to be recorded on separate lists of losses.[26] Guidelines provided information on who was to carry which records out of the building if worse came to worst. From Saarbrücken, the president of the Higher Regional Court in charge reported that the court had been set on fire by fifty incendiary bombs; when the fire finally spread from the roof timbers to the floors below, the fire brigade had brought the records stored there out of the building, which is why "the personnel records, the general and administrative records, furthermore the records of the political department, the records of Department II, which comprises the letters M to Z, were almost completely salvaged." Going forward, important documents were stored on the ground floor.[27] From Greifswald came the useful hint that "the heavy land registers" would, "if possible, be passed out of the window and then from hand to hand in a chain formation." In Stuttgart, an administrative circular gave the instruction to "make baskets and sacks immediately available at a certain place" in order that helpers could start salvaging the records. In Cologne, appropriate precautions had apparently been taken, enabling helpers to transport practically all of the records "packed in large sacks … down the fire escape."[28]

And if prevention had been unsuccessful despite all efforts, there was still the—admittedly inconvenient—possibility of reinstatement in the end. In 1942, the Reich Ministry of Justice made it possible for the first time to reinstate destroyed documents without having to replicate the records recorded in them.[29] Even in the case of handwritten wills, a procedure followed in 1944 to enable their reinstatement, if not in form, then at least in content.[30] The courts now drew up detailed lists of the offices from which one could ask for a duplicate record. In addition, general legal life experience, so to speak, helped. That is, if records burned at a higher regional court, one could ask the lower courts from which the matters of appeals or revisions had emanated. Lawyers, notaries, youth welfare offices, or other offices involved were available for this purpose; for general or personnel records, the Reich Ministry of Justice could also be considered.

It is difficult to estimate how successful these efforts were. In September 1944, a report came from Königsberg stating that the last air raid had completely destroyed the seat of the Higher Regional Court, which had also affected all the records, "with very few exceptions." The unflinching announcement that at least the personnel records could be "easily produced" was followed, in the very next report by, the subdued admission that the restoration of the records would require "a great deal of effort" and would "take up numerous forces."[31] After two attacks in the spring and summer of 1944, the local court manager of Stettin had to announce the loss of virtually all records. From land records to probate files, registers of associations and foreclosures, to bankruptcy files and more than 150,000 criminal files, as well as over 700,000 civil case files, all records were lost. After being asked to report on "what has been done," the official made the almost megalomaniac claim that "The reinstatement of the lost records is in full swing."[32] In Dresden, where the air raids had destroyed practically all the courts, laborious attempts were made to reconstruct at least the administrative files on the holdings of the local courts from the surrounding area, plus a few trial files.[33] Still shaken by the loss he had just suffered, a lawyer from Ellwangen, visibly agitated, struggled to regain an overview of his legal affairs. In January, 1945, he stated that "Our typist Dahlmann has been killed! I now ask you to send me all documents still in your possession, in particular the statement of claim we have currently sent you! Heil Hitler!"[34]

Thus in practice, there could be no cues for a uniform handling of records. However, a lively exchange between the ministry and the legal staff on the ground eventually resulted in a sort of handbook for the air war. Any destruction was countered with a bundle of bureaucratically meticulous measures. Those who properly respected the blackouts, who applied fire retardants and cleared out the attics, reduced the risk of their own building going up in flames in the event of an attack. If it did go up in flames, air raid wardens and company fire departments were able to prevent the worst. If the worst could not be prevented, at least the most important records and necessary inventory were to be saved. If there was nothing more to be done, the other courts from the district contributed their excess furniture and searched their cellars for copies of records. The belief in administrative self-healing powers was not abandoned until the end of the war, not even when the bombing raids from the summer of 1944 onward reduced German cities, one after the other, to rubble. Emergency services were supposed to prepare for emergencies, alternative quarters were inspected in advance, and blank signs were available so that, in an emergency, the new location chosen only had to be filled in. Even the question of when a "large-scale attack" actually existed, and what distinguished it from a "normal attack," received a standard treatment.[35]

Official Duties: Legal Service as Military Service

This bustle of activity paid off. In February 1944, the Security Service observed with satisfaction that a suspension of law had so far "not occurred, or only for a very short time"; even "under the most difficult conditions," the judiciary had set an example to the population that "the work of the authorities and courts continues despite the damage caused by the terrorist attacks."[36] The meaning of such unobstructed administrative functioning went far beyond the concrete services provided therein. The judiciary was a model, a bastion, a haven of peace and a guarantor of order, a stern but just friend of the frightened masses. To this end, Reich Minister of Justice Otto Thierack informed his high court presidents and general prosecutors that the people were "in need of an example"; judges held a prominent position and were therefore obliged to "give support and strength" to anyone who turned to them.[37]

Showing a good administrative response after an air raid gradually became integrated into the conventional ethics of civil service duty. The Civil Service Act of 1937 had elevated civil service to be a "mark of confidence from the state leadership," demanding "unconditional obedience and the utmost fulfillment of duty," and then unfurled this demand, without regard for redundancy, into a whole catalog of internal and external instructions for conduct: "genuine love of the fatherland, willingness to make sacrifices …, full commitment of labor, obedience …, comradeship …, example of faithful fulfillment of duty …, diligent fulfillment of one's official duties, loyalty to the Führer … until death."[38] Reminiscent of a marriage vow, the relevant literature extracted from this the tenderhearted demand that the office bearer owes "loyalty to the Führer in good and bad days."[39]

These oaths of allegiance had concrete consequences when dealing with dangers from the air. No one was allowed to exempt themself from cooperation in air protection, certainly not in exchange for money.[40] On 15 March 1944, Thierack sent out an administrative circular describing the behavior of a judge who had been absent from court the morning after a large-scale attack in detail. As an excuse, the judge had claimed that his means of transportation had been unavailable; because of a foot injury, he had been unable to make the longer trip on foot, and he had also suffered from depression. His superior had then accused the official of "a deplorable lack of sense of duty and responsibility" and prosecuted him under criminal law. Thierack now made this incident known throughout the Reich; he used the opportunity to admonish "that all members of the judiciary be reminded of their duties during and after air raids." Especially from judges and public prosecutors he expected "complete dedication with disregard for personal interests."[41]

Judicial service thus gradually became war service. From the beginning of the war, security and order on the internal front were repeatedly touted as indispensable prerequisites for military victory, and the civil servant was therefore no less in combat duty than the soldier.[42] Roland Freisler's characterization of the judge as a "soldier of the Führer" was passed down, as was State Secretary Curt Rothenberger's call for a "heroic nature."[43] On the tenth anniversary of Hitler's accession to power, Thierack added to these words of wisdom the maxim that judicial business must "work as quickly, resolutely, energetically, powerfully and precisely as the mighty wheels of our victorious army."[44] The martial rhetoric had become a reality. The longer the war lasted, "the more burning are all things that concern air raid protection," the head of air raid protection at the Greifswald Regional Court, Chief District Judge Riensberg, let his colleagues know in richly unsuccessful metaphors. After a subsequent tour de force through the necessary stock of gas masks, air-raid-prevention steel helmets, and axes, he once again forcefully reminded them that it ultimately depended on "the courageous and combative determination of each individual" to "act purposefully with cool superiority" despite the threatening flames. It was known, after all, "that just as the Führer demands of every soldier at the front the hourly sacrificial commitment against all enemy weapons of murder, so he also expects of *Volksgenossen* (members of the German nation) remaining in the homeland the ruthless commitment where necessary to victoriously fight the terror bombings."[45]

In June 1943, the Armed Forces High Command (the OKW) issued instructions that civilians were also in action "for Germany's greatness" during air raids, and that casualties among them should therefore also be designated as "wounded" or "fallen."[46] In April 1944, judicial officers learned that they could receive military awards for bravery after air raids, even if they were not members of the Wehrmacht, although it was subsequently emphasized that mere performance of duty was not sufficient for this purpose. As a rule, "service under direct shelling, under projectile weapons or otherwise endangered by bombs or bullets" was required.[47] The president of the Cologne Regional Court gave his judges the consistent instruction that "no hostile threat, no terror and no destruction, neither personal concern nor personal loss" should make them "slacken in the performance of their duties."[48] From this, the president of the Düsseldorf Higher Regional Court developed a personnel policy proviso to pay attention to "toughness of will" and "soldierly attitude" when selecting managers in the future; he contemptuously described how the regional court presidents of Mönchengladbach and Kleve had immediately "folded" after the last attack.[49]

But even those at the staff level were obligated to play their role in ensuring uninterrupted functioning legal services, regardless of the mortal dangers at stake. In Stettin, the president of the Regional Court was incensed that, after particularly serious attacks, his cashier clerks had only attempted to salvage the cash register on his orders, despite the fact that this had been their duty anyway; they had not even been "smoke-blackened." On the other hand, he was able to praise another employee because she had "rescued, at risk to her own life, important records, documents and cash from the court cashier located in the burning old building of the regional court during the fire."[50] A notary from Stettin lamented the loss of his deed register, which the otherwise reliable custodian had forgotten in the building; in the attempt "to make up for what he had missed after the full alarm, he perished in the building" and, with this terse note, the greetingless letter ends.[51] The regional court president of Verden reported, full of appreciation, that a judge—himself completely bombed out—and a bailiff had carried personnel and general records, as well as eight typewriters, from the burning local court of Geestemünde. In Cologne, numerous records, typewriters, and "two good bicycles of the criminal police" were rescued from the burning regional court. In Stuttgart, "all typewriters, two calculating machines, a duplicating machine, and part of the manual files, as well as the personnel records that had been in the building" were salvaged from the presidium of the Higher Regional Court, while the fire had "spread at breakneck speed."[52]

Bundled together and condensed into a register of official duties were descriptions of the heroism of the civil service in May 1944, when the presidents of the higher regional courts and the attorneys general met at the picturesque Reichsburg Kochem to discuss the effects of the air raids with representatives of the ministry. From Frankfurt, Hamburg, Hamm, Kassel, Cologne, and Berlin, the top legal practitioners reported on their experiences with explosive, incendiary, and phosphorus bombs, on the advantages of water over sand, and of wells over fire ponds in fighting fires. The head of a judicial agency, it was stressed several times, had to get to the courthouse immediately after an attack. If there was unrest in the prisons, the Berlin attorney general had the tried-and-true recommendation that "a shot in the air" would "usually calm things down." Above all, however, the air-raid shelters from the first years of the war were to be restored categorically; securing one's own employees was "the first duty," an idea that Thierack also took up when he warned in drastic terms against "human traps," not without expressing a certain cluelessness, however, when he added in conclusion: "Everyone must help himself."[53]

That was not quite supportive after all. Thierack came back to the subject a few months later when, in an administrative circular of September 1944, he emphatically pointed out that the heads of the judicial agencies also had to take over air-raid night watch duties. He himself had taken similar action as president of the People's Court (*Volksgerichtshof*), and he also remembered how his company commander had taken on highly risky post duties under heavy barrage during the Battle of the Somme in 1916, thus earning the unconditional respect of his men.[54] The anecdote could easily be applied—*a maiore ad minus?*—to the judiciary, which was also under barrage, and its employees, who were expected to sacrifice their own lives if necessary to ensure the unobstructed operation of legal services.

A Functioning Service and Its Heroes

The administration for the consequences of war was therefore designed in two manners: on the one hand, there was the attempt at standard characterization whilst, on the other, there were expectations of the individual civil servant's unconditional fulfillment of duty. The countless manuals for the protection of documents, inventory, and buildings, added to the illusion that even aerial warfare could be administratively tamed by firefighters and clean-up workers. The realities contradicting this pipe dream were shifted such that they were the responsibility of the acting personnel. There, the unpredictability of total war was in good hands. Even when large-scale carpet bombings showered down on German cities in the summer of 1944, the civil servants acted as if they had expected them: dutifully, obediently, and ready to make sacrifices. In the last months of the war, there was an attack somewhere or another almost every day, and judicial buildings were almost always affected. Total war ate its way through the entire German Reich, but hardly any of the reports written about it lacked the defiant closing formula at the end: "Legal services were maintained." Here is a small selection, in loose succession—without regard to city and countryside, center and periphery, wartime urgency, and wartime indifference—that began the last major wave of enlistments in 1944:

A large-scale attack on Hamburg in August 1944 partially destroyed the Higher Regional Court. The sheer weight of the bombs penetrated all floors, in addition to time fuses that continued to detonate long after the attacks. The time fuses were also the reason why some court hearings had to be cancelled; apart from that, the president of the Higher Regional Court reported to Berlin, "the course of justice ... was never impeded."[55] In Königsberg, the entire city center was destroyed shortly thereafter. The Higher Regional Court burned out completely and all records were lost. At the local and regional court, where the fire had spread only to the upper floors, the houseless judicial authority found shelter. The immediate judicial service also took place there: "It seems to me worth mentioning," the Higher Regional Court President concluded his report, that the next morning "at 9 o'clock, i.e., 7 hours after the end of the attack, a criminal chamber held a session in the building, which was still partly somewhat on fire, in which four out of five cases were heard."[56]

The destruction of Stuttgart in September 1944 was even more devastating. Practically no building in the city center was spared, fires broke out everywhere, and the supply of water, electricity, and gas came to a halt. Nine explosive bombs and numerous incendiary bombs fell upon the large judicial building block, the seat of all Stuttgart's courts. Records and books were destroyed, almost without exception. Almost half of the building was destroyed, and the rest was severely damaged. Nevertheless, it was not without pride that the Attorney General was able to report to Berlin that, on the morning after the attacks, "still in plumes of smoke, a number of criminal trials had already been held in the few considerably damaged rooms still available."[57]

For the judiciary in Hanover, the autumn began with the loss of heating and electricity, the result of an attack in October that had severely damaged the judicial buildings. Thanks to hasty cleanup work, the Special Court and civil chambers were at least provisionally restored to such an extent that legal services in Hanover were "maintained in full operation."[58] The Heilbronn judiciary was "In full operation" again soon after the December attacks, although not in Heilbronn, where all institutions had been destroyed, but in Öhringen, 25 kilometers away.[59] In Detmold, the regional court lost all of its window panes in an attack on New Year's Eve, but this was no reason to interrupt legal services, even in winter: "Legal services continue unhindered," it was reported to Hamm the very next morning.[60] The local court in Ahrweiler also had no windows and no heating after an attack in early January 1945. Two ovens ensured that "the most urgent work" could nevertheless get done.[61] At the local court in Hillesheim, where work had already been going on for weeks without light, water, telephone, post and transport links, windows and doors were also destroyed shortly afterwards. Here, too, the court was able to defy the winter cold and continue its operations in a makeshift room.[62] The same was true of the Vienna Regional Court: during the attacks on 15 January, one of the two court buildings was almost completely destroyed. In the other, which had lost all of its windows, legal service continued immediately: "The hearings scheduled for the following day … were held without any problems," the president of the Regional Court announced.[63]

Three rooms were left of the Bad Kreuznach local court after an attack, the rest had burned out or collapsed, and there were virtually no records left. Asylum was found with a notary public, who soon announced that "legal services have been resumed."[64] After an attack in Rheinbach, the five undamaged rooms had to be shared with a convalescent home, and the supply of light, water, and gas was interrupted. Nevertheless, legal services continued "as far as is still possible."[65] At the Osnabrück Regional Court, the incendiary and demolition bombs had not left a single room undamaged. Six days later, the standard news followed: "Legal services have resumed in the heavily damaged buildings."[66] And in Bensberg, on the right bank of the Rhine, it was even worse. There was not one undamaged room left, not to mention a huge hole in the outer wall, and the building was also under constant artillery fire. But here, too, it was true, regardless of losses: "Legal service will be maintained to a large extent, so long as it is possible."[67]

At the local court in Schwäbisch Hall, all windows and some doors were lost, and numerous buildings in the surrounding area were destroyed. They made do with front windows and cardboard panes, reporting to Berlin that "legal services continue for all judicial authorities in Schwäbisch Hall."[68] At the same time, the third major attack in Leipzig had left devastation in its wake. The Reich Supreme Court was also affected: the president's apartment was destroyed, and from then on he lived, along with a fellow judge's family, in the basement of a constable's apartment. However, it was reported that "legal services continue without restrictions."[69] The same was true for Aschaffenburg: a large bomb penetrated the roof of the justice building and all floors below but then remained in the hallway without exploding. Because a small incendiary bomb was also quickly extinguished, the summary read: "Legal services were not interrupted."[70] And in Reutlingen, too, the firefighters ensured undisturbed legal business. Their "energetic intervention" kept the fires in the vicinity away from the courthouse; an incendiary bomb in the roof truss was "extinguished by the immediate intervention of the chief constable Schweikle and his son. … The continuation of legal services to the previous extent is assured."[71] In Göppingen, it was the judge himself, who lived in the court, who was able to extinguish a fire bomb "immediately after the attack." Therefore, "legal services in the local court are not disrupted."[72] The president of the regional court there described Hildesheim as "pretty much completely destroyed," but immediately undermined this peculiar superlative by claiming that "legal services in the regional court building could be maintained in full after the necessary cleanup work had been completed."[73] And also from Ulm, which the Stuttgart Attorney General declared to be "now completely … destroyed" after several attacks, came the usual proviso: "The business of the public prosecutor's office was not interrupted."[74]

Lack of space, loss of records, cold, darkness, and, on top of that, death. In Bonn, the judiciary resided on a pile of corpses after the large-scale attack of 6 January 1945. The public air raid shelter located under the court received a direct hit, and well over 200 people were killed. Gas, electricity, and water were out for several day throughout the city. People moved to the neighboring building of the local court, where they took refuge in the air-raid shelter. The smell of decay must have been everywhere. "According to the precautions taken," the report concluded, "the maintenance of an orderly judicial business is assured."[75] In Bielefeld, too, the corpses in the prisoners' own cellars did not disrupt official business. About forty prisoners had been buried in an attack. It was not known who was still alive, the regional court president reported, but nevertheless declared the attack to be "instructive," since it had once again demonstrated that "air-raid shelters under multi-story buildings [would become] mass graves in the event of a direct hit." And, of course, "However, as far as possible, work operations are to be continued here."[76]

These reports about the heroism of one's own performance of duty were interest-driven, of course. But their very number speaks against the fact that they were greatly exaggerated. Also, the potential for any gain or loss was negligible. The hero of the immediate action could expect a military distinction, while the one who rejected it was threatened with no more than a disciplinary sanction somewhere on the broad spectrum between "sanction" and "revocation of pension."[77] Moreover, the authors of the reports could count on confidentiality if the accounts were transmitted via the situation reports written by the presidents of the higher regional courts and were, in any case, under special protection as secret Reich matter. What's more, military and propaganda considerations ensured discretion. There was therefore little reason for whitewashing the reports. "One does not like to find that one can go no further," read one, demonstrating that praxis breathed life into the ministry's strained, bureaucratic watchword. Without windows, without doors, without records, without walls, without roofs, without light, without electricity, without heating, without courts, and without cities, legal life still somehow went on.

Final Efforts

And so the last civil servants whom the war had left or discarded sat in their offices and did their duty: old, frail, damaged, bombed out, cut off from their records, their books, their prisoners, often freezing due to smashed windows and rationed heating, sitting at unlit desks to save electricity, aimless in their industriousness due to missing paper and typewriters, all the while hungry and tired because of how isolated their places of work had become. Like the imposing palaces of justice of the Kaiser Wilhelm II era, their ruins became a conspicuous expression of "fossilized legal culture";[78] the morbid spirit of doom wafted through the concrete jungle. Hastily established courier services mediated between the outposts of the isolated bureaucracy and desperate inventories gave the institution its last legs.

In Saarbrücken, the courts worked only in shifts during the day so that merely a portion of the judicial staff would be exposed to the dangers of the constant attacks.[79] From Rottweil came the complaint that regular work was impossible because of the constant air raids and that two hours of rest was "already a lot."[80] In Eisenach, negotiations continued in the air-raid shelter when the air-raid alarm sounded, even though this led to conflicts with the other shelter-seekers, who complained about losing their seats.[81] In Neubrandenburg, due to a lack of fuel, all law firms and offices shared the only room in which it was still possible to heat.[82] The chief public prosecutor in Stettin complained that his 59 staff members had just twelve rooms at their disposal, and that some of them had to work in the corridors without lighting.[83] From the Zweibrücken Higher Regional Court, it was reported that the judges would alternately spend one day working at the Siegfried Line and one day doing their official business.[84] In Cologne, the last departments of the public prosecutor's office were moved to the detention rooms in the basement after the air raids of February 1945—Cologne itself looked like a dystopian vision of Dante.[85] In Koblenz, they moved into two rooms in a bunker.[86] At the Kochem Local Court, legal services continued in the judge's private apartment.[87]

People met anywhere to administer law, martial law, emergency law, improvised law, to decide on the last land register entries, alimony suits, divorces, neighbor disputes, insults, thefts, lootings, violent crimes, and whatever the whims of chance brought into their offices. In general civil law, the volume of business had fallen sharply since the beginning of the war, but the number of matrimonial and alimony cases had virtually exploded. In criminal cases, jurisdiction had shifted because the judiciary regularly lost out to the persecution apparatus of the Gestapo and the Security Service. However, in the general crime domain, there were still enough cases left and the politicized law matters that came before the Special Court were in high demand. In December 1944, Ministerial Director Vollmer, after his visit to the Cologne Higher Regional Court district, which had already been partially occupied by the Allies, emphatically stated that the judicial authorities were "still actively being called upon," not only in criminal law, but also in civil matters. The courts, he said, were striving to continue their legal operations smoothly and had, so far, been "essentially" successful in doing so.[88] Even from Koblenz, which had been completely destroyed, the Regional Court president reported in February 1945 that the guardianship and probate courts were active relatively frequently, and that there were "still a modest number" of divorces.[89]

In Hanover, in the days before the end of the war, the local court dealt—among other things—with a senior post office clerk who had accused the police of "dirty tricks," "foul play," and "corruption" during a police check. The local court sentenced him to a fine of RM 500, although his tirade had escalated to the accusation that even the Weimar police had been "better than the present one"; he was generously given credit for being in a state of agitation after an air raid. A marriage swindler, on the other hand, was sent to prison for eight months. He had forged his passport in order to appear "younger and more desirable," and, through this, had obtained bread and butter and a dinner worth RM 10 from a chance acquaintance who was willing to marry. The court in Hanover last convened on 6 April 1945, the day U.S. and British troops entered the city. The judges sanctioned three thefts with a fine and additionally handed down prison sentences of between two and eight months to ten people for offenses against the war economy and to three for receiving stolen goods.[90]

The Freiburg Local Court has a record of a hearing in a maintenance case in which the legal parties present—judge and clerk—recorded for 22 February 1945 that "no one" had appeared when the case was called. However, since at that time there had been "acute air danger with bombing," the absence of the summoned persons was justified. The last session in the Freiburg Local Court took place on 19 April 1945, when the parties met to negotiate the modification of a judgement of support. The divorced husband claimed that his ex-wife was now able to work again, that he himself had also remarried, that he had to care for a child brought into the second marriage, and that he had now also taken in his mother. Instead of RM 130 per month, he wanted to pay only RM 60. The court ruling was set for 24 April.[91] This did not happen as, two days after the hearing, French troops entered Freiburg.

The small local court in Kirchheim unter Teck also met for the last time on 19 April. A farmer named Schmid had sued his daughter-in-law, who had moved into Schmid's house in 1937 with Schmid's son. The son was supposed to work for his father, so they had agreed on a modest monthly rent of only RM 10. But the son had fallen in September 1943, and now the father was stuck with the daughter-in-law, who did not work for him and lived with him far too cheaply. In March 1945, his lawyer sued for a rent increase. At an opening hearing on 12 April, the defendant agreed to an increase in rent to the amount of RM 20. Schmid, however, wanted RM 25, and therefore the remaining RM 5 still had to be decided. On 19 April, the day of the next hearing, the Americans were already in the neighboring village. The highway bridges were hastily blown up, and from noon on low-flying planes shelled the town. The town chronicle states: "The inhabitants of the town had for the most part holed up in the air-raid shelters; only there could one feel reasonably safe."[92] Regional Court Director Fach and his loyal clerk, Justice Inspector Staudacher, apparently felt safe in court as well. There was nothing to do and Staudacher recorded: "When the matter is called, no one appears: for the plaintiff, for the defendant, no one." Apart from the two dutiful court clerks, no one else had ventured out onto the street.[93]

For the local courts of Greifswald and Stralsund, the documents for the hearings provide an insight into the activities of the criminal courts during the last months of the war: insults, war-related economic offenses, and mainly thefts—from raisins to the army postal service—were tried. Contact with prisoners of war, with whom the defendants had "chatted," "socialized," "had sexual intercourse," "had especially sexual intercourse," "had especially frequent sexual intercourse" was also brought before the court.[94] The last Stralsund file documents the theft of a bicycle. The defendant, a refugee from the East, claimed that he had had to leave his own bicycle behind in his hometown and therefore asked for "lenient punishment." Legally, of course, this was irrelevant: on 24 April 1945, he was sentenced to six months in prison.[95] In Greifswald, the court worked until 27 April, a Friday. The agenda provided for the five cases of embezzlement, receiving stolen goods, theft, a breach of labor contract, and a violation of the Reich Benefits Act (*Reichsleistungsgesetz*).[96] Three days later, the Red Army moved into the city.

In Dresden, business was as usual on 30 April 1945. The scheduled hearings had been postponed after large-scale attacks, with a formal statement issued that read, "as a result of enemy attack on 13 February 1945," the court building had been "destroyed."[97] One of the last sessions of the local court was devoted to an ornamental garden in a Dresden suburb. At the end of March 1945, a homeowner had filed a suit against his tenant, whom he had contractually granted part of the garden behind the house in order to plant perennials and create a goldfish pond there. Now, he wanted to grow vegetables there himself, citing the general food situation, an appeal by the provincial agricultural leader to get "the last out of the soil," and, finally, the unfortunate circumstance that he could not easily sidestep it for the piece of garden in front of the house. After all, flowers were already growing there, and a vegetable garden would "not exactly contribute to the beautification of the front of the house." The defendant, who considered his collection of perennials to be scientifically important and estimated its value at a ludicrous RM 12,000—roughly the annual salary of an adept lawyer—referred to the contractual agreement, in addition to the notion that the garden had "always given pleasure," not least to the plaintiff himself. On 26 April 1945, a peaceful agreement was reached: the defendant agreed to clear a "6m-wide strip in its entire extension of length," the costs of the legal dispute (RM 2) was imposed on the plaintiff.[98]

The last word, however, belonged to the small local court of Aue in Saxony, which, like the entire Schwarzenberg district, remained without foreign occupation for a few weeks after the surrender. There sat Judge Martin Zweynert, born in 1908, who had been a judge in Saxony since August 1939. Zweynert was a knuckling down type. On 23 May 1945, he issued a default judgment because the plaintiff, who was seeking an outstanding payment of RM 73.88, had failed to appear at the hearing. The judge, on the other hand, could not be accused of defaulting. He had only a worn-out form from the despised Weimar era at his disposal, which still bore the long outdated verdict formulation: "In the name of the people (*Im Namen des Volkes*)." But Zweynert did not put up with these conditions; with courageous intervention, he rejected the demons of the past. While in Flensburg the Reich government under Hitler's successor Karl Dönitz was being arrested, Zweynert corrected his form with a small handwritten addition that ensured that this last legal act of the Thousand-Year Reich would still be promulgated "In the Name of the *German* People (*Im Namen des Deutschen Volkes*)."[99]

Fiat iustitia

What the "Third Reich" had wanted from its judiciary was delivered. Judicial business was also, in the eyes of those in power, "one of the most important guarantors" of the "solidarity of the inner front," as Thierack had recalled in his New Year's speech in 1944.[100] A total war could not be waged without secure order and the stable routine of everyday life. The columns of death needed a reliable ground on which to march. Justice created this ground, especially where it indulged in a supposedly apolitical formalism. Particularly in the final phase of the war, when National Socialist propaganda conjured up a kind of Last Judgment of the world, the contours of earthly jurisdiction had to remain recognizable so as not to lose the horizon of the future. The continued normality of legal services between, underneath, and beside the rubble outshone the musty present and laid out a trajectory toward a better future. This trajectory took a form of the kind: today the statement of claim (with duty stamps), next week the reply, in two weeks official certificates of service with summonses to the hearing, in four weeks the hearing in court, with judge, robe, and clerk, then the taking of evidence, witnesses, documents, and perhaps even a visual inspection and, at some point, a title and access to the state's enforcement apparatus. Which of these steps actually took place was ultimately futile, as long as there existed the prospect that they might take place.

This continuum of normality was not to be interrupted by any suspension. Again and again, those involved emphasized the psychologically beneficial effect of providing a service that was not swayed by the world-shaking events. Even a rather insignificant political figure such as the chief magistrate of Gemünd suddenly saw himself elevated to the position of people's guardian. Rebelling against the announced closure of his court due to proximity to the frontline, he reported to his regional court president on 15 November 1944: "With the many external and internal stresses to which the population is subjected by enemy action and by rumors, continuous administrative services offer reassurance." He himself was now occupied "in a previously unimagined way" with "taking care of the population mentally and thus keeping them ready for action and work."[101] The latent functions of the judiciary superseded what little remained of its manifest possibilities. The realm of normality dispensed its soul balm: the world was sinking into rubble, but the law was unflinchingly erecting its legal idyll.

The hearts of the judicial officers themselves also found some warmth in their offices. "The professional official," says Max Weber in *Economy and Society*, "is chained to his activity with his whole material and ideal existence ..., a single link, entrusted with specialized tasks, in a restlessly on-running mechanism that can be induced to move or to stop only from the highest point, but not (usually) from his side, and which prescribes for him an essentially bound line of march."[102] The legal workers were fused with their legal existence; the formal rationalism of the bureaucratic apparatus protected their lives against all semblances of the improper. The happenings of their everyday lives disappeared behind business operations, official calendars, and civil servant duty, until the civil servants became administrative functionaries of themselves.[103] On 12 January 1945, the president of the Stuttgart Higher Regional Court wrote to the courts in his district that in Heilbronn "all robes [had] been destroyed by enemy action. I therefore ask retired judges and the relatives of fallen or deceased judges of your district to inquire whether there are still usable robes in their possession and whether they are willing to dispose of them, and if so, at what price."[104] By the end of the month, robes and berets had been gathered from various stocks for five judges. The living borrowed the vestments of the dead, while they themselves judged toward their demise.

Fiat iustitia et pereat mundus? The jurist is indignant about the supposed fanaticism of the subjunctive. Yet it is precisely the *realis* that is much more disturbing: And if the world perishes, justice takes place.

Notes

1. See Introduction.
2. Chronologie: Schutzverordnung of 4 December 1943 (Reichsgesetzblatt I, 666–668), AV (*Allgemeinverfügung* or "AV," defined as a "general order" addressed to a larger audience) RJM, 22 December 1943, in: *Deutsche Justiz*, 1944, 39.
3. Protocol in HStAW, Thüringisches Oberlandesgericht Jena No. 906, p. 302. Short reproduction in Schubert, 530; the Higher Regional Court President of Celle to the Regional Court President of Detmold, 22 February 1944, in: LAV NRW-OL, D 20 B No. 2002, pp. 325 et seq.
4. The Higher Regional Court President for Rostock to the Reich Ministry of Justice (or "RJM"), 30 April 1942, in: LHAS, 5.12-6/4 No. 851 (unpaginated), also in LHAS, 5.12-6/4 No. 46. Subsequent quotations are from this source. See also the status reports from the Higher Regional Court President of Rostock to the RJM, 1 May and 1 July 1942, the BA, R 3001 No. 23385, pp. 19 et seq.
5. The Higher Regional Court President for Rostock to the RJM, 30 April 1942, in: LHAS, 5.12-6/4 No. 851 (unpaginated).

6. The Higher Regional Court President for Rostock to the Senate chairmen and the Regional Court Presidents, 27 May 1942, in: LHAS, 5.12-6/4 No. 857, p. 169.
7. The Higher Regional Court President for Cologne to the RJM, 29 July 1942, in: LAV NRW-R, Ger. Rep. 255 No. 469, p. 8–10; Manthe, *Richter in der nationalsozialistischen Kriegsgesellschaft*, 107 et seq.
8. RJM memo dated 4 June 1942, in: BA, R 3001 No. 22761, pp. 17 et seq. The simplification ordinance of 1 September 1939 (Reichsgesetzblatt I, 1656–1658) was used and it was important that the parties involved should not suffer any prejudice. During the next major attack on Cologne, a *Justitium* was no longer considered; cf. the Regional Court President for Cologne to the Higher Regional Court President for Cologne, 15 May 1944, in: LAV NRW-R, Ger. Rep. 28 No. 206, pp. 186 et seq.
9. Correspondence between the Regional Court President for Duisburg, the Higher Regional Court President for Düsseldorf and the RJM on this matter, in: BA, R 3001 No. 22761, pp. 250 et seq., 254.
10. Status report from the General Prosecutor's Office in Zweibrücken, 8 August 1942, in: BA, R 3001 No. 23389, pp. 85 et seq.
11. The entire process is documented in StAM, 263 OLG Kassel No. 5.
12. The Higher Regional Court President for Dresden to the RJM, 27 December 1943, in: BA, R 3001 No. 22328, p. 21.
13. AV RJM, 7 August 1943, in: BA, R 3001 No. 22328, pp. 31 et seq.
14. Circular decree of the RJM, 4 April 1941, in: BA, R 3001 No. 22327, pp. 1 et seq.; AV RJM, 15 December 1942, in: BA, R 3001 No. 8463/18 (unpaginated); AV RJM, 14 August 1943, in: *Deutsche Justiz* 1943, 404; a *Rundverfügung* or "RV," i.e., a circular issued by a ministry, in this case the RJM, addressed to subordinate authorities such as the Higher Regional Courts, 1 March 1944 and 8 May 1944, both in: BA, R 3001 No. 8463/21 (unpaginated); RJM Conference, 3–4 February 1944 (Schubert, 517 et seq.).
15. AV RJM, 30 April 1943, here according to LHAS, 5.12-6/4 No. 849, p. 122.
16. AV RJM, 27 July 1943, in: BA, R 3001 No. 8463/20 (unpaginated).
17. AV RJM, 21 August 1943, in: BA, R 3001 No. 8463/20 (unpaginated). The report itself can be found in BA, R 3001 No. 22317, p. 7–10; very similar to the status report from the Attorney General's Office in Hamburg, 30 September 1943, in: BA, R 3001 No. 23366, p. 118.
18. See, for example, for the Regional Court for Stargard, the reports in GStA PK, XV. HA Rep. 76 Stargard No. 672.
19. RV RJM, 13 July 1943, in: BA, R 3001 No. 22734, p. 19. Further: RV RJM, 31 May 1942, in: BA, R 3001 No. 22317, p. 174; RV RJM, 19 October 1942, in: *Deutsche Justiz* 1942, 686 et seq.; RV RJM *Deutsche Justiz* 1943, 24 et seq.
20. Status report of the Higher Regional Court President for Hamburg, 27 November 1943, in: BA, R 3001 No. 23366, p. 122.
21. Both reports are undated, probably late 1943, in: HStAW, Thüringisches Oberlandesgericht Jena No. 34, unpaginated.
22. The Senior Public Prosecutor for Stettin to the Regional Court President for Stettin, 12 May 1944, in: LAG, Rep. 76 Stettin (neu) No. 129, p. 100–102.
23. Correspondence (December 1944) in HStAS, EA 4/001 Bü 646, Vorgänge 5/1, 5/14, 5/15.
24. AV RJM, 6 December 1944, in: BA, R 3001 No. 22317, p. 241.
25. AV RJM, 5 April 1944, in: BA, R 3001 No. 8463/21 (unpaginated.). The report of the Higher Regional Court for Celle – which goes somewhat beyond this – can be found in BA, R 3001 No. 22317, p. 135–139.

26. AV RJM, 9 August 1944, in: BA, R 3001 N. 8463/22 (unpaginated). Similarly AV the Higher Regional Court President for Stettin, 5 September 1944, in: LAG, Rep. 76 Stettin (neu) No. 650, unpaginated.
27. Status report of the Higher Regional Court President for Zweibrücken, 8 August 1942, in: BA, R 3001 No. 23389, pp. 85 et seq., 90 et seq.
28. Address by the air-raid warden of the Regional Court for Greifswald, 13 November 1943, in: LAG, Rep. 76 Greifswald No. 61, pp. 9 et seq.; RV the Higher Regional Court President for Stuttgart, 21 October 1942, in: StAL, F 254 II Zugang vom 29.4.1988, Bü 195; the Regional Court President for Cologne to the Higher Regional Court President for Cologne, 15 May 1944, in: LAV NRW-R, Ger. Rep. 28 No. 206, p. 187.
29. Ordinance, 18 June 1942 (Reichsgesetzblatt I, 395).
30. AV RJM, 2 June 1944, in: *Deutsche Justiz*, 168.
31. Status report of the Higher Regional Court President for Königsberg, 9 September 1944 and 30 October 1944, in: BA, R 3001 No. 23375, pp. 258 et seq. and 273.
32. Manager of the Local Court in Stettin to the Regional Court President for Stettin, 24 April and 5 September 1944, in: LAG, Rep. 76 Stettin (neu) No. 129, p. 90 and 145.
33. See, for example, the Regional Court President for Dresden to the Chief District Judge for Riesa, 3 March 1945, in: HStAD, 11091 No. 19, p. 16; the Higher Regional Court President for Dresden to the Local Court in Zwickau, April 9, 1945, in: StACh, 30145 No. 5650 Volume II (AG Zwickau, 15 C 225/44).
34. Regional Court for Ellwangen R 45/1945, in: StAL, E 341 IV Zugang vom 14.11.1988 P 61 No. 307.
35. Form (January 1944) in BA, R 3001 No. 22733.
36. Security Service Report, 21 February 1944, in: Meldungen, 6346 et seq.
37. Thierack's address at the meeting of the higher regional court presidents in Weimar, 3–4 February 1944, in: HStAW, Thüringisches Oberlandesgericht Jena No. 1166, p. 123. The account is somewhat different in Schubert, 501. In addition, Stolleis, "Nachwort," 338.
38. All quotations from §§ 1 and 3 German Civil Service Law (*Deutsches Beamtengesetz*), 26 January 1937, in: Reichsgesetzblatt I, 39–70.
39. Eschrich, Beamtenrecht, 21 et seq. See also Kershaw, Das Ende, 387 et seq.
40. This practice was banned several times, see RV RJM, 5 September 1942, in: BA, R 3001 No. 22308, p. 191, and AV RJM, 5 January 1943, in: *Deutsche Justiz* 1943, 41.
41. AV RJM, 15 March 1944, in: BA, R 3001 No. 8463/21 (unpaginated).
42. Compare Stuckart, *Führung und Verwaltung im Kriege*, particularly 46.
43. Supporting evidence in Majer, *Grundlagen*, 112 et seq.
44. Thierack, "Sammlung der Kräfte!," 65 et seq.
45. Address dated 13 November 1943, in: LAG Rep. 76 Greifswald No. 61, pp. 9 et seq.
46. See RV RJM, 15 June 1943, in: BA, R 3001 No. 8463/19 (unpaginated).
47. AV RJM, 24 April 1944, in: BA, R 3001 No. 8463/21 (unpaginated), amended on 1 June 1944 and 17 June (ibid.).
48. The Regional Court President for Cologne to the Local Court for Cologne, 18 October 1944, in: LAV NRW-R, Ger. Rep. 255 No. 198, p. 7.
49. Status report from the Higher Regional Court President for Düsseldorf, 29 November 1944, in: LAV NRW-R, Ger. Rep. 203 No. 191 (unpaginated).
50. Report of the Region Court President for Stettin, 7 February 1944, in: GStA PK, XV. HA, Rep. 75a OLG Stettin No. 629, Vorgang 26.
51. Notary (*Justizrat*) Flamme to the Regional Court President for Stettin, 28 August 1944, in: LAG, Rep. 76 Stettin (neu) No. 129, p. 157.

52. The Regional Court President for Verden to the Higher Regional Court President for Celle, 29 September 1944, in: LAH Hann. 173 Acc. 123/87 No. 161, p. 17; Report of the air-raid ward in Cologne, 1 May 1944, in: LAV NRW-R, Ger. Rep. 255 No. 178, p. 112; Report of the Higher Regional Court President for Stuttgart and the General Prosecutor's Office in Stuttgart to the RJM, 27 September 1944, in: HStAS, EA 4/001, Bü. 646, p. 7.
53. Thiearck had also said this word-for-word at the Weimar meeting a few months earlier (3–4 February 1944, in: HStAW, Thüringisches Oberlandesgericht Jena No. 1166, p. 123). Reports from Kochem are reprinted in Schubert, 547–550.
54. RV RJM, 28 September 1944, quoted here according to: HStAS, EA 4/001 Bü 646.
55. Status report of the Higher Regional Court for Hamburg, 5 August 1944, BA, R 3001 No. 23366, p. 138.
56. Status report of the Higher Regional Court for Königsberg, 9 September 1944, in: BA, R 3001 No. 23375, pp. 258 et seq.
57. Reports of the Higher Regional Court President for Stuttgart and the General Prosecutor's Office Stuttgart, 27 September 1944, in: BA, R 3001 No. 22328, p. 6–9; General Prosecutor's Office Stuttgart to RJM, 3 October 1944, in: BA, R 3001 No. 23387, pp. 61 et seq.
58. The Regional Court President for Hannover to the Higher Regional Court President for Celle dated 1 November 1944, in: LAH, Hann. 173 Acc. 123/87 No. 161, p. 25.
59. Report from the Higher Regional Court President for Stuttgart, 23 December 1944, in: HStAS, EA 4/001 Bü 646, p. 48.
60. The Regional Court President and Senior Public Prosecutor for Detmold to the Higher Regional Court President for Hamm, 1 January 1945, in: LAV NRW-OL, D 20 B No. 2155, p. 12.
61. Report of the Chief District Judge for Ahrweiler, 10 January 1945, in: LAV NRW-R, Ger. Rep. 255 No. 327, p. 134.
62. Report of the supervisory judge for Hillesheim, 26 January 1945, in: ibid., p. 128.
63. Report dated 1 February 1945 in: BA, R 3001 No. 22734.
64. The Regional Court President for Koblenz to the Higher Regional Court President for Cologne, 29 January 1945, in: LAV NRW-R, Ger. Rep. 255 No. 327, p. 124.
65. Report of the Chief District Judge for Rheinbach, 7 February 1945, in: ibid., p. 127.
66. The Higher Regional Court President for Oldenburg to the RJM, 31 March 1945, in: BA, R 3001 No. 22734, p. 11.
67. Report of the Chief District Judge for Bensberg, 1 March 1945, in: LAV NRW-R, Ger. Rep. 255 No. 327, p. 138.
68. The Higher Regional Court President for Stuttgart to the RJM, 27 February 1945, and the report of the local court manager for Schwäbisch Hall, 26 February 1945, in: HStAS, EA 4/001 Bü 656, Vorgänge 143 and 152.
69. President of the Supreme Court of the Reich (*Reichsgericht*) to the RJM, 2 March 1945, quoted according to Glöckner, "Die Auflösung des Reichsgerichts," 437.
70. The Higher Regional Court President for Bamberg to the RJM, 22 March 1945, in: BA, R 3001 No. 22734, p. 10.
71. The local court manager for Reutlingen to the Regional Court President for Tübingen, 3 March 1945, in: HStAS, EA 4/001 Bü 656, Vorgang 153.
72. The local court manager for Göppingen to the Higher Regional Court President for Stuttgart, 2 March 1945, in: HStAS, EA 4/001 Bü 656, Vorgang 154.
73. Report of the Regional Court President for Hildesheim to the Higher Regional Court President for Celle, 27 March 1945, in: LAH, Hann. 173 Acc. 123/87 No. 171, p. 174.

74. Reports of the Attorney General for Stuttgart, 12 January, 2 and 10 March 1945, HStAS, EA 4/001 Bü 646, p. 46, 81, 85.
75. The Higher Regional Court President for Cologne and the Attorney General's Office in Cologne to RJM, 9 January 1945, in: the State Archives in Duisburg, Gerichte Rep. 255 No. 365, p. 214, and the report of the Regional Court President for Bonn to the Higher Regional Court President for Cologne, 8 January 1945, in: ibid., p. 216.
76. Report of the Regional Court President for Bielefeld to the Higher Regional Court President for Hamm, 24 February 1945, in: BA, R 3001 No. 22734, p. 3.
77. The service penalties according to § 4 Reich Service Penal Code (*Reichsdienststrafordnung*) dated 26 January 1937, in: Reichsgesetzblatt I, 71–90.
78. Gephart, "Versteinerte Rechtskultur," 401–431.
79. Report of Wittmann, 10 November 1944, in: BA, R 3001 No. 25017, p. 52.
80. The Regional Court President and Senior Public Prosecutor for Rottweil to the General Prosecutor's Office for Stuttgart, in: HStAS, EA 4/001 Bü 656, Vorgang 146.
81. Report of the Regional Court President for Eisenach to the Higher Regional Court President for Jena, 28 June 1944, in: HStAW, Thüringisches Oberlandesgericht Jena, No. 1988, p. 228.
82. Statement of the Chief District Judge for Neubrandenburg dated 7 February 1945, in: LHAS 5.12-6/4 No. 396 (unpaginated).
83. The Senior Public Prosecutor for Stettin to the Regional Court President for Stettin, 10 November 1944, in: LAG Rep. 76 Stettin (neu) No. 120, p. 59.
84. Inspection report of Wittmann, 10 November 1944, in: BA, R 3001 No. 25017, p. 55.
85. The Attorney General's Office Cologne to the RJM, 8 February 1945, in: LAV NRW-R, Ger. Rep. 255 No. 327, p. 120.
86. Attorney General's Office Cologne note, 24 January 1945, in: LAV NRW-R, Ger. Rep. 449 No. 46, p. 168.
87. The Higher Regional Court President for Cologne to the RJM, 20 February 1945, in: LAV NRW-R, Ger. Rep. 255 No. 327, p. 133.
88. Report of Dr. Vollmer/Fechner, 8 December 1944, in: BA, R 3001 No. 25017, p. 48.
89. General report of the Regional Court President for Koblenz to the Higher Regional Court President for Cologne, 14 February 1945, in: LAV NRW-R, Ger. Rep. 255 No. 175, p. 83.
90. Chief Postmaster: Court Session and Verdict, Local Court for Hannover dated 20 March 1945, in: LAH, Hann. 172 Acc. 15/61 No. 35; Marriage Swindler: Court Session and Verdict dated 14 March 1945, ibid. No. 12; Further offenses, ibid. No. 3 and No. 28. The last dates are obtained from the criminal case register, in: LAH, Nds. 725 Acc. 2004/112.
91. Air Strike: Local Court for Freiburg 2 C 99/1944, in: StAF, E 159/1 Packet No. 418; Maintenance Case: Local Court for Freiburg 2 C 133/1944, ibid. No. 424.
92. Frasch, *Kirchheim unter Teck*, 425.
93. Local Court for Kirchheim unter Teck C 8/1945, in: StAL, Bestand 276 III, Zugang vom 14.11.1980 No. 7.
94. Terminated by 4 May 1945; see altogether LAG, Rep. 76 Greifswald No. 1136.
95. Local Court for Stralsund 4 Ds 51/1945, in: LAG, Rep. 77 Stralsund No. 5023.
96. This is shown in the overview in LAG, Rep. 76 Greifswald No. 1136.
97. Minutes of the Higher Regional Court for Dresden, 30 April 1945, 5/10 U 145/43, in: HStAD, 11045 AG Dresden No. 221, p. 7, Form, ibid., p. 2. Similarly, incidentally, AG Freiburg, E 1/1945, in: StAF, E 159/1 Packet 23 No. 509.
98. AG Dresden 36 C 505/45, in: HStAD 11045 AG Dresden No. 284.

99. StACh, 30100 AG Aue Nachtrag 112. The Local Court for Aue continued services until 16 July 1945, when it was closed and Zweynert was dismissed (Report of the Local Court for Aue, 27 July 1945, in: HStAD, 11380 No. 238).
100. Thierack, "Deutsche Rechtswahrer!," 1. Quite similar, Altstötter, "Rechtspflege," 253.
101. The Chief District Judge for Gemünd to the Regional Court President for Aachen, 15 November 1944, in: LAV NRW-R, Ger. Rep. 198, p. 10.
102. Weber, *Wirtschaft und Gesellschaft*, 669. Weber's considerations are based on "legal government," which admittedly is not applicable in the case of the Nazis.
103. This formulation is based on Adorno/Horkheimer/Kogon, "Die verwaltete Welt," 121, 124.
104. HStAS, EA 4/001 Büschel 256, pp. 1 et seq.

Chapter 2

Good People's Law

On the Trail of the German Soul

Neustadt, a Montage

"Neustadt" is not a name that attests to its founders' particular originality. Dozens of places in Germany have this name. The *Court organization of the German Reich*, printed in 1944, lists fifteen Neustadt local courts alone, whose individuality relied on additional geographic descriptors such as "Aisch," "Tafelfichte" or "Waldnaab." The Neustadt described here—the correct name should probably be Neustadt a.W. (am Wassersturz)—does not appear in the list. Neustadt a.W. is a patchwork of the remnants of other courts. The core of the collection is the source material of two smaller courts; missing fragments were occasionally supplemented by reference to two other smaller courts. In the background, files from the big, wide world rustle. The synthesis of this source material has created an impression, a condensation, a collage, cut together from the legacy of local courts such as Landsberg and Freiburg, Friedland and Kirchberg—inconspicuous, peripheral places where events may have occurred as described below. At the end was Neustadt a.W. with its small local court. No circumstance has been added or embellished and changed. All the cases took place in this number and with the empty splendor described here: the judges filled out their personnel forms, the lawyers earned their money, the good people visited the court office and filled the judicial statistics—just not in Neustadt.

In the Shadow of the Forest

Neustadt is bordered by forest on three sides. The town lay at the end of a valley that a river had carved through prehistoric rock formations. The water flowed from a ridge, poured over a moderately powerful waterfall—somewhat too opulently known as the "Neustadt Plunge"—into the hollow in which Neustadt had found its place, and then flowed peacefully through the valley, accompanied since time immemorial by a narrow road that, despite its meager appearance, served as the gateway to the world for the people of Neustadt. In all other directions, one came more or less immediately upon densely and highly overgrown chains of hills, whose gloomy impression was heightened by the town's somewhat recessed location.

The original inhabitants of Neustadt probably settled here to mine iron ore from the rocky subsoil of the surrounding area. A document from 1137 first mentions iron ore successfully mined by the "*Herren vom Neuenstadt*" ("lords of Neustadt"), the date also generally used for the founding of the town. This remained only a faint memory by the twentieth century, apart from perhaps a certain appreciation for the metalworking industry. For a long time, the forest had been the closest ally of the modest entrepreneurial spirit of the people of Neustadt. Those who did not work in agriculture made use of the natural alliance with wood and shrubs, sawing, planing, carpentry, wood turning, or working in one of the two paper mills. The Neustadt forest was treated with correspondingly meticulous care. The overriding maxim was to ensure "eternal permanence for the forest," for which the doyen of German forestry, Georg Ludwig Hartig, had chosen the constant "re-growth of wood" as the tried and tested means in 1791.[1] Eternal forest, eternal life! The people of Neustadt could never be accused of disregarding this principle.

What else could there be? For the sake of completeness, the following should be mentioned: the old grammar school, a small village church and two respectable town churches, the miniature porcelain collection of Baron Mintz, a lovingly maintained collection of old coins and stamps on display in the town hall, a spacious indoor swimming pool and, of course, the Neustadt waterfall, which was not unjustly considered a nationally renowned landmark. Given the restrictions of geography, one could hardly hope for more impressive sights, even after the railway had made its way through the valley at the end of the nineteenth century and the population had risen to over 10,000.

But impressing the world was the last thing anyone cared about in Neustadt anyway. The tranquil, remote, reassuringly predictable atmosphere was much more to the liking of the people of Neustadt. The centuries had deprived the town of a true golden age, but as its inhabitants traditionally had the gift of keeping their aspirations in healthy harmony with external opportunities, they could look back on something like a solid existence. For decades, the rumor persisted that Goethe had spent a night in Neustadt while passing through in November 1806 and, visibly impressed by the almost omnipresent forest, attributed a "shadowy existence" to the town. Although no reliable evidence could be found for this assessment—nor for Goethe's visit at all—this "shadowy existence" formed an integral part of Neustadt's identity. That this did not describe a deficit was self-evident to the majority of Neustadt residents. According to the common interpretation, Goethe expressed his appreciation for thoughts and actions that, over the centuries, had followed an unerring instinct for what was appropriate and what was not, without regard for fashions or appearances. What mattered was God and homeland, with a distrust for the distorting powers of passion—life had no need for escapades to give it meaning and fulfillment. After all, two birds in the bush never trump the one in one's hand; one does not leap far, but one does not fall either. Moderation, down-to-earth sense, and prudence, fear of God, and a healthy patriotism were therefore the hallmarks of the true Neustädter. Of course, calling this "shadowy" was up to each individual, and especially to a man like Goethe; the educated Neustadt residents nevertheless secretly considered "bucolic" to be the more appropriate attribute for the most famous of poets. The rest of the population, on the other hand, preferred the simpler statement that the people of Neustadt were simply "good people."

Under the Germanic Sun

As with all good people, the law has a long tradition among the people of Neustadt. The intersection of the fifteen authentic Neustadt legal histories looks something like this: since the depths of the Middle Ages, various authorities have asserted claims on the resident population, resulting in a somewhat confused juxtaposition and succession of various jurisdictions. Since the direct settlement of disputes was not only a matter of political symbolism but was also practically enforced by the unfavorable traffic conditions, a large number of Neustadt judicial lords and institutions had accumulated over the centuries. From the court tree, the Gogericht, and the venerable Thing, to peasant and feudal courts, burgrave, mayor, and salt count courts, a wide variety of offices, free courts, courts of reprimand and governments, right up to patrimonial courts, virtually every court form that German legal history has to offer was documented in Neustadt at some point. For a long time, legal disputes were heard on the market square, where benches and chairs were brought from the town hall and—as required—the pillory erected. At some point, the benches were given a roof, which was first made of wood before being built in stone at the beginning of the modern era thanks to a generous donation from a local paper merchant. Eventually, the entire courthouse was permanently incorporated into the town hall.

Nevertheless, for a long time, the people of Neustadt were not entirely comfortable with the confusing course of their past. Perhaps they were even a little uncomfortable, as it made their so proudly declared cool-headed minds appear somehow dim and short-sighted. However, two events almost completely healed this mistrust of their own history. The first was the new Courts Constitution Act of 1877, with which the newly created German Reich uniformly regulated the courts and judicial bodies. The now almost universally applicable standard of local court, regional court, higher regional court and *Reichsgericht* ("Supreme Court of the Reich") was practical in every respect, but at the same time had a monotony that suddenly made the convoluted history of the new Neustadt Local Court appear charming, and its often inexplicable transformations seem fascinatingly mythical.

The second major step came in 1933. The torchlit marches from Berlin had lent the flight of the German soul a historical coherence that also had a reassuring effect on Neustadt's self-perception. The questionable nature of Neustadt's legal culture, which had initially aroused shame and then modest research ambition, was now transformed into a universally praised advantage, as it was irrefutable proof in the new order that Neustadt had always been on the right side of history. Only in the unfathomable could true German inwardness find a home and unfold, far from the Romanesque craving for surface and splendor; precisely where the traces were lost in the darkness of the Middle Ages, where the life of law—undisguised by academic conceit—had played out on pastures and shoals, and where its influence could be sensed more than researched, there one could suspect the sources of a truly German common law. The previously inconspicuous shadowy realm of Neustadt was the new Germanic sun.

Far From the War

Neustadt was therefore well prepared for the next thousand years. Overnight, its own way of life had become avant-garde. The *Volksgemeinschaft* ("national community") found in Neustadt a considerable reservoir of healthy and reliable comrades, who willingly joined forces in the NSDAP and SA to celebrate Aryan superiority. The town's silvan setting was now a locational advantage, the dwelling place for the German soul, a natural dome of the master race and the root of its ethnic existence; a conspicuous sign with the inscription "Jews are not welcome in our German forests" was the logical consequence.[2] There had only been six Jewish families in Neustadt anyway, five of whom had sought refuge abroad by 1938; only the sixth had to be evacuated "to the East" in 1942. As the character of Neustadt had not been conducive to the development of pacifist, communist, or other extreme tendencies, the town could essentially consider itself to have been brought into line as early as March 1933.

The local court was no exception. Two judges and two lawyers moved within its orbit, along with the usual staff of clerks, registrars, secretaries, constables, and a senior judicial inspector who was in charge of the public prosecutor's office. Those who followed the Führer's call and joined the party took this official step more for the sake of good order, as there was no doubt about the political reliability of the Neustadt legal administration. Otherwise, there were not many other opportunities to demonstrate one's own convictions. Neustadt's legal proceedings were as transparent, measured, and modest as the people of Neustadt themselves: neighbors who had to be called to order by the courts, disagreements over how to repair storm damage, dairy cows that were sold and gave too little milk, defective repairs, unpaid bills, rent disputes, household disputes, petty thefts, fights, insults, whatever complications life in a small town had in store. Even if the majority of these missteps—presumably unavoidable even among good people—could be resolved without much effort with the help of penalty orders and dismissals of proceedings, the legal staff in Neustadt were kept quite busy in peacetime. After all, in addition to administering criminal and civil law, they also had to maintain land registers, supervise guardianships, and deal with the court's internal administration.

The war only slowly disrupted these peaceful conditions. The young men, like everywhere else, were sent to the front. Like everywhere else, forced laborers from East and West provided replacements. By the end of the war, a good 1,500 of them were working in Neustadt's agriculture and forestry. However, the town was not attractive for air raids. The Allied bombers found a more productive target in Lundheim, almost 50 kilometers away, with its armaments industry and airport. It was there that the enemy planes were seen flying from 1942 onwards, and from there more and more bombed-out survivors had to be taken in, their lamentations on the destruction reverberating. Despite all the horror, this also triggered a secret satisfaction, as the metropolitan arrogance in the faces of the new arrivals had all too clearly given way to pale envy about the safe, comfortable life in the small town. In Neustadt, there was no more intimate knowledge of the war to be gained.

Even as the war escalated into an all-out war, the Neustadt townscape remained untouched. The local court in particular escaped unscathed. In fact, there was less and less to do. In 1931, there were over 1,500 cases to be handled. After that, things went steadily downhill, a trend that accelerated even further during the war. In 1939 there were 350 cases left, after which around a quarter of the remaining business was lost every year of the war, so that by 1944 there were just 61 meager cases. In criminal law, the decline was somewhat slower. The loss of young men, who usually accounted for the largest influx of crime statistics, was clearly noticeable. But bombed out and forced laborers provided some balance, and the war also created conditions in which respect for mine and yours no longer played a central role. In 1944, a good 90 incidents still required criminal prosecution.

The small Neustadt Local Court should therefore not have survived the great wave of closures that rolled over the justice system in 1943. Even with all the farmsteads, hamlets, and ponds in the surrounding area, there were not 20,000 court residents in total whose need for legal services could, from a normative point of view, have been easily met by another court. It was obvious that Neustadt's legal system had no strategic importance under any circumstances. But here, protected by the forest and its whims, even the totalitarian state reached its limits. The train came only twice a day, and the narrow road that gave Neustadt access to the Reich was too often impassable, especially during the winter months, to be able to refer the Neustadt residents to another court. The judicial administration soon came to an understanding, not so much because of the centuries-long judicial tradition that the people of Neustadt had established, but out of consideration for the railroad timetable, which made out-of-town appointments without an overnight stay almost impossible. There was no question that it was difficult to sacrifice two working days for a witness statement or even a land register matter. The shadow of the forest therefore not only protected the people of Neustadt from the Allied attacks, it also saved their local court from wartime closure.

The Province's Law Enforcers

This is not to say that the war did not have a noticeable effect on the business of the local court. In 1940, first a judge and then a lawyer were drafted. And yet: the judiciary and the legal profession, each a one-man operation from the second year of the war onwards, were allowed to continue running their small empire even after Stalingrad and Goebbel's proclamation of total war. The war had left behind Local Court Judge Eugen Thalmann, who had been working at the Neustadt court since 1914, and Karl Dürr, who had been a lawyer since 1925. Although both were from the area, they were not born in Neustadt and initially viewed their work in the district as a transitional period that would eventually end with a call to higher office. However, the call never came, and so the transition eventually became permanent.

Attorney Karl Dürr had studied with modest success; he took up the legal profession out of genuine interest and evidently developed a good instinct for it. The global economic crisis coincided with the founding phase of his law firm—not a bad time for a lawyer, which is why Dürr was able to make a steady income from the meager conditions in Neustadt early on. In October 1933, however, when asked in a pub, he gave the legal opinion that "there was no legal obligation to salute Hitler's flag," which earned him a fine and a notice in the newspaper. His income was halved to 2,300 Reichsmarks a year. Dürr made the best of the situation: he joined the SA, the *Rechtswahrerbund* ("National Socialist Association of Legal Professionals") and the *Volkswohlfahrt* ("National Socialist People's Welfare Organization"), but stayed away from the party itself and left the SA again after a few months, citing his unwavering Catholic faith. This distant relationship with the regime, he reported in retrospect, brought him "increasing harassment from year to year": interference, summonses, inquiries, a legal dispute in 1936 that went through three instances in order to obtain the pious nickname Ignatius for his second son, and in 1937 even a poster with the inscription "Zum Judenknecht Dürr" ("To the Jew's Servant Dürr") on his office because he had "represented the Jews living here … until the end."[3]

Maybe so. Nevertheless, Dürr was not an oppositional spirit. For all the difficulties he reported, it should be noted that they were more than compensated for financially by the monopoly position he enjoyed since 1940. The small world of Neustadt proved to be a lucrative place for Dürr in the long term. His income increased year after year after 1934, until it reached the impressive figure of 11,173 Reichsmarks in 1943. Eugen Thalmann, who was already in the top salary bracket thanks to his extensive professional experience, did not even make 9,000 Reichsmarks as a judge.[4]

Thalmann was quite happy with this. He was a poor jurist with poor exams and a scar on his face. After completing his studies, he worked variously as a lawyer and as an assistant to the public prosecutor before being appointed local court judge in Neustadt in 1914. A burn on his foot saved him from the war, but his limited talent stood in the way of any major career advancements, so Thalmann remained local court judge in Neustadt. He married a resolute woman, adopted a son—the illegitimate child of a farmer's maid, whose criminal father he had met as a defendant in the courtroom—left the church, and became involved in the Anthroposophical Society. After 16 long years in the profession, Thalmann did not attract any negative attention, which is why the judicial administration finally gave him a promotion in 1930 at the age of 55. However, as Thalmann had also not attracted any positive attention up to that point, his career leap could only be seen with a microscope. Thalmann was promoted from local court judge to local court councilor, based in Neustadt. Everything remained as it was. On 1 May 1933, he joined the NSDAP on the recommendation of the *Richterbund* (Association for Judges), and shortly afterwards the *Rechtswahrerbund* and the *Volkswohlfahrt*; he became an air raid warden and district legal advisor. In 1939, a certificate from the president of the local court summarized, "He is diligent and punctual. His conduct and character are good, but he is somewhat sensitive and easily offended. He loves truth and justice. Politically, I am not aware of anything detrimental about him, nor do I have any reason to doubt his personal commitment. He is in good health."[5]

Circumstances were kind to this unspectacular activity. In criminal law, Thalmann was usually the only fully qualified jurist in the courtroom; hardly any of the defendants could or wanted to afford a lawyer, and the district attorney was more of an administrator than a jurist. Thalmann saw himself, in all modesty, as something like the wise man of Neustadt: affable, down-to-earth, unlike "the high-ranking gentlemen" at the Higher Regional Court or even in Berlin, none of whom he knew, but whom he nevertheless perceived as a vague intellectual threat. National Socialism and the war significantly reinforced this feeling. The ideological aversion to formal rigor and the ever-increasing impossibility of complying with the procedural rules of the Code of Procedure down to the last detail had elevated even the most repressed judicial bureaucrats such as Thalmann to the status of judicial kings, especially in the small local courts. The Reich Ministry of Justice had repeatedly called for criminal cases of minor importance to be generously dismissed,[6] which Thalmann then interpreted generously, seeing it as a general mandate not to attach too much importance to legal issues. A wise word here, a stern admonition there, that weighed more than all legal subtlety. When the directive came to reduce the reasoning behind a verdict to a folksy minimum, particularly in criminal law,[7] Thalmann finally saw himself as the herald of a higher wisdom, whose advice was sought less for his legal expertise than for his insights into the mysteries of life.

Annual Chronicle of Neustadt Criminal Law

It was Dürr and Thalmann, these two commonplace legal figures, who were responsible for the administration of Neustadt's legal affairs, which even during the war had remained commonplace legal affairs—decimated in number but still as close to the richness of life as in peacetime. In any case, Neustadt was not responsible for the worst transgressions of the citizens. The political corruption was left to the authorities in Lundheim: the *Volksschädlinge* ("public enemies" or, literally, "public vermin"), looters, draft dodgers, defeatists, black marketeers, ration card fraudsters, who could expect to be dealt with in a disturbingly routine manner. At least, that was what Karl Dürr had reported in a private moment. After the last major air raid, he was one of the few law enforcement officers who had not been bombed out and had been asked to go to the Lundheim Special Court for immediate deployment. Eugen Thalmann thought to himself at such moments that he really had not had it that bad in Neustadt.

And so, in 1945, under the patronage of the Neustadt Justitia, he distributed his magic spells among the good people. From January to April 1945, the records show two new cases every week, brought together from all corners of the criminal universe: tiny infractions, minor offenses, major crimes. Judging by the file numbers, about half of them survived. The whereabouts and contents of the remaining files are unknown; whether they were the victims of accidental loss or planned destruction could not be determined. It can therefore not be ruled out that they contain messages from the dark side of the moon; however, a review of several comparable collections has not provided any evidence to this effect.

The annual chronicle of Neustadt's criminal justice system begins with a snowball fight. Some youngsters were having fun in the snow on New Year's Day, until one of them seized the opportunity and threw a snowball in the face of a neighbor he disliked. When confronted, he initially pretended to be shocked, but soon became abusive, and finally got carried away with a light slap in the face. Consternation everywhere, police activity, a swift indictment. Thalmann reacted mildly. After a short meeting, he downgraded the assault, which had undoubtedly been realized, to "boorishness" and a "rascal's prank," reprimanding the delinquent for having nevertheless "gone too far." This meant that he would have to spend a weekend in jail, while the state, which was after all watching over everything, had to bear the costs. That was on 10 January 1945,[8] and the framework for the next few months was set: the Neustadt pastoral resonated even in the misdeeds of the residents and could usually be dealt with in one or two lenient sentences without much legal fuss.

Youthful sins: three apprentices threw stones at a house as a joke, damaging 23 bricks worth a total of 40 Reichsmarks. Thalmann called this "outrageous shenanigans" at a time when labor and materials were in short supply. The result was two weeks of juvenile detention.[9] A 16-year-old forged a collection slip for two suitcases and redeemed them from the train station storage. This was met with such bitterness by his father in view of his son's prolific criminal history that he hissed at the main hearing in early February that it would be best "if the boy were beaten to death." It didn't work out that way either; Thalmann calmed things down, mediated, and ended up with four weeks of juvenile detention.[10] At the beginning of March, another 16-year-old saw an unguarded Waffen SS car standing around and took it for a spin: driving without a license and stealing fuel, but a good reputation and a reliable commitment to the Hitler Youth—five days of juvenile detention should be enough.[11]

The adults also behaved peacefully on the whole. One gentleman took a lady out to dinner; his presumed ulterior motives threatened to be thwarted by a downpour, whereupon he pocketed two umbrellas for himself and his companion in the restaurant. Thalmann showed sensitivity, labeling the thief an "unfortunate cavalier" and fined him 200 Reichsmarks—a mere half a week's salary for the criminally untalented perpetrator, but enough for most Neustadt residents to see the lack of umbrellas at least symbolically recognized.[12] Thalmann also found the right words for two Frenchmen who had stolen a fat rabbit from a garden plot. He imposed only three weeks' imprisonment because, "there was a strong temptation to procure a holiday roast."[13] Another Frenchman, however, had to be dealt with a little more firmly. He was already being held in the court prison, where he found a set of keys that eventually brought him to the institution's meat room, from which he took a total of 17 kilograms of meat and twelve pairs of sausages over the course of several days. Such unrestraint upset even Neustadt's deep peace of mind. Sure, Thalmann attested to "intense hunger," and a German fellow eater was also arrested, but the mountains of meat he devoured were nevertheless so excessive that the five months' imprisonment that Thalmann handed out for it[14] was secretly considered a testament to Germanic gallantry.

The small community of Neustadt was, on the whole, quite content with itself. Very little happened that could not be understood. On 11 March, the seventh anniversary of Austria's grand transformation into the Ostmark, the fluff piece *Wir bitten zum Tanz* ("We Invite You to Dance") was shown in the city's only cinema, even though the authorities had not approved this schmaltzy reminiscence of old Vienna for the day. Fifty Reichsmarks made up for the faux pas.[15] A farmer's wife hid a goose and 16 chickens during the livestock census so that she could offer a lavish feast at her daughter's wedding. The concept of the *Volksgemeinschaft* was well understood, but if the individual was not doing well, then the people could certainly not be doing well either, and so the often-preached priority of the common good needed a logical foundation in self-interest. In any case, the victim received a penalty order for 200 Reichsmarks, which she took to Dürr, who advised her to appeal—not so much because of the substantive legal situation, which was difficult to assess in such matters, but rather because of his long experience with Neustadt customary law, according to which an appeal against a penalty order would generally result in it being halved. This was also the case here.[16]

Another Neustadt resident, who had also briefly privatized his membership in the *Volksgemeinschaft*, was brought back into the Reich with 50 Reichsmarks. He had falsely claimed to a bombed-out engineer from Lundheim that he had no more beds and therefore could not take anyone in. He claimed at the court hearing that rest meant a lot to him, that his wife had a heart condition, and that he did not want the last bed to be contaminated. In the Neustadt cosmos, these were not far-fetched arguments. It was only a minor case, Thalmann said of the accused, but as "his behavior was unpleasant," a fine of 50 Reichsmarks was nonetheless unavoidable.[17] Things were even more economical for a defendant who had opted for a strategy of compliant obstruction: "When the Weitner family, consisting of three people, was to be accommodated at her place on 8.XII.1944, she behaved in such a way that the people were happy to leave again," an act of spitefulness that Thalmann punished with a fine of 30 Reichsmarks.[18]

A Matter of Honor

Things only got sordid in two cases. A severely injured soldier, who had been working as a janitor since his return from the front, had twice been observed having "taken out his genitals with his front facing the street … and rubbed them until he ejaculated." Well, that was not acceptable. To be sure, everyone knew that the man concerned had had little prospect of female intimacy even before his war injury; his remorse was credible simply because of the public disgrace, the risk of a repeated incident was generally ruled out. Thalmann did not want to waive two weeks' imprisonment from a general prevention point of view but reduced the penalty to a fine of 150 Reichsmarks in view of the glaring shortage of janitors in Neustadt.[19] A somewhat different case took place at the end of February. A foreign worker from the East lived out his sexual desire with a cow while standing on a milking bucket. A colleague had recommended this technique, but the main reason he used it, according to the protocol, was "because I was stupid." Thalmann sentenced him to four weeks in prison. The full justification: "He is an inferior human being who will never become a valuable member of the *Volksgemeinschaft*. He could not have sacrificed too much human dignity with his actions."[20] Such a person, they found in Neustadt, executed himself.

After a few minor offenses of a more technical nature—a forgery of documents, a breach of employment contract, four small-scale black market slaughterings, all of which the perpetrators confessed[21]—Thalmann soon had to judge a truly tragic case. A young woman had put her one-and-a-half-year-old child to bed in the evening and then gone to a neighbor's house, where the heating was supposedly better. Her husband, it was known, had been drafted to Hanover. An air raid alarm delayed her return; when the woman finally came home, the whole room was full of smoke because some logs had slipped on the stove and had started to smolder. The child was dead. Thalmann only needed one sentence to resolve the case: "It was unquestionably a certain amount of carelessness not to supervise the stove and the wood piled up behind it, but the defendant has already been severely punished by the death of her child." A prison sentence of one month would have been called for, but with the payment of 150 Reichsmarks "justice should … be done."[22] One month in prison or 150 Reichsmarks for a dead child—on the previous day of the hearing, Thalmann had pronounced a one-month prison sentence for the foreign worker's intimate relationship with the cow, and two weeks later he imposed a fine of 150 Reichsmark for the public double ejaculation. Justice took a strange path; as soon as it entrusted itself to the law, it made completely incomparable things unpleasantly comparable.

Only when these procedures threatened to turn the law into a forum for private squabbles could one not hope for much in Neustadt. Insults were treated seriously, that's true; the witnesses did not hide, the police investigated extensively. But there was little to be gained here. For the verbal attack "I'll beat you crooked and lame. Even if you are the father of the local group leader, I'm not afraid of you," Thalmann imposed a 10 Reichsmarks fine; the threat was not meant seriously, the insult behind it "insignificant."[23] On the basis of similar considerations, the rude "I'll stab you in the guts!" with which the defendant intended to disrupt the local party leader's examination of her cover-up measures, was met with a fine of 25 Reichsmarks.[24] A drunk man who had insulted a police officer as a "sausage dog," "simpleton," and "half-wit," and had also caused a disturbance in the drunk tank was fined 60 Reichsmarks and sentenced to 14 days' imprisonment; the latter, however, was suspended on payment of 140 Reichsmarks, as the defendant had no criminal record and (allegedly) had to carry out armaments-related work. [25]

The people of Neustadt only once forced their valiant local court judge to go to extremes: Thalmann actually had to dismiss a case that he deemed insignificant. In a house on the outskirts of the city, there had been for months heated arguments between the tenants, one of whom was said to have repeatedly listened to the radio at night, slammed doors, fetched coal, and shaken the oven, which regularly resulted in colorful insults. The parties involved argued so bitterly that Thalmann suddenly found himself dealing with two lawyers for the perpetrators and witnesses, with Dürr and an out-of-town colleague ultimately expressing "truly justified doubt" as to whether it was "at all acceptable in today's circumstances" to involve four jurists, the defendants, joint plaintiffs, and countless witnesses in such a "trivial matter." Thalmann asked himself that question, too. But one could never be sure, so he preferred to summon all parties involved to the court for the main hearing.

After that, even Thalmann had enough. Who had thrown cigarettes out of the window, beat carpets, left the toilet dirty, and who had been labeled a "pig" or even a "lazy pig" and by whom—it was plain impossible to tell from the wild confusion of witnesses. With the blessing of the senior public prosecutor, Thalmann closed the proceedings, but not without a final appeal: "The court expects both parties—especially in this tense time of war—to avoid anything that could lead to further friction in the house."[26] An *obiter dictum*, Thalmann thought with humanistic emotion, certainly not legally necessary, but somehow a Solomonic saying.

The Final Struggle for Law

Civil law had also remained fairly civil during the war. Admittedly, the war had also opened up temptations for the people of Neustadt that not all good people were able to permanently resist. More and more illegitimate children appeared, for whom a guardian had to be appointed, and, above all, a father obligated to provide support had to be found—this rarely happened without an unappetizingly detailed examination of the intimate lives of individual women. About a quarter of the court's workload was now taken up by this business. However, the alarming erosion of modesty was still primarily the responsibility of the superior local court in Lundheim, where, it was reported, marriages were now being dissolved on a regular basis.

Neustadt's civil law therefore consisted primarily of tenancy law. This was nothing new in itself, but tenancy law had increased in two ways during the war. First, the state had already attempted for some time to quash more and more private disputes until, apart from the unavoidable maintenance cases, only tenancy law remained for the local courts. And then the bombs fell. The many refugees from abroad who had to be taken in in Neustadt inspired the local population to a previously unknown rigidity of principle. In the courtroom, Georg Friedrich Wilhelm Hegel's Absolute Spirit, Ernst Jünger's *Storm of Steel*, and Adolf Hitler's *Mein Kampf* came together to sell even the most narrow-minded adherence to principles as a manly fight for justice. The common good, civic solidarity, ethnic coexistence—all this was self-evident, but nevertheless right did not have to give way to wrong. The highly educated lied to themselves with Martin Heidegger. "For the philistine, struggle is always only discord, strife, quarrel, and a disturbance," the Freiburg forest philosopher said in 1934, but for "the essential man," "the struggle is the *great test* of all existence, in which it is decided whether we are servants to ourselves or masters."[27] "Essential men," without a doubt, is what the Neustädters wanted to be, especially in the national struggle of their time.

Whatever the case, they took legal action without reservation. Even the first quarter of 1945 brought sparse growth to the judicial statistics, although new cases were added on a weekly basis. By April, a total of 14 cases had been filed. A good two-thirds of these have been preserved; there is no information about the rest. From what has survived, it can be seen that the Neustadt residents were truly essential contemporaries. This is exemplified by a complaint filed by Dürr on 2 March 1945. The court wished to "oblige the defendant to,

1. clean the house every other week, including sweeping the sidewalk around the entire house, the access to the front door, the cellar and attic stairs, and the attic area, and to remove snow in the event of snowfall,
2. not throw kitchen waste, such as bones and vegetable scraps, onto the walkway leading to the front door outside the house or onto the roof of the chicken coop,
3. pay the amount of 45.00 Reichsmarks and from April 1, 1945, 15.00 Reichsmarks per month on the first of each month,
4. bear the costs of the legal proceedings."

The Neustadt residents' sense of purity and orderliness was on full display, and in this case even extended to family sociology: the defendant was the plaintiff's brother-in-law, lived in the same house, and the lawsuit was the third between the parties within a year. The defendant denied some of the accusations, considered himself justified in reducing the rent—"In wartime, there is no rent increase"—and moreover in league with world history: "The whole thing is so ~~rid~~ petty that one would have to assume that, with the enemy so close to this country, this would not even be accepted by a local court." "Ridiculous" was too strong a term; after all, they were already conducting the third trial over the supposed marginalia, but no one could really deny that the cleaning week and leftover vegetables seemed "petty" in the face of the threat of Allied occupation.

The court convened a week later. Embarrassed, the court remained silent about the defendant's history remarks—it didn't take much legal expertise to recognize that the war had no relevance to tenancy law. Thalmann carefully created a measure of legal peace. With the active support of Dürr, who repeatedly and forcefully persuaded his client, the parties reached a settlement in which the defendant undertook to "clean the house every second week, starting on Sunday, 25 March 1945, and to properly remove the snow when it snows" and also to "no longer throw kitchen waste, such as bones, vegetable scraps, etc., onto the roof of the chicken coop." No agreement was reached on the rent, but it was still a considerable achievement to have at least partially settled the notorious dispute.[28] Thalmann was satisfied.

And this is what the civil law activity in Neustadt looked like in the last months of the war: no matter was too small, no dispute too venomous to be resolved somehow in court. When it served the purpose, Thalmann did not shy away from inspecting the situation, taking his clerk with him, inviting the parties involved to the scene, and inspecting front courtyards, cellars, apple orchards and garden plots in large numbers. On 22 March—which had begun so hopefully with the settlement over the weekly cleaning services—the parties gathered in a beautiful apartment building where they had made each other's lives a living hell. Here, too, the negotiation resulted in a settlement: in the future, the laundry would be hung up in the attic on a rotating basis, the plaintiff would be allowed to receive visits from her sister—even overnight, in case of illness; the potatoes were to be stored in one way, the apples in another, and finally: "The defendant agrees that the plaintiff will keep her hand trolley, her ladder, the fruit crusher and the fruit hook in the barn; it is agreed that the key to the barn door will be hung up on a nail to be fixed behind the front door. On the other hand, the defendant cannot guarantee that any subsequent tenant of the barn will also tolerate the storage of the aforementioned objects belonging to the plaintiff in the barn."[29]

In another shared house, the defendant agreed "to run the motor vigorously at 7:30 a.m., 10 a.m., 12 noon and 6 p.m. for the purpose of drawing water, so that a sufficient quantity of water can also be drawn by the plaintiff. The defendant must notify the plaintiff of the time at which water is to be drawn by means of an electric bell signal and the plaintiff is obliged to inform the defendant if he does not draw any water."[30] On a property on the outskirts of the town, Thalmann gathered ten people, including spouses, experts, and witnesses to reorganize an inconvenient access road. Previously, there had been talk of a "campaign of violence" and "extortion," but now, face to face, they exchanged parts of the property for a small fee, ultimately leaving both sides in a better position than before.[31] On behalf of the plaintiffs, Dürr accused another homeowner, who had removed the wash tubs with malicious intent, of having created a "harmful and culturally unacceptable situation." Big words. The matter was resolved without incident when the plaintiffs moved out.[32] Dürr reported from another location: "Doors are constantly being slammed shut. Between 10–11 o'clock in the evening, people are still washing up and banging around in the kitchen." In addition, the plaintiff was told that she "couldn't die, otherwise the devil would have taken her long ago!"[33] The matter was dropped for the time being.

Thus, the Neustadt residents gradually litigated toward the final victory. On 6 April, the court heard the case of an elderly gentleman who wanted to get rid of his tenant, who had suffered bomb damage. Her children had called him "a cheeky fellow," and the regular visits from unknown men did the rest.[34] This was followed by another meeting, the subject of which was the "restoration of a hedge." In one of his baroque lawsuits—an annual profit of 11,000 Reichsmarks had to be earned—Dürr had described how the defendant, a baker, had arbitrarily chopped down a 50-year-old hedge over a length of 23.50 meters "and put up a sloppy wire fence in the same place." The plaintiff, an architect, "resents this disfigurement of his villa property;" just because "the hedge had not been trimmed during the war due to a lack of workers," the defendant was by no means entitled to "take such a radical measure." True enough. But what should restitution in kind look like here? Even Dürr seemed to be at a bit of a loss. So Thalmann resorted to the last resort and shelved the matter due to a lack of urgency.[35] For once, he thought, it must be allowed.

And that was almost the end of it. The National Socialist legal system in Neustadt only had one case left to process, albeit one that had been with them all year. On 29 December 1944, Dürr had filed a lawsuit on behalf of a working-class widow who felt harassed, bullied, insulted, and threatened by her tenants—her daughter and her daughter's husband. Finally, her son-in-law had announced that he would "beat her half to death if she didn't give up her husband's bed." She then sued for termination of the rental agreement, saying that an exchange apartment was available. On 15 January, it was agreed in court that the tenancy would be terminated immediately, with the defendants only having to move out when a "suitable" replacement apartment was available. The suitability of various housing offers subsequently continued. The housing office deemed the first replacement apartment too large. A proposed exchange also failed. Meanwhile, the dispute continued to escalate. On 13 April, the plaintiff appeared in court, reported physical assaults and filed criminal charges against her son-in-law. Dürr, who, although the plaintiff's lawyer, had known nothing about all of this, then intervened. On 18 April, he wrote to the court and asked "for the court files to be made available for inspection." The distances were short, and therefore such requests were merely an announcement of an imminent visit to the court office. On 21 April, Dürr set off and received the files in person. "Sent for inspection for 1 week. Transport fee—0—as collected in person," noted the court clerk. "Transport fee 0": This meticulous oxymoron brought the National Socialist legal system in Neustadt to an end.[36]

Resistance through Omission

The 21st of April was a Saturday. The enemy, it was known, was close. The noise of battle had taken on an unpleasant intensity, and the party officials had become ominously agitated. On 22 April, Thalmann stayed in his study. Sunday was normally a day of peace and quiet, an exchange of ideas, and idleness, but Thalmann stared tensely out into the drizzle of a dreary spring day. At eight o'clock in the evening, two young women rang the doorbell, identified themselves as employees of the district leadership, and delivered the order for Thalmann to report to the local court at midnight to hold the court martial there.[37]

That was too much. Joining the party: yes, *Rechtswahrerbund* and *Volkswohlfahrt*: yes, *Gleichschaltung*, beatings, murders, deportations, war: yes, yes and yes again, but now National Socialism was threatening to get too close to him. Thalmann stammered his consent in order to get rid of the messengers of doom. When he was alone with his wife, the two decided to flee. Under cover of darkness, they went out into the cold and rain and entrusted their fate to the forest, the eternal, German, Jew-free forest that had protected Neustadt from hostile forces for so long and now also embraced the old Thalmann couple in its benevolent arms. For two days they wandered through in the forest, in the echo chamber of the soul, where spirit, ideals, cultural past, poetry and the whole truth are at home, always worried that they might still be discovered by the henchmen of their own regime.

On Wednesday, they returned. Neustadt was unchanged. Only the Nazis were gone. The pragmatic sense of the population had saved the town from a fanatical defensive battle. Fighting for a lost cause did not suit the people of Neustadt; even the mayor had only made a few tired efforts, but obviously without any real conviction. In the end, he had made off on his bicycle. The court martial had been dispensed with, and when the first white flags appeared, the nightmare was over. The Allied troops made their entry—not a triumphant one, certainly—and were met with cautious curiosity.[38]

Thalmann, too, was no longer a Nazi. What's more, now that the war had been lost, he was able to give an unbiased account of his true self again for the first time, and this self-examination led him to the realization that he had never actually been a Nazi. On Thursday, 26 April, he went back to court. On 28 April, the Allies came and presented a questionnaire, which took him almost the whole day to complete. Thalmann's conscience was clear. His judgment, he found, was beyond reproach. The political concessions he had made were easily explained by his unsuspected desire for a career. His escape from the court martial was practically an active act of resistance, the humiliatingly meager promotion from local court judge to local court councillor, when viewed in the light of day, even made himself a victim of National Socialism. "Have you ever been restricted in your commercial or professional freedom for racial or religious reasons …?" Of course! "As an anthroposophist, I was denied promotion to the position of court chairman by decree, and a colleague 20 years younger than me was put in front of me as deputy head of the court."[39]

Nothing further happened. Thalmann remained in office. Even the military government was evidently overwhelmed by the omnipresence of the forest and refrained from closing the small Neustadt Local Court; the court was the only one in the district to receive a special permit "for particularly urgent cases."[40] Therefore, a suspension of law never came to pass in Neustadt. During the war, the topography of the town had made the mere existence of the court a matter of vital importance for the war effort; now, under the opposite circumstances, it ensured a lasting importance for peacetime.

In May, Thalmann's activities were limited to sending out a few enforceable copies of various titles and otherwise keeping the files in order. The people of Neustadt remained calm, and the former civilian workers, now called forced laborers, were only rarely abusive. Attorney Dürr reappeared on 7 May. The speed with which the capitulation in Neustadt had taken place had spared him the *Volkssturm*. Outwardly unscathed, he returned the borrowed court files,[41] actually a week late, but formalism was really not the order of the day now. Dürr was now in the clear because he had not joined the party; he only had to justify his brief membership in the SA, but he soon received official confirmation of his license to practice law.[42] At the end of May, regular court proceedings resumed. After all, life in Neustadt had not come to a standstill in the meantime: on 14 May, a previously upstanding citizen had stolen a bicycle to fetch vegetables from his garden a little further away. On 25 May, he was arrested and immediately brought before Thalmann, who just as immediately ordered him to be remanded in custody; in view of the "existing political circumstances," he argued there was a risk of absconding. On 1 June, a wandering apprentice was sentenced to six days' short-term detention for stealing, roasting and eating a rabbit.[43] On the same day, Thalmann sent out the first summonses for civil court dates. On 15 June, the bicycle thief was sentenced to three weeks in prison. He had Dürr declare that he agreed to the trial "without an indictment and without observing the summons period"; his sentence was deemed to have been served because he had already been remanded in custody.[44]

On 18 June, civil proceedings resumed, starting with the court's most recent legacy, the tenancy law battle of the worker's widow against her daughter; the question of whether an offered replacement apartment was "suitable" was still in the air. Thalmann issued an order for evidence, and on 25 June they went together, first to the new, then to the old apartment, measured, compared, evaluated: the offered replacement "makes a friendly impression and is close to the forest. The apartment also has a small garden," according to the minutes, but the previous home was also "bright and friendly." Neustadt simply had many beautiful homes to offer. When the building authority finally agreed to add a third room to the new apartment with a partition wall, there was nothing left to prevent the defendant from moving out. At a hearing scheduled for 23 July, which was merely a precaution, the minutes of the local court noted: "At the call appeared: Nobody."[45] This case, too, ended well.

Rule of Law

Except for Thalmann. The minutes of 23 July were the first to be signed by someone else. On 17 July, Robert Röll had been appointed by the Higher Regional Court as chief magistrate in Neustadt. After his apartment had been completely bombed out, he had moved to Neustadt. Röll was actually already retired, but the first request to reactivate him had already been made in March 1945, even though he had always kept his distance from the party as a devout Catholic and former member of the Center Party. Röll had resisted at the time, but now, shortly before his 67th birthday, he agreed.[46] Thalmann, on the other hand, was removed. Party members were no longer well-liked in the higher judicial service. What he did over the next few months is unknown. On 17 August 1945, he applied for employment "as a qualified legal assistant at the Neustadt Local Court, where I had worked as a judge for more than 30 years. I have already signed the oath dissolving my National Socialist ties twice."[47] He also completed the questionnaire again, not without pointing out once more that he had been denied a promotion because of his anthroposophical beliefs and that a colleague 20 years younger had been preferred instead. The application was nevertheless rejected. Shortly beforehand, the new government had advised former party members to seek re-employment as assistants in order to recommend themselves for a return to judicial office. But the military government did not appreciate such lazy compromises. Thalmann's time in Neustadt was irretrievably over.

In order to be able to work again, he began to press ahead with his denazification proceedings with determination. He hired a lawyer: Dürr, of course. He gathered exonerating witnesses. He summarized his case in an unassailable manner: he had only joined the party because the Association of Judges had recommended it, because in 1933 no one could have seen "that we were dealing with criminals," because he had wanted to prevent the wildest excesses, because leaving would have landed him "in a concentration camp along with the priests of the Christian Community." "District legal advisor" was a completely insignificant office. He had never enjoyed any advantages, on the contrary: "as an anthroposophist, I was excluded from promotion to supervisory judge." And then of course: resistance! His escape into the Neustadt forest was "active resistance," after all, it was only thanks to the occupying troops that he was "still alive at all."[48]

The denazification court (the *Spruchkammer*) had no use for this. Party, *Rechtswahrerbund*, air raid warden, district legal advisor: on 19 November 1946, it declared Thalmann a *Mitläufer* ("follower") and imposed a special contribution of 600 Reichsmarks on him. The worst accusations had been refuted, and Thalmann had "no more than nominally" participated in National Socialism. But his escape had only taken place at a time when the Allied invasion was "imminent and the person concerned had suffered no disadvantage as a result." It could therefore not be considered active resistance.[49]

Thalmann was shocked. He wrote to the ministry, but to no avail. His resolute wife was equally shaken. She also wrote to the ministry to recount the drama of the escape, which had apparently been mistakenly chalked up to a "romantic walk in the woods." Escape had been the last alternative to suicide; she had often had to lay her "very heart-sick husband … on bundles of brushwood," and despite the rain and cold they had not dared to "seek shelter in a village or farm" for fear of the Gestapo. Finally the wise wife pleaded: "My husband must not find out about this letter," concluding with her plea as a (even wiser) judge's wife: "As a judge's old wife, I now hope that justice will be done."[50]

Justice was no longer to be found. Thalmann resigned himself to his fate. In January 1947, the military government approved his reinstatement, but by then he had already been a "qualified legal assistant" at the local court in Hausen, a good 25 kilometers from Neustadt, for several months. In April 1947, he became a local court clerk there. In 1948, his wife made another (secret) attempt to "vindicate her good husband" in order to "help the future sense of justice to get back on its feet a little."[51] Shortly thereafter, Thalmann also applied for reinstatement, arguing that he could provide new witnesses. Nothing was successful. The good man from Neustadt remained branded a *Mitläufer*. Only his later years were made a little sweeter: in 1950, he received the long-awaited promotion to chief magistrate, albeit only in title due to the lack of a position. He retired in 1951.

In Neustadt itself, it was up to his successor to pick up the loose ends of Neustadt's legal system and tie them together in a postwar-compatible manner. Dürr helped where he could. The swastikas had to be removed from the stamps, seals, and letterheads—a laborious task, but denazified paraphernalia were not available for the time being. Judgment forms, too, were only available in the outdated version, which solemnly proclaimed a legal verdict "In the name of the German people," which was now hastily corrected to the ideologically unobjectionable phrase "In the name of the law." Such doctored forms remained in use until 1948. Dürr also had to cross out "Adolf-Hitler-Str." separately on every letterhead for years to come, and he also kept a small supply of wastepaper on hand to paste over the symbol of the National Socialist Association of Legal Professionals.

This cosmetic treatment was now appropriate in all areas of law. Admittedly, not many of the proceedings under National Socialist criminal law remained, and by no means can everything that had happened in the meantime be reconstructed from the files. The Frenchman who had so unrestrainedly abused the prison sausages was gone. All that remained was the determination that he was a member of the Allies and that "further enforcement measures" therefore had "no prospect of success."[52] The careless cinema operator paid his fine on 16 August 1945,[53] the horny janitor paid his on 15 November.[54] Also in November, the youth who had taken the SS vehicle for a joyride was summoned because he still had five days of youth detention outstanding. The public prosecutor's office in Lundheim informed Röll that, according to Section 62 (4) of the Juvenile Courts Act, which had only been reformed in 1943, the sentence could be waived if the convicted had been "called up to the Wehrmacht, the Reich Labor Service or a similar service." During the trial, it emerged that none of this was true, but that the 16-year-old had spent three months in US captivity, which Röll generously categorized as a "similar deployment." Did the Allies ever find out about this bold analogy? In any case, this put an end to the sentence.[55]

There was more to do in the civil law area. As far as the state was involved, that went without saying. In the countless maintenance cases, it was usually the Youth Welfare Office that kept an eye on the orderly progress of the matter. These cases sometimes dragged on for years; only the reports generated by Nazi race theory proponents were now more sparingly used. If there were questions of fees still awaiting a decision, Röll could rely on Dürr or his external colleagues, who were fairly reliable in such matters.[56] For other minor matters, a party or a lawyer would usually get in touch from somewhere and withdraw the last remnants of a pending lawsuit.[57] If nothing at all was heard, Röll would contact the parties following a comprehensive revision of the files, which he had carried out at the beginning of 1949. Most of them then declared that they were withdrawing their action. And what else? The landlady, who allegedly could not die because otherwise she would have been taken by the devil long ago, appeared at the court in July 1946 to record a number of further outrageous statements. Shortly afterwards, Dürr translated the epochal turnaround into lawyerly prose:

"The trial was suspended due to wartime conditions. Recently, further insults have been made." Now the wartime conditions were over, so the dispute continued until the matter was settled in March 1947 when the defendants moved out.[58] Only with regard to the cut hedge, whose fate had been suspended since 6 April 1945,[59] did no one take action. The revocation was never issued, and so the defendant's sloppy wire fence ultimately managed to establish a permanent existence for itself.

The Right Life in the Right Life

And so, life in Neustadt went on as usual. The people of Neustadt accepted whatever joys and sorrows the plan of creation had in store for them, sought idleness in the forest when the work of the day and week was done, and enjoyed the blessings of civilization, which remained heralds of progress even under the adverse conditions of the time. The German soul was in good hands in Neustadt. "The diversity of German talents, the coexistence of military, technical-organizational, but also theoretical-philosophical, poetic and musical talents is sometimes perceived by the Germans' neighbors as something uncanny, because it makes their reactions in individual cases unpredictable," wrote Walter Mühlmann, one of the leading German ethnopsychologists of his time, in 1944.[60] Reich Minister of Justice Otto Thierack added to this psychological profile from an official perspective in his New Year's appeal in 1944, in which he attested that the German people had a "fine sense of law and justice."[61] Léon Degrelle, a senior official of the Waffen SS, discovered a German "sense of discipline down to the most extraordinary details" during his last tour through the destroyed city of Berlin in April 1945, which also made the downfall appear "really beautiful,"[62] and Franz Scholz, a self-absorbed administrative judge with a penchant for literary bombast, added the layman's assessment, but one that is likely readily applicable from an ethnopsychological perspective: "Since time immemorial, the judge has been seen as the 'bastion of justice' in all civilized countries. … The German people, in particular, demand a judge. After all, they have a very sensitive sense of justice, which often manifests itself in a stubborn 'struggle for law'."[63]

That was in 1955. The German soul had survived the times well. It had retained its sense of the essential when the rats swarmed in the rubble of the cities, fat on corpses, and now, as the post-war years gradually spread their palliative mildew, it was even more essential. The good people had remained good at heart. And anyone who might have wished for less shadowy advocates to nurture the German soul also found encouragement. After all, Neustadt was just a projection of posterity, a rapture that cheerfully mixed actors, places, and ideas, as if Neustadt could be anywhere and as if historical truth were not a serious matter but a literary gimmick. But what can be everywhere can also be nowhere. The concern for such an invention, everyone in Neustadt agreed, could therefore be left to others.

Notes

1. Hartig, *Holzzucht*, V.
2. See Zechner, *Der deutsche Wald*, esp. 163–193; generally Wildt, *Volksgemeinschaft*, esp. 176–218; ibid., "keine Juden," 117–134.
3. Quote and information from the denazification file of Karl Dürr, questionnaire of the military government with attachments, 9 December 1946.
4. This and the following from Eugen Thalmann's personnel file.
5. This was an assessment made by the responsible LGP in 1939 (ibid.).
6. See e.g., the *Allgemeinverfügung* ("AV," defined as a "general order" addressed to a larger audience) of the Reich Ministry of Justice (or "RJM") of 20 December 1944, in: BA, R 3001 No. 8463/22 [unpaginated]).
7. Decree of 13 August 1942 (Reichsgesetzblatt I, 508–512). See also Richterbriefe No. 5 and No. 18, 1 February/1 December 1943, reprinted in: Richterbriefe, 68–81, 225–250.
8. Local Court of Neustadt, judgment of 10 January 1945, Ds 1/1945.
9. Local Court of Neustadt, judgment of 15 March 1945, Ds 11/1945.
10. Local Court of Neustadt, judgment of 8 February 1945, Ds 5/1945.
11. Local Court of Neustadt, judgment of 19 April 1945, Dls 11/1945.
12. Local Court of Neustadt, judgment of 18 January 1945, Ds 4/1945.
13. Local Court of Neustadt, judgment of 16 January 1945, Ds 2-3/1945.
14. Local Court of Neustadt, judgment of 8 March 1945, Dls 1/1945 and Ds 13-14/1945.
15. Local Court of Neustadt, penalty order of 28 March 1945, Cs 16/1945.
16. Local Court of Neustadt, judgment of 25 January 1945, Cs 1/1945.
17. Local Court of Neustadt, judgment of 1 March 1945, Ds 6/1945.
18. Local Court of Neustadt, penalty order of 2 March 1945, Cs 9/1945.
19. Local Court of Neustadt, judgment of 15 March 1945, Ds 12/1945.
20. Local Court of Neustadt, judgment of 22 February 1945, Ds 10/1945.
21. See the proceedings of the Local Court of Neustadt, Ds 7/1945, Ds 8/1945, Ds 20–24/1945.
22. Local Court of Neustadt, judgment of 1 March 1945, Ds 9/1945.
23. Local Court of Neustadt, judgment of 5 April 1945, Ds 26/1945.
24. Local Court of Neustadt, penalty order of 21 February 1945, Cs 15/1945.
25. Local Court of Neustadt, judgment of 13 February 1945, Dls 3/1945.
26. Local Court of Neustadt, discontinuation order of 12 February 1945, Dls 4/1944.
27. Heidegger, "Abiturium," 283 et seq.
28. Local Court of Neustadt, settlement of 22 March 1945, C 5–6/1945.
29. Local Court of Neustadt, settlement dated 22 March 1945, C 1/1945.
30. Local Court of Neustadt, partial settlement of 16 February 1945, C 2/1945.
31. Settlement dated 7 April 1945, Local Court of Neustadt, C 7/1945.

32. On 24 March 1945, the plaintiff found a replacement apartment; Local Court of Neustadt, C 56–57/1944.
33. Brief dated 10 January 1945, Local Court of Neustadt, C 3/1945.
34. The tenants were given notice. Local Court of Neustadt, judgment of 6 April 1945, C 12–13/1945.
35. Local Court of Neustadt, decision of 6 April 1945, C 11/1945.
36. Local Court of Neustadt, C 60–61/1944.
37. This and the following information is taken from Eugen Thalmann's personnel file and from the file of his denazification proceedings.
38. Similar accounts in Stephenson, *Hitler's Home Front*, 314.
39. Thalmann, questionnaire from the military government, 28 April 1945, identical wording in the personnel file and in the denazification file.
40. No general files have survived, but the process is evident from correspondence with a lawyer from June 1945, which is documented in the Local Court of Neustadt, C 60–61/1944.
41. The return receipt can be found in the file Local Court of Neustadt, C 60–61/1944.
42. The confirmation came on 21 November, the swearing-in on 4 December 1945 (denazification file of Karl Dürr).
43. Local Court of Neustadt, judgment of 1 June 1945, Ds 29–30/1945.
44. Local Court of Neustadt, judgment of 15 June 1945, Ds 31/1945.
45. Local Court of Neustadt, decision of 18 June 1945, settlement of 25 June 1945, and minutes of the hearing of 23 July 1945, C 60–61/1944.
46. Robert Röll personnel file: born in 1878, Catholic, he passed two state examinations with distinction ("good"), was a judge since 1906, served at the Higher Regional Court since 1929, retired in 1945 and was subsequently reappointed to the Higher Regional Court. From 1922 to 1933 he was a member of the catholic *Zentrum* party. He was not a member of the NSDAP, but belonged to the *Beamtenbund* (Civil Servants' Association), the *Rechtswahrerbund* and the *Volkswohlfahrt*.
47. Thalmann to Spruchkammer, 17 August 1945, in: Personnel file of Eugen Thalmann.
48. Thalmann to Spruchkammer, 13 September 1946, in: Denazification file Eugen Thalmann.
49. Spruchkammer, decision of 19 November 1946, in: ibid.
50. Letter from Ms. Thalmann to the Appeals Chamber, 18 December 1946, in: ibid.
51. Letter from Mrs. Thalmann to Karl Dürr, 23 March 1948, in: ibid.
52. Order of the public prosecutor's office, 20 February 1947, Local Court of Neustadt, Dls 1/1945, Ds 13–14/1945.
53. Local Court of Neustadt, Cs 16/1945.
54. Local Court of Neustadt, Ds 12/1945.
55. Local Court of Neustadt, Dls 11/1945.
56. Cost decisions from October and November 1945 can be found, for example, in Neustadt, C 56-57/1944 and Local Court of Neustadt, C 7/1945.
57. E.g., in Local Court of Neustadt, C 5-6/1945.
58. Local Court of Neustadt, C 3/1945.
59. Local Court of Neustadt, C 11/1945.
60. Mühlmann, *Die Völker der Erde*, 133.
61. Thierack, "Deutsche Rechtswahrer!," 1.
62. Quoted from Kempowski, *Echolot*, 76.
63. Scholz, *Rechtssicherheit*, 69.

Chapter 3

Parceling Death

The Auschwitz Local Court and the IG Farben Land Register

Image of the World

The land register describes a world of its own. Before its introduction, in the dark centuries of the German Middle Ages, a complex symbolism was employed to legally validate the sale of a plot of land. One person came, the other went, and so that everyone could see this, the seller would extinguish the hearth fire, jump over the fence, or hand the buyer a clod of earth, a stick, or a stalk, thus giving some kind of sign that he had left the land and was now transferring it to the other person. *Ufgegebin* and *ufgelazin*, *upseggen unde uplaten*, *vertygen* and *opgelaten*: long-practiced phonetic adaptation eventually turned this into "*Auflassung*" ("declaration of conveyance"), and this is what the transfer of real property was called from the thirteenth century onwards.[1] The general mechanization of the world banished the accompanying ritual to the quiet sphere of paper. As early as the Middle Ages, the first towns drew up lists of house plots and their sales in order to quickly and reliably determine land ownership. In the nineteenth century, this apparatus grew beyond the city limits, covering meadows, fields, groves and forests until there were practically no gaps left. The *Civil Code* gave the land register access to the entire Reich, a process that was completed in 1935 with a new Land Register Ordinance. "The land registers are maintained by the local courts," the description now stated in dignified style. And further: "These are responsible for the properties located within their district."[2]

Without land registers, nothing could be done anymore. Anyone wishing to trade in real estate first entered into a purchase agreement, which had to be notarized by a court or a notary, after which both parties went to the land registry and declared their agreement. Because this was a rather solemn affair despite all the technical details, the *Civil Code* took the precaution of adding the parenthetical phrase "*Auflassung*" ("declaration of conveyance") after the "agreement between the alienor and the acquirer" in Section 925 in discreet reference to the term's Middle High German roots; in such matters, a short basic course in the vocabulary of German private law is indispensable.

At the same time, the land register itself was interlinked behind the scenes with the cadasters, the old land and building tax registers. These were originally created for fiscal purposes: in order to determine the tax burden, the authorities measured the size of properties and recorded the boundary, location, and use. As early as 1786, Johann Georg Krünitz' *Oekonomische Encyklopädie* contained the prophecy that in future, "not a hand's breadth of land will remain hidden" from the official boundary markers.[3] This soon turned into a barter deal. The cadastral offices reported to the land registries what they had found when surveying the land, and in return they received information about changes in ownership. The land register sorted out the world of law, the cadaster dealt with the harsh reality.

However, the norms prevailed over the facts. The land register remained connected to reality but was hierarchically superior to it. The *Civil Code* stipulated that the contents of the land register were "presumed to be correct" (Section 892), even if they did not adequately reflect the actual circumstances. If, for example, the surveying authorities had determined that a property boundary actually ran ten meters further east than previously assumed, the land register could still only be adjusted with the consent of the affected owners. Until then, incorrectly documented legal positions could be acquired in good faith, a somewhat peculiar variant of the old saying *quod non est in actis, non est in mundo*—only with recognition in the land register was reality authenticated in its existence.

This marked the end of the bureaucratization of turf; the *ratio scripta* had completely replaced the old symbolism of hearth fires and fence jumping. The parcels of land in the world became properties in the legal sense. Two plots of land could only be combined "if there was no risk of confusion," as the land registry regulations of 1935 repeatedly emphasized. Each plot was given its own sheet, each sheet a corresponding file to document purchase contracts, certificates of inheritance or any applications, and each municipality its own book. The entire land was translated into the silent data series of hectares, depreciations, rights, and encumbrances, neatly divided into sections, columns, and serial numbers. By the mid-1920s, the land registers had been completed in almost all German states.

What a success of civilization! And what a tremendous victory for German virtues: "German love of the soil, German sense of transparency, German conscientiousness, and loyalty to the civil service have come together over the course of centuries in the land register," rejoiced Justus Wilhelm Hedemann in 1936, full of National Socialist fervor.[4] The paper duplicate of the world: in the land register, the German soul found itself.

Measuring the Lebensraum

The invasion of Poland, however, brought disorder into this idyllic world. The Wehrmacht's victories and the hectic annexations in the East opened up new scopes of application for the German land register, which legally speaking was unprepared for this war of aggression. When the Sudeten German territories were taken over, a three-step process was prescribed for the new land registers: first, a draft had to be produced, this then had to be interpreted in order to be able to record objections, after which the Reich Minister of Justice would finally declare the land register "established."[5] But these regulations were not suited for the conquered territories in Poland. The Reich Ministry of Justice had presupposed that the entries in the existing land register would serve as the starting point for the new draft. Polish land registers, however, were linguistically almost inaccessible to German officials, and their content was structured quite differently. Some followed Prussian law, some Austrian law, and still others French law, while in the parts of the country where Russian law had applied, there were often no land registers at all.[6] The task of keeping records of the Wehrmacht's route to the East therefore required not only detailed legal knowledge and an eye for technical details, but also a certain amount of improvisation. The German land register encountered unknown regions.

And so it came to Auschwitz following the German invasion of Poland. By the time the Germans reached Auschwitz, the small town already had a long history. Even the *Brockhaus Enzyklopädie* noted in 1864 the impressive 800 years that the inhabitants of the Duchy of Auschwitz had spent in a border region, sometimes belonging to Silesia, sometimes to Krakow, sometimes to Bohemia, before the entire area, along with Galicia, fell to Austria after the partition of Poland in 1795. Two small tributaries, the Sola and Przemsa, flowed into the Vistula here, and not far away there was "an ancient castle on a steep hill" to marvel at, as the *Brockhaus* reported.[7] The Treaty of Saint-Germain, which finalized the dissolution of Austria-Hungary, transformed Auschwitz back into Oświęcim in 1919 by transferring Galicia to Poland. At the turn of the twentieth century, the population grew to over 5,000 inhabitants, and by 1939 there were already a good

14,000, more than half of whom were Jewish, which led them to confidently declare that they were living in the "Jerusalem of Oświęcim."[8]

On the very first day of the war, the city came under heavy bombardment from the German Luftwaffe. A mass exodus soon began: Polish soldiers and civilians tried to make their way to Krakow or Romania. Those who remained were primarily the few ethnic Germans and a few elderly people, whose memories of the "good Austrian times" led them to expect nothing bad from the Germans. On 4 September, the Wehrmacht was at the gates of the town, and the next day the first Einsatzgruppe marched in to immediately take "the necessary measures for pacification," as was reported to Gleiwitz in grim triumph.[9] Within a week, Oświęcim was once again called Auschwitz, and where a traditional market square formed the center of the town, an "Adolf Hitler Square" now signaled the dawn of a new era. Within a few weeks, the Jewish population was dispossessed, their businesses confiscated, their bank accounts frozen. Throughout the region—Eastern Upper Silesia and the so-called "Eastern Strip"—the occupiers destroyed synagogues and Jewish cemeteries, the unleashed violence culminating in countless arbitrary executions. On 8 October, Hitler issued a decree establishing the Kattowitz administrative district, which was to be incorporated into the Province of Silesia "including adjacent territories." The decree came into effect on 26 October.[10] Auschwitz now belonged to the German Reich.

However, this did not solve a fundamental problem: there were virtually no Germans living in Auschwitz. A census in December 1939 revealed—despite all the myths about the "original German tribal area"[11]—a total of 61 ethnic Germans in the town itself, and none at all in the surrounding area. There was not even a National Socialist-approved suitable candidate for the post of mayor. Only a madcap subsidy program gradually attracted ethnic Germans from the Old Reich. "In the East" there were favorable prospects for power, quick riches, and the rapid rise to the status of a master race. A particularly vile form of National Socialist gold-rush mentality therefore spread in the area around Auschwitz: the coal mining area around Kattowitz promised lucrative profits for decades to come; tax breaks attracted investments of all kinds; the de facto lawlessness of entire groups of people provided a rich pool of businesses, villas, furniture, and accessories from which the visiting officials could help themselves more or less freely. The *völkisch* ideology ennobled even the most ordinary crime as a valuable service to one's own race.

The judiciary initially had little place in this aggressive Germanization race. Auschwitz had long had a solid judicial institution, which had now been declared a German local court and been incorporated into the German court system, subordinate to the Bielitz Regional Court and, above that, the Breslau Higher Regional Court.[12] The street on which it was located was renamed "Hermann-Göring-Straße" after a few days. This was now a German court at a fairly German address, but otherwise there was nothing: no staff, hardly any usable files, and not even an adequate building. An inspector sent by the Reich Justice Administration shortly after the occupation described his impressions of his visit to the site with downright disgust: the building was located almost at the edge of the town, belonged to a Jewish refugee, and was "in a poor, partially neglected condition," with no electricity and only an inadequate water supply. Only two rooms were in use: the "extremely poorly furnished" room of the supervising judge and the office, in which only one employee spoke German. Of the original four judges, two had fled, one had committed suicide, and the fourth had applied to the civil administration in Krakow. The files and 121 volumes of land registers were largely intact; however, all the cadastral records had been removed.[13]

Who was to serve there? In Berlin, three posts were quickly created for the new German local court. However, there was only one lawyer who wanted to go to Auschwitz, and his application was presumably successful only because it was the only one. The new official had never held an office before. Werner Günther was 26 years old, fresh from his legal traineeship, and now, without any practical experience, was tasked with establishing an independent German judiciary. Until then, his career had been unremarkable. Günther's father was a moderately successful publisher in Reichenbach, Silesia, and he had spent his studies and legal clerkship in Silesia, with brief excursions to Rostock and Jena. His exams were solid, his Protestant faith relaxed, his political views robust: in 1933, he joined the SA, and in 1937 he became a member of the NSDAP.[14] On 1 November 1939, Günther began his service in Auschwitz. At that time, the local court was the only German civil authority in the city and Günther was the only judge there, a lonely, insanely young outpost of German law and order in the middle of a relatively foreign region. And even this brave fighter was granted the greatest possible distance from the newly conquered *Lebensraum*: his official residence remained Bunzlau, deep in western Silesia; in Auschwitz, he moved into merely a furnished room, with a year and a half's daily allowance of 3.50 Reichsmarks to ease the burden of the good 320 kilometers that the German reorganizing plan had installed between Günther's office and Günther's dining tables.[15]

Remaking of the East

And so, in the first year of its existence, the new local court—like the judicial administration in the annexed East—was a makeshift arrangement with few resources and few staff.[16] Günther administered a space with no order. In January 1940, he was assigned a judicial constable to assist him. This constable had been given a pistol with a bayonet and five cartridges at his previous post in Ratibor along the way,[17] thus elevating the Auschwitz newcomer, in a sense, to the sword of justice. No further support was to be expected for the time being. Not even lawyers or notaries could be found; until the invasion of the Wehrmacht, nine had been licensed in the town, but now there was not a single one left.[18] It took a year to find a lawyer and notary, but as a native Hungarian and long-time employee of the railroad, he had only found his way to the law and to German-ness through a second educational path. This may have been acceptable for a transitional period, but because the late-appointed legal worker was unwavering in his belief that he could also represent Polish compatriots in court,[19] he was removed from office again in September 1942.

Günther himself repeatedly attempted to make the move to the new location more attractive to new employees. However, the limited leeway afforded by development bonuses, separation payments, and daily allowances only offered modest options. The judiciary could hardly compete with the shady entrepreneurship of the private sector. To the great annoyance of the civil servants, Auschwitz was placed in Local C Class, which provided only meager bonuses. Housing, food, and all the necessities of everyday life were either unavailable in Auschwitz or exorbitantly expensive. In November 1940, Günther justified financial support for a legal secretary on the grounds that food prices in Auschwitz were 15 to 20 percent higher than in the Old Reich, that there were hardly any German merchants or craftsmen, that the only distraction was "a single—primitive—German restaurant," and that there were no cultural facilities at all.[20] However, even these observations had to be accompanied by a meticulous list of all the extra costs—overnight accommodation, first and second breakfast, "newspaper 0.20 RM" etc.—before the suffering employee finally received an additional daily allowance of 5 Reichsmarks.[21]

Above all, there was a lack of living space. Furnished rooms were not available, Günther complained to the judicial administration, "because 70 to 80 percent of the population are Jews," which another judicial employee dramatized into the claim—favorable for a relocation allowance—that the city was "90 percent Jewish."[22] In fact, the Jewish population had increased after the German occupation due to numerous deportations from other parts of the country. The Old Town soon functioned as a kind of open ghetto, which was later isolated from the rest of the town by a police cordon. As a result, there were virtually no vacant apartments in the city itself. The prospects were even worse in the surrounding areas. The periphery was firmly in the hands of the SS. In the southwest, west, and north, confiscations swallowed up more and more villages, farms, and towns in the surrounding area until the SS finally had an "area of interest" which, at a good 40 square kilometers, was many times larger than the urban area of Auschwitz. By the end of January 1940, it had been decided to build a concentration camp of monstrous size around an empty barracks site. In the spring, around 300 Jewish men were conscripted to build the camp; on 14 June, the new institution, designed for 10,000 prisoners, began operations.

And now, in the gloomy shadow of the camp, civilian life in the city began to flourish. Over the summer, several thousand SS men and their families gradually moved into the town. In a short time, a settlement with kindergartens, schools, doctors' offices, a library, a soccer stadium, and a swimming pool was built, an enclave of stone for the new Aryan elite. The economy followed suit. At the end of 1940, IG Farben gave the region its next investment boost. The decision was made to build a new plant for the production of synthetic rubber in Dwory, a few kilometers east of the city.[23] A massive construction program was to be launched for Auschwitz itself, both to attract the necessary skilled workers and at the same time demonstrate the National Socialist determination to reclaim the vastness of the East for their own race. Here, as was emphasized at every opportunity from then on, a bulwark of German spirit and German energy was to be created: at the founding meeting of IG Auschwitz in April 1941, Otto Ambros affirmed on behalf of the entire IG board the intention that "this industrial foundation will become a solid cornerstone for a strong, healthy Germanness in the East." Heinrich Himmler raved about the "model of German settlement in the East" that was to be created in Auschwitz. Gauleiter Fritz Bracht became almost hysterical a few weeks later when he exclaimed: "Upper Silesia must become so German that there will be no district more German in the entire Reich. Whatever is in and around us must be German!"[24]

As a result, the small town on the outskirts suddenly found itself at the center of the action. To the west lay the endless concentration camp, to the east the new Buna plant, which, at around 25 square kilometers, also far exceeded the size of the city. The IG needed land, labor, and living space, all resources to which the SS had almost unlimited access. This presented a profitable trade for both sides. The SS received the building materials they needed to expand the camp. In return, the IG received everything it needed for its facility. Because the camp was designed for gigantic capacity from the outset, there was an almost inexhaustible pool of prisoners available that the IG could draw on cheaply; the daily rate for a worker from the camp was just 3 to 4 Reichsmarks. Furthermore, in February 1941, the SS began deporting the Jewish and parts of the Polish population of Auschwitz at breakneck speed. Six weeks later, the city was half-empty; there were no more Jews, and the remaining 7,000 or so Poles had to watch as exactly 660 Reich Germans and 161 ethnic Germans secured the most luxurious houses for themselves.[25]

This marked the beginning of a strange era for Auschwitz, a time of brief, explosive, and morbid growth. Squeezed between the world's largest concentration camp and a massive branch of the world's largest chemical company, urban planning visions admittedly faced strict limitations. The cooperation between the professional murderers on the one hand and the slave drivers on the other yielded beneficial by-products also for the city. It was worth investing in the city's quality of life simply because of the skilled workers to be recruited from all parts of the country and thus, as the IG leaders put it in their crude telegram style, to create the "basic condition for the settlement of inhabitants who were willing and eager to work."[26]

In addition, the poor urban infrastructure caused high—but avoidable—transaction costs for transporting slaves from the camp to the IG factory. Every day, first a few hundred, later more than a thousand, prisoners trekked through the city to get from the camp to the construction site, a walk of a good ten kilometers that opened and closed the workday. At some point a—rather unreliable—freight train was deployed. Rapid transport to the main camp had to be guaranteed even after the IG had opened its own concentration camp on the company premises in autumn 1942, both as a credible threat to work-shy prisoners, but also for practical reasons, as malnourished, sick, or otherwise unproductive workers were singled out for the gas chambers on a weekly basis; even the IG managers considered it unreasonable to operate gas chambers in their own factory.

The city's infrastructure therefore continued to function as a "gruesome human assembly line" between the camp and the factory,[27] and the IG ensured that this assembly line ran smoothly. The first convoys of prisoners built a road from Auschwitz to Dwory. Soon afterwards, work began on a railway embankment to connect the factory to the railway network, and another commando readied expropriated houses in the city for occupancy. The IG supplied the city with water, electricity, and district heating, and invested in apartments, housing estates, and green spaces— "without regard to costs of any kind"[28]—according to its claim. This was with almost unconditional support from the Reich government, which classified every construction project in Auschwitz as a top priority and provided millions in subsidies and tax breaks.

The efforts were increasingly paying off. Buna was still not in production, but at least parts of the facility were now in operation. Companies from related industries followed the IG to Auschwitz and eventually provided the concentration camp with 38 economically oriented sub-camps. By October 1943, the town had grown to 28,000 inhabitants, a good 7,000 of whom had moved from the old Reich, and the majority of whom were connected to IG in some way. A new residents' registration office monitored the influx and departure of citizens, a building inspectorate and a traffic office monitored the numerous building sites, a welfare office looked after the socially disadvantaged members of the community, and a street cleaning service ensured that the roads were cleared in both summer and winter. After the war, mayor Heinrich Gutsche proudly recalled that Auschwitz was "soon known as one of the cleanest towns in the district."[29] In addition to the 2,825 Germans, IG Farben employed approximately 20,000 foreign workers and a good 10,000 prisoners from the camp. In the concentration camp, four crematoria worked tirelessly toward the Final Solution, enveloping the entire area in the sweet stench of burnt flesh.

The city was now indisputably a German legal and cultural area. In the same year, it was included in the guide book of the German bourgeois traveler: in 1943, the *Baedeker Generalgouvernement*, Hans Frank's personal propaganda project, noted that the railroad line from the occupied territories to Krakow ran via Auschwitz, "an industrial city of 12,000 inhabitants, formerly the capital of the Piast duchies of Auschwitz and Zator." Whoever was inspired by this dry information, found the genre-typical addendum: "Hotel Zator, 20 beds."[30]

"Ethnic Land Consolidation"

A new era began as well for the judicial administration when the first convoys of prisoners began to develop the IG Farben lands at the end of April 1941. On 1 February—the deportations had just begun—Günther received his appointment as a local court judge, and in March—half the town had been deported—he reported that he had now found an apartment in Auschwitz, "partly accommodated with confiscated furniture"; if he were granted the reconstruction allowance for the East, he was prepared to give up the separation allowance he had previously received and move to Auschwitz. This was also a sensible plan from the perspective of the judicial administration. Günther officially lived in Auschwitz from 1 June 1941.[31]

Legal staff were also able to contribute to the unexpected economic miracle in eastern Germany. On 17 September 1940, Hermann Göring, as Commissioner for the Four-Year Plan, issued a *Decree on the treatment of assets belonging to members of the former Polish state*, which allowed the seizure and confiscation of property belonging to Jews and Polish refugees, as well as the appropriation of anything else that was "needed in the interests of the defense of the Reich or the consolidation of German nationhood."[32] If this concerned an agricultural holding, then according to Section 12, the Reich Commissioner for the Consolidation of German Nationhood, i.e., Heinrich Himmler, was responsible and could have confiscations carried out for the SS through the shortest possible channels. However, to ensure that the property of a fellow citizen was not confiscated by mistake, Section 13 provided for something resembling a legal process: if someone claimed to be a German national, the proceedings were to be suspended and a corresponding decision was to be obtained from the local court president, against which an appeal could then be lodged with the Reich Minister of the Interior if necessary. A number of threats of punishment in Sections 20 and 21 in turn countered this administrative procedure, making legal recourse appear not a particularly attractive option: anyone who "in any way impaired the effect of the confiscation" and thereby "acted against the political reorganization" was to be punished with death.

The political goal was therefore clear: the complete "Aryanization" of the real estate market, supported by capital punishment if necessary. This was a considerable imposition for the formalized rigor of the land register. Hitler's stated goal of "ethnic land consolidation"[33] came up against an extraordinarily inflexible branch of the law, even by legal standards. Even confiscation was not easy to implement under land registry law. As a matter of principle, only items whose validity depended on entry in the land register could be entered in the land register. A confiscation by Göring or Himmler, however, did not affect the ownership at all, but was merely a law enforcement ban on disposing of the property. It was obvious that such a measure did not depend on the correct recording in the land register. After months of uncertainty, it was agreed to indicate the prohibition on sale by a colored sticker on the file cover, as a kind of unregistered warning against non-registration.[34] However, the fact that the validity of the confiscations depended on the ethnicity of the persons concerned could no longer be represented in the land registry. The SS had already made formal determinations in this regard. But these assessments could at least theoretically still be challenged with a complaint, especially as the entries on the German People's List (i.e., the Nazi classification of inhabitants of Nazi-occupied territories) in Upper Silesia only began in April 1941, meaning that the ethnic affiliations were still open to interpretation.

And that was not even the worst of it: the ethnic land consolidation was to be immediately followed by an economic one, so that the German Reich or any bona fide purchaser would not take over the mortgages of the previous Polish owners. Only in the case of agricultural holdings was the legal extinguishment of all encumbrances provided. Otherwise, the local courts had to ensure that any old debts were first settled between the seizure and the final confiscation, before the new owners were recorded in the land register. Here, too, racially defined exceptions were added.[35] In the case of properties chosen for IG Farben, however, there were not even any land survey records because the Polish authorities had removed the cadasters before the German occupation. It was therefore unknown whether the properties had been legally seized and what liens were attached. Indeed, it was not even known whether the affected parcels were even "properties" in the sense of land register law or whether the legally relevant boundaries lay elsewhere.

As the land registry office, the Auschwitz Local Court was designated to resolve these difficulties. From the summer of 1941, hundreds of confiscation orders began arriving there. These orders had been issued by Himmler, as Reich Commissioner for the Consolidation of German Nationhood, in order to be able to sell the land for the new factory to IG Farben.[36] Legally, none of this was of any use. Confiscation prevented the previous owner from continuing to dispose of his property, but did not create any new ownership, neither for the German Reich, nor even for the IG Farben. The invasion of Poland had left the land registry system untouched: without a land register, there was no ownership, and without a cadaster, there was no land register. The IG Farben placed its important wartime multi-million-Reichsmark project on a piece of land that would belong to other owners for years to come.

The IG's legal department was therefore alarmed. "The question of the land registry treatment of our land acquisition," a memo noted, "probably plays the most important role of all in our land purchase."[37] It was pointed out during an initial meeting that there were no land registers for the properties in question, all attempts to find them proved to be unsuccessful. There was therefore no alternative but to have the confiscated properties surveyed first and then to replace the land register, which had previously been maintained according to Austrian law, with a newly created German one. Soon the land surveyors from the Bielitz Cadastral Office were busy in Dwory parceling out the confiscated land, recording the location, type of use, area, and yield measurement, and ultimately creating seven impressive plots from the thousands of small and very small plots—everything from 300 square meters to 80 hectares. The lists read like medieval landscape descriptions: flood channels, paths, ponds, pastures, located "south of the Vistula," "north of the large fish pond," "northeast of the large fish pond," "on the border with Zaborze," "south of the Reichsstraße," "on the border with Dwory II," or simply "in the village," used as forests, farms, courtyards, paths, dams, and bodies of water.[38] Just as Johann Georg Krünitz had prophesied centuries earlier, not an inch of land remained hidden, which, of course, could be attributed not only to the loyalty of German officials and German conscientiousness, but certainly equally to the fact that anyone who resisted this racially cleansed world view was threatened with the death penalty. By the summer of 1942, around half of the site had been properly parceled out and the cadastral registers were "clean and clear," as the IG stated with satisfaction at a construction meeting in September 1942.[39] A first substantial set of data was sent to the court.

Legal Ground Staff

The Auschwitz Local Court was initially hopelessly overwhelmed by these tasks. Only the accompanying rhetoric remained bombastic as usual. Karl Buchholz from the Posen Higher Regional Court rejoiced in his own successes, claiming that in September 1939 they had found "a legal vacuum" in Poland, in which German law had been applied without further ado.[40] Fritz Fechner from the Reich Ministry of Justice expressed the transfer of law with even more gravity: "The German people who had retaken possession of the German East brought their law with them, so to speak," emphasized in bold type so that even the casual reader would not miss the world-historical significance of this mission.[41]

The practice of land registry law, however, forced German legal experts to adopt a rather subdued tone. If Werner Günther, as a brave guardian of Eastern European law, had brought his own German law with him to the new territories, then this gift certainly escaped him. A few months after taking office, he contacted the ministry in Berlin directly and began with the disarmingly honest question of whether German land registry law already applied in his court. Günther was also unclear about a number of other things. He wanted to know from his superiors whether he should continue to maintain the existing Polish land registers or whether he could expect to receive German land registers, whether he would also have to create land files and, finally, whether he could base his proceedings on the German fee schedule.[42] Apart from his carefully cultivated respect for the official channels, the fully qualified German lawyer had actually brought nothing with him.

But there were no other staff. The court still eked out a meager existence. Günther was still the only judge on site,[43] of six positions in the land registry office, just two were filled. For these scattered members of the judiciary, the IG Farben land registry soon became a kind of life insurance policy. Without the Buna factory, the court would probably have been closed; its existence depended on the state's plunder. Only as long as there were still stolen lands to be legally cleaned up could it be justified to withhold able-bodied legal workers from the war effort.

Günther had already been declared indispensable upon his assignment to Auschwitz. The growing symbiosis between the court and the land registry became the decisive argument to further justify this. On 23 April 1942, the president of the Kattowitz Higher Regional Court—which had been established a year earlier and had since then held jurisdiction over Auschwitz—announced that the "major construction projects of IG Farben" would require a "*considerable* number of land registry orders, numbering in the thousands." Günther was the only judge in the district who was "privy to the many difficult issues," which made him "hardly replaceable until the construction projects were completed." IG Farben therefore attached "considerable importance" to Günther remaining in his job. At almost the same time, IG Farben wrote to the Military Recruitment Inspectorate that "for the acquisition and development of the extensive land in Auschwitz," on which "a factory of the highest wartime importance" was to be built, it was "absolutely necessary to draw up a land register in accordance with the German model," which only Günther could do, as he had already been involved in the preparatory work. Two weeks later, the president of the Higher Regional Court reiterated this assessment: "The situation is indeed such that a judge other than the one who carried out the very difficult preparatory work would hardly be in a position to complete it properly."[44] The land register became a guarantee against conscription. Günther remained.

His fellow associates felt the same way. The land register needed them, and they needed the land register. Otto Schmiegel, born in 1900 and most recently a court clerk in Kassel, came to Auschwitz at the end of 1940 and was quickly promoted to legal secretary. Günther attested that he had already opened 934 IG Farben land files and that his duties "mainly consisted of processing confiscation applications."[45] When Schmiegel was absent for two weeks due to illness, the court immediately asked for a replacement "as work on the land register was in full swing."[46] Schmiegel's work was also more important than the war; from 1942 onwards, his exemptions from military service were routinely justified with "known urgent work."[47] The same formula also benefited Erich Pretzsch, a judicial employee from Görlitz, whose work for the Buna-Werke had also earned him a promotion and subsequently saved him from military service.[48]

Even Polish personnel proved indispensable. Since the beginning of 1940, Sebald Godulla, a Germanophile Pole, had been employed to facilitate communication with the population and to access the Polish files.[49] When Godulla left in April 1943, he was immediately succeeded by Anna Brzezinski, whose appointment was expressly justified by the "rush of business due to the new creation of the land register."[50] Even Albin Jaskiewicz, a Pole whose entry in the German People's List was rejected, found employment, against all regulations. Born in Auschwitz in 1885, he had been working at the court there since 1904. He initially retired in 1939, then returned to the court and was now summarily declared indispensable by Günther: "Jaskiewicz takes care of the frequent land register extracts related to the I.G. Farben factory and the Auschwitz concentration camp," he explained to the President of the Bielitz Regional Court in June 1942, adding that Jaskiewicz would also be "indispensable for the soon-to-be-expected registration of the I.G. Farben factory's properties in the land register." To avoid any misunderstanding, Günther once again emphasized that the work was "urgent" and had to be completed "at an accelerated pace."[51] As late as the end of 1943, Jaskiewicz's continued employment was justified by the "imminent commencement of the creation of the land register in accordance with German law for the area of interest of the local IG Farben factory." To be on the safe side, it was pointed out that the land registry office was so separate from the other departments of the court that Jaskiewicz "could not familiarize himself with anything other than land registry business."[52]

Land Conveyance

Political cartography posed a final difficulty in 1943. The exact boundary between the city of Auschwitz and the SS concentration camp had long been the subject of dispute, with the civilian authorities finally even making the both naive and macabre suggestion to rebuild the camp "at a different location" in order to "ensure adequate development opportunities for all parties involved in the future."[53] The IG also tried to settle the dispute. In the end, they were successful. In the spring of 1943, the border to the SS area of interest was finally determined; the city renounced some disputed areas in return for preferential municipal treatment—it received its own mayor, its own municipal coat of arms, and, finally, the consolidation of its eastern border: Dwory and Monowitz, the two villages where the IG had settled, belonged predominantly to the municipality of Auschwitz from 1 April.

But this meant that the Buna factory, as politically privileged, financially strong, and important to the war effort as it may have been, was tied to the town of Auschwitz in terms of land registry law, a disaster for IG Farben. The land registers could by law only be established for the municipal district in its entirety. Accordingly, the IG could only hope to have its land register when the entire municipal area of Auschwitz had been properly recorded. In this respect, however, it was clear to everyone that there was no hope. The countless deportations, destruction, re-zoning, and new construction had left Auschwitz in a state of property law chaos that would take years to re-survey.

It took Otto Thierack, the Reich Minister of Justice, himself to intervene to break the land registry partnership between the factory and the city. Thierack readily recognized the predicament of an investment of millions in an unresolved ownership situation. He divided the city into two land register districts. At the end of 1943, he declared the Auschwitz II land register officially created; the Auschwitz I land register implied by this was never created. The crowning moment came on 22 March 1944. By then, almost 30,000 people were working on the construction site, a good 7,000 inmates were held in the IG's own concentration camp, and the "transfer reports to Birkenau" repeatedly recorded hundreds of departures—diagnoses of "weakness," "diarrhea," or "collapse" meant death in the gas chamber[54]—and now, in a final step, the lawless interregnum on the company premises came to an end. *Ufgegebin* and *ufgelazin*: the Auschwitz Local Court recorded a purchase agreement between IG Farben and the German Reich, which promised IG Farben almost 2,500 hectares of land, for which the latter in turn paid a purchase price of 4.062 million Reichsmarks.[55] The Hungarian Jews, who arrived by the thousands from mid-May onwards, were enslaved by IG Farben under clarified ownership. Now the area was truly ethnically cleansed.

The long-awaited legalization of their multi-million Reichsmark project must have brought considerable relief to IG Farben. The thousands of human lives that this prestigious war project had already claimed by this point could be integrated into a brutal, yet somehow still economically viable, logic by referring to the Führer and the world market: resolute action was required to maintain the regime's goodwill. Moreover, a great deal of money had been invested that demanded a return and, last but not least, the SS could be brought in when it came to getting one's hands dirty. The rough terrain of white-collar crime, however, must have remained a source of unease for the rulers of IG Farben. The respectable businessman could not afford a dirty collar. Up to that point, a good 500 million Reichsmarks had been sunk into the racially unreliable land register of eastern Upper Silesia. The construction of the company concentration camp alone had cost five million, and in the meantime 20 million had been paid to the SS for the slaves from the main camp, and the city's infrastructure had also eaten up huge sums. It would have been embarrassing to explain at the annual general meeting why this enormous sum had been sunk into a construction site that IG Farben had control over thanks to the beneficence of the SS, but not in its own right. Contact with a public prosecutor could have been even more unpleasant: company law was already full of criminal provisions regarding actions that were detrimental to the company or were based on false statements. The embezzlement offense under Section 266 of the Criminal Code, which was only reformed by the National Socialists in 1933, gave the hazardous investment at Auschwitz further criminal relevance.

Whether the professional discomfort of their legal gamble ever bothered the decision-makers at IG Farben is unknown. The shareholders asked no questions; the public prosecutors stayed away before 1945 and even more so after 1945. The collar remained white. The pseudo-legal circumstances of property acquisition provided welcome opportunities for participation for all involved. In the face of the monumental significance of the land register, even the dictates of Göring and Himmler shrank to the puny size of sticky notes. "Property" as a core area of civil society remained beyond the brute grasp of the prerogative state, at least according to the records; the land registry offices, credit institutions, shareholders and other dignitaries of the *Volksgemeinschaft* ("national community") were able to enjoy a legal normality for which even the construction of a death factory was primarily a problem of proper documentation. The land registry also defended its paper empire against the Wehrmacht by declaring itself indispensable. The merchants' self-image remained untarnished—proper papers were simply needed for the journey into the thousand-year future. And anyone who could gaze into the mirror of the law so fearlessly had every reason to consider themselves normal.

Resolution

This largely fulfilled the purpose of the small local court in Auschwitz. The deal was done. By March 1944, the court had become superfluous. As far as the concentration camp was concerned, it flew under the radar anyway; the SS found the legal ground staff of the local court incapable of satisfying the SS. It is unlikely that there were any connections through party affiliations either: Otto Schmiegel as cell leader, Sebald Godulla as block leader, and Werner Günther as propaganda and training leader of the Auschwitz local NSDAP branch, which had only existed since August 1940, were the highest dignitaries at the court. Relations with the IG also yielded only a few crumbs. One court employee reported to the administration that his 15-year-old daughter was now working for a monthly wage of 60 Reichsmarks as an office trainee at the IG factory in Auschwitz; he asked the court to consider that he would still have to cover the costs of clothing and laundry when calculating the child benefit.[56] Another changed sides completely at the end of 1943 and joined the IG Farben factory "for an indefinite period."[57]

For most, however, the only war-critical business left was the war itself. Werner Günther, who had so valiantly pushed ahead with the Germanization of the court and the creation of the new land register, was forced to leave Auschwitz even before the culmination of his years of hard work. After three and a half years of reorganization work in eastern Upper Silesia, he was drafted for military service in February 1943. For the first few months, he was stationed in Liegnitz—from May onward he was a member of the Auschwitz municipal council—but by 1944 at the latest, he was assigned to the 108th Panzer Grenadier Regiment, an emergency formation formed from the remnants of the 6th Army, which had been destroyed at Stalingrad. With this regiment, he was deployed primarily in Romania, Lithuania, and Latvia.[58] Sebald Godulla, the Pole who felt German and who had served in the Polish army in the distant past, pursued his Germanization with bitter seriousness; in return, he was entered in the German People's List in 1942 and called up to the Wehrmacht at the beginning of 1943.[59] Erich Pretzsch was called up on 10 September 1943,[60] Otto Schmiegel, the indispensable land registrar, was declared fit for military service in early 1944;[61] his further fate is unknown.

After IG Farben had sorted out its land registry affairs, legal services were only offered sporadically on site. Anna Brzezinski was still there to provide Polish translations, while the Pole Albin Jaskiewicz remained at the court on the grounds that the ethnic Germans were no more reliable as they often had Polish relatives and wanted to "ostentatiously make themselves popular with Poles again."[62] A widow with five children came every day for eight hours to keep the court clean.[63] After Werner Günther was called away for the war, Günther Hindemith—a moderately talented lawyer from Lower Silesia—supervised the court in 1943.[64] In 1944, it was Gerhard Thiele, a politically servile careerist, who traveled from Krzepice, 140 kilometers away, to record the purchase agreement between the German Reich and IG Farben.[65] There was no longer a judge in Auschwitz itself.

Escape and Integration

When Auschwitz was evacuated in January 1945, the now rather sleepy local court was not a particular cause for concern for anyone. The SS were interested in the concentration camp, IG Farben in the factory. On 21 January, the Kattowitz Higher Regional Court reported to Berlin that most of the judicial authorities in the district were working "without disruption," and that at least the most important business in Bielitz could "by and large still be carried out." It was added that only in Auschwitz "disruptions are to be expected."[66] This was not entirely wrong. IG Farben had been working on emergency and evacuation plans for months, which now had to be implemented within a few days.[67] On 16 January, the first Russian planes appeared over the city, a day later the evacuation of the non-working population began. Due to the constant air raids, work in the factories practically came to a standstill. On 19 January, the SS drove the first columns of prisoners on a death march to the west, and the following day the evacuation order for the factory was issued. The last remaining employees began to deliberately paralyze the operations and burn compromising documents. On 23 January, the factory management inspected the premises once again and supervised the removal of secret files and key technology. The evacuation was then reported complete.

On the same day, the aforementioned disruptions also reached Kattowitz itself. The Wehrmacht there had repeatedly emphasized that it was virtually impossible for the Red Army to advance as far as the Silesian coalfields. On 23 January, it was learned that the waterworks were already completely in the hands of Soviet soldiers and that the railway only had enough coal for a few days. The next morning, Kattowitz received the evacuation order. Important files were destroyed, others were loaded into a truck that could still be found, the guillotine was dismantled, the individual parts were buried, and finally the gallows were removed. The President of the Higher Regional Court and the General Prosecutor drove through their district one last time; their experiences were harrowing: "Westward-bound Wehrmacht columns, convoys of refugees, and repatriated concentration camp inmates and prisoners made the journey difficult. Mothers fleeing on foot with their small children in their arms pulled their last belongings behind them on sleds. The corpses of concentration camp prisoners lay along the road. Military columns marched along in a disorganized manner. Advancing troops and military guards were nowhere to be seen. It was a picture of a disorderly retreat and immense refugee misery. The people were freezing due to the severe cold. Quite a few children died from freezing to death. It was a desolate, depressing impression that even old soldiers among us had never experienced on such a scale."[68]

It is almost impossible to determine what happened to the lawyers working at Auschwitz after their time at the local court. Günther Hindemith was taken prisoner by the British, became a laborer in a cardboard factory in March 1946, then served as an assistant to the defense in the Nuremberg trials against the southeastern generals, and subsequently a simple judicial officer. Due to his constant efforts and in recognition of his five children, he was promoted in 1956 and became a local court judge in Geilenkirchen.[69] Nowhere in his personnel files is it noted that he was ever in Auschwitz. Gerhard Thiele's legal career, on the other hand, was over—his personnel file initially remained in the Reich Ministry of Justice, was then sent from Berlin to the Federal Archives in Koblenz, and when it was supposed to be returned to Berlin after 1990, it was lost and has since disappeared.[70] Werner Günther's path led via a Silesian military hospital and the final battles in Guben to Schwerin, and a few months later to Hof, where he was initially unemployed, then worked for Siemens and finally became a lawyer. When it came to his integration into West German society, he resorted to the usual narratives: his memberships in the NSDAP and SA had actually been forced upon him from other organizations, he had always stood up for Poles, even Jews, and in doing so accepted open confrontation with superiors. Albin Jaskiewicz, the indispensable land registry clerk, and Sebald Godulla, who had wanted to be Germanized at all costs, served as key witnesses. A small network of Silesian refugees—namely Erich Pretzsch and Sebald Godulla, who had also ended up in Bavaria—confirmed the many exaggerations, evasions, and lies. An elusive Silesian, Otto Schmiegel, was unanimously heavily incriminated. On 16 December 1946, Günther received a first-class acquittal with a rating as "exonerated." The statements on "active resistance"—not leaving the church, "lack of interest" in party affairs, "salary upgrades for all employees in his office"—make up about half of the explanation. Günther's description of his activities, "in particular, preparation for the conversion of the land register from the Austrian to the German system," sounded unemotionally bureaucratic, and the cute "small" appendix, which Günther, following the popular terminology of the German judicial administration, attached to his local court in Auschwitz, rounded off the impression of a rural idyll: he had worked in a sleepy Upper Silesian village where, as Günther picturesquely summarized, "the foxes said 'good night' to each other."[71]

Land Register of Memory

And so it is that almost no traces of the small Auschwitz Local Court can be found today. For a long time, three meager files were kept in the relevant archive in Bielsko-Biała, of which only the confiscation orders from the Land Registry are of some interest.[72] Four volumes from the Opole State Archives were recently added, documenting the career of the office assistant Maximilian Schmidt, who tirelessly worked his way through the Silesian province during his professional career, including a brief stop in Auschwitz.[73] Not even the land register, which the local court so devotedly endeavored to maintain, has survived beyond the smallest fragments; apparently only a "list of properties entered in the land register of the Auschwitz Local Court for the Saybusch estate" survived, which, however, does not refer to the city of Auschwitz.[74]

Only one single collection reached the post-war period almost intact: the personnel files of the local court. Their metamorphosis from court records to historical records took place in a peculiar way. They were originally located in Kattowitz, the seat of the higher regional court. From there, at the end of 1944, they were transferred as a precaution to the town of Neisse, a good 130 kilometers to the west, on the other bank of the Oder. When town after town had to be hastily evacuated in January 1945, it was only at the last moment that a Reichsbahn wagon was organized to transport the files to Dresden on 13 February. A radio message steered them in a different direction once again, thus avoiding the bombing of Dresden; after a lengthy odyssey, they finally perished in Ronneburg in Thuringia.[75]

It is not known why the US troops, who usually requisitioned files in large numbers, were not interested in the Kattowitz legacies. The Soviet military government also limited itself to abruptly interrupting an initial inventory in the summer of 1945. But in 1946, a systematic overview was begun. As a result, in May 1947, the Altenburg District Council, now responsible for the matter, compiled an overview of the remaining Kattowitz holdings. The last coal reserves from the Upper Silesian mining area had been used two years earlier in the final battle to send the files a good 600 kilometers to the west by rail. The list seemed endless: registers, administrative processes, legal literature, general files, lists of names, decrees, estates, calculation sheets, calendars, official seals, 20 typewriters, three radios, a 1946 forestry calendar, twine, file tabs, 36 pencils, 200 ink pens, 120 bags of ink powder, eight ink pads (five small and three large), a letter basket, 10,000 sheets of draft paper, two pairs of scissors and two rulers, a box of valuables, whose trustee, Local Court President Dr. Hermann, was imprisoned and therefore "could not be questioned" about its contents. And so it went on, a total of 150 densely printed pages full of the oddities of the Upper Silesian judiciary, and somewhere hidden in this withered florilegium were the personnel files of the legal workers at Auschwitz.[76]

After this inventory, the way was clear to transfer the files from Ronneburg to the newly founded "Central Archive in the Soviet Occupation Zone," where they witnessed the founding of the GDR and spent relatively uneventful years until 1990. After socialism in Germany had become history, the files were moved once again. Since then, they have been housed in the Secret State Archives of the Prussian Cultural Heritage in Berlin-Dahlem, assigned to the Province of Silesia and there, in turn, to the Breslau Higher Regional Court.

Is this the final resting place? The journey of the files—Kattowitz, Neisse, Ronneburg, Merseburg, Berlin—was bundled together in the archive in a provenance that is essentially completely false. Even the assignment to Breslau is incorrect, as the Auschwitz Local Court had been under the jurisdiction of the newly founded Kattowitz Higher Regional Court since 1941. But the rest is also wrong. In the almost 1,000 years of its vivid existence, Auschwitz was located in Poland, Poland-Lithuania, Austria, and Bohemia. It was part of various duchies and, at one point, a duchy itself. It belonged to the Holy Roman Empire and, in the nineteenth century, to the Kingdom of Galicia, making it part of the Austro-Hungarian Dual Monarchy. Unlike the rest of Galicia, however, it was also a member of the German Confederation. The penultimate chapter in this history was the annexation by the German Reich, which converged its cruel dialectic of Germanization and extermination in Auschwitz. The current chapter began in 1945, when the city became part of the resurrected Poland and has been called again Oświęcim ever since.

However, Auschwitz was never Prussian. Its small local court was established at a time when, following the "*Verreichlichung*" ("Reich-ification") of the judiciary, there was no longer even a Prussian judicial administration. The fact that the local court was retroactively Prussianized in the archival provenance process is just another bizarre twist in the city's complicated history. Almost like in real life: even the land register of memory takes no account of the cadasters of political geography.

Notes

IG Farben was a chemical and pharmaceutical conglomerate, formed in 1925 from a merger of six major chemical companies and, at its time, the largest chemical company in the world.

1. Olechowski, "Auflassung," Sp. 339–342.
2. § 1 Allgemeinverfügung (or "AV," defined as a "general order" directed to a wider audience), 8 August 1935 (Reichsministerialblatt 637).
3. Volume 14, "Flur"; Volume 7 "Dorf=Buch."
4. Hedemann, *Grundbuchrecht*, 2.
5. AV of the Reich Ministry of Justice (or "RJM"), 12 December 1939, in: *Deutsche Justiz* 1939, 1899–1901.
6. An overview of this can be found in the memorandum of the President of the Breslau Higher Regional Court on the status of the reorganizational work on 1 December 1940 of the court organization in the eastern territories incorporated into the Breslau Higher Regional Court district, in: BA, R 3001 No. 20283, pp. 1–39, pp. 26 et seq.
7. Volume 2, "Auschwitz."
8. For a summary of the history of Auschwitz up to 1939, see Steinbacher, *"Musterstadt" Auschwitz*, 22–47.
9. Report of the Einsatzgruppe to the General Command of the VII Army Corps, 5 September 1939, quoted from ibid., 55.
10. Decree of the Führer and Reich Chancellor on the division and administration of the eastern territories, 8 October 1939, in: Reichsgesetzblatt I, 2042 et seq.
11. See the quotes in Steinbacher, *"Musterstadt" Auschwitz*, 78.
12. Memorandum (op. cit.), here p. 10; thereafter: Decree on the division of courts in the incorporated eastern territories, 26 November 1940, in: Reichsgesetzblatt I, 1538 et seq.
13. RJM, note on the inspection of the local court in Auschwitz (Oswiecim), undated (probably mid-November 1939), in: BA, R 3001 no. 8531, pp. 132 et seq. See also Higher Regional Court President of Breslau to RJM, 30 May 1940, in: BA, R 3001 no. 20829, p. 7; Auschwitz Local Court to the RJM, 28 June 1940 (BA, R 3001 No. 20814, p. 108).
14. All information from PA [personnel file] Günther, in: GStA PK, XVII HA Rep. 222a No. 2161 (Volume 1). His exams were each graded "good," the third of seven grades.
15. OLGP Breslau, 26 January 1940, in: GStA PK, XVII. HA Rep. 222a No. 2161 (PA Günther Vol. 1), p. 154.

16. An overview is given in the memorandum (footnote), here pp. 18 et seq. On the development of the judiciary as a whole, see Becker, *Deutsche Justiz*, 59–69; with a focus on the region in Iluk, "Das deutsche Amtsgericht in Saybusch," 199–221.
17. Manager of the Local Court in Ratibor to the Higher Regional Court President of Breslau, 26 January 1940, in: GStA PK, XVII Rep. 222a No. 3590, Bl. 257.
18. Higher Regional Court President of Breslau to RJM, 21 November 1940, in: GStA PK, XVII. HA Rep. 222a No. 1902, Bl. 1.
19. Minutes of the meeting of 18 June 1942, in: GStA PK, XVII. HA Rep. 222a No. 1902, Bl. 22 (PA Matthäus Fazekas).
20. Supervising Judge of the Local Court of Auschwitz to the Regional Court President of Beuthen, 25 November 1940, in: Personnel File of Otto Schmiegel, Vol. 1, GStA PK, XVII. HA Rep. 222a No. 3681, p. 209. See also similar reports in PA Bernhard Kleczka, in: GStA PK, XVII. HA Rep. 222a No. 2578, p. 42; PA Erich Pretzsch, in: GStA PK, XVII. HA Rep. 222a No. 3449, p. 34; Status report from the Higher Regional Court President of Danzig to the RJM, 1 July 1940, in: BA, R 3001 No. 23360, p. 6–10; also Steinbacher, *"Musterstadt" Auschwitz*, 224.
21. Handwritten list by Otto Schmiegel, 4 December 1940, in: GStA PK, XVII. HA Rep. 222a No. 3681 (PA Vol. 1), p. 212.
22. Judicial employee Sebald Godulla via Local Court to the Regional Court President of Beuthen, 6 December 1940, in: GStA PK, XVII. HA Rep. 222a No. 2073, p. 16. Percentage figures in the letter from the supervising judge of the Local Court of Auschwitz to the Regional Court President of Beuthen, 25 November 1940, in: Personnel file of Otto Schmiegel, GStA PK, XVII. HA Rep. 222a No. 3681 (PA Vol. 1), p. 209.
23. See Wagner, *IG Auschwitz*; White, *IG Auschwitz*; Hayes, *Industry and Ideology*; Setkiewicz, "Ausgewählte Probleme," 7–147; ibid., *The Histories of Auschwitz*; Schmaltz, "Die IG Farbenindustrie," 33–67.
24. Ambros: Report on the founding meeting of IG Auschwitz in Kattowitz, 7 April 1941, Nuremberg Doc. NI-11117, in: TUB ZfA and NMT 8, 383–386; Himmler: Bericht über die Gründungssitzung der IG Auschwitz in Kattowitz, 7 April 1941, here quoted from Wagner, *IG Auschwitz*, 64; Bracht: Kattowitzer Zeitung, 1 August 1941, here quoted from Steinbacher, *"Musterstadt" Auschwitz*, 215 footnote 49.
25. Report in Adler, *Der verwaltete Mensch*, 123 et seq.
26. NI-11125 IG on-site meeting, 26 August 1941, in: TUB ZfA.
27. Hayes, "Die IG Farben," 144.
28. Carl Krauch to Otto Ambros, 25 February 1941, Nuremberg Doc. NI-11938, in: NMT 8, 358–360. Similarly, the founding meeting, 7 April 1941, Nuremberg doc. NI-11117, in: TUB ZfA, where it is stated that the Buna plant was to be built "with all possible speed."
29. Gutsche, Auschwitz-Stadt. Eine kommunalpolitische Betrachtung (1960), in: BA, Ost-Dok. 13/17, p. 1–10. Gutsche was the district commissioner of Auschwitz before the introduction of the municipal code.
30. Baedeker, *Das Generalgouvernement*, 10.
31. Werner Günther to the Higher Regional Court President of Kattowitz, 13 June 1941, in: GStA PK, XVII. HA Rep. 222a No. 2161 (PA Günther Vol. 1), p. 233.
32. The land register offices had already been instructed in November 1939 not to make any entries without prior notification to Göring (*Rundverfügung* or "RV," i.e., a circular issued by a ministry) RJM, 1 November 1939, in: BA, R 3001 No. 20814, p. 16.
33. Hitler used the term as early as September 1939; see Herbert, *Best*, 241.

34. See the AV Higher Regional Court President of Danzig, 24 July 1940, in: BA, R 3001 No. 20814, p. 190; see also Becker (op. cit.), 108 with footnote 22.
35. The entire procedure was governed by the so-called Debt Settlement Ordinance, 15 August 1941, in: Reichsgesetzblatt I, 516–525. For explanations, see von Gagern, "Ursachen und Auswirkungen," 2505–2509; Klee, *Die bürgerliche Rechtspflege*, 180–184; Breithaupt, "Feststellung," 251–256; Wirsich, "Bedeutung," 373–376.
36. In this respect, it makes perfect sense that these confiscation orders (dated 14 March, 8 April, 24 July, 3 October, 3 November, 22 November, 25 November, 4 December 1941) have survived the test of time: APBB, 13/554 No. 2 and No. 3. The appendices there list close to 900 confiscated businesses; it is not possible to determine how many there actually were.
37. Memo from the IG Farben legal department, 19 December 1943, in: UA BASF, PB 4/898 Abt. 6 (unpaginated).
38. Copies of the surveying administration in: UA BASF, PB 4/898 Dept. 6 (unpaginated). Apparently, no documents have been preserved in Polish archives.
39. 20th construction meeting IG Auschwitz, 8 September 1942, Nuremberg Doc. NI-11138, in: TUB ZfA.
40. Buchholz, "Zur Ostrechtspflegeverordnung," 2477.
41. Fechner, "Das bürgerliche Recht," 2482. See also Breuning, *Die Beschränkung der deutschen Gerichtsbarkeit*, 115.
42. Local Court of Auschwitz to RJM, 28 June 1940, in: BA, R 3001 No. 20814, p. 108. The reply of 12 July, ibid., p. 201. Most importantly: the Polish land registers were to be continued.
43. From 1 October 1941, Dr. Franz Langer was nominally chief magistrate in Auschwitz. However, Langer had already been called up for military service in 1939; after his court activity in Bielitz, he began his military service again in March 1941 as a private (Infantry Regiment 444) and probably did not even come to Auschwitz temporarily. See the information in the Personnel File of Franz Langer, in: BA, R 3001 No. 83691, and BA (PA), Dr. Franz Langer.
44. Correspondence April/May 1942, in: GStA PK, XVII. HA Rep. 222a No. 2161 (PA Günther Vol. 1), pp. 261–263. The founding of the Higher Regional Court (Deutsche Justiz 1941, 395) was preceded by the division of the Province of Silesia, as a result of which the administrative districts of Kattowitz and Oppeln were combined to form the Province of Upper Silesia.
45. Evaluation by the Supervising Judge of the Local Court of Auschwitz, 5 May 1941, in: Personnel File of Otto Schmiegel Volume 2, GStA PK, XVII. HA. Rep. 222a No. 3681, p. 60.
46. Supervising Judge of the Local Court of Auschwitz to the Higher Regional Court President of Kattowitz, 4 June 1943, in: ibid., p. 110.
47. Regional Court President of Bielitz to Wehrbezirkskommando Bielitz, 14 August 1942, in: ibid., p. 86.
48. Regional Court President of Bielitz to Wehrbezirkskommando Bielitz, 2 June 1942, in: GStA PK, XVII. HA Rep. 222a No. 3449, Bl. 55.
49. The information is all taken from the personnel file of Sebald Godulla, in: GStA PK, XVII. HA Rep. 222a No. 2073.
50. Supervising Judge of the Local Court of Auschwitz to the Higher Regional Court President of Kattowitz, 29 April 1943, in: GStA PK, XVII. HA Rep. 222a No. 1669, p. 9. Similarly, the Regional Court President of Bielitz to the Higher Regional Court President of Kattowitz, 31 March 1943 (GStA PK, XVII. HA Rep. 222a No. 2073, p. 102).

51. Supervising Judge of the Local Court of Auschwitz to the Higher Regional Court President of Kattowitz, 5 June 1942, in: Personnel File of Albin Jaskiewicz, GStA PK, XVII HA Rep. 222a No. 2419, p. 16. The deployment of Polish forces was a frequently lamented problem. Overview in Becker, op cit., 83.
52. Supervising Judge of the Local Court of Auschwitz to the Higher Regional Court President of Kattowitz, 22 October 1943, in: Personnel file of Albin Jaskiewicz, GStA PK, XVII HA Rep. 222a No. 2419, p. 32.
53. Meeting 15/16 January 1943, quoted from Steinbacher, *"Musterstadt" Auschwitz*, 236.
54. Transfer lists of the Monowitz prisoner infirmary, Nuremberg Doc. NI-14997, Case VI, Prosecution Exhibit 2266, reel 035, sheets 5-318 (POL). The reports from 25 and 26 March 1944 include a total of 200 names.
55. A copy of the purchase contract can be found in UA BASF, PB 4/898 section 6 (unpaginated). The entry in the land register itself cannot be traced; only a few fragments of the Auschwitz land register have survived.
56. Otto Schmiegel to Oberjustizkasse Breslau, 9 May 1942, in: GStA PK, XVII. HA Rep. 222a No. 3681 (PA Vol. 2), p. 83.
57. Supervising Judge of the Local Court of Auschwitz to the Regional Court President of Beuthen, 24 February 1944, in: GStA PK, XVII. HA Rep. 222a No. 2578, p. 59. The further career path is unclear.
58. See BA (PA), Werner Günther, and Werner Günther's personnel file, in: GStA PK, XVII. HA Rep. 222a, pp. 279 and 282, and the information on the questionnaire, 3 February 1946, in: StAB, K 100/4 No. 3467, p. 3.
59. The Regional Court President of Bielitz to the Higher Regional Court President of Kattowitz, 16 April 1943, in: GStA PK, XVII. HA Rep. 222a No. 2073, p. 103.
60. The Regional Court President of Beuthen to the Higher Regional Court President of Kattowitz, 13 December 1943, in: GStA PK, XVII. HA Rep. 222a No. 3449, p. 79.
61. The Regional Court President of Bielitz to the Higher Regional Court President of Kattowitz, 27 February 1944, in: GStA PK, XVII. HA Rep. 222a No. 3681 (PA Schmiegel Vol. 2), p. 114. Maximilian Schmidt was preventively seconded to the court as a substitute on 15 June 1943, but was apparently no longer entrusted with land register matters there (GStA PK, XVII. HA Rep. 222a No. 3675 [Personnel file of Schmidt Vol. 3], p. 59).
62. Supervising Judge of the Local Court of Auschwitz to the Higher Regional Court President of Kattowitz, 22 October 1943, in: Personnel file of Albin Jaskiewicz, GStA PK, XVII HA Rep. 222a No. 2419, p. 32.
63. Personnel file of Sofie Smolarek, in: GStA PK, XVII. HA Rep. 222a No. 3848.
64. Günther Hindemith, born in 1900, studied in Breslau and Berlin, passed both state examinations with the grade of "sufficient" (the fourth of five grades), from 1933 onward was a Party member and block leader, from 1938 was Local Court counselor in Striegau (all this from the personnel files LAV-R, NW-Pe no. 2563 and BR-Pe no. 13284. 2563 and BR-Pe No. 13284). His activities in Auschwitz can only be deduced indirectly from references in the personnel files of others, see for example GStA PK, XVII. HA Rep. 222a No. 1669, 2419, 2578, 3449, 3681).
65. See the copy of the purchase contract, in: UA BASF, PB 4/898 Abt. 6 (unpaginated). Gerhard Thiele, born in 1905, studied in Breslau, passed two fully satisfactory state examinations (the third of five grades), completed his doctoral dissertation in law in Breslau in 1928 (*Die Bestrafung des Treibers beim Jagdvergehen des § 292 StGB*, cum laude), was a member of NSDAP, *Rechtswahrerbund*, *Wohlfahrt,* and *Reichsbund der Deutschen Beamten* since 1 May 1933, local court judge in Pitschen since 1 December

1934 and in Krzepice since October 1941. In 1944, Thiele had to assess the latest territorial confiscations of the Waffen SS for the Auschwitz Local Court, which he summarily completed with the assessment that, as an act of state sovereignty, they were "beyond judicial review" (Higher Regional Court President of Kattowitz to RJM, 11 February 1944, in: BA, R 3001 No. 20815, pp. 208 et seq.). All other information from: Reichsjustizkalender 1941; Richterkartei Reichsjustizministerium Bundesarchiv; Personnel file of Thiele, in: GStA, XVII. HA Rep. 222a No. 4001.

66. Higher Regional Court President and General Prosecutor Kattowitz to RJM, 21 January 1945, in: BA, R 3001 No. 23372, p. 300.
67. This and the following according to Walther Dürrfeld, *Bericht über die Kriegsereignisse in und um Werk Auschwitz vom 13. Januar bis 24. Januar 1945*, Pirna, den 7.2.1945, Nürnbg. doc. NI-11956, in: TUB ZfA; the report is categorized in Wagner, *IG Auschwitz*, 275–280.
68. Higher Regional Court President and GStA Kattowitz (currently Neisse) to RJM, 1 February 1945, in: BA, R 3001 No. 23372, pp. 302–305. Similarly, GStA Kattowitz (currently Neisse) to RJM, 1 February 1945, in: BA, R 3001 No. 24051 (unpaginated).
69. All this from his personnel files, LAV NRW-R, NW-Pe No. 2563 and BR-Pe No. 13284.
70. I owe this information to Andreas Grunwald of the Bundesarchiv, Berlin.
71. Werner Günther to the Hof/Stadt Trial Chamber, 24 November 1946, in: StACo, Hof/Stadt Trial Chamber No. 985 (unpaginated). The "small" court, the job description, and the route to Hof are explained in the lawyer's personnel file (StAB, K 100/4 No. 3467, p. 8), the acquittal of 16 December 1946 can be found in StACo, Spruchkammer Hof/Stadt No. 985 (unpaginated).
72. APBB, 13/554 No. 1–3. Also preserved is a register of old files and a relatively insignificant criminal case from 1942 (unauthorized border crossing by a Polish woman, four months in a penal camp).
73. Maximilian Schmidt's personnel file, four volumes, APBB 13/554 no. 4–7. They were transferred from Opole to Bielsko-Biała in September 2018. There is a parallel tradition in GStA PK, XVII HA Rep. 222a No. 3675. Schmidt left Auschwitz on 1 May 1944, and became a senior judicial secretary in Gleiwitz.
74. APBB, 13/908 No. 1274, mentioning properties in Brzeszcze, Jawischowitz, Przecieszyn and Skidziń.
75. See report of the Higher Regional Court President of Kattowitz (currently Neisse) to RJM, 16 February 1945, in: BA, R 3001 No. 22730, p. 14; memo RJM, February 1945, in: BA, R 3001 No. 24052, p. 38; Higher Regional Court of Kattowitz, memo, 22 August 1945, in: HStAW, Oberlandesgericht Erfurt, No. 95, p. 124.
76. The lists are preserved in HStAW, Oberlandesgericht Erfurt no. 95, pp. 124–276, and BA, DP 1 no. 563, camp unit 2 (unpaginated). There are 13 personnel files relating to Auschwitz; only that of Chief Judicial Inspector Raiwa (born 6 November 1912; present in Auschwitz as an official of the public prosecutor's office) could not be found.

Chapter 4

Severance Pay

The *Sondergericht Aachen* and Its Last Judge

Hans Keutgen: A Normal Life

The last judge of the *Sondergericht* ("Special Court") in Aachen, was not an atypical representative of his kind. His father designed patterns in the textile industry, his mother was a housewife, and only having five younger siblings clouded with recurring financial worries what would otherwise have been a lawyer's classic middle-class socialization. The family had been rooted in the western Rhineland for generations; Keutgen himself was born in Aachen in 1912, was—naturally—baptized Catholic, and—just as naturally—attended the humanistic Kaiser-Karl-Gymnasium. Endowed by nature with gifts, he showed a strong interest in school life, even if Keutgen's thirst for knowledge was not great enough to independently motivate him. At Herz-Jesu Primary School, it was "strokes of the cane and hours of detention" that drove him to study, as he himself admitted in retrospect. No such disciplinary methods were used at the Gymnasium: "If you did nothing," Keutgen explained, "the most you'd get was a bad grade, the consequences of which you couldn't yet grasp at the time." In the face of this new freedom, Keutgen lapsed into an intellectual apathy during his early years at secondary school, which ultimately forced him to repeat a year.[1] That was too much. Soon thereafter, his teachers observed an "almost excessive diligence" in him,[2] which benefited his performance in almost all subjects. Admittedly, he did not really like ancient languages and had neither musical nor artistic prospects waiting for him. Otherwise, his grades were all good, and even very good in French.

But Keutgen's results on the final *Abitur* were poor. He failed three out of five subjects, although he was by far not the only one in this situation. This generally diagnosed "exam psychosis" was met with generous understanding by the teachers' conference; after extensive deliberation, the teachers agreed that "the bleak conditions of the time … should probably be held responsible."[3] Indeed. The circumstances of the examination were depressing, although not in the sense that Keutgen's teachers probably had in mind. The 1932 graduating class—after all, the only one whose entire school career had taken place within the short life of the Weimar democracy—was allowed to reflect on the topic: "Germany's geographical location its destiny" [*sic*] as proof of their maturity.[4] Keutgen, whom the school had already generally attested to being "deeply inwardly enthusiastic about lofty and noble ideas,"[5] felt inspired. In eight pages, he summarized all the world-historical wisdom available to a teenager, lamented the "irreconcilable quarrel" with France, Russia, and England, expressed outrage at the "cry … for large areas of German soil," reverently quoted the Kaiser's prophecy: "Our future lies on the water!" and hailed the flag of the German fleet, which flew "proudly … in the ports of Japan and China" and brought "home greetings to the Germans in Brazil, Chile, and Argentina." Finally, he noted with emotion the "admirable" fact that the German Reich still existed at all, which Keutgen attributed with gratitude to those "who steered the ship of state through the rolling waves, to our happiness and to the blessing of the whole world."

A bleak time. Keutgen's sweeping global political attack was unsuitable even for his humanist educational institution. The teacher considered his explanations to be linguistically inadequate and useless in terms of content, sometimes even a "superficial and incomprehensible distortion of history." Keutgen also failed the examinations in Greek and mathematics. He was saved by his respectable performance during the school year, a C in gymnastics, and an A in French. On 26 February 1932, he graduated school with his *Abitur*.

Keutgen began studying law the summer semester of 1932 in Cologne, where he would remain without interruption until his final exams. The fact that he spent his entire studies close to home may well have been in keeping with the breadth of his intellectual horizons, but it was also a consequence of his parents' limited financial resources, which did not allow for major detours. As is usual with lawyers, his choice of study itself was not motivated by any particular professional inclination, but rather from the outset was the result of a cool, measured calculation of means and ends. Upon graduating from Gymnasium, Keutgen admitted that he was "virtually forced" to study at university, as his father had invested so much in his education that he could not simply complete an apprenticeship. Because the career prospects in the economy were poor, he wanted to study law "for purely practical reasons." "Capable jurists" are "still needed everywhere today," "with the greatest diligence" one can get ahead professionally "despite the overcrowding," and—perhaps most notable for a high school graduate—in terms of career path, a jurist can "adapt more easily … than anyone else."[6]

He pursued his studies with the uncompromising diligence he had cultivated in school. Roman private law, Roman legal history, German legal history, the core legal subjects, plus shipping law, mining law, civil service law, canon law, international law, press law, securities law, financial and tax law, criminology. There were few courses that Keutgen missed.[7] He also readily embraced the new spirit. In May 1933, he joined the Nazi Students' League and the SA and had "all the more joyfully placed himself at the service of our Führer's movement," as he himself explained in detail that such activities had previously been off limits to him due to the prohibition of the Gymnasium and the prohibition of his father, who worked in a Jewish business. Now he listened to Gotthold Bohne's explanations of eugenic criminal policy as well as Carl Schmitt's brisk overview of Reich and state law. According to Keutgen, he devoted what free time he had left "entirely to the movement."[8]

Keutgen even allowed himself a brief digression into the matter of justice shortly before his exams and included the legal and political philosophy of the recently habilitated Hans Welzel in his program, a further reservoir of lofty and noble ideas. Welzel had proclaimed the goal of overcoming the "senseless, brutal construction of reality of naturalistic positivism," developing a new "metaphysical synopsis" and thereby simultaneously providing the ideological background for "what has already achieved the most vivid reality in political and state life."[9] Keutgen was thus well-equipped. He knew the textbook reference for every technical detail, and the dark whispers of Nazi metaphysics gave him a sense of education. In December 1935, he completed his studies with a solid first state examination ("good," the third of seven grades) and was now entitled to call himself a "certified law candidate." That he had also completed his metamorphosis into a man of law internally is demonstrated by his signature, which he ended with a period from this time onwards, i.e., he signed with "Hans Keutgen.," as if his name, contrary to all the rules of syntax, was already a meaningful sentence.

Textbook Jurist

But that was not the end of the story. Keutgen decided to follow his studies with a dissertation to obtain a diploma in his trade—again, not atypical for his profession. Of course, this was not seriously about refining a process of intellectual maturation. It took Keutgen a whole four months to complete the tedious study on "Private and Public Atonement in Criminal Law. [*Private und öffentliche Sühne im Strafrecht*]."[10] Atonement! A big word. Keutgen dismantled the powerful text until it was legally compliant and, at the same time, tailored to the needs of those in power, for whom private ambitions were particularly repugnant in criminal law of all things. "Everything that still exists in criminal proceedings today to grant the individual a position of control over the state can no longer be upheld, for the simple reason that it is not in line with our new understanding," it stated, *pour prendre le ton*, right in the preface. At 78 pages, the work was actually relatively detailed, but this only served to emphasize the intellectual wasteland.

The introduction offers the usual delve into the historical treasure chest—18 pages devoted to atonement in law from Rome to the present day—followed by a multitude of detailed, often anxious presentations, well-written and full of discussions on the "essence" and "nature" of legal forms of thought, the typical product of a legal science that doggedly defends the perfect world of its realities against the touchstone of the intellect. The only surprise came in the concluding paragraphs, in which Keutgen cautiously recommended the introduction of a justice of the peace for cases of minor crime, justifying this with the blatantly self-serving argument that this would also create an opportunity to "relieve the plight of fully qualified jurists without alienating them from their life's work."

Even after the required revision, Albert Coenders, the supervisor, could only bring himself to concede that Keutgen's dissertation was "now a reasonably adequate study." The second reviewer, Gotthold Bohne, added the customary "Agreed." The final examination went slowly, and it was the new subject "People and State" of all things that ensured that Keutgen passed at all and was ultimately awarded his doctorate with the lowest passing grade of *rite*.[11] But so what? The thesis was not aimed at any reader, but from the outset designated only for Keutgen's CV. And in this respect, it fulfilled all his wishes. After being awarded a doctorate in law, Keutgen's signature mutated once again: the dinky "Hans" was erased and Keutgen now proudly signed as "Dr. Keutgen."

His dream of a civil service career was now within reach. Keutgen remained loyal to his hometown during his legal clerkship and completed his assignments at the often small and remote local courts within the Cologne Higher Regional Court's jurisdiction. He became a member of the NSDAP in 1937.[12] The militant nationalism and—for his fellow citizens—the caring socialism of the party may well have appealed to Keutgen. He probably did not share the obsessive anti-Semitism in the same way, but as a good Catholic he probably also did not reject outright either, lest he jeopardize his own career—after all, the Civil Service Act that had just come into force required a civil servant to "support the National Socialist state without reservation at all times" (§ 3), which was tangibly proven by joining the party. During the obligatory weeks at the Hanns Kerrl community camp in Jüterbog, Keutgen made a good impression in every respect. His special suitability for judicial office was expressly confirmed,[13] he again passed the second state examination with a mark of "good." Keutgen thus demonstrated outstanding credentials: a fully qualified lawyer with a doctorate and two honors degrees; "clearly above average," noted the first professional assessment,[14] politically on track, and a gifted orator, as was repeatedly reported later—apart from what he actually said, one could just as easily have believed the opposite.

Was there anything in this career not at his disposal? Certainly not "education." In his legal training, Keutgen confirmed, almost ideally, what the sociology of law would systematically grasp only much later: studying is a stopgap solution for those who do not know what else to do. Keutgen could not develop a passion for reflection, artistic distance, or even doubt, because this would have contradicted the legal *comme il faut*. Freedom of opinion, originality, and brilliance are not viable currencies in the world of law; a good lawyer goes unnoticed. It was therefore entirely in keeping with the logic of the profession for Keutgen to direct his not unfavorable aptitude with unerring instinct to where professional advancement was in sight.

And what else? Faith in God will certainly have guided him. Keutgen considered himself a Catholic throughout his life. He wanted to have his religious affiliation noted on his high school graduation certificate, he remained a member of the church even during the Third Reich, and after the war he was active in several Christian organizations. For the man of law that he primarily was, the earthly order remained the decisive factor. But from his connection to the higher powers, Keutgen must have gained the unshakeable confidence of someone who knows that he is on the right side. Keutgen's goal was not Catholic legal practice, and yet in his legal work he was always also a metaphysical messenger; with his pronouncements he could transcend earthly legislation if necessary.

A solicitor like Keutgen therefore fitted in perfectly with the requirements of the judiciary: receptive, objective, and ambitious, conscious of the fully accessory nature of his own existence, which offered secure protection against individuality, extravagance, and other extreme ideas. The dependence on the prevailing conditions turned the official channels into something like a moral authority; thoroughness and diligence replaced the lack of creativity; the pronounced ambition found a secure foothold in a resilient opportunism; in short: a jurist.

Public Enemies, Black Marketeers, Ration Coupon Forgers

Before Keutgen could devote himself to legal practice, the war caught up with him. His second state examination took place on 26 September 1939; he was subsequently appointed an assistant judge, before being drafted into the Wehrmacht at the beginning of 1940. He was assigned to the 206th Infantry Division, a unit consisting mainly of East Prussian troops, with which he was briefly deployed in Poland, but was not involved in combat there or in the six months in France, where his unit subsequently served. After the armistice in the West, Keutgen was granted a six-month leave of absence from the war. He became an assistant judge at the Aachen Regional Court before returning to the Eastern Front in March 1941. He and his division took part in the invasion of the Soviet Union. As part of the reserve of Army Group North, the unit moved through what was then Lithuania and Belarus for a good three weeks without encountering any major resistance. Combat did not break out until mid-July, with the storming of a Russian troop camp near Polotsk, a good 250 kilometers northeast of Minsk. This was successful after a few days, albeit with massive losses.[15]

Keutgen was also seriously wounded: shrapnel in his thigh and back, and a grenade pierced his right foot. He was hospitalized near the front, transported back to East Prussia through Belarus and Lithuania, until he was finally transferred from Tilsit to Gütersloh and from there back to Aachen. In January 1942, severely wounded by the war, he left military service with the rank of non-commissioned officer. How he experienced the war, as a spectacle of nature or a journey through hell, which battles and crimes he took part in, whether the army's male bond meant security or arrogance to him, which experiences remained engraved in his memory—lack of conscience, camaraderie, fear, the dark spirits of collective disinhibition—we do not know. Like so many others of his generation, Keutgen avoided talking about the war. He was now a civilian through and through. On 1 March 1942, he joined the Aachen Regional Court as an assistant judge and administrative clerk, and on 1 January 1943, he finally received the position he had longed for as a regional court judge. At the same time, he became an associate judge at the Aachen Special Court.

Keutgen had thus found an institution that corresponded to his field, but also the spirit of the times, in a manner as discreet as himself. There was hardly ever any particular excitement to report in the Aachen judiciary. The Palace of Justice, located just outside the old town, was the seat of everyday life in the Prussian province. Even when the special court moved in there, it was initially just a by-product of the nearby city. There had been a special court in Cologne since 1933. As elsewhere, it was initially used for cases of high treason and perfidy, but since 1939 it had jurisdiction over almost all offenses involving any form of political deviation. At some point, it became too much. Because Cologne was fully booked for months in advance, thus jeopardizing the desired efficiency of the special court, Aachen received its own special court on 10 February 1941.[16] It was composed as befitted a special court, with judges "who not only possessed professional competence but also inner determination, were able to take a tough approach where necessary, but also worked thoroughly and conscientiously, not for the sake of praise" and were also distinguished by "impeccable professional and private conduct," as the regional court president emphasized.[17] Spectacular cases were rare. The Aachen Special Court handled just under 1,000 cases between its foundation and its demise. Almost 700 files have survived.[18] And in this comparatively favorable record, there is a single file that the court itself considered significant enough to save from oblivion. The cover is adorned with the meaningful imperative, "To be preserved as a matter for the state archives." Behind this lies a regrettable, but ultimately completely insignificant case from today's perspective, in which a young woman defrauded the War Damages Office and received compensation for a burned suitcase that had not actually belonged to her, but to her brother at the front. Keutgen was an associate judge when she was sentenced to 18 months in prison in 1943 as a *Volksschädling* ("public enemy" or, literally, public vermin).[19] One of 1,000 cases. The court found nothing worth remembering in the rest of the cases.

In fact, the proceedings were predominantly legal mass-produced goods. Overall, it was less ideology than the war that determined the court's day-to-day work. Because the expansion of commercial law increasingly criminalized free trade, the courts in Aachen primarily dealt with the diverse violations of the necessities of the war economy: illegal slaughtering, illegal butter-making, fraud with ration coupons, violations of currency and price regulations, prohibited trade in foodstuffs, the sale of clothing without the required ration coupons, plus repeated false declarations of air raid damage—a potpourri of scarcity in which small and large scams were widely regarded as a tried and tested means of somewhat mitigating the hardships of war.

The provinces produced run-of-the-mill cases, to which the court reacted with ideologically adapted, but rarely truly excessive, responses. As has always been the case among lawyers, bourgeois ways of life were met with more sympathy than other milieus; this sentiment was not new, but it was now much easier to present in legal terms. The very notions *Volksschädling* and *Gewohnheitsverbrechern* ("habitual criminals") provided the handy terminology. But even beyond this, the assessment of the accused left plenty of room for traditional resentment. For example, if English radio was listened to by someone with a "correct patriotic attitude," it was less dangerous than if it were a communist.[20] Support for deserters, when provided by women, often resulted in moral connotations that lawyers found unseemly and for this reason alone had to be rigorously punished.[21] And in general, where female sexual life unfolded beyond marriage, the judiciary could easily convert its traditional mistrust of non-binding forms of cohabitation into legal arguments thanks to the elevation of race and nation. A woman who abandoned her fighting husband or even made common cause with the enemy had to expect relentless severity in punishment.[22]

Thanks to this bourgeois preservation of tradition, a certain equanimity in routine legal work could develop even in particularly politically contaminated areas. Even after massive restrictions on defense and legal recourse, the proceedings retained a distinctly legal character. Insults and curses against the Führer could hope for prison sentences of only a few weeks. One defendant had blamed Hitler for the war and, in a conversation with an acquaintance on the street, declared that someone should "pour petroleum on him and set him on fire!" For this, she was sent to prison for three months in 1941 because the court was of the opinion that the statement had not been made publicly. In early 1942, a Dutch woman received a suspended sentence of six weeks for exclaiming, "The Führer is a criminal, the greatest straw man who is merely pushed forward." She was credited with having responded to the insult that the Dutch were "rabble" in a heated exchange. In mid-1943, a defendant—a party member married to a Polish woman—received a three-month suspended sentence for saying, "Look at how our SS men behaved in Warsaw. Every woman and child runs off the street when they see an SS man." As late as 1944, the ten months in prison received for the unequivocal statement, "The bastards brought this on, these rat bastards, they should be shot to death" were suspended after just three months because the accused's excitement after an air raid had to be taken into account as a mitigating factor.[23]

Legal outliers were rare, in every respect. There was no need to look for political obstruction or even acts of resistance; equally rare, however, were the infamous death sentences for stealing trivial items after an air raid. In fact, capital punishment remained something of a last resort in Aachen; the special court executed a total of 14 people in the three and a half years of its existence, including four members of a smuggling gang that had repeatedly driven cattle across the nearby border into Belgium—still drastic compared to peacetime, but a far cry from the conditions in the military courts, other special courts, or even the *Volksgerichtshof* ("People's Court").[24]

Special Judges and Agitators

Keutgen must have felt quite at home in this institutionalized mediocrity. His colleagues were as locally rooted as he was; anyone not born in Aachen or Cologne could almost be considered exotic. The major purges in the judiciary and administration in the spring of 1933 had caused a stir, but were now almost ten years in the past, and there had been no Jewish colleagues among either the judges or the lawyers since 1938. The special court jurisdiction was experiencing a great upswing at the moment that Keutgen was released from war duty. Especially for the general prosecutor's office, it was often more advantageous to bring charges before the special court in order to restrict the rights of the defense, shorten the legal process, and generally avoid the risk of accidentally placing a political offense under the responsibility of the ordinary courts. From 1942 onwards, the special court became the standard court of the German criminal justice system; its jurisdiction encompassed, as the Reich Ministry of Justice resignedly stated, "all criminal cases of any significance."[25] This was also evident in Aachen. By 1942, the number of cases at the special court had risen from an initial 20 to 40 new cases per month, necessitating the establishment of a second chamber. Keutgen became an associate judge in the chamber of Paul Losenhausen,[26] who also served as the permanent deputy of the court president, but was approaching retirement age, had a generally weak physical condition, and frequently had his deputy, Josef Schwengers, represent him.[27]

Others dominated the scene. Walther Fritz enjoyed particular authority at the special court. A judge since 1929, chairman of the chamber, he was an outstandingly qualified jurist, bureaucratically gifted, full of drive,[28] whose formative role was not seriously jeopardized when he was called up for military service for a few months at the end of 1943 and found an equally experienced and hands-on deputy in Paul Howahrde.[29] Although he had only joined the party in 1942, Fritz was considered to be politically absolutely reliable. He was an "open-minded person who put National Socialist legal views into practice with full affirmation and out of inner need," his superior explained shortly after the outbreak of war. In 1933, he refrained from joining the party, "because he did not want to be seen as a mucky-muck," and later so as not to degrade his National Socialist convictions to a "cheaper springboard"[30]—a narrative that, as can be imagined, could easily be reinterpreted after 1945 as a hidden opposition activity.

The general prosecutor's office was largely dominated by two rabble-rousers, Konrad Höher and Paul Zimmerath. Neither was a particularly good lawyer, but both were useful: both were party members, and together they not only took on the vast majority of the upcoming hearings, but also used them for particularly high-profile criminal charges—two "notorious general prosecutors," as an Aachen lawyer wrote after the war, who regularly outdid each other to secure "bestial punishments."[31] Ludwig Kuhnert, born in 1910, was influential in a different way and quickly developed into a kind of factotum at the court. Although Kuhnert had been a member of the Social Democratic Party for four years, he was able to attribute this to the overpowering influence of his father—a trade unionist—and compensated for his youth transgressions by joyfully committing himself to the movement and joining the NSDAP in 1937, a career that also remained compatible to all interpretations. In 1940, he became a judge at the Aachen Regional Court; two years later, after several military exemptions, at the special court. Finally, in January 1944, when a number of call-ups required a reshuffle, he was seconded to the local general prosecutor's office.[32] He therefore knew the regional and special courts like no other; there was no one in the senior civil service who Kuhnert would not have had as a colleague at some point.

Keutgen himself was too young and too legally inexperienced to play a decisive role at the special court. Nevertheless, he did not remain a marginal figure. Presumably thanks to his rhetorical skills, he took over the local judicial press office in his very first year. It had been conceived as a kind of miniature version of the Ministry of Propaganda, in which Keutgen acted as the primary public informant for the next few years. At the special court itself, he likely served as an associate judge a good 40 times, dealing with the full range of cases that Aachen's provincial law had to offer: any illegal slaughter and other violations of the war economy, broadcast crimes, thefts, which generally resulted in moderate prison sentences; but also serious crimes, violent offenses, and repeat offenses that resulted in long prison sentences. And finally, Keutgen was involved in cases in which the National Socialist spirit was allowed to flow more or less unfiltered into the proceedings. The theft of a carpet and washing utensils during clean-up operations qualified the previously blameless perpetrator as a *Volksschädling* and justified a prison sentence; the same applied to false loss reports after an air raid, the large-scale fraud with food ration coupons, and the continued theft of food under cover of blackout.[33]

Keutgen also provided the support expected of him even when the goal was to finally eradicate such identified *Volksschädlinge*. While still an assistant judge, he served as an associate judge in a spectacular trial against a local group leader who had run the Würselen consumer cooperative in a lordly manner for years, eventually resulting in a food shortage of more than 300 tons of food. In September 1942, the special court sentenced him to death amid excessive public and party interest.[34] A few months later, two more death sentences were handed down within three days. One delinquent had systematically stolen field mail,[35] another—with multiple previous convictions—had posed as a detective or customs officer to confiscate money, food, and spirits from foreign forced laborers, occasionally using a party badge. Such behavior deserved death, the verdict stated, because it "shook the victims' trust in the German police" and undermined the "reputation of the party."[36] Might the forced laborers have lost their otherwise intact trust in the German police apparatus? And did this damage the NSDAP's unshattered reputation? It is hard to imagine that Keutgen or his colleagues believed this themselves. The verdicts were reviewed after the war and classified as "unobjectionable."[37]

Evacuation of the City

Aachen and its special court only became a special case because of the war. Not so much because of the possible destruction—the air war had been ravaging Aachen regularly since 1941, repeatedly causing severe damage. But it was no different in any other major city in the West, and optimism was maintained for a surprisingly long time. As recently as May 1944, after the most severe attack to date, the judicial administration was granted 90,000 Reichsmarks to bring about "complete reconstruction to its original state."[38]

But Aachen was the first major city to be attacked from more than just the air. In the late summer of 1944, the Allies approached by land. After almost 70 air raids, the city was largely destroyed and its population more than halved. Even now, the focus remained on the future, albeit without any optimism, driven instead by fanaticism. Already after the landing of the US forces in Normandy, Hitler had issued the order that civilian life in the operational area was to continue in the event of "the advance of enemy forces into German Reich territory."[39] Unauthorized evacuations were prohibited. On 5 September, Martin Bormann reiterated that, apart from cases of "extreme danger," the decision to evacuate was reserved for Hitler.[40] On the same day, Gauleiter and *Reichsverteidigungskommissar* ("Reich Defense Commissioner") Josef Grohé requested permission to evacuate Aachen.

Initially without success. The symbolism weighed too heavily. Aachen stood for more than just the imminent loss of a city. Its occupation by the enemy would have irrefutably proven that the defenders had much less to offer against the Allied attacks than the propaganda claimed. The "struggle for Aachen," according to Goebbels' propaganda staff, was "generally regarded as the indicator of our fighting strength in the West."[41] There was no middle ground between successful defense and total annihilation. Hitler himself gave the uncompromising order: "Every bunker, every block of houses in a German city, and every German village must become a fortress where the enemy either bleeds to death or buries its occupying forces in hand-to-hand combat."[42]

Within the judiciary, the prospect of a military decision triggered a peculiar mixture of determination and fatalism. On 5 September, the President of the Cologne Higher Regional Court informed his governors in the districts close to the border of the military leadership's instructions. No job could be abandoned without an express order from the superior authority, and "a particularly energetic official" would monitor conditions on the ground.[43] At the same time, preparations for an evacuation began, rather discreetly. Great effort was devoted to the actual raw material of criminal justice: the files and the defendants. In this respect, the success was considerable. Of the prisoners, only "150 short-term prisoners" remained in Aachen, otherwise the prison and the detention centers in the surrounding area were evacuated.[44] The files also left the city, at least in part. In the chaotic days before the evacuation, there was no longer any capacity to remove them from the regional and local courts. However, the special court relocated "a significant proportion of important files" or, if they could not be taken, destroyed them, as the General Prosecutor reported. The only painful loss to be lamented in this respect was the criminal registers, which were relocated to Geilenkirchen, where they fell into the hands of the Allied troops.[45]

In other respects, however, people were under remarkable illusions. Alfred Hellbach, a Nazi loyalist in theory and practice,[46] who had come to Aachen from Brünn in June 1944 as the successor to the late chairman Paul Losenhausen, scheduled trials into October, completely ignoring military events.[47] On 5 September—a Tuesday, and so a regular court day—a defendant who had stolen items of clothing from a cellar was declared a *Volksschädling* and sentenced to three years in prison, likely the last Aachen sentence to be passed in Aachen itself.[48] On Thursday, 7 September, when the evacuation of the city had already been requested, the last court sessions appear to have taken place, although no one other than the court staff themselves were able to attend. All that remained to be ascertained was the transport of the defendants to Siegburg on the east bank of the Rhine, whereupon, at the request of the general prosecutor's office, the decision was made to postpone the case "indefinitely." Even here, however, Hellbach demonstrated his blindness to reality by marking the minutes with the obstinate instruction "Resubmission after 2 weeks."[49]

The unfavorable outcome of this main hearing nevertheless seemed to have made him realize the futility of his efforts. On the following Friday, he set about—again in a bizarre overestimation of his remaining options—canceling the previously scheduled appointments and dismissing the participants "as far as possible."[50] Hellbach still considered himself in control of the proceedings. That same day, a lawyer requested that his client be given a suspended sentence for the last five months of his sentence; the elderly offender had slaughtered a large pig without permission but consumed the meat exclusively for himself and his wife, and had already served ten of his 15 months prison sentence. Hellbach was not impressed. "With continued good behavior," he stated, "I am in favor of a conditional suspension of the last three months."[51]

There was not much time left. On 10 September—a Sunday—Heinrich Himmler appeared in Aachen. After a meeting with the party, the Wehrmacht, and the administration, he announced to the citizens that the enemy would not reach Aachen, and that evacuating the city was therefore out of the question. The following Monday, Hellbach returned to the office to cancel several appointments, some of which were now accompanied by an appropriate "Immediately!"[52] This was, by all appearances, the end of the special jurisdiction in Aachen.

That same day, in view of the military situation, Hitler was persuaded to authorize the evacuation of the city. The news arrived in Aachen around 5 pm. The military situation necessitated haste, but because of the fighter bombers, they had to wait until nightfall. Special trains were frantically requested during the night, and the population was informed the next day, knowing full well that an orderly evacuation was no longer possible. The first shells had already hit the city; the police, administration, and large sections of the party had fled; and ongoing air raids made evacuation by train even more difficult. On the evening of 12 September, long treks of civilians set off on their own. At three o'clock in the morning, the evacuation was declared complete. Twenty thousand to thirty thousand inhabitants remained in Aachen, without electricity or water, at best sporadically supplied by a municipal emergency administration. After weeks of fighting, the city surrendered on 21 October, now completely destroyed.

The Front Is Close: Alternative Accommodations

It is not possible to determine how Keutgen fared during this time. All that is certain is that he, too, left Aachen during the evacuation. "At his own request,"[53] he was seconded to the small Gemünd Local Court, 50 kilometers away, deep in the Eifel region. Keutgen took up his post there on 19 September 1944, in a court reduced to two rooms, which was only still in operation because the traffic conditions made it unreasonable to refer the population to an outside institution.[54] He stayed there for a good two months, but no records have survived that could provide information about his activities.

His Aachen colleagues, on the other hand, followed their authorities. Only at the local court was there a suspension of law with the evacuation of the city.[55] The regional and special courts continued to operate, but geographical cohesion was lost along with the court's location. The administration moved far to the east bank of the Rhine and from then on resided in Gummersbach Local Court. Some of the female defendants were sent to the women's prison in Frankfurt-Hoechst, so that a special court in Aachen could operate there on a case-by-case basis.[56] The general prosecutor's office and Aachen Special Court moved 30 kilometers east, where they were able to use the Düren Local Court building, which had only opened in 1940. It did not take very long for the apparatus to be recalibrated. That same working week, on 16 September—just four days after the evacuation—the special court convened in Düren.[57]

Three general prosecutors and Regional Court Director Fritz had moved from Aachen to Düren, and they were able to call on four colleagues from Düren and a local court judge from St. Vith, which had also been evacuated.[58] Hellbach, who was clearly overwhelmed by the situation in Aachen, was sent to Gummersbach to head the court administration there. Walther Fritz, thirsty for action, seized the opportunity. He soon became the undisputed head of the court. An official appraisal noted that Fritz had presided over the special court, criminal and civil chambers in an exemplary manner under constant bombardment and "the most severe air terror" and had generally proved his worth during these "extremely difficult weeks."[59]

There were only a few new cases. A report by the General Prosecutor explained that they were primarily dealing with cases of looting during the evacuation. The investigations were proving extremely difficult: witnesses were rarely to be found, and the police had more important things to do at this point anyway. But the Aachen officials did not miss the opportunity for heroism. Ten kilometers from the front, under regular artillery fire, two sessions of the special court and one of the juvenile court were held every week, and even a death sentence was handed down.[60] Two direct hits in the court were only commented on by the officials with a sparse passive construction: "The question of whether orderly judicial business was still possible under the given circumstances was answered in the affirmative."[61]

The superior authorities took note of this with satisfaction. The Reich Ministry of Justice seized on the Aachen judges' devoted performance of duty as proof of the judiciary's dedication and willingness to make sacrifices. In this respect, it was sufficient to point out "that the special court is still in session today in Düren, a town 34 km west of Cologne and under artillery fire," the Ministry wrote to the organizer of the *Volkssturm* ("German Territorial Army") on 17 November 1944.[62] Too late. The praise of Aachen's bravery was outdated by the time it left the Ministry's post office. On 16 November, a half-hour-long carpet bombing had completely destroyed the entire city center of Düren. The Aachen Special Court had again lost its place of work: there were no more buildings, no telephone, no official car, and the senior general prosecutor, a passionate National Socialist who had been given the fitting name Hans Führer by a favorable fate, was dead.[63]

The Aachen judiciary moved eastwards once again. Two days later, a new temporary seat was found in nearby Bergheim. The local court judges there were spontaneously appointed judges at the special court, and a daily commuting courier kept the connection to Siegburg, a good 50 kilometers away, where the regional court and public prosecutor's office had retreated.[64] Admittedly, Bergheim was not even suitable as a temporary solution. Even after a month, not a single new criminal case had arisen there, but the front had approached the town so threateningly that the seconded local court judge Schmitz asked to be released, partly to be able to prepare the relocation of Bergheim Local Court—for which he was actually responsible—and partly to bring his private collection of paintings to safety. A replacement was found for him, as the Jülich Local Court, which had been bombed out in the meantime, had also moved to Bergheim and its leadership could now take over the business of the Aachen Special Court, but there was nothing more to do than oversee the withdrawal.[65] They left Bergheim in mid-December and moved on to Siegburg.

All the conditions for a longer stay were met there. The courthouse was in good condition. Although the prison was severely overcrowded, some of the Aachen prisoners on remand and their files had been transferred to it. For this reason, some officials had already moved to Siegburg earlier, without the detour via Düren. The regional court and public prosecutor's office had dispensed with the detour to Bergheim, and now the entire staff was reunited. They temporarily lived in shared quarters in the prison, but that soon changed. There was also plenty of work. On 30 January 1945, the General Prosecutor reported to the Ministry that, although the Aachen Regional Court district was largely under enemy occupation, there was "still so much work" that the Chief Public Prosecutor and two other officers were "fully occupied."[66]

Tour of the Reich

And with that, Keutgen was in demand again. On 28 November 1944, he received his secondment from Gemünd back to the special court, and shortly before Christmas he took up his old, but at the same time completely different, position in Siegburg. He could not stay there for long, however. A large number of the pending cases could not be processed because the associated prisoners on remand had been transferred to Bautzen during the evacuation of Aachen. It had therefore been planned for some time to send staff to Bautzen. In Düren, this plan had apparently failed due to the destruction of the court, which made other matters more urgent. It was taken up again in the relative calm of Siegburg. Two officials were required: a prosecutor to represent the prosecution on site and a judge to decide on the case. Hans Wickmann, a servile man of practice with two dismal exams and involvement in the NSDAP and SA, was chosen as the public prosecutor.[67] Keutgen was chosen as the judge.

Why these two were designated to fill the positions in Bautzen is unknown. Keutgen was severely wounded in the war, Wickmann had three small children and a wife in need of help due to severe hearing loss. In terms of age and seniority, both lacked the necessary administrative experience for this secondment into the unknown. For the same reason, however, both were at the bottom of the institutional food chain, which may ultimately have been the deciding factor. Be that as it may, Keutgen set off on his journey on January 1945. First, he traveled to Brilon in the Sauerland region, where his heavily pregnant wife had been evacuated; on the same day as his daughter's birth, he had to continue his journey in the evening.[68] It took him almost three days to cover the 500 kilometers to Bautzen due to the destruction and air raid alarms. There he met Wickmann and around 180 prisoners on remand from Aachen and Cologne. There were no files. Keutgen and Wickmann worked hard. By their own admission, they succeeded in reconstructing and concluding the proceedings in approximately 60 cases.[69] Some young people who were considered "Germans on probation" and had evaded military service were released. The Aachen officials secured convictions for other offenders. After the war, one of the affected reported that he had been taken from Aachen to Bautzen via Siegburg while on remand; after several months, he was taken to the courthouse there, where a room was marked "Aachen Chief Public Prosecutor's Office." In addition to him, four other defendants were tried there. He himself was sentenced to 15 months in prison as a *Volksschädling* because of his actions—he had recycled and reused food and tobacco ration coupons on a large scale—but was released on parole shortly afterwards.[70] Another stated that he had also been declared a *Volksschädling* for stealing fabrics, clothing, and rabbits under cover of darkness in Bautzen, but was sentenced to only nine months in prison.[71]

However, the events of the war soon turned Bautzen into a stopover. Keutgen stayed there for less than four weeks. Bautzen had become a kind of holding center for many prisoners from the now occupied eastern territories. The prison was hopelessly overcrowded, and the front was inexorably approaching. The special court retreated westward to Ichtershausen in Thuringia, almost 300 kilometers away. Keutgen followed the prisoners, but not directly. In a three-day train journey, he traveled home to care for his wife and newborn child, both of whom were seriously ill. Shortly after his arrival, his daughter died, and shortly thereafter Keutgen had to return to his official duties. After another three days on the train, he reached Ichtershausen on 23 February 1945.

In the neighboring Arnstadt Local Court, the Aachen lawyers were given a courtroom room for the remaining 120 or so prisoners with the tacit approval of the President of the Higher Regional Court in Jena. By all appearances, further proceedings were practically nil. Only one single verdict from the Ichtershausen period has left its mark—albeit a verdict that intertwined everyday life, war, and ideology in a particularly symptomatic way. On 22 March 1945, a switchman for the Reichsbahn, who as a result of his broken marriage had begun to embezzle food parcels in order to cook in his garden shed the meals he no longer received at home, was sentenced to two years in prison as a *Volksschädling*.[72]

This verdict was handed down during the final phase of the Aachen Special Court. After the war, Keutgen testified that he had served in Thuringia until 29 March 1945, a statement that is entirely plausible: 29 March was Maundy Thursday; over Easter, Arnstadt was on almost continuous air raid alert, on the next working day—3 April—the US artillery bombardment began, and a week later the town was taken. The Ichtershausen prison's entry book also contains no more entries after 29 March 29. If this 29 March is therefore taken as the last working day of the Aachen Special Court, a strange coincidence arises. On 29 March 29, two wagons full of files and private items arrived in Ichtershausen from Berlin, with which the Reich Ministry of Justice was relocating some departments. It was confidently announced that they were now in a position to "fully resume business."[73] The Aachen Special Court and Berlin Reich Ministry of Justice: united for a brief moment in the in-between world of Ichtershausen.

What's more: when Keutgen placed his "Dr. Keutgen." under the final verdicts, his special court essentially no longer existed. Aachen had been occupied for more than half a year, Düren had been destroyed for four months, Bergheim had long since been evacuated, and the final battle was raging in Siegburg. The special court had lost its alternative homes, and only a few meager remnants of the Cologne Higher Regional Court remained active in Waldbröl.[74] Keutgen's expedition had degenerated into management without a mandate. The Allies had closed all the courts they found in their occupied territory, and the Reich Ministry of Justice was well aware of this.[75] In Aachen itself, the post-war period had therefore already begun.

On 4 March, the untainted lawyer Philipp Bohne was appointed as the new Regional Court President,[76] and the first civil sessions were held at the end of the month, as the local court recorded in a historical self-reflection in 1962.[77] While the Ministry's files give 1 April 1945 as the date the Aachen courts reopened, this date cannot be correct[78]—1 April 1945 was Easter Sunday, and it would have been contrary to the blind zeal of the German civil service even at that time to open a new agency on a Sunday, especially the most important Christian holiday at that. Presumably, the opening date was set *post festum* at the beginning of the month, while business had *de facto* already begun beforehand.

But if the first post-war sessions actually took place in March, then, contrary to all normative expectations, two parallel universes would be visible for a brief moment. While the judicial authorities in Aachen themselves obeyed the imposed rule of law, Keutgen unwaveringly served National Socialist law from afar and brought the last of Aachen's *Volksschädlinge* to justice: a synchronous clash of anachronous systems, which can hardly be represented in legal terminology. Did Keutgen's Aachen Special Court still have jurisdiction over Ichtershausen at the time, even though an ordinary Aachen Regional Court had already been established again? Was it part of the German jurisdiction, even though its home authority had long since only been able to act with the authorization of the occupying power? And was it even still a "state court," as required by Section 15 of the Court Constitution Act? As one might imagine, no one asked these questions in Keutgen's time. And no one later did either.

Aachen's Ordinary Judges, Familiar Faces

The lawyer can adapt more easily than anyone else. Now, at the age of 33, Keutgen had the opportunity to fulfill his post-pubescent prophecies. It is not clear from the files exactly when he returned to Aachen. One thing is certain: on 15 August 1945, the military government readmitted him to practice as a judge,[79] even though he had practically everything that, even by the most lenient criteria, would have led to at least a temporary ban from the profession: membership in the SA and—albeit late—the NSDAP, legal adviser to the Hitler Youth, special court, and involvement in death sentences. As is well known, however, even in the new order such a concentration of grounds for exclusion did not necessarily cause harm, neither in Aachen nor elsewhere. Those who only do their duty need not worry, even if times should change. On 29 January 1946, the military government appointed Keutgen as a judge—he had already been serving as such for almost half a year—and two months later he submitted the obligatory questionnaire. His explanations completely convinced the review committee. He had, in fact, never been a member of the party—in 1944, he had still been aware of a membership number—but had remained merely a candidate. As a devout Catholic, he had been forced to reject National Socialism, and he had only joined relevant organizations when "it was absolutely necessary to achieve my professional goals, without which I would never have felt truly satisfied." When appointed legal advisor to the Hitler Youth, where this explanation clearly did not suffice, Keutgen resorted to the usual explanation: that he had taken up the position in order to prevent worse and "to protect the youth from the unbelieving and radical elements otherwise common in these positions," which he had indeed succeeded in doing. The admission was crowned by the confirmation of an English friend, a vicar of the High Church there, who conscientiously expanded on Keutgen's inner life and whose character study culminated in the repeated affirmation, graphically emphasized as a precaution: "*You were never a Nazi!*"[80]

Brief difficulties arose only in June 1947, when the British military government, likely spurred on by a newspaper article, reviewed his case and ordered his dismissal; apparently, they deemed the confluence of the SA, NSDAP, legal advisor to the Hitler Youth, and special court to be too much. However, his appeal was immediately successful. Keutgen mobilized his entire legal and ecclesiastical network: lawyers, defendants, convicts, their families, the regional court president, court employees, two chaplains, a priest, a religious teacher, and a youth minister. In all, a total of 22 statements were submitted—"I am in a position to provide a large number of further testimonies at any time"—in which the statements that had already been presented were presented again. In the end, Control Council Law No. 4, which unequivocally demanded the removal from office of judges "who directly followed the punitive practice of the Hitler regime," was set aside by marginalizing Keutgen to deputy associate judge, a position he had in fact only actually held in 1944. After such an array of embellishments, distortions, and outright lies, even the active National Socialist Keutgen was soon seen as a *Mitläufer* ("follower").[81]

Certainly, the fall of the Third Reich had not left such superficial traces on all career paths. Hellbach, in whom narrow-minded bureaucratism and ideological fanaticism had formed a particularly disastrous combination, had made himself intolerable; he was retired and died in 1953.[82] Fritz, who as emergency chairman of Düren and Siegburg had risen to the position of administrative grand vizier on immediate deployment, was recommended for reinstatement, but a position at the Aachen Regional Court was considered "inappropriate"—so much political sense still remained;[83] he first became an administrative judge in Münster and finally President of the

Senate at the Essen Regional Social Court. In addition to the new Regional Court President Philipp Bohne, there was also a new senior public prosecutor, Arnold Heitzer; as a former SPD member, Heitzer had suffered repeated backlash during the National Socialist era.[84]

But at the working level, familiar faces soon emerged. Josef Schauergans, who had been a member of the NSDAP for a short time before the Hitler Putsch and then long-term from 1933 onwards, and had been involved in at least three death sentences as a special judge, was one of Keutgen's old-new colleagues.[85] Hans Wickmann, his traveling companion in the East, was first classified as a *Mitläufer* after the war, then a public prosecutor, then elevated to "exonerated" in a new trial, then first public prosecutor, and finally senior public prosecutor.[86] Ludwig Kuhnert, the court's factotum, initially remained in Aachen, where he finalized his move from the judge's office to the public prosecutor's office; in 1953, he rose to the position of senior public prosecutor in Essen.[87] Even the expert witness Walter Stillger, who had been called in regularly until 1945 to assess the mental state of the accused, was, naturally, back in the courtroom.[88] The list of questions he had compiled was, of course, only partially usable; the standard query about the functions of Hermann Göring and Joseph Goebbels, among others, was omitted.

And so, they set about rebuilding the judiciary together, which at this time consisted to a large extent of clearing away the rubble of the previous years.[89] Parts of the courthouse were still in danger of collapsing months after the end of the war, and the intact rooms had to be shared with the military government and the city administration for an extended period. Qualified and politically acceptable staff were scarce, and only half of the 27 permanent posts at the court were still filled after a year. Paper, stationery, typewriters, and coal remained in short supply, and in winter, work was carried out at ten degrees below zero without heating. There was plenty to do; the judiciary was kept busy above all with thefts from the evacuated apartments, the black market flourished, as it did everywhere, and the flood of divorces continued unabated.

There were also plenty of old cases. The special court's 1,000 or so proceedings were stuck at various stages. Some investigations were still pending, others had already led to an indictment but the main trial had not yet begun, in still others a verdict had been reached but the developments of the war had made it impossible to carry out the sentence. None of these procedural steps were ineffective. A catalog of National Socialist laws, the special courts, and the *Volksgerichtshof* were repealed. However, the sentences handed down by the abolished institutions or under application of the incriminating laws were not. Law No. 1 of the Military Government ordered that sentences that had not yet been carried out and the severity of which were deemed contrary to the new era were to be revoked. This was reiterated in Control Council Proclamation No. 3 for convictions unjustly handed down "under the Hitler Regime on political, racial, or religious grounds."

What exactly this meant and how a corresponding pardon was to be implemented still required considerable clarification. In the British zone, various directives instructed the judicial authorities that upon a prisoner's release by the Allies, their sentence was to be considered served; anyone who escaped without authorization could be pardoned, and anyone who had been in preventive detention was now on probation.[90] At the same time, this meant that in every legal act, a contaminated element had to be identified and eliminated, while an independent, neutral element could certainly remain alongside it. The *Volksschädlingsverordnung* ("Ordinance on Public Enemies"), part of the ideological heart of the old regime, was, from a legal perspective, no more than an aggravated factor like many others—with the only difference being that, under the Control Council's legislation, it could no longer be applied. Anyone who had looted after air raids was no longer a *Volksschädling*, but still a thief.

Cologne relied on two decrees to address these complications. On 21 January 1946, the President of the Higher Regional Court issued a decree declaring political crimes exempt from punishment and the remaining sentences imposed by the special courts to be halved.[91] In June 1947, the Central Judicial Office for the British Occupation Zone, which had been created in the meantime, again ordered a reduction in sentences.[92] But even these legal acts had no direct impact on legal reality. What the special courts had left behind remained *ipso iure* until the now competent institutions announced otherwise. The public prosecutor's office was declared responsible; if a party so wished, a court could subsequently consider the matter and decide by order without a new trial. In the case of the Aachen Special Court, this meant that the necessary corrections now lay with the Aachen Regional Court and its public prosecutor's office.[93]

Vigilante Justice: "File It"

And so the former special jurists, now mutated into ordinary jurists, sat together pouring over the old cases to determine which of their old rulings could still claim validity in the new order. Ludwig Kuhnert played the most peculiar role. As an assistant to the public prosecutor, he was involved in virtually every case in which an outdated legal system had to be adapted to the post-war situation. Kuhnert closed open investigations, withdrew charges, referred to the amnesty decrees that had since been issued, or resorted to the clemency route, ideally condensed into a bureaucratic panacea: "1. No further action. 2. File it."[94] But in many cases, it was not possible to resolve one's own past so casually. The provincial conditions in Aachen had created a constellation of profound peculiarity: because in many cases the National Socialist and democratized officials were the same, it was often necessary to review the legacy of colleagues, but not infrequently also one's own judgements. Kuhnert concluded numerous proceedings in the postwar period in which he himself had previously played a key role. He requested the reduction of sentences that he himself had helped to decide as a judge, reduced them himself, or suspended them, withdrew his own indictments, or granted clemency where he himself had rejected them before 1945.[95] The indifference with which the court's own contingency budget was exhausted is demonstrated by a verdict from 1943 that Kuhnert had supported as an associate judge. A defendant had been sentenced to six years in prison as a *Volksschädling* for stealing a few items of clothing and jewelry after an air raid. Although she had no criminal record, the verdict at the time had emphasized, she had "acted in a highly reprehensible manner." It was precisely in these "fateful hours" that the "harshest stigmatization and strictest punishment of the accused" was necessary. As a post-war public prosecutor, Kuhnert wrote to the court in 1946 in the same case, asking for the sentence to be corrected because he considered it "too high" even after applying the amnesty decree. Nothing more. The sentence was reduced to two years.[96]

But the judges were also expected to adapt, and they, too, repeatedly had to subject themselves to a revision when reviewing the old judgments. Schauergans had to deal with the ominous past of colleagues in several cases,[97] but was also confronted with his own past at least once: in 1943, a city employee had given a friend countless ration coupons, which she in turn used for her own supply or resold at exorbitant prices. The death penalty was also considered at the time, but in the end, both were sentenced to six years in prison as *Volksschädlinge*. Schauergans had been an associate judge in the previous trial, now he was an associate judge again; Kuhnert modified the indictment in accordance with the rule of law, and the presiding judge of the responsible criminal chamber was the equally reformed Keutgen. Together, they paid homage to the new constitutional state: there were no longer any *Volksschädlinge*, and apart from that, the imposed sentence was "excessively high." Both offenders were now sentenced to 18 months in prison, with the coupon user additionally fined 500 Reichsmarks.[98]

Keutgen also had plenty to do. He corrected the jurisprudence not only of Schauergans, but also of other colleagues, he intervened in proceedings for which Kuhnert had shared responsibility as a judge, and he reconsidered sentences that Kuhnert had initiated as a public prosecutor.[99] A death sentence in a looting case, requested by Wickmann and commuted by the Reich Ministry of Justice to a ten-year prison sentence, he now reduced to 13 months' imprisonment.[100] Finally, Keutgen was given several opportunities to reconsider sentences based on his own preliminary work. In 1943, the special court had to judge a case in which a defendant had severely abused his wife and children on several occasions. The general prosecutor charged him as a violent criminal. The special court did not agree but nevertheless sentenced the defendant to four years in prison. Keutgen, then associate judge, now chairman, reduced the sentence to 15 months in 1947. To justify his decision, he reverted to the tried and tested rhetoric of the impersonal: "the criminal chamber" could not avoid the impression that the verdict of the special court—despite its legal assessment to the contrary—was "significantly" influenced by the harsh indictment.[101] In another case in 1949, Keutgen disguised his involvement in the conviction of a *Volksschädling*—ration coupon fraud—with the routine, transpersonal statement that further enforcement "should *not* be appropriate."[102]

Naturally, it is impossible to determine the extent to which such corrections strained the environment-adapted identity of those involved. But the legal self cannot have survived these transformations unscathed, even taking into account the high degree of indolence that usually characterizes the legal world. Not even a hardened trustee like Kuhnert would have chalked it up as an everyday occurrence when he was told by a lawyer about a decision he himself had initiated as a public prosecutor that he was dealing with "one of the horror sentences typical of the Third Reich" and that in 1946, still a public prosecutor, all he could do was to request more lenient treatment for the former *Volksschädlinge*.[103]

So how could the legal identity be preserved over time? Part of the decision-making process could be externalized by referring to the Allied Control Council's legislation that had since been passed—the *Volksschädling* had just been abolished. Moreover, the consequences of the review were too limited to seriously test the judicial ethos. The primary target of the Aachen judiciary was the files themselves. Hardly any of the reduced sentences were enforced; some were deemed to have been served through mitigation, others were suspended.[104] And for the Allies, this paper-based service was evidently too convoluted to grasp who was actually being called upon to take the law into their own hands. In some districts, it was expressly stipulated that the review of old political cases could not be carried out by the very judges who had been involved in the original case. This allowed the clear legal conclusion, *e contrario*, that there was no need to be concerned about the postwar judges' old wartime everyday cases.

Legal gestures took care of the rest; habitus and rhetoric were still the most reliable heralds of the inevitable. The possibility that any of Aachen's legal practitioners might have lost some of their purely objective judgment on the long road from National Socialism to the constitutional state was not even considered in any of the proceedings. Jurists were simply servants of necessity. The *Reichsgericht* ("Supreme Court of the Reich") had, in a wonderful circle, expressed the self-affirmation that judges are obliged to apply state law neutrally, which is why they must declare themselves biased as soon as a conflict of conscience arises. If they declare that they do not feel biased, then "even from the reasonable standpoint of a defendant, there can be no reason to doubt the impartial exercise of the judicial office by this judge."[105] A rare acknowledgement of the illocutionary power of legal language: the judges were not biased as long as they themselves claimed so. *These* principles were undoubtedly adhered to in Aachen as well.

The Provincial Prince

And with that, the Third Reich could be consigned to the foggy realms of memory. In 1950, Keutgen applied for a review of his categorization as a *Mitläufer* in accordance with the new *Regulation on legal status after periodic review in denazification proceedings*, which in his opinion should not have been issued "if the available evidence had been properly taken into account."[106] On 6 June 1951, the military government's decision was overturned by the Special Commissioner for Denazification because Keutgen had indeed inwardly rejected National Socialism and had only committed himself to his positions out of "pure motives."[107] Keutgen was now officially exonerated, his past legally expunged. As a result, not only did the already heavily watered-down references to Hitler Youth and party membership disappear from his service records, but Keutgen's career start was only dated to 1946, and even his engagement as press officer, which he had started in 1943, was shortened in retrospect by the war years.

Keutgen therefore no longer had to fear what came next. When he appeared in the GDR's *Brown Book campaigns* at the end of the 1950s, they were content to simply inform him of the situation without comment.[108] In response to these attacks, the Ministry of Justice of North Rhine-Westphalia nevertheless decided to review the death sentences of the special courts in general; this the outcome already predetermined when it was stated that in the case of "particularly suitable judges," a special determination would be made as to whether there had been a "significant violation of constitutional principles."[109] None of the Aachen judgments were challenged. A final farewell from the past, which Keutgen received in 1965, was treated with complete indifference. A certain "wise guy," probably a former Nazi victim, had contacted the Ludwigsburg Central Office to denounce Keutgen, claiming that Keutgen had "imposed several death sentences ... at the Special Court in Cologne for minor reasons" and that "the hypocrite" had also "previously been a fierce advocate of the death penalty" and "a zealous servant of the Führer." This ultimately culminated in the—strangely tame—request: "Take immediate steps." The Cologne Higher Regional Court responded with perfect detachment: "Nothing can be done in response to the petition."[110]

The time in the East also soon became an episode from days gone by. Wickmann spoke about it in considerable detail in his denazification proceedings, describing how he had worked with Keutgen to improve the detention conditions for the foreigners and had released a "considerable number" of them—sometimes against explicit orders.[111] Keutgen, on the other hand, limited himself to the blanket statement that "judicial business" had taken him to Bautzen and Ichtershausen.[112] Was his conscience still stirring here? He was twice asked for an official statement when defendants claimed after the war that they had already been sentenced by a relocated special court in Aachen. In one case, he confirmed the information with lengthy explanations of the convicted person's career and prospects,[113] in the case of another defendant who claimed a relatively favorable sentence for himself and claimed that his various thefts under cover of darkness had only led to nine months in prison, he left it at a terse "Not correct! K."[114]

Although the assignment had officially taken place in 1945 and had been reported to the Reich Ministry of Justice via the General Prosecutor's Office, few now wanted to remember it. Interrogating police officers openly speculated that the defendants were "deliberately naming a location in the Russian zone" because their statements "could then no longer be verified."[115] The judicial administration repeatedly initiated lengthy correspondence with courts in Bautzen to search for the files of the ominous special court.[116] A newspaper article from the 1960s only stated that Keutgen had been evacuated "with the prisoners"—which was not true—to Bautzen and Ichtershausen—which was also false—from where he had returned in 1944 (*sic*!), which was completely nonsensical.[117]

In Aachen, Keutgen soon became a kind of provincial prince. Official evaluations praised him in the highest terms as a "jurist with exceptional skills and knowledge," with "excellent general knowledge," "commendable diligence" and "rare decisiveness," who was "'up to any workload,' "of very high character," "straightforward, open-minded," and "a good, always helpful colleague."[118] From 1956 to 1963, he was nominated as a federal judge every year, then three times as Senate President; the files do not reveal why the promotion was not carried out.[119]

The press was also well-disposed toward him. As press officer, Keutgen was responsible for the court's public relations work, and he carried out this task as conscientiously as all other duties. In 1953, his superiors attested that he had "maintained contact with the press with great skill in difficult times,"[120] and the press obviously took a similar view. His (alleged) silver jubilee—by which time he had actually been in office for 28 years—was universally noted with favor.[121] When he switched from criminal to civil law in 1964 and took over the chairmanship of a chamber there, all three Aachen daily newspapers published articles, expressing their great regret over this step and at the same time their hope that he would nevertheless remain press officer.[122] The correspondent of the *Aachener Zeitung* went the furthest, using the change as an opportunity for a comprehensive portrait, at the end of which he gave Keutgen himself a chance to speak: "After 18 years in the criminal court, I wish to pursue a more peaceful role as a civil judge. That should be understandable"—a concern that the newspaper man devoutly commented on: "One should respect the decision of a wise man."[123]

Equalization of Burdens

There was only one thing left for the wise man to do. Hans Keutgen, the indefatigable special, ordinary, criminal and civil judge from Aachen, had been forced to serve far from home from 12 September 1944. A civil servant does not have to accept such a cut in his lifestyle without compensation, then as little as today. According to the *Relocation Expenses Reimbursement Act* of 3 May 1935, civil servants were entitled to reimbursement of their travel and relocation expenses. What's more, Section 11 also granted him a separation allowance if he was "transferred to another place of employment for official reasons" but was prevented from setting up his own household there "due to a lack of accommodation."[124]

Keutgen gratefully accepted the offer of a special allowance. Even in Gemünd, he had only needed three days to bring his sense of order and self-interest into play and request reimbursement of his additional relocation-related costs from the judicial administration, which had itself been evacuated. Because, as Keutgen stated on the form, "it is currently impossible to obtain a new accommodation at the place of employment under the current conditions," he applied to the President of the Regional Court for a separation allowance, and because apparently no one doubted that the war-related evacuation was an "official reason," the request was granted. The same was true for Siegburg, Bautzen, and Ichtershausen; after all, it was obvious that an accommodation could not be obtained under the existing conditions. And since it was not known how long the absence from Aachen would last, but an imminent return seemed to be out of the question, the separation allowance was granted as a lump sum until the end of 1945.[125]

This entitled Keutgen to a substantial bonus to somewhat mitigate the hardships of his frequent relocations. The usual daily rate was 8 Reichsmarks, plus a kind of start-up allowance of an additional 10 Reichsmarks per day for the first week. For January 1945, the separation allowance therefore amounted to 310 Reichsmarks—a good half of his salary—for February 224 Reichsmarks, and for March 248 Reichsmarks,[126] plus reimbursement of travel expenses. Because these benefits would add up to a considerable amount over the course of a year, Keutgen received an initial installment of 500 Reichsmarks that January. Everything else was reserved for the postwar period.

On 22 May 1946, a few weeks after the denazification proceedings were completed, the President of the Cologne Higher Regional Court contacted Keutgen to find out from which sources he had received remuneration and compensation following the evacuation of Aachen.[127] The process proved to be quite convoluted. It was unclear by when the separation allowance was due, as Keutgen had returned to Aachen long before 31 December 1945. It was also not easy to determine what expenses he had incurred on his travels across the German Reich. Furthermore, it remained unclear whether two further installments, transferred to Keutgen by postal check in February and March, had reached their destination. And finally, it had to be investigated whether Keutgen had possibly unnecessarily extended his official trips by visiting home on the occasion of the birth and death of his daughter.

Keutgen was genuinely interested in shedding light on these events. He described in detail his odyssey during the last months of the war, his assignment to Bautzen, and the onward journey to Ichtershausen, a good 2,500 kilometers in total. On 15 January 1945, he left Siegburg and traveled to Brilon for 13.10 Reichsmarks to assist his wife during the birth of their daughter. She was born on 17 January, so he went to Bautzen in the evening as instructed (travel costs: 36.20 Reichsmarks), where he arrived three days later. During the evacuation of the Bautzen remand prison, he had received a telegram stating that his wife and child, both now in Erwitte, were seriously ill. Therefore, he had traveled from Bautzen to Erwitte on February 15 (39.20 Reichsmarks) and, after a short vacation there, from Erwitte to Ichtershausen on February 23 (23.80 Reichsmarks), which, given the conditions at the time, had taken three days each way. The trip home, Keutgen explained his legal opinion, was "already reimbursable because even without a valid reason, the separated civil servant is allowed to travel to his relatives once every three months." Until the end of his official duties on 29 March, he could generally only claim a daily rate of 8 Reichsmarks as separation allowance, but the increased rate of 10 Reichsmarks during the first seven days in the new location was available to him three times—modesty is not called for in such moments—namely for Siegburg, Bautzen, and Ichtershausen.[128]

Keutgen's contribution to clarifying the facts of the case was obviously appreciated by the judicial administration. The President of the Aachen Regional Court forwarded Keutgen's letter to the President of the Higher Regional Court just one day later with his own assessment, in which the various secondments were all confirmed with reference to the files or the statements of colleagues. While approval for relocating the place of employment from Bautzen to Ichtershausen had been necessary, it had not been possible to obtain it "in view of the current circumstances." With regard to the intervening journey home, there had certainly been an important reason, according to the inductive conclusion; after all, "the child's life-threatening illness … is documented by the fact that the child died on 20 February 1945." Because it was no longer possible to determine "how many days the journey from Bautzen to Ichtershausen would have taken without the detour via Erwitte, given the traffic conditions at the time," Keutgen generously agreed to allow the entire journey to count toward his leave. Therefore, "taking into account all the circumstances of this case, in particular the difficult and dangerous business trips, as well as the poor and disproportionately expensive overnight accommodations," Keutgen's application "should be subjected to a favorable review."[129]

Now the matter could be settled. The Higher Regional Court made minor adjustments, but there was no doubt as to the eligibility for reimbursement. Separation allowance, daily allowance, accommodation allowance, travel expenses, travel allowance, employment allowance in Bautzen (local class B), employment allowance in Ichtershausen (local class C), employment travel allowance: the last service under the Aachen special law, the last 180 *Volksschädlinge*, conscientious objectors, black marketeers, ration coupon forgers, and usurers had incurred additional costs of 956.24 Reichsmarks in their special judicial treatment.[130] Keutgen's months-long assignment to the then Central and now East German prisons was thus compensated. And why not? There was no Radbruch formula for the reimbursement of relocation allowances, and in any case, the official duties in Bautzen were described with the innocuous nature of travel law as "handling the remaining criminal cases," while the work in Ichtershausen was—strikingly logically—described as "continuation of the criminal proceedings."[131] Only one point indicated that the bureaucratic follow-up was not a normal case: the return trip to Aachen was neither reimbursed nor did Keutgen even request reimbursement. It was clear to everyone that Keutgen had left as a special judge but had not been able to return as a special judge.

Man of the Law

Additional costs of 956.24 Reichsmarks. Nothing comparable has been recorded for Wickmann, whose expenses must have been no less. But what does that mean? Perhaps he had been forgotten, or perhaps he had no reason to take action on his own initiative in view of sufficient advance payments. In Keutgen's case, these advances amounted to a good two months' salary, and multiple applications for relocation expenses prove that he was in good need of the money. Moreover, the initiative for the proper accounting of his official duties did not come from him, but from the judicial administration, and it is almost in the nature of things that he was stubbornly meticulous in his search for reimbursable items.

The jurist can adapt more easily than anyone else. Keutgen died on 5 February 1999, at the blessed age of 86.[132] In his eventful career, he had numerous opportunities to put his presumptuous statements into action. In 1976, he received a certificate of honor for 40 years of service, which again omitted the wartime period. The fact that he had actually worked for 44 years upon reaching retirement in 1977 only played a role in calculating his pension; when it could be translated into hard cash, Keutgen was once again heard to acknowledge his time as a special judge.[133]

Service to order as a way of life: someone like Dr. Keutgen—formerly Hans—could always be relied upon. In one of the few public statements of his that has survived, Keutgen followed this up with an explanation. "With the criminal judge"—unlike the civil judge—he told an audience at the Aachen Bürgerbräu in 1964, the jurist comes second; "first and foremost," "the human element" should be applied. That certainly sounded like vigilant humanism. But Keutgen's humanity went in a completely different direction: the criminal judge must, he continued, "use his own personality to stand up for the law, even to the point of his own dissolution."[134] A remarkable ideal. The jurist should make himself an instrument of his profession. To be "human" means precisely to cast off the human element. Keutgen is not guilty of anything wrong in this respect. But if the primacy of humanity itself suggested to him that he should dissolve himself, then nothing else could be expected.

Notes

1. All this after Keutgen's request for admission to the school-leaving examination of 1 December 1931, in: Stadtarchiv Aachen, KKG, Abitur 1932, Klasse OI b (unpaginated).
2. Expert opinion of the class conference, 7 December 1931, in: ibid.
3. Preliminary consultation on the oral examination of 22 February 1932, in: ibid.
4. This was one of four topics from which the students could choose; there is no explanation as to why it was set in this garbled form. In German: "Deutschlands geopgraphische Lage sein Schicksal."
5. Report of the class conference, 7 December 1931, in: Stadtarchiv Aachen, KKG, Abitur 1932, Klasse OI b (unpaginated).
6. Application for admission dated 1 December 1931, in: Stadtarchiv Aachen, KKG, Abitur 1932, Klasse OI b (unpaginated).
7. For the course of studies, see the documents on the college funds in UA Köln, Zugang 604, no. 161–168.
8. My curriculum vitae (doctoral file, UA Köln, accession 42 no. 3210).
9. These quotations are all from Welzel, *Naturalismus und Wertphilosophie.* Welzel elaborated on these considerations more comprehensively—albeit in another most vivid reality. C.f. *Naturrecht und materiale Gerechtigkeit.*
10. Keutgen, *Private und öffentliche Sühne*, from which the following quotations are taken.
11. Doctoral file, UA Köln, Zugang 42 No. 3210.
12. On his personnel form, Keutgen gave the membership number 4.194.114 and the rank of block leader (Archiv OLG Köln, Ersatz-Personalakte des OLG betreffend Dr. Hans Keutgen, p. 2).
13. This is the assessment of Keutgen's time in Kerrl (25.4.–18.6.1938), in: Archiv OLG Köln, Personalakte des Referendars Hans Keutgen (unpaginated).
14. Assessment dated 14 January 1943, in: Archiv OLG Köln, Ersatz-Personalalalakten OLG betreffend Dr. Hans Keutgen (unpaginated).
15. A brief description of these stations in BA (PA), Dr. Hans Keutgen. See also: Tessin, *Verbände und Truppen*, 23–27.
16. The Reich Ministry of Justice (or "RJM") to the Higher Regional Court President for Cologne, in: LAV NRW-R Ger. Rep. 255 No. 213, p. 55. Official report in Deutsche Justiz 1941, 223.
17. Report of the Regional Court President of Aachen to the Higher Regional Court President of Cologne, 28 February 1942, in: LAV NRW-R, Ger. Rep. 255 No. 174 (unpaginated), also in: Situation report of the Higher Regional Court President of Cologne to RJM, 1 March 1942, in: BA, R 3001 No. 23374, pp. 67–72.
18. The most comprehensive review of these files is by Vurgun, *Staatsanwaltschaft*, 40–44. Vurgun's precise, albeit not very stimulating writing has made access to the files much easier.
19. Judgment of 23 March 1943, in: LAV NRW-R, Ger. Rep. 113 No. 313.
20. See the proceedings ibid., nos. 304 and 306: one case resulted in two years' imprisonment, the other in one year's imprisonment.
21. Ibid., nos. 198, 201, 217, 229, 242, 396.
22. In Aachen, this even applied to cases in which rape was suspected (e.g., LAV NRW-R, Ger. Rep. 113 No. 258, also Nos. 214, 218, 300, 203, 355).
23. See ibid., nos. 303, 325, 307, 310.
24. See Vurgun, *Staatsanwaltschaft*, 374–379.

25. *Rundverfügung* (or "RV," i.e., a circular to a larger audience) of 5 July 1943, in: BA, R 3001 No. 22489, pp. 151–155. For corresponding local reports, see the Regional Court President for Aachen to the Higher Regional Court President for Cologne, 27 July 1943, in: LAV NRW-R, Ger. Rep. 255 No. 213, p. 98, 100–104.
26. Losenhausen had been a member of parliament for the Deutsche Volkspartei [German Peoples' Party] since 1925 before joining the NSDAP on 1 May 1933. His fragile state of health is documented several times. Relatively little case law has survived in his case. Losenhausen died after an air raid on 12 April 1944.
27. In purely quantitative terms, Schwengers was a very active judge, see Vurgun, *Staatsanwaltschaft*, 534. After moderate examinations, he became a judge at the Bonn Regional Court in 1928. His personnel file apparently no longer exists; an overall positive report from the Higher Regional Court President for Cologne, dated 27 December 1944, considers Schwengers fit for promotion, but warns that sometimes he "lacked commitment" (LAV NRW-R, Ger. Rep. 255 No. 138, p. 152).
28. Walther Fritz was born in Aachen in 1901 and studied in Bonn and Greifswald. After his legal clerkship in Stettin, he worked briefly as an assistant judge in Berlin before becoming a regional court judge in Trier in 1929. He then worked in Aachen from 1934, where he was promoted to regional court director in 1941 after a short period of military service. See in total the personnel file LAV NRW-R, NW-Pe No. 399. The regional court president himself, Dr. Walter Graeschke, apparently played no role at the special court.
29. Howahrde, a Protestant from the Rhineland, had passed his exams, had become an assistant judge in 1918 and had been a regional court judge since 1926. More information in his personnel file in: BA, R 3001 No. 61328. In Aachen, he was by far the most active judge of the Special Court; more than a quarter of all cases were decided under his chairmanship (Vurgun, *Staatsanwaltschaft*).
30. This from an assessment by the Higher Regional Court President for Cologne dated 22 December 1939, in: LAV NRW-R, Ger. Rep. 11 No. 1535, p. 184.
31. Letter from the lawyer Lauber to Aachen Regional Court, 11 February 1946, in: LAV NRW-R, Ger. Rep. 113 No. 360. Höher was appointed to the People's Court in November 1944; Zimmerath worked for the General Prosecutor's Office in Prague from March 1944. After the war, both had considerable difficulties in obtaining reinstatement. For Höher, see the personnel file in LAV NRW-R, NW-Pe No. 3711 and the denazification file in ibid., NW 1049 No. 37731. Biographical and other information on Höher can be found in Vurgun, *Staatsanwaltschaft*, 195–202, 490 et seq., and on Zimmerath in ibid., 215–224, 491–493.
32. All this from the multi-volume personnel file of Ludwig Kuhnert, in: LAV NRW-R, NW Pe No. 8002 and ibid., NW-Pe No. 6063.
33. See the judgments of 15 February 1943 (LAV NRW-R, Ger. Rep. 113 No. 408), of 23 March 1943 (ibid., No. 313), of 10 June 1943 (ibid., No. 286), of 4 June 1942 (ibid., No. 204).
34. The files can be found in BA, R 3001 No. 163394–163395, see also the description in Vurgun, *Staatsanwaltschaft*, esp. 411–420. In the denazification proceedings, Keutgen claimed to have been the driving force behind the proceedings (LAV NRW-R, NW 1079 No. 1145) and to have enforced the conviction against the will of the party, which, however, can hardly be true, since Keutgen had not even been officially appointed at that time.
35. Judgment of 27 March 1943, S Ls 55/1943, recorded in LAV NRW-R, NW 1213 No. 43, Sonderheft III. The file itself could not be found.

36. Judgment of 30 March 1943, in: BA, R 3001 No. 162245, in Vurgun, *Staatsanwaltschaft*, 423–425.
37. This was the assessment of the Ministry of Justice in 1960 in LAV NRW-R, NW No. 43 1213, Sonderheft III.
38. The destruction is almost completely documented in LAV NRW-R, Ger. Rep. 255 No. 343, here pp. 259 et seq.
39. Füherorlass of 13 July 1944, reprinted in: Moll, 426–428.
40. Letter from Reichsleiter Bormann to the Gauleiter, 5 September 1944, quoted from Rass/Rohrkamp/Quadflieg, *Gerhard Graf von Schwerin*, 32. The following account of the events is based primarily on this report.
41. Report of 17 October 1944, quoted from Henke, *Die amerikanische Besetzung Deutschlands*, 154.
42. Order of 16 September 1944, quoted from Henke, ibid., 154 footnote 23.
43. Letter from the Higher Regional Court President for Cologne to the Regional Court President for Aachen, Cologne, Trier, Koblenz, 5 September 1944, in: LAV NRW-R, Ger. Rep. 255 No. 553, p. 195. The Aachen experience, in turn, was put to the test, so to speak, and turned into administrative decrees *post festum*. See the summary letter from the Plenipotentiary General for the Reich Administration, 18 September 1944, hereafter: GStA PK, XV HA Rep. 76 Stargard No. 675, pp. 187–189.
44. Note on the telephone information from the General Prosecutor's Office in Cologne, 9 September 1944, in: BA, R 3001 No. 25017, p. 69.
45. Situation report General Prosecutor's Office in Cologne, 30 September 1944, in: BA, R 3001 No. 23374, p. 145.
46. Details can be found in the personnel file (LAV NRW-R, BR-Pe No. 1046 and NW-Pe No. 446) and denazification file (ibid., NW 1037 RS No. 1949, NW 1079 No. 15400 and NW 1048-40-00110). As chairman of the special court at the German Regional Court in Brno, Hellbach was involved in at least six death sentences (BA, R 137 II); at the end of 1944 he was seconded to the Cologne branch of the People's Court (LAV NRW-R, Ger. Rep. 449 No. 47).
47. See the proceedings LAV NRW-R, Ger. Rep. 113 No. 402. Dates in the second half of September can be found in ibid., Nos. 211, 216, 269, 270, 384, 390, 396, 397, 398, 399, 400, 401.
48. LAV NRW-R, Ger. Rep. 113 No. 212, 389.
49. Ibid., nos. 385 and 386. According to the minutes, Hellbach, local court judge Dr. Gliesche, assistant judge van Kempen and public prosecutor Dr. Marx were present. Also on 7 September a witness was summoned for a meeting on 16 September; see ibid. no. 398. According to information received by telephone, the GStA Cologne dates the removal of the prisoners to 8 September (note on this in BA, R 3001 no. 25017, p. 69).
50. See LAV NRW-R, Ger. Rep. 113 No. 209, 380, 387, 388, 394.
51. Ibid., no. 344.
52. LAV NRW-R, Ger. Rep. 113 no. 211, 384, 397.
53. Cf. his letter to Regional Court Director Fritz, 19 September 1944, in: Archiv OLG Köln, Ersatz-Personalakte des OLG betreffend Dr. Hans Keutgen, p. 4.
54. Oberamtsrichter ("OAR") Gemünd to the Regional Court President for Aachen, 15 November 1944, in: LAV NRW-R, Ger. Rep. 255 No. 198, p. 10.
55. Higher Regional Court President for Cologne to OAR Ahlen, 30 September 1944, in: LAV NRW-R Ger. Rep. 255 No. 202, p. 75.
56. See LAV NRW-R Ger. Rep. 113 No. 217 with the investigation file in No. 396. The judgment is dated 27 January 1945.

57. The interruption of judicial activity was "only of insignificant duration," noted the Cologne Higher Regional Court (memo Higher Regional Court President for Cologne, 25 January 1945, in: LAV NRW-R, Ger. Rep. 255 No. 326, p. 233).
58. See the personnel overview of 16 September 1944 (LAV NRW-R, Ger. Rep. 255 No. 202, p. 74); for the general prosecutor's office, see the report of the chief public prosecutor in Aachen, 14 October 1944, in: LAV NRW-R, Ger. Rep. 449 No. 46, pp. 133 et seq.
59. Personnel file of the Higher Regional Court on Walther Fritz, assessment dated 23 December 1944, in: LAV NRW-R, NW-Pe No. 7244 (unpaginated).
60. Judgment of 10 October 1944, in: LAV NRW-R, NW 174 No. 200.
61. However, it is added that the evacuation order is awaited. See GStA Cologne report dated 14 November 1944, in: LAV NRW-R, Ger. Rep. 449 No. 28, p. 160; for the situation in Düren as a whole, see also the situation reports of the General Prosecutor's Office in Cologne dated 30 September 1944 (BA, R 3001 No. 23374, p. 145) and 22 October 1944 (ibid., p. 150).
62. Letter from State Secretary RJM to Commander-in-Chief Friedrichs, 17 November 1944, BA, R 3001 No. 22266 (unpaginated).
63. Travel report MD Dr. Vollmer, 24 November 1944, in: BA, R 3001 No. 25017, p. 25. See also personnel file Hans Führer, in: LAV NRW-R, BR-Pe No. 7577.
64. All this according to a letter from Regional Court President for Aachen to the Higher Regional Court President for Cologne, 23 November 1944, in: LAV NRW-R, Ger. Rep. 255 No. 215, p. 50, and memo dated 20 November 1944, ibid., p. 48; official travel report MD Dr. Vollmer, 24 November 1944, in: BA, R 3001 No. 25017, p. 32; situation report Higher Regional Court President for Cologne, 1 December 1944, in: BA, R 3001 No. 23374, p. 155.
65. Letter from the Regional Court President for Aachen to the Higher Regional Court President for Cologne, 14 December 1944, in: LAV NRW-R, Ger. Rep. 255 No. 215, p. 52.
66. Situation report GStA Cologne, 30 January 1945, in: BA, R 3001 No. 23374, p. 162. See also the report on the business trip Dr. Vollmer/Fechner, 8 December 1944, in: BA, R 3001 No. 25017, pp. 46 et seq.
67. In the first state examination he received the grade "sufficient," in the second he failed once and ended up with "sufficient" again when he retook it; see the personnel file of the North Rhein-Westphalia (*Nordrhein-Westfalen* or "NRW") Ministry of Justice (LAV NRW-R, NW-Pe No. 6190); Vurgun, *Staatsanwaltschaft*, 210–215.
68. Letter from Keutgen to the Higher Regional Court President for Cologne, 17 January 1945, in: Archiv OLG Köln, Ersatz-Personalakte des OLG betreffend Dr. Hans Keutgen, p. 14.
69. Letter from Hans Keutgen and Hans Wickmann to the Higher Regional Court President for Jena, 28 February 1945, in: HStAW, Thüringisches Oberlandesgericht Jena No. 909, p. 67.
70. The proceedings can be found in the holdings of the Sondergericht Aachen LAV NRW-R, Ger. Rep. 113 No. 401, here pp. 26 et seq.
71. Ibid., no. 386, p. 172.
72. LAV NRW-R, Ger. Rep. 113 No. 402, p. 16. The convict was sent to Untermaßfeld Prison for execution on 27 March 1945; the date of the sentence was communicated from there after the war, ibid., p. 18. In another case, two prisoners on remand confirmed after the war that they had served time in Ichtershausen without a trial having taken place there; see the case in: LAV NRW-R, Ger. Rep. 113 No. 385, pp. 34 et seq.

73. Letter from RJM currently Ichtershausen to RJM, 29 March 1945, in: BA, R 3001 No. 24471, pp. 136 et seq.
74. The Higher Regional Court was still in operation until 9 April 1945, see report Higher Regional Court President for Cologne to the Justice Ministry for NRW ("JM NRW"), 1 April 1947, in: LAV NRW-R, NW 189 No. 1181, p. 26.
75. See the Security Service (*Sicherheitsdienst* or "SD") report on the situation in the occupied territories of October 1944, which already contains Law No. 1 and Proclamation No. 1, in: BA, R 3001 No. 25017, pp. 64–66.
76. See Birmanns, "Aachener Justiz," 217 footnote 34.
77. Aachen Local Court, memorandum dated 1 October 1962.
78. See, for example, the reports of the Higher Regional Court President for Cologne to JM NRW, 1 April 1947 (LAV NRW-R, NW 189 No. 1181, p. 28) and 15 November 1947 (ibid., Ger. Rep. 255 No. 84, p. 151), or the occupation lists in ibid., Ger. Rep. 563 No. 23. The literature seems to rely on this report; see Raim, *Justiz*, 85 with footnote 362.
79. See the questionnaire in the denazification file LAV NRW-R, NW 1079 No. 1145 (unpaginated).
80. Keutgen, explanation to the questionnaire, 28 March 1946, in: Archiv OLG Köln, Ersatz-Personalakte des OLG betreffend Dr. Hans Keutgen, p. 30. Ibid., p. 36, is the decision of the Review Committee dated 16 April 1946.
81. See Einreihungsbescheid, 19 July 1947, and Berufungsbescheid, 2 September 1947, in: LAV NRW-R, NW 1079 No. 1145 (unpaginated); also letter of appeal, 28 July 1947, in: NW 1037 No. 1984 (unpaginated).
82. See personnel file Dr. Alfred Hellbach, in: LAV NRW-R, BR-Pe No. 1046.
83. See the decision of 9 April 1946, in: LAV NRW-R, NW-Pe No. 7244 (unpaginated).
84. Heitzer was taken into protective custody for several months in 1933; after 20 July 1944, he evaded arrest by fleeing and hid until the Allied invasion.
85. For Schauergans, see the personnel file and the denazification file in: LAV NRW-R, BR-Pe No. 13373 and NW 1079 No. 17007.
86. See the personnel file LAV NRW-R, NW-Pe No. 6190 and the denazification files, ibid., NW 1037 RS No. 1106 and NW 1079 No. 1789.
87. See Ludwig Kuhnert's personnel file, in: LAV NRW-R, NW-Pe No. 8002.
88. For example, in the proceedings in: LAV NRW-R, Ger. Rep. 113 No. 386. Questionnaires from Stillger can be found in the proceedings LAV NRW-R, Ger. Rep. 113 No. 386, pp. 132–144 or ibid., No. 196, pp. 53–68.
89. The following information comes mainly from the situation reports of the Regional Court President for Aachen to the Higher Regional Court President for Cologne, LAV NRW-R, Ger. Rep. 255 No. 176. They begin on 24 September 1945, and are submitted every six months from January 1946. The reports on the reconstruction work in LAV NRW-R, Ger. Rep. 255 No. 343 and 344 have also been consulted.
90. Referred to here according to a letter from the Military Government to the JM NRW, 30 May 1947, in: LAV NRW-R, Ger. Rep. 255 No. 288, p. 186. See also the references in Wrobel, *Verurteilt zur Demokratie*, 154 et seq.
91. Decree on the granting of impunity of 21 January 1946, in: JBl. Köln 1946, 6.
92. Ordinance on impunity of 3 June 1947, in: Verordnungsblatt British Zone 1947, 68.
93. See the Ordinance on the Transfer of Criminal Proceedings in Abolished Courts, 4 December 1946, in: VOBl. BZ, 1947, 8.
94. See, for example, ibid. no. 292. Cf. incidentally the proceedings in: LAV NRW-R, Ger. Rep. 113, nos. 291, 373, 380, 381, 382, 383, 384, 387, 388, 389, 390, 391, 392, 393, 395, 397, 398, 399, 400, 402.

95. Application: ibid., nos. 349, 356, 407, 409; reduction: ibid., nos. 296, 300, 301, 304, 317, 325, 326, 354; probation: ibid., no. 347; withdrawal: ibid.; in case no. 208, Kuhnert withdrew an indictment with which he had been involved as a judge; clemency: ibid., no. 289.
96. See ibid., no. 369.
97. See, for example, ibid., nos. 262, 268, 288, 337.
98. Ibid., no. 331.
99. The former: ibid., nos. 349, 356, 357, 369; the latter: ibid. no. 410.
100. Ibid., no. 205.
101. Ibid., no. 206.
102. Ibid., no. 286. Incidentally, Schauergans was also involved in the judgment of the special court.
103. Ibid., no. 375. To be fair, the sentences before 1945 were harsher than he had requested.
104. Some rare exceptions: No. 204 (sentenced in 1942 to eight years in prison with preventive detention for grand larceny; preventive detention lifted in 1946), No. 206 (aggravated assault: reduction from four years in prison to one year and three months, summons to appear for sentencing in May 1946).
105. Reichsgericht, *Juristische Woche* 1930, 2560 No. 26.
106. Hans Keutgen application, 21 April 1950, in: LAV NRW-R, NW 1037 RS No. 1984 (unpaginated). The ordinance itself can be found in Ministerialblatt NRW 11/1950, p. 497.
107. Decision of the Special Commissioner for Denazification in the State of North Rhine-Westphalia, 6 June 1951, in: LAV NRW-R, NW 1037 RS No. 1984 (unpaginated). It is probably superfluous to add that no new evidence was submitted for this decision, but only the evidence already available to the military government was re-evaluated.
108. Letter from the Cologne Higher Regional Court to Hans Keutgen, 13 May 1959, in: Archiv OLG Köln, Ersatz-Personalakte des OLG betreffend Dr. Hans Keutgen, p. 145. Keutgen is mentioned in two brochures (*Hitlers Sonderrichter*, 6; *Wir klagen an*, 20), which was carefully recorded in the JM NRW (LAV NRW-R, NW 1213 No. 3). The mention in Koppel, *Justiz im Zwielicht*, 89, 160, 174, plays no role in Keutgen's personnel file.
109. Note of the meeting of the Higher Regional Court President with JM, 25 March 1960, in: LAV NRW-R, NW 1213 No. 43, p. 3.
110. Letter from the Ministry of Justice of North Rhine-Westphalia to the President of the Higher Regional Court of Cologne, 17 March 1965, and memo from the President of the Higher Regional Court of Cologne, 20 April 1965, both in: Archiv OLG Köln, Ersatz-Personalakte des OLG betreffend Dr. Hans Keutgen, p. 216–218.
111. Hans Wickmann, undated attachment to the questionnaire, probably at the end of 1947, in: LAV NRW-R, NW 1079 No. 1789 (unpaginated).
112. This from the denazification file, in: LAV NRW-R, NW 1079 No. 1145 (unpaginated).
113. See the procedure in: LAV NRW-R, Ger. Rep. 113 No. 401, p. 27.
114. Ibid., no. 386, p. 172. The note is handwritten; Keutgen's authorship can only be deduced from a comparison with other handwritten statements. The evidence is therefore not unambiguous.
115. Thus in the proceedings in LAV NRW-R, Ger. Rep. 113 No. 386, p. 172.
116. See, for example, ibid., no. 401.
117. Aachener Zeitung, 5 December 1964.
118. Regional Court President for Aachen, assessment dated 25 October 1950, which ends with the somewhat peculiar phrase: "He knows what he wants." (Archiv OLG Köln, Ersatz-Personalakte des OLG betreffend Dr. Hans Keutgen, p. 86).

119. Regional Court President for Aachen, assessment dated 28 October 1970 (Archiv OLG Köln, Personalakte über den Vorsitzenden Richter am LG Dr. Hans Keutgen [unpaginated]).
120. Regional Court President for Aachen, assessment dated 5 November 1953 (ibid.).
121. See the notes in *Aachener Zeitung*, 1 February 1961; *Aachener Nachrichten*, 1 February 1961; *Aachener Volkszeitung*, 1 February 1961.
122. *Aachener Volkszeitung*, 1 December 1964; *Aachener Nachrichten*, 1 December 1964; *Aachener Zeitung*, 1 December 1964.
123. *Aachener Zeitung*, 5 December 1964.
124. Reichsgesetzblatt I, 566, in conjunction with the Reich Finance Minister's implementing decree of 7 May 1935, Reichsbesoldungsblatt, 40, from No. 25, from which the above quotations are taken.
125. Regional Court President for Aachen, 9 January 1945, in: Archiv OLG Köln, Ersatz-Personalakte des OLG betreffend Dr. Hans Keutgen, p. 13.
126. Calculation and monitoring sheet for separation compensation, 9 January 1945, in: Archiv OLG Köln, Ersatz-Personalakte des OLG betreffend Dr. Hans Keutgen, p. 38.
127. Letter of the Higher Regional Court President for Cologne to Hans Keutgen, 22 May 1946, in: Archiv OLG Köln, Ersatz-Personalakte des OLG betreffend Dr. Hans Keutgen, p. 27.
128. Letter from Hans Keutgen to the Higher Regional Court President for Cologne, 10 February 1947, in: Archiv OLG Köln, Ersatz-Personalakte des OLG betreffend Dr. Hans Keutgen, p. 53.
129. Regional Court President for Aachen to Higher Regional Court for Cologne, 11 February 1947, in: Archiv OLG Köln, Ersatz-Personalakte des OLG betreffend Dr. Hans Keutgen, p. 51.
130. Travel expense report of the Aachen Regional Court, 11 February 1947, in: Archiv OLG Köln, Ersatz-Personalakte des OLG betreffend Dr. Hans Keutgen, pp. 44 et seq., pp. 51, 56.
131. Archiv OLG Köln, Ersatz-Personalakte des OLG betreffend Dr. Hans Keutgen, sheets 37 and 44.
132. Obituary in *Aachener Zeitung*, 10 February 1999; obituary ibid., 11 February 1999.
133. The case can be found at the end of Ersatz-Personalakte des OLG betreffend Dr. Hans Keutgen (Archiv OLG Köln). One of the issues discussed was whether Keutgen had been granted special leave to complete his dissertation.
134. Quoted from *Aachener Nachrichten*, 21 April 1964. A few references to Keutgen's image of the judge also in Keutgen, "Kritische Betrachtung," 47–61.

Chapter 5

On the Run

The Relocation of the Judicial Authorities in the Winter of 1944/45

The Beginning

At the end of 1943, the Stettin Higher Regional Court's administrative department left its original location. The city had experienced its first major air raid that spring, although the judiciary was barely affected—the files remained virtually intact, the Stettin Regional Court President announced, and the courts could still be visited at their usual addresses.[1] However, the Higher Regional Court, prominently located in Stettin Castle, had to expect that it would not survive further attacks unscathed. As Plenipotentiary General for the Reich Administration, Wilhelm Frick issued an order in July that precautions be taken to ensure that authorities could continue to carry out war-critical tasks immediately even after the destruction of their offices; if necessary, they should be relocated to the surrounding area.[2] As the administrative department of the Stettin Higher Regional Court was not expected to attract large numbers of visitors, there were no objections to its relocation. In August, a few typewriters and some important but nevertheless dispensable documents—older personnel files, building files, entailment and fiefdom files—were transferred to the Köslin Regional Court, and in September concrete plans began for the relocation of the entire administrative department to the Pomeranian hinterland.[3]

The project was ambitious. Shipping companies were struggling with fuel shortages and the Reichsbahn was operating at full capacity. A move to more remote areas could not be allowed to hinder the judicial system's ability to function, which is why particular attention had to be paid to rail and bus connections. However, the many quiet towns in the district, which offered good conditions in this respect, were often already so overcrowded due to evacuations from the air-ravaged West that accommodating the judicial employees proved impossible. In addition, there were the usual defensive reflexes: the Schneidemühl Regional Court President claimed that while there were still rooms available in some of his local courts, they were only suitable for housing furniture and equipment. The Köslin Regional Court President, evidently endowed with particular ingenuity in this respect, regretfully announced that even important works in his library, such as Palandt, Schlegelberger-Hoche, Löwe-Rosenberg and, moreover, the entire tax code, were out of date,[4] which he himself apparently did not consider to be disruptive for his own jurisdiction, but was unacceptable for the administration of the Higher Regional Court.

The solution finally agreed upon was intended to hurt no one and therefore satisfied no one. Between September 1943 and January 1944, the Stettin administrative department was distributed among no fewer than seven alternative locations. The local court in the tiny municipality of Bublitz, almost 200 kilometers east of Stettin, became the seat of the Higher Regional Court President. His deputy moved to the even smaller and even more distant village of Pollnow, and further staff were installed at the local courts in Köslin, Bärwalde, and Tempelburg. Only the court treasury remained relatively close by and continued to operate in the Pyritz Local Court, located about 40 kilometers south of Stettin. Legal proceedings continued to be held in Stettin, where the trainee judges were also able to attend their training sessions as before. The Higher Regional Court President concluded in his report to the Reich Ministry of Justice that in future mail should be addressed to "the staff of the Higher Regional Court in Bublitz, Local Court."[5]

This asylum was not chosen with particular care. The effort required for the relocation alone was considerable. The first shipments of office furniture and files were handled in September: a specially converted van from the Gollnow prison took over what the shipping company was unable to load. The bulk of the move then took place in December, and no restraint was exercised. In addition to the usual items—tables, chairs, filing cabinets, filing racks, typewriters, forms, books, paper, gas masks, safes—the traditional trappings of bourgeois representation were still considered indispensable: massive writing desks traveled along, as did lecterns, flower stands, sofas, upholstered chairs, armchairs, even a chaise longue and a chandelier found their way to the temporary quarters in the countryside. The employees' personal belongings were also taken without any major reservations, and a good two dozen trips brought a colorful hodgepodge to the province: beds, mattresses, blankets, bedside tables, oil paintings, tubs, buckets, mirrors, carpets, curtains, decanters, lamps, dressers, lockers, cupboards, a grandfather clock, sacks of briquettes, potato stocks, as well as ten rolls of toilet paper and 15 towels.[6] A major attack on Stettin brought the operation to a halt in January 1944, and the move was not completed until the end of February. But it was impossible to truly settle into the new circumstances. Bureaucratic practices suffered considerably from the spatial fragmentation, especially given the increasingly unreliable postal and transport conditions. The temporary quarters in Köslin soon had to be abandoned because the Wehrmacht set up a military hospital there. The staff in Bublitz, Pollnow, and Bärwalde also left their asylum after a few months and attempted to reestablish a center for the fragmented administration at the Stargard Local Court, only 50 kilometers east of Stettin. Once again, accommodations had to be found, and once again files, desks, and mattresses went on the move.[7]

Of course, this was only an interim step. While the administration slowly returned to its original headquarters, Stettin's city center was largely destroyed in a major air raid in August 1944. The castle burned down completely. Divisions of the Higher Regional Court and the Local Court, which had remained there until the end, lost all their rooms, files, and inventory; together they moved into a less damaged building of the Regional Court—a small palace of justice, albeit one clearly created by necessity: all three instances united under one roof.[8] Shortly thereafter, the presidium of the Higher Regional Court also returned to Stettin to take up residence in the local court in the eastern suburb of Altdamm. After its rather erratic odyssey through the Pomeranian hinterland in the past twelve months, this was now its ninth alternative location.

The threat situation had changed radically during this time. The danger no longer came from the air, but from the east. In September 1944, the first top-secret preparations for an emergency began. Aachen was lost in the west, and soon after, Memel and the surrounding areas had to be evacuated. Pomerania was still a long way from the front, but it was also clear in Stettin that salvation no longer lay in the east. After the Russian winter offensive, things moved quickly.[9] The first towns in the district were evacuated at the end of January 1945, a Gestapo commando shot at least 600 prisoners in the nearby Sonnenburg prison, and the *Volksgerichtshof* ("People's Court") in Stettin hanged seven perpetrators of high treason at the beginning of February. Shortly thereafter, the telephone connections to Berlin broke down, and the Stettin General Prosecutor consequently declared himself authorized to make clemency decisions on death sentences in the future. In mid-February, a standing military court was set up in Stettin and staffed by two judges from the local court; the first death sentence followed in the days after. The final battle could begin.

Code Word "Spring Festival"

No one involved had ever experienced anything like it, that is, an enemy occupation of one's own country. Not from the First World War, from which administrative practice had learned so many important lessons. The beginnings of the current war had provided modest illustrative material, albeit in a completely different context. In order to withstand a French military response to the invasion of Poland, various zones were designated during the construction of the so-called West Wall, which were to be evacuated in an emergency. The "Red Zone," around 20 kilometers wide, ultimately stretched a good 500 kilometers between Aachen and the Swiss border. At the end of August 1939, more than half a million people were evacuated from the area and brought into the interior of the German Reich, in some cases with good organizational preparation, but often in a senseless rush. The population was not privy to the details of the plan and generally knew neither when they had to leave their homes nor where they were going. They were allowed to take hardly any possessions with them.

Hospitals and nursing homes, but also government agencies and other civilian institutions fared considerably better. This was especially true for the judiciary. With the outbreak of war, many of the so-called *Freimachungsgebiete* ("clearance zones") received new *Sondergerichte* ("Special Courts"), which tightened the network of political criminal law even more than in peacetime.[10] Some of the ordinary courts, on the other hand, were relocated from the western border to the interior of the country, where they had to remain for about a year. No one really had to move far; due to the relatively narrow width of the restricted area, they could remain within the jurisdiction of their own higher regional court. Zweibrücken was the only higher regional court forced to vacate its seat and move to Ludwigshafen. Of the regional courts, Zweibrücken and Saarbrücken, along with six local courts, found accommodation in Kaiserlautern, while three other local courts were accommodated elsewhere. From the Cologne district, the Trier Regional Court, which was relocated to Koblenz, and a good handful of local courts were affected. The 100 kilometers or so eastward by which the Merzig Local Court was moved is probably the greatest distance an institution had to cover at the time.[11]

But unlike the rest of the population, the courts were well prepared for the relocations. As early as mid-August 1939, confidential evacuation plans were distributed for emergencies. Reception quarters and storage facilities were inspected in a timely manner; files, seals, and inventory were carefully packed; standby services ensured the ability to react at any time.[12] Sophisticated seismographs announced the outbreak of war well in advance, even at the lower courts. From 21 August 1939, local courts near the border received an increasing number of notifications from parties or witnesses that they were unable to attend appointments due to conscription into the Wehrmacht, a phenomenon that intensified over the next few days.

When the evacuation order was finally issued (the code word being "Spring Festival"), an intact infrastructure was in place to actually carry out the planned measures: means of transportation, accommodation, and food. The normative framework was also still intact, the hierarchies clear, the official channels undamaged. The supervising judge at Saarburg Local Court, for example, refused to comply with several evacuation orders because they "did not originate from a judicial authority." Only after receiving confirmation by telephone from the Regional Court President and the general prosecutor did he agree to evacuate the prison, a procedure that apparently met with no objection from either the military or the party. There was even time to properly place the keys "on the key rack in Room No. 4," although the—quite useful—additional information was laid bare that the key for No. 4 was itself "in the door."[13] Bureaucratic support for the civilian population accompanied these steps: a decree on the "judicial support for the population in clearance zones" clarified the new responsibilities, and "aid measures for lawyers and notaries from the clearance zones" endeavored to re-employ the unemployed legal administrators.[14] Therefore, there was no need to complain about a suspension of law.

Of course, not everything went smoothly. Employees and civil servants had to be regularly reminded to report for duty on time, even when far from home.[15] There were also repeated disputes with the Wehrmacht over the use of office buildings. But after the gradual return in the summer of 1940, there was no dissatisfaction. In general, things continued as before. The Bergzabern Local Court One presented one of the few exceptions: after just under a year in Speyer, the headquarters—which had since been seized by the Wehrmacht—was found to be "badly damaged." Furniture was scattered haphazardly throughout the rooms, chairs were left outside, a large land register shelf had only been discovered by chance in a company, and a small one was still missing. It will therefore take a "considerable amount of time" to set up again. And the President of the Zweibrücken Higher Regional Court hastened to add to this somewhat fuddy-duddy stocktaking that it had proved to be far too pessimistic. It was also noted that "we must be grateful to Providence" that the "elemental force" of this war had largely spared Germany. In September 1940, one year after the invasion of Poland, it was possible to conclude that the courts had all returned to their former places of work and had resumed their activities there "without a hitch."[16]

Hope of Return: "Currently"

The experiences of 1939 were hardly suitable as a model for measures to be implemented in 1944. In the late summer of 1944, the Allied troops in East and West were approaching the borders of the German Reich. The "Red Zone" became red again. Unlike in 1939, however, the affected areas were evacuated not to allow the German army to advance, but because the Wehrmacht had nothing left to oppose the Allied troops. From Zweibrücken came the resigned report that the district had now once again become a war zone and that large parts had once again been cleared, "although there is no doubt that an evacuation today would take place under much more difficult circumstances." Almost all towns had been destroyed, the judicial staff had been reduced by 80 percent, and the remaining employees were worn down by air raids and trench work.[17] The Higher Regional Court itself relocated to Kirchheimbolanden. Whatever files and inventory could still be saved did not remain in the vicinity, if possible, but were sent to Bamberg, several hundred kilometers away—Zweibrücken was part of the Bavarian Palatinate.

The possibility of an enemy occupation had already become apparent in the preceding months, initially on the Western Front following the American landing in Normandy at the beginning of June. Hitler issued an initial decree "on command authority in an operational area within the Reich" as early as 13 July 1944. It stated that even if foreign troops occupied German Reich territory, civilian agencies should continue their activities in the operational area. At the end of September, when the area around Aachen was already in US hands, this directive was renewed. The Reich Defense Commissioner—who was also the NSDAP head of the district (or *Gauleiter*)—was responsible for taking the necessary measures himself, while Heinrich Himmler, as Reich Minister of the Interior, was to oversee uniform implementation in practice.[18] To this end, the Plenipotentiary General for the Reich Administration, Wilhelm Frick, in explicit coordination with the Ministry of Justice, laid down guidelines for the "relocation of authorities from clearance zones," which were sent to the responsible authorities in a secret express letter. Most important was the introductory maxim that an office should only be relocated "in the event of an acute enemy threat" and even then, only "by express order." Where possible, they were to remain within their own district; further relocations or closures were to be ordered by the responsible ministry. Civil servants who were no longer needed were to be transferred to the Wehrmacht or armaments factories.[19]

Almost simultaneously, Reich Minister of Justice Otto Thierack issued "Guidelines for Measures by Judicial Authorities in Operational or Combat

Zones," which spelled out these principles once again. Personnel were to remain on site until orders to the contrary were issued. If accommodation was no longer possible, the court had to be relocated "until further notice"; staff were to go to the designated reception center, if possible, or at the very least report to the nearest judicial authority. The purpose of the relocation was also made clear: "The authority will continue its official activities at its new location under its previous name." This directive obviously grossly misjudged the military situation. But political blindness was also cultivated with surprising devotion in the Ministry at this time: if necessary, personnel were to be left behind to ensure that the remaining population "could continue to receive judicial support in the most important areas, especially non-contentious jurisdiction, in the event of the enemy occupation of the territory."[20] It was actually assumed in Berlin that the Allied occupiers would also make use of the services of the German judiciary.

This was clearly not a scorched earth policy. The state leadership had a vital interest in making the administrative withdrawal appear to be a strategically intended operation, or at least a controlled one. Considerable resources were therefore made available, particularly in the western districts. Many of the Zweibrücken courts relocated for the second time during the war. The Merzig Local Court now moved to Ottweiler, a good 60 kilometers away,[21] the Trier Regional Court went to Bernkastel-Kues,[22] where the Perl and Saarburg Local Courts were later also located.[23] The evacuation of Aachen, although ordered far too late, ultimately proved not too damaging for the judiciary; via Düren and Bergheim, they finally reached Siegburg, while administrative business continued from Gummersbach. The courts in the annexed territories of Belgium—Eupen, Malmedy, Sankt Vith—and five smaller local courts from the district of Aachen were forced to cease operations, but at least a post office was established for them at the Gummersbach Local Court.[24] The Jülich Local Court relocated to Titz, where it met up with its colleagues from the destroyed town of Düren, with whom it then moved to Merzenich and later to Lechenich, before finally relocating to the land registry office in Bergheim.[25]

These sometimes quite costly relocations were preferred where they were not necessarily seen as a precautionary measure against impeding occupation but could be integrated into the air-raid protection activities that had been common practice since at least the summer of 1943. On 3 November 1944, some of Cologne's judicial authorities left the largely destroyed city to settle on the east bank of the Rhine: the Higher Regional Court President and General Prosecutor in Eitorf, the Regional Court in Wiehl, the criminal chambers of the Regional Court, the Special Court and Local Court in a school in Königswinter.[26] Only the civil courts remained in Cologne. The Karlsruhe Higher Regional Court also moved eastwards at the end of the year. This was a reaction to the US invasion of Straßburg at the end of November but could just as easily have been explained as a consequence of the air raids on 4 December. The Higher Regional Court remained in Sinsheim until the end of the war, and the General Prosecutor in neighboring Eppelheim.[27]

There was still comparatively little to do in the east at this time. In November, three regional courts and 20 local courts in Memelland had to be closed, while the remaining authorities were consolidated in Königsberg. On the border with the General Government for the Occupied Polish Region, the local courts of Ostenburg and Scharfenwiese also received new offices.[28] For the rest, efforts focused on planning for what was widely believed to be imminent: temporary evacuations, even far behind the front, due to a Soviet offensive. Long lists defined the "most important and irreplaceable" working material: political files, secret files, wills, land registers, personnel files, pension files, registers, typewriters, telephones, radios, money.[29] On 9 September 1944, the Danzig General Prosecutor distributed detailed evacuation plans for the seven prisons in his district. It listed the code words to be expected ("*Strömung in Erwartung*," "*Strömung I*," "*Strömung II*," or Flow in Anticipation, Flow I, Flow II), which prisoners were to be evacuated immediately, how evidence was to be handled, how many supplies would be needed for the retreat, which machines would have to be prepared for a transfer, which files were to be taken along and which were to be destroyed. In addition, they also included details of security measures, marching columns, assembly points, and reception centers.

But here, too, the signs were pointing toward return. Any files that could not be taken with them were to be "stored as fireproof as possible," the General Prosecutor announced, evidently guided by the confidence that the files could be processed after the fighting. An instruction was also issued for the prisons, aimed at facilitating their return to their previous status: "The evacuated prison buildings are to be properly locked and the keys are to be deposited in the office of the prison director, except for those required for the final external lock," while those "keys required for the final external lock" were to be handed over to the responsible district judge or, if unavailable, to the respective district administrator.[30] Even for the evacuated Memel region, the President of the Higher Regional Court in Königsberg expressed hope that the population might be able to return "shortly," and then "the judicial authorities would also resume their activities."[31]

The spatial separation was therefore intended as a temporary intermezzo, and the work in an alternative location was intended to bridge this interim period. The authority and its headquarters were dissociated so that the former could continue to operate, even if the latter was—temporarily!—no longer accessible. In Cologne, there was even an explicit demand that the courts in the occupied cities should continue to operate, at least formally, so as not to give the impression that these areas were being abandoned in any way.[32] The time horizon had darkened, but it was not yet closed. In October, a "Central Information Office for Repatriated Persons" was set up at the Berlin police headquarters to centrally record the relocation of offices. Anyone forced to relocate by the front was to send their new address there "in duplicate on a postcard form in a sealed envelope," and the highest Reich authorities would then be supplied with updated lists on a weekly basis.[33] In official communications, the interlude was therefore clearly marked as a mere episode. A defiant "currently" on the respective form, clearly visible between the names of the authority and place of residence, prevented any misunderstandings from arising: Special Court of Aachen, currently Düren; Higher Regional Court of Cologne, currently Eitorf; Higher Regional Court of Karlsruhe, currently Sinsheim. The interregnum was clearly marked, the realm of authenticity under threat, but on the whole still undamaged.

The Power of Paper

However, the legal line of defense could only be maintained where there were files. There were no points of reference for legal posterity where legal matters had completely lost their paper existence and only existed in the memories of those involved. In the continuum of time, the files took the place of the lost space. Only through this media representation did the temporal limitations of the alternative locations become plausible in the first place. The courts administered districts whose existence increasingly evaporated into the realm of the virtual. The files remained the last material links to the world outside the courtroom. They were therefore the most important item for a successful relocation of the court authorities. And at the same time, their sheer quantity alone made them the greatest obstacle, even more recalcitrant than the prisoners, whose inevitable transfer was also discussed in detail during the preparations for evacuation. If necessary, the prisoners could be moved on foot. Escape was to be avoided, but if a "departure occurred," a prisoner "dropped out," had to be "liquidated," or did not "arrive at the destination," a note in the file and the prospect of better organization for the next transport was sufficient.[34] The loss of prisoners was bearable; the loss of files was not. Without wills and land registers, without civil and commercial registers, without trial and personnel files, it was no longer possible to determine who owned what, who wanted what from whom, who had paid what fees and provided what evidence, and in general who was who.

Wherever a court had to be relocated, the files were therefore given the greatest possible care. Wherever possible, they were sent on their journey as a preventative measure. In December 1944, the Reich Ministry of Justice ordered the immediate retrieval of all important files for the areas on the west bank of the Rhine. Two railroad wagons filled with land registers and other important documents were sent from Zweibrücken to Bamberg.[35] In Brühl, the presiding judge managed to organize a car through personal acquaintances; the clerks and judges were ordered to remove the legally binding divorce decrees from the files and prepare them for transport. In Cologne-Mühlheim, a twelve-ton truck arrived to secure the land registers and shelves. Nearly 600 land registers—weighing more than seven tons—were removed from Kerpen.[36]

For the small Bitburg Local Court, however, the order came too late—an administrative drama, because a large portion of the Cologne land registers and subsidiary civil registers had been transferred there. The land records themselves had been burned in Cologne. In Bitburg, parts of the documents had been photocopied and thousands of replacement sheets produced, but now a good 2,700 land registers remained on site, many of which were the only surviving evidence of the ownership of Cologne properties. Concern was correspondingly great. Walter Müller, the staunchly National Socialist President of the Cologne Regional Court, mobilized his contacts in the party, and the Bitburg supervisory judge was given blanket authority to use every possible means of transport, whatever the cost. It was all to no avail. On 24 December 1944, heavy air raids began on Bitburg, almost completely destroying the town. A few judicial employees were still holding out in the court cellar, without food, electricity, or heating, trapped with over 40 tons of files. In the end, they marched the 200 kilometers to Wiehl over four days and nights, in temperatures well below zero, to report the situation at the judicial administration's temporary headquarters there. Even though the President of the Cologne Higher Regional Court commented on the failure with the utmost dispassion—"further processing of the Cologne land register cases in Bitburg … is unlikely to be possible for the time being"—they were not yet ready to write off the files completely. In an act of madness, a 64-year-old fugitive, half-frozen, suffering from rheumatism and an open hernia, was to be sent back to Bitburg to retrieve the files and, if possible, "five valuable accounting machines (Elliot-Fisher system)" from the court. After the bureaucratic hubris subsided, they did manage to find a motor vehicle, but by the time it was halfway there, the US troops had already occupied Bitburg.[37]

Such tales of woe made the need for careful planning clear to everyone. Thierack informed the border authorities as early as September 1944 that the relocation of files should be considered "at a much earlier date" than the relocation of people. The most important documents were to be identified immediately and transferred to reception centers in less endangered areas.[38] In Danzig, for example, alternative locations were established for the courts east of the Vistula, and the senior general prosecutors were instructed to "remove from enemy access" all files needed to continue operations. Registers were to be removed immediately, as were forms, paper, and typewriters that would be needed to resume business after the office was relocated.[39] By the end of the year, the most important files—wills, registers, personnel forms—had been moved to the west of the district, to Krone, Berent, and Neustadt, with the bulk of the items going to the Konitz Regional Court. "Care has been taken," it was emphasized hopefully, "to ensure the ongoing processing of the seized files."[40]

Where appropriate steps had been neglected in a timely manner, however, subsequent care was all the greater. When Memel was evacuated on 9 October 1944, the President of the Königsberg Higher Regional Court immediately dispatched a truck to retrieve the "particularly important files and some typewriters." What remained was later secured by the officials "in cold blood and in an exemplary manner," often even under artillery fire, the President reported proudly. The Königsberg files were taken across the Vistula in November and finally arrived via Neustadt, Stolp, Margonin, and Flatow in the area around Schneidemühl—now in the Stettin Higher Regional Court district, a good 350 kilometers from Königsberg—where three collection points for the criminal files, criminal records, land registers and wills were set up. Here, too, efforts were made to continue operations despite the great geographical distance. It was emphasized that there had been no association with the receiving authorities and that accommodation under the same roof had been "purely coincidental." Seconded judicial employees followed the files, primarily to continue processing the land registers and criminal records, and the corresponding official seals also traveled with them.[41]

But who was going to transport it all? The files were a stubborn object. Their contents alone could pose great difficulties. Confidential material had to be specially protected from unauthorized readers or even loss; it required escorts, safe deposit boxes, and trustworthy recipients at the destination.[42] And then there was the sheer volume! Even if the 40 tons from Bitburg were an extreme case, the paper was not light elsewhere either. In Köslin, 12,000 land register pages, 230 personnel sheets, and countless public registers were waiting to be transported from the local and regional courts, a total of almost two and a half tons of material.[43] In neighboring Kolberg, where they wanted to limit the transport to personnel sheets, land register pages, and wills, two and a half tons of paper were also collected, whereupon it was "immediately" decided that means of transport could not be provided.[44]

The small Bublitz Local Court, formerly a temporary asylum for the Stettin Higher Regional Court, reported on 26 January 1945 a total of 15 hundredweight of important papers for clearance papers under the heading, "Extremely urgent!" Even deducting the telephones, typewriters, clocks, and vacuum cleaner, which were intended to survive the chaos of war in Bublitz, there remained well over half a ton of land register tables, registers, and personnel files, the removal of which threatened to fail simply because they could not be packed due to a lack of boxes. "Assistant Justice Seargeant Ziemer" wrote the supervising judge to Stettin, "will now provide some nails from his private property and make boxes."[45]

Expectation of Doom: "Still"

This was obviously desperation speaking. The winter of 1944–45 fundamentally changed the psychological effects and propaganda justifications for the court postponements. The Battle of the Bulge stalled soon after Christmas, and hardly any of the promised miracle weapons were deployed. By the start of the Russian offensive in East Prussia on 12 January 1945, at the latest, the belief in a merely temporary abandonment of the evacuated territories had vanished. The stubborn "currently" was increasingly mixed with traces of a fatalistic "still." From Königsberg, reports on 25 January 1945 affirmed that "work was still being done" and that the city was "still calm." The next day it was announced that the attitude of the "officials still present"—who were "still working in the courthouse on Adolf Hitler Platz"—was "still quite good." Shortly thereafter, it was reported that Bartenstein was "still in our hands";[46] a little later, reports came from Danzig on the situation in the "parts of the *Reichsgau* still not occupied by the enemy."[47] The Regional Court President in Neisse wrote on 9 February that activities at two of his local courts had "ceased of their own accord" due to enemy occupation, and continued gloomily: "Only time will tell whether it will be possible to resume services at these locations in the foreseeable future after the enemy has been driven out."[48] The interim accommodation was no longer followed by a return to the headquarters, but inevitably by further *reformatio in peius*, almost as if it were a law of nature that at some point the front would be overtaken and driven into the interior of the crumbling Reich.

The symbolism was correspondingly poisonous. As the transfers took place in a country that was now largely destroyed, the organizational effort involved was immense. The President of the Higher Regional Court of Leitmeritz, for example, reported that it now took five days to travel to the outermost courts in his district—some 450 kilometers away.[49] However, preparations made for the evacuation should under no circumstances give the impression that a premature retreat or even an escape was being initiated. At the end of November 1944, the Reich Ministry of Justice announced in a civil tone that anyone who left their workplace without authorization when threatened by the enemy would be "held accountable through disciplinary action," with anything up to the death penalty possible.[50] Now the vocabulary became soldierly. Wilhelm Frick, as General Plenipotentiary of the administration, instructed the authorities in the eastern districts on 23 January 1945 to continue their work "until the last moment" and to take "immediate and severe" action against "slackers." On 29 January, Heinrich Himmler clarified what this meant: a head of an agency who left his post without orders was to be punished with death. The police chief of Bromberg, according to the deterrent example, would be dealt with accordingly because of his attempt to flee, and three other officials had been sent to the front on probation to take on "particularly difficult and dangerous tasks." On 1 February, these letters reached the Reich ministries, with Frick requesting that they also ensure that in their respective "areas of responsibility work continues in an orderly and calm manner"; they were in the "full view of the public," which is why the "firm and determined attitude" of the civil servants was of paramount importance.[51]

Otto Thierack immediately processed this information into a tailored circular for the judiciary. Under the heading, "Conduct in the Event of Enemy Approach," he informed his officials on 7 February 1945 of the requirements for the coming weeks, largely repeating verbatim what Frick had told him. To lend even more emphasis to the—already somewhat sinister—announcements, Thierack replaced Himmler's examples with incidents from his own department: the President of the Higher Regional Court and the General Prosecutor of Königsberg as well as the Chief Public Prosecutor of Kattowitz had fled to the West in breach of their duties. All were immediately arrested, two of them shot themselves, and the Königsberg President was facing trial before the *Volksgerichtshof.* In true Frick style, Thierack noted that he expected the heads of his authorities "to continue working in complete peace in their areas of responsibility" for as long as it was possible. If the agency's evacuation was ordered, it would require on-site monitoring and support; "neglect of duty" and "dishonorable" actions are unforgivable, especially since the judicial authorities are in the "public eye" and therefore the "firm and determined attitude" of the officials is of fundamental importance.[52] There was not much room for misunderstanding after this. To dispel any remaining doubts, on the same day Martin Bormann, Hitler's personal secretary, promised "draconian measures" with which "all orders … would be enforced under all circumstances."[53] Himmler declared shortly afterwards that relocation orders could only be issued by the commander-in-chief of the responsible army group, and that "leaving the post without this order" would result "immediately in the death of the person concerned." He quickly added that "alleged instructions from Berlin authorities" would not be accepted as an excuse.[54]

The course of action was thus clear: hold out until the end. The "still," intended to suppress any impulse to flee, was extended across the board. The price for this was high. Anyone who was not yet in the Wehrmacht could now expect to be conscripted into the *Volkssturm* (the German territorial army). In the event of an acute enemy threat, only an indispensable emergency administration was to remain in place. An orderly evacuation was practically impossible: anyone who took measures in time to have a chance of success was suspected of treason. Anyone who waited for the evacuation order, on the other hand, essentially had no chance of bringing files, inventory, or even their own employees to safety in a controlled manner.

Resuming Service

To continue legal proceedings despite the approaching Allied troops—and even "in complete peace"—required considerable legal (self)maneuvering. People did not flee their place of work, but from reality. The President of the Breslau Higher Regional Court announced on 5 February 1945 that the situation in the district could "currently be considered much more relaxed," a truly ludicrous statement—the Higher Regional Court itself had already moved to Görlitz due to an acute enemy threat, and two regional courts with over 20 local courts were already occupied by the Red Army.[55] At the same time, the President of the Danzig Higher Regional Court described in detail the disintegration of the party and the Wehrmacht, the hopeless chaos of the flight, and the hasty abandonment of almost all courts in the last week of January, only to then offer the completely counterfactual self-description: "In Danzig, the courts continue to operate without disruption."[56] And in Cologne, too, no one was prepared to grant the occupation of their own judicial district a special historical status. They contentedly noted that the reputation of the judiciary had been preserved by their perseverance in place for as long as possible, apart from "the chatter of ignoramuses and complainers," who, as a handwritten note added in demonstrative denial of any historical anomaly, stand out "on such occasions always."[57]

Such placatory formulas were based on a confusing interplay of bureaucratic megalomania, ideological overzealousness, and fear. The result was a toxic brew. The unexpectedly rapid advance of the Red Army and the persistent denial of reality on the German side meant that what had been officially described with the reassuring formula of "repatriation" soon became an aimless flight, sometimes to the east, sometimes to the west, sometimes back again. Time and again, those fleeing were forced to change direction by some command post or other. On 11 January, the President of the Karlsruhe Higher Regional Court reported to his colleague in Stuttgart under the remarkably neutral subject line "Service" about the "surprising invasion of Alsace by the enemy," which had prompted many court officials to flee on their own initiative, certainly including the neighboring district of the Stuttgart Higher Regional Court. "Despite the strengthening of the military situation in the meantime," many had not returned, so the colleague was asked to ensure that the non-resident judicial staff "return to their previous places of employment without delay."[58] Of course, the President of the Karlsruhe Higher Regional Court, a National Socialist to the core, clearly did not believe in the military reassurance he was preaching to his subordinates. Before he called his staff back to Alsace, he had taken the precaution of setting up a "Central Office for Processing Alsatian Legal Matters" at the Wolfach Regional Court, meaning that he himself had long since moved his office out of Alsace.[59]

After his escape, the President of the Memel Regional Court come to Danzig, from where he was sent on 3 February to Konitz, 120 kilometers away, to check on the situation in the supposedly prematurely evacuated town. He found the regional court building almost completely occupied by the Wehrmacht, and the judicial staff had fled with the exception of one judge and one general prosecutor. On 4 February, a Sunday, he took over the leadership of the court and chaired the significantly reduced special court. Because he found that the situation eased after a few days, he decided to "reoccupy" the surrounding local courts of Heiderode and Tuchel, which had long been deserted. After further Russian advances, this plan remained at the experimental stage; on 13 February, Konitz was also evacuated.[60]

On 6 February 1945, the Stettin General Prosecutor reported that the evacuation order had been issued for Stargard. The district legal advisor, Dr. Johannes Paulick, a committed member of the party, an energetic judge of the special court and soon afterwards the court martial, immediately objected. So far, only the "dispersal" had been ordered; women and children were to leave the city, but the heads of government agencies were to return immediately. The Reich Defense Commissioner had reiterated the maxim that anyone who left their post without an express order was to be punished with death.[61] So they went back. Five days later, however, on a Sunday, an evacuation order was issued "unexpectedly." That same afternoon they marched twelve kilometers. Those not present were informed of the need to flee immediately by a "notice in the courthouse entrance." After a short night's rest, they set off at 3 a.m. to continue westwards, but were soon caught in a heavy snowstorm, prompting the regional court president to turn back. In the evening, the news spread that they could return to Stargard, as the authorities had been given the appropriate order. On 14 February, the judicial employees were back together on site, and the regional and local courts reported that they were able to operate.[62] Operations remained uninterrupted for three days. On 18 February, an almost continuous air bombardment began, severely damaging the court. The regional court president decided to stay on site to secure the last files. The court only left Stargard on 4 March, one day before occupation by the Red Army. Demmin in Pomerania was chosen as an alternative location. There they found the "complete peace" that Thierack had desired—for about six weeks. At the end of April, the foreseeable capture of the town by the Soviet troops triggered a mass suicide among the population. When the Red Army finally arrived, there were countless rapes and lootings, and the town was almost completely destroyed.

Special Special Courts

In this increasingly hopeless situation, the judiciary also began to pursue a scorched-earth policy. What remained to be decided related to a future that would no longer exist anyway. The last offenders encountered a landscape of ruins—and not just metaphorically: on 27 January 1945, the General Prosecutor's Office in Königsberg reported by telephone to Berlin that the special courts would now be hearing cases without interruption, that efforts were being made to destroy the files, and that "preparations were being made to blow up the courthouse."[63] But the legal system was also in ruins. During the last major draft in the summer of 1944, Königsberg had come up with the idea to prevent foreseeable staff shortages in the judiciary by preemptively appointing all judges in a district as special judges. As soon as any general prosecutor's office filed a corresponding charge anywhere, a special court would convene there "for immediate trial," whereby "all those brought in … were to be sentenced immediately—if possible, on the same day."[64] This procedure was copied in other locations near the front and on 15 September 1944, the Reich Ministry of Justice made it a general recommendation for the border districts: it was advisable to establish a special court at each regional court and, as a precaution, to appoint "*all* judges of the regional court district" as members of the special court.[65] Germany, a giant special court: this legal innovation, a creation of the judiciary itself, began to take effect long before the drumhead courts martial and the military courts began to exercise their reign of terror. In a strange dialectic of form, ordinary jurisdiction both authenticated and marginalized the ordinariness of its existence. Special courts could now form ad hoc, even in places where there had previously been neither special courts nor special judges at all.

This possibility generated a unique dynamic. In November 1944, the Cologne General Prosecutor reported succinctly by telephone to Berlin that it was now intended "that the special court should move around."[66] In the district of Breslau, the number of special courts increased eightfold at the beginning of February 1945. Even the small town of Waldenburg was given its own special jurisdiction, although there had not yet been a regional court there.[67] The same happened to the Gotenhafen Local Court in the district of the Danzig Higher Regional Court.[68] It is difficult to gauge how busy these special courts were. To tailor their work to the needs of the time, they specialized from the outset in offenses that were particularly typical of people fleeing, primarily looting cases. Collective flight was given its own order and its own personnel. At the Stolp Local Court, for example, the newly established special court was staffed directly with judges who had fled from the East and who had to judge the criminal offenses of their compatriots who had not yet fled, before they then fled together to the West.[69]

In many cases, however, the new special courts seem to have existed only nominally. The President of the Thorn Regional Court, who could still report diligently on the orderly destruction of files, had to admit in shame that the evacuation had devolved into a frantic flight, which is why the special court—which was, of course, properly staffed—had ceased to operate.[70] In Oppeln, after the evacuation of the city, only the special judges remained from the judiciary; they moved into a hotel "for better cohesion." Meanwhile, forced laborers set fire to the court. As the police and fire department had also already left, it burned down completely. After two uneventful days, the judges also left the city to make their way—on foot—to the alternative location in Neisse, 50 kilometers away. There, however, they were immediately instructed to move "further west." The Oppeln Special Court did not manage more than two days in the hotel.[71] The President of the Breslau Higher Regional Court could only report that after the occupation of Glogau, the Glogau Special Court had first moved to Sagan and then, after the Soviet offensive on the town, to Weißwasser, where, as he wrote in apocalyptic rhetoric, "a few things would still be settled" before they would proceed with their own dissolution.[72] The futility of their own actions became increasingly clear. In the minutes of the Breslau Special Court, the discussion immediately jumped back to the old days, when wishing still helped. The judicial administration summarized the plan after the escape to Hirschberg,[73] saying that the matters "from the earlier period" would be dealt with—as if the time when place and court were still in agreement had not only passed a few days ago, but was already the dream of a long-gone era.

Files and Stamps: Burning, Burying, Destroying

This omnipresence of the past soon also reached the files. They were registered or forgotten, carried along or ignored, left behind or burned, depending on how quickly the front was approaching, how closely the officials were connected to their paper shadow, and how robust their contacts with the party were. Whatever could not be taken away had to be destroyed. Large-scale destruction was therefore one of the last to-do items on-site. At the Neisse Local Court, the personnel forms were removed from the files and then all personnel files were burned.[74] In Kolberg, the chief magistrate only managed to issue the evacuation order when the noise of battle and pools of blood in the streets proved irrefutable evidence of the impending occupation. Before fleeing, the official took all the secret files from the safe and destroyed them together with the court seals, of which only one was left and given to a fleeing senior judicial inspector.[75] In neighboring Belgard, there was just enough time to burn the secret documents, stamps, and seals, but not enough to bury the "Church, Jewish, and Dissident Registers" as planned.[76] Burn, bury, destroy—on 5 April 1945, when the front had reached the heart of the Old Reich, the President of the Hanover Regional Court wrote to his superior: "I submit the two enclosed destruction proceedings," a self-contradiction that artfully combined a sense of duty and insubordination, which is why posterity was able to trace, right down to the file numbers, that the paradoxically hardened official had destroyed not only the compromising files but also the "Secret" and "Secret Reich Matter" stamps.[77] In Dresden, all compromising personnel and general files,[78] which had been left by the air war, were burned at the beginning of April. In Schwäbisch Gmünd, an attempt was made to transport the outsourced personnel files of the Stuttgart Higher Regional Court to Ravensburg, but this failed just as much as their controlled burning: the file covers refused to catch fire. [79]

And even if—which was a rare exception—means of transport could still be found for the transportation of files, it was unclear where to send them. The war was now everywhere. After the erratic moves of 1943 and 1944, the Stettin criminal records office was still in Pyritz when the town was already under Russian fire. All recovery attempts failed; a truck was forced to turn back by a firefight and the Higher Regional Court's file van hit a mine.[80] In Kattowitz, at the beginning of February 1945, the President of the Higher Regional Court surprisingly managed to save the district's treasury and personnel files by sending them west, partly by horse-drawn wagon and partly by truck. Finally, a Reichsbahn wagon was ready to transport the files to Dresden—on 13 February of all days, when the city center of Dresden was destroyed. A radio message stopped the cargo somewhere along the way.[81] At the small Bendsburg Local Court, a focal point of Jewish persecution in the years prior, personnel files, cash registers, typewriters, the "most politically sensitive files" and—for whatever reason—"the remaining bed linen from the single men's home" were diligently collected in boxes and taken to the district administrator, who had organized a truck. But where the truck was headed remained a mystery to the capable local court director because, as the judge had to admit to his superior, the district administrator "did not disclose the truck's destination."[82]

The greatest uncertainty, however, befell the President of the Thorn District Court, who had to leave his home at the end of January. He loaded his luggage onto a sled on 22 January, in the freezing cold and under enemy fire, and set off on foot, walking almost 30 kilometers to the nearest train station in Kulmsee. Thorn was already deserted, the party, the Wehrmacht, and civilians had practically all fled, and any belief in a return had been extinguished. Only the language retained its carefully crafted administrative detachment. Even the end of his official duties, the top jurist prudently reported that there was nothing to report: "The buildings were locked around 12 noon, and the keys were left in the lock; there was no one there to give them to."[83]

"Ambulatory Business"

The institutions now depended on chance. The initial plans for an emergency operation had not foreseen that the war would significantly spill over onto German territory. Accordingly, the first guidelines for the border districts from September 1944—still declared a "Secret Reich Matter"—were not sent to Danzig or Breslau. By February 1945, this restraint had become pointless. On 13 February, secrecy was lifted, and on 19 February, all judicial authorities throughout the Reich received new instructions on how to proceed with "clearance zones." In the event of partial evacuation, operations should continue at the nearest possible location. If the entire district was evacuated or occupied, however, the authority was to be "considered closed until further notice," and there would be no reception or alternative quarters. Administrative staff would only be set up for administrative activities, registry matters, and cash transactions. Legal proceedings, on the other hand, were to be suspended.[84] Above all, as stated in a separate letter, the impression that individual authorities were "only being continued for their own sake" had to be avoided.[85] Internally, there were further instructions to ensure that correspondence with the administrative staff was "limited to the bare essentials."[86] The following day, similar instructions were repeated, this time focusing on the needs of the individual official. After fleeing, they were to report to "the nearest available judicial authority," which would decide on further assignment. It was possible to be deployed in the judicial service itself, given a need, but also to be released for the Wehrmacht or for armaments work.[87] And another thing: the Führer was not to see the full extent of the misery. Alternative quarters "in *Gau* Salzburg or in Berchtesgaden-Reichenhall and Traunstein" were not desired, as was emphasized several times.[88]

In practical terms, these guidelines were of little use. They were addressed to the higher Reich judicial authorities, in particular to the presidents of the higher regional courts and the general prosecutors. When the term "district" was used, it must initially have meant their districts. However, the military strategy of declaring individual localities to be "fortresses" had the concrete consequence that, with the exception of Posen, by April 1945 no higher regional court district had been "completely evacuated or fully occupied by the enemy," as required by the guidelines for decommissioning. So what happened to a local or regional court that was already fully occupied, but whose staff could still be relocated within the higher-level district? And could a higher regional court that had already been relocated for a long time continue to hold court at its new location if a tiny local court in its home district was still working and holding down the fort?

What might have been a central overview of the realities of German jurisdiction up to this point was now disintegrating. Institutions were torn apart and reassembled or were permanently lost in the no-man's-land of German history. The German judiciary was increasingly atomized, controlled, administered in a climate of fear—fear of the Allied enemies, of partisans and saboteurs, but also fear of their own government, whose phobocratic terror in these weeks could even affect previously well-liked party members. The Central Information Office for Repatriated Persons, which had just shortly before boasted that it would document the relocations in weekly overviews, seems to have ceased its activities, if they ever existed, after the heavy air raids on Berlin on 3 February 1945. The Reich Ministry of Justice therefore compiled its own list of the new addresses. But even there it was no more than a makeshift document: the clerk handwrote a three-page address list, without an introductory title, without a final signature, without a date, and without a file number,[89] almost as if the overview served more the private collecting interests of a judicial employee than official purposes.

And in any case, the Berlin table was far too static for the conditions on the ground. It was evidently inspired by the relocations on the Western Front—the move from Karlsruhe to Sinsheim is the first entry—and subsequently updated several times, but only systematically up to the beginning of February 1945, as the destruction of Dresden on 13 February is not recorded. The last major entry concerns the splitting of the Munich judiciary: the President of the Higher Regional Court moved to Fürstenfeldbruck, a criminal division with a special court chamber to Buchloe, another criminal division with another special court chamber to Landshut, a third special court chamber and the general prosecutor's office were moved to Dachau.

The register was therefore unable to capture the most severe upheavals in court architecture, even in terms of time. The first post-war descriptions from the Soviet occupation zone, in whose territory many institutions were stranded at the end of the war, spoke of entire "administration treks,"[90] while in the West they were mockingly referred to as an "ambulatory business."[91] Both labels are too broad. At the beginning of 1945, the German Reich had 34 higher regional courts, around 200 regional courts, and over 2,000 local courts. In the East alone, hundreds of courts would have had to be sent on their way to safety from the front. That didn't even come close. But at least they did what they could: the Higher Regional Courts of Danzig and Königsberg opened administrative offices at the Rostock Higher Regional Court, which, of course, had itself no longer resided in Rostock since the devastating attacks of April 1942, but had moved to Schwerin.[92] The Posen Higher Regional Court moved via Frankfurt an der Oder and Riesa to Weißenfels,[93] the Kattowitz Higher Regional Court via Neisse, Ottmachau, Dresden and Radebeul to Gera,[94] the Breslau Higher Regional Court to Görlitz and later to Krummhübel in the Riesengebirge,[95] the Dresden Higher Regional Court to Döbeln,[96] the *Volksgerichtshof* first to Potsdam and then to Bayreuth,[97] while a kind of collection point for the judicial authorities from the occupied commissariats in the east was established in Frankfurt an der Oder,[98] until the regional court there was itself relocated to Fürstenwalde.[99] The Lyck Regional Court moved to Stolp,[100] the Schweidnitz Regional Court to Waldenburg,[101] the Hohensalza Regional Court to Waldheim,[102] the Köslin Regional Court to Greifswald, the Schneidemühl Regional Court to Anklam, the Stettin Regional Court also to Greifswald,[103] the Bautzen Regional Court to Marienberg,[104] the Plauen Regional Court to Falkenstein,[105] the Cosel Local Court to Leobschütz,[106] the Stettin Local Court to Stralsund, the Ueckermünde Local Court to Barth,[107] the Kolberg Local Court to Stralsund,[108] the Fiddichow Local Court to Greifenhagen,[109] and the Plauen Local Court to Oelsnitz.[110]

In the West, a similar dynamic set in somewhat later, but also affected a large number of institutions: the Düsseldorf Higher Regional Court relocated some divisions to Wuppertal in March 1945,[111] the Düsseldorf

Regional Court moved to the suburb of Gerresheim,[112] the Hamm Higher Regional Court transferred some offices to Altena and Werl,[113] the presidium of the Stuttgart Higher Regional Court first relocated to Tübingen and then to Ravensburg at the beginning of April.[114] The Kerpen Local Court moved to Bergheim, the Prüm Local Court to Hillesheim, the Gemünd Local Court to Blankenheim and the Trier Local Court to Neumagen.[115] The Koblenz Local Court, which had already moved to Ehrenbreitstein on the other side of the Rhine following the destruction of the city, relocated to Montabaur at the beginning of March and the administration was housed in Dierdorf.[116] The Cologne judicial authorities, most of whom had been out of the city since November 1944, were also on the move once again in March 1945. The Higher Regional Court and the General Prosecutor's Office moved from Eitorf to Waldbröl, the remaining administration went to Wissen and Daaden, the Regional Court moved its criminal chambers first to Wiehl, then to Gummersbach, and the members of the General Prosecutor's Office and the Special Court marched on 10 March from their first alternative location in Königswinter to Marienheide—a car could no longer be found for the 60-odd kilometers—but had to make do with the spa house at the entrance to the town because the rooms intended for them were already occupied by the Gestapo.[117]

The Reich Ministry of Justice was not spared either. By February 1944, entire departments of the Ministry had been relocated to Leitmeritz, Böhmisch-Leipa and Prenzlau; mainly criminal law remained in Berlin, while the mail was sent via Dresden.[118] In October 1944, the Bohemian locations were abandoned, and some were relocated to the Berlin-Lichterfelde Local Court and some to the Prenzlau Regional Court, with one of the departments there being transferred to the Zehdenick Local Court.[119] In March 1945, the last departments moved to Greiz in Thuringia and from there on to the Ichtershausen Correctional Facility. A train car loaded with files traveled along, containing personnel files, budget files, secret files, a total of over 28,000 volumes of files, which were to be forwarded "under all circumstances," as the ministry instructed the station managers en route, otherwise they would be destroyed.[120] On 29 March, Ichtershausen reported that it was now in a position to "fully resume business."[121] On the same day, the artillery bombardment of Ichtershausen began, and at the beginning of April it was occupied by US troops. On 10 April 1945, the ministry received another call, presumably from Prenzlau. "In response to a telephone inquiry," the Rostock General Prosecutor (at the moment Schwerin) was informed that "neither alternative offices nor administrative staff had been established for the authorities of the Higher Regional Courts of Cologne, Düsseldorf, Frankfurt/M., Darmstadt, Zweibrücken, or Kassel."[122] The Reich had become small.

Subsequent Deployment

Who moved where and how, what they did there and where they next traveled was therefore a matter of luck and misfortune, skill, relationships, determination, and fate. Everyone withdrew somehow, ended up somewhere, and reported to someone, received a salary, was perhaps assigned a task, processed land registers, punished *Volksschädlinge* ("public enemies" or, literally, "public vermin"), was sent to do armaments work, or retired. The Higher Regional Courts in Stettin and Dresden became something of a catchment area for the dissolving institutions from the East, and in the hinterland there was Rostock, where many civil servants were waiting for a transfer. Efforts were made to register all new arrivals and record their new addresses. The success was modest. In Rostock, 279 displaced judicial employees were recorded by March, 28 of whom were judges.[123] No records exist for Dresden; only the associated Freiberg Regional Court has numerous reports of judicial employees who fled.[124] From Stettin, probably the more important point of contact because of its port, a total of nine "lists of repatriated members of the East" have survived, sorted by district.[125] But although all ranks were recorded, written and oral reports were accepted, wives were included on the lists and even reports from those displaced about others displaced were recorded, in the end there were fewer than 500 people whose fate was even roughly known. Most came from the Stettin district itself, moreover 164 from Königsberg, 37 from Danzig, 13 from Posen, two each from Kattowitz and Breslau—a negligible percentage in view of the presumably tens of thousands of employees affected.

The displaced often had little more to do than wind up their final duties. A loyal judicial inspector from Löbau Local Court in West Prussia brought with him several personnel files, a list of outstanding land register applications, and finally, money: 100.55 Reichsmarks in cash, 105.93 Reichsmarks in stamp duties, and postal stamps worth 3.50 Reichsmarks, all delivered to the Celle Local Court, where he arrived on 8 February. He received nothing more for his efforts than the bureaucratic, all-purpose formula "FYI."[126] On his ten-day flight from the vicinity of Posen, a senior court clerk took 3,876.25 Reichsmarks with him, of which around 300 Reichsmarks had not been properly accounted for. After a further ten days of investigations, the Cottbus Regional Court forced him to confess "that under the current circumstances it will not be possible for me to make a final accounting of around 300 Reichsmarks." He claimed that "in the current state of excitement," he had failed to properly count the money entrusted to him. The matter was apparently left to rest.[127] In the East Prussian town of Guttmannstadt, an employee pocketed 377.75 Reichsmarks in stamp duties and 42.17 Reichsmarks in cash, which he handed over to the court treasury in Stade on 1 March 1945. He also asked for a decision on where he should deliver the keys to his home court, which he had also secured. He, too, was given a standard protocol note: "The keys are to be kept in office custody."[128]

The displaced could not recommend themselves for further employment, neither with their knowledge nor with the treasures they had rescued. Their legal expertise was not needed in the final battle. The President of the Stettin Higher Regional Court included the following note in his report on displaced persons to the Reich Ministry of Justice on 12 February 1945: "Insofar as the members were needed in my district, I have assigned them to the courts in my district." To avoid sounding overly optimistic about the need, he added a handwritten note to the draft: "This only applies to a few."[129] A judge from East Prussia was assigned to the Stettin Regional Court but was drafted into the Wehrmacht the very next day. A judge from Thorn found a new position at the Stettin Higher Regional Court,[130] while a judge from Köslin was assigned to unspecified "displaced persons matters."[131] At the Greifswald Regional Court, a judge from Zempelburg took over administration, supervision, and library duties,[132] and at the town's local court, a displaced higher regional court judge from Kattowitz was given responsibility for foreclosures and bankruptcy.[133] The President of the Breslau Higher Regional Court listed five judges from the evacuated areas to whom he had been able to grant "provisional service assignments" in his district: three judges at local courts and two at special courts.[134] His colleague in Rostock was able to use ten of the 28 judges who had made their way to his district.[135]

The outcome for Schneidemühl was also sobering. Of all the judges from the entire regional court district, including all the local courts, new employment was found for only two: one was supposed to go to Anklam Local Court, but requested a leave of absence due to a faintness caused during his fleeing. Another, intended for Ueckermünde Local Court, immediately applied to be allowed to return to his home court, the Siegen Local Court. All the others had fled to an unknown destination or were unusable—a very meager return in view of almost 40 vacant posts. The report by the President of the Schneidemühl Regional Court, who had also made his way to Anklam, clearly reflected the awareness of his own dispensability. On 15 March, the official sent his superior a memo that painstakingly translated the futility of his legal existence into the lowlands of administrative language: "To date, the need for judicial activity for the repatriated population of the Schneidemühl district court district has not yet emerged."[136] Life was obviously more important to the displaced than their legal business.

Magnanimity

The Berlin headquarters had also made provisions in this respect. The German citizen, who had "carried his rights with him" to the East from 1939 onwards, as was formulated at the time with patriotic pathos,[137] was now also allowed to pack his or her cases in their luggage for the escape back to the Old Reich. In December 1944, the Reich Ministry of Justice had issued the directive that the courts in the displaced persons' respective places of residence should continue proceedings upon request. Legally, this was problematic because the jurisdiction is generally determined by residence, which, in addition to the actual residence, also requires a corresponding legal intention to reside there. However, it was obvious that those displaced had not left their hometowns voluntarily. In a colorful juxtaposition of superlatives and fictions, the Reich Ministry of Justice therefore appealed to the generosity of its employees: the forced change of location could—against better judgment—be interpreted as establishing a new place of residence, the discussion of jurisdiction should not impair the substantive work any more than the loss of files, the displaced seeking justice were to be "supported to the greatest extent possible … with advice and assistance," and in general the judge should "show magnanimity" in all related matters.[138]

That was a nice way of putting it: immediate legal assistance for the fellow citizen in need, easily and unbureaucratically available. However, the legal triad of definition, subsumption, and outcome does not provide for forays into the emotional landscape. Magnanimity is not a legal concept. Practitioners therefore preferred to stick to the conventional tools of the trade. In Stettin, a plaintiff lawyer from Thorn actually achieved the incredible: in April 1945, while his client was stationed in Stettin, he located the defendant's address in Vogtland. He then asked the Stettin Regional Court to continue the pending case—a divorce. The response was as narrow-minded as one would expect from a legal professional in normal circumstances: a business residence, the court wrote on 28 April 1945, did not constitute a domicile, and as far as Vogtland was concerned: "A summons cannot be served there."[139] That was the end of the matter.

And that was already far more than most of the other parties achieved. The continuation of their own legal disputes was generally low on the list of priorities for the displaced, coupled with the problems caused by the loss of files or participants. Although the Posen General Prosecutor had managed to relocate his institution to Riesa and some of the prisoners to Dresden, the hearings that had originally been planned before the Posen Higher Regional Court, which had also been moved to Riesa, failed because there was little possibility to bring the defendants from the detention center to court after the attacks on Dresden.[140] The Local Courts of Jülich and Düren had been run by just one judge in Nörvenich since their third transfer at the end of November 1944. "In practice, of course, this judge can only work to a limited extent," conceded the superior judge, although he was "only used to this extent."[141] The Gemünd Local Court, which had relocated just 25 kilometers to Blankenheim, had virtually nothing to do at the alternative location; only in the area of voluntary jurisdiction was there "little business activity in family law and probate matters."[142] And the president of the Koblenz Regional Court, who had moved the last remnants of his judicial services to Montabaur and Dierdorf at the beginning of March 1945, also expressed an anxious view of the future when he reported to his superior: "I doubt, however, that any productive work can be done under the current conditions."[143]

No, it was no longer productive. But the administration of right and wrong is a categorical matter that does not ask about costs and benefits nor even the sensitivities of its henchmen. "Even if a civil society were to be dissolved by the consent of all its members (e.g., if a people inhabiting an island decided to separate and disperse throughout the world), the last murderer remaining in prison would first have to be executed so that each has done to him what his deeds deserve and bloodguilt (*Blutschuld*) does not cling to the people for not having insisted upon this punishment; for otherwise the people can be regarded as collaborators in this public violation of justice," wrote Immanuel Kant in 1797 in his *Metaphysical Foundations of the Doctrine of Right*.[144] The German judiciary at the end of the Second World War was guilty of very little in this respect. The last murderers, the last traitors, the last *Volksschädlinge* were executed as orderly as was appropriate for the legal doctrine of duty, which had been trimmed down to one semester. The last thefts, assaults, and insults were punished according to the rules, and even with the last forms, cash balances, travel expense reports, stamp pads, and service calendars, the military justice system meticulously ensured that it could hand over its legacy to posterity free of any *Blutschuld*; in Breslau, divorces were still being pronounced at the end of March, when the city had already been surrounded by the Red Army for weeks.[145]

Only the very last concern was completely un-Kantian. Starry skies, moral law, all well and good, but even dutiful legal professionals know that food comes before morality. On 6 February, the President of the Rostock Higher Regional Court reported that 17 members of the judiciary from the East had arrived at his office. At least six of them had previously worked at the Higher Court Treasury of the Königsberg Higher Regional Court. They were housed in the Schwerin courthouse; new arrivals from the district of the Königsberg Higher Regional Court were encouraged to go there as well. The Königsberg court treasury therefore resumed operations far from home—the displaced persons' work was even given its own organizational chart.[146] And they certainly got busy: a good 300 payment slips from the Königsberg Higher Regional Court have been preserved, arranged alphabetically, and neatly sorted according to senior, superior, middle, junior, and even prison service, for February, March, April and May, most of which were issued at the end of May and processed via the "Mecklenburger Bank." The last official act was for the assessor Dr. Werner Gruenhagen, who received remuneration of 558.90 Reichsmark for February and March. The cash order was signed: "Schwerin, 30.5.45."[147]

The End

And after all this, the odyssey of the Stettin judiciary, which had led them to the surrounding area in the fall of 1943 and back to Stettin in the fall of 1944, reached yet another stage. On 9 March, the order was issued to evacuate Stettin. Over the next few days, the Higher Regional Court and the Regional Court moved to the tranquil town of Greifswald, where they were able to find last-minute alternative accommodations in the Regional Court at Domplatz, around 120 km from home; the Local Court traveled on to Stralsund. Before leaving, a major legal feat was accomplished: on 13 March, the final contingent of the Stettin Special Court sentenced three postal workers who had embezzled mail from—of all places—the Red Cross, to long prison sentences and one of them to death.[148] On 20 March, the artillery fire became so heavy that the heads of the agencies were given permission to leave their posts. Two days later, "some stragglers were taken out of Stettin" in a truck belonging to the general prosecutor's office.[149]

It was no longer truly orderly. Files continued to arrive in Greifswald in large numbers. But the massive writing desks and chandeliers that had so hopefully been used to decorate the Pomeranian provincial courts in 1943 and 1944 were no longer an option. Colleagues from Greifswald supported the new arrivals with a few modest gifts; in the end, 53 employees of the Stettin Regional Court shared 15 desks and four typewriters.[150] Of course, even this meager displacement operation was far from descending into chaos. The apparatus quickly regained a resilient structure. With generous foresight, an organizational chart defined the responsibilities for the rest of the year: a good two dozen judges were distributed among the local court, which had been moved to Stralsund, the regional court operated with one criminal chamber and four civil chambers, plus the special court, five divisions at the higher regional court, the general prosecutor's office, and the administrative department. Even the unpopular entailment cases received their own clerk, and finally the junior staff also found a contact point: "Dr. Müller handles the business of the Examination Office."[151]

The civil chambers met on Wednesdays and Thursdays, criminal law on Fridays, and Saturdays were for the special court.[152] The other ingredients for proper business operations were also diligently gathered. A lawyer who had fled to Rostock requested exemption from the obligation to appear before the Stettin Higher Regional Court: he had not found an apartment in Greifswald, did not know where his clients were, and, moreover, had been unable to bring any files with him from Stettin. The request was denied. "In the interest of judicial business, ... every effort must be made" to conclude matters ready for trial. On 10 April 1945, a Higher Regional Court judge stated that "with the absolutely quiet front in front of Stettin" during the previous two weeks, it was "easily possible to obtain files and office material from Stettin," and that the housing market in Greifswald had since eased somewhat. The lawyer should therefore set up an office in Greifswald as quickly as possible and also provide the addresses of other lawyers in Stettin. On 20 April the Higher Regional Court ordered the deputy president of the bar association, who had reported his flight to Flensburg, to return to the court district "within two weeks" because he is "constantly needed here."[153]

Of course, the words were louder than the deeds. The office was largely empty. A few divorces were still trickling in, an inheritance dispute was being finalized, a maintenance case required a statement, several evidentiary proceedings were pending, 14 Frenchmen were in custody, a verdict had to be reached on two *Volksschädlinge*, a civil servant was asked to file a criminal complaint for defamation so that action could be taken against the perpetrator. An abusive husband was forced to vacate the matrimonial home by temporary injunction, a plaintiff was told that he could "not expect his divorce proceedings to be carried out in the near future," and a plaintiff received notice that the evidence she had requested was "not feasible at the moment."[154]

The main task was self-administration. On 3 March 1945, the Köslin Regional Court President, who had also fled to Greifswald, received 16 special passes for tonics for intellectually active individuals so that he could continue to run his skeletal agency.[155] On 7 April, the Stettin Regional Court President requested that he be exempted from the obligatory quarterly overview of the employment situation in his district. As "the vast majority of the local courts under my authority had been vacated or occupied by the enemy," he felt unable to prepare the overview.[156] Two days later, a different matter almost came to a head. The Stettin Regional Court President complained to his Higher Regional Court President that, contrary to "all previous practice," the Higher Regional Court had repeatedly ordered his employees to operate the heating system, which undermined his efforts to maintain full authority over his employees "even in these difficult times."

In his agitation, the official even wanted to force a decision from the Reich Ministry of Justice. A verbal discussion prevented this escalation,[157] the end of the heating season or the approach of the Red Army may have encouraged the parties' willingness to compromise. On 29 April, the employees were gathered once again to review the files for incriminating material and destroy it, if necessary. That night burned "fires in all ovens."[158] The following day, Greifswald was surrendered without a fight.

However, the last official act here was also a dip into the judicial coffers. Anyone who was "transferred to another place of employment for official reasons" but was unable to set up their own household there due to a lack of housing was granted a separation allowance in accordance with Section 1 of the *Relocation Expenses Reimbursement Act* of 3 May 1935. This amounted to a daily rate of 18 Reichsmarks for the first week, followed by 8 Reichsmarks thereafter. The last general decrees of November 1944 stipulated an exception if a relocated employee was deployed "at or near the receiving location."[159]

This was undoubtedly the case here: the lawyers from Stettin worked in Greifswald and also lived there. The legal world became fragile. But the forms were patient. "Daily return to the place of residence is not possible," the form began, and the applicant added by hand: "as Köslin is in enemy hands."[160] Was this an official reason? And was Greifswald even a "receiving location" or just a fortuitous temporary solution? At this point, the officials truly displayed the magnanimity that they had been encouraged to show in their treatment of their fellow displaced persons. The judicial administration granted well over a hundred of them the usual compensation—in accordance with Section XVIIa Part IX Subpart 2a—generously limited to 31 March 1946, to be on the safe side.[161] Apparently, no one was listening to the sermons about the approaching final victory with too much faith.

And one more thing: the last separation allowance was approved by the Stettin Regional Court President on 22 May 1945, and paid out via the usual cash order. From an administrative point of view, the situation was finally clear. Previous employment authority: "Stettin Regional Court in Stettin." New employment authority: "Stettin Regional Court in Greifswald." Reason for the discrepancy: "Relocation of the Stettin Regional Court to Greifswald."[162] It was obvious that neither the invasion of the Red Army nor the unconditional surrender had been able to change this strikingly clear state of affairs.

Notes

1. Announcement of the Regional Court President for Stettin, 26 April 1943, in: GStA PK, XV. HA, Rep. 75a OLG Stettin No. 620, p. 60.
2. Plenipotentiary General for the Reich Administration to Reich Defense Commissioners, 31 July 1943, in: BA, R 3001 No. 22328, p. 33.
3. See the overviews in: GStA PK, XV. HA, Rep. 75a OLG Stettin No. 620, pp. 1 and 10; similarly, in: LAG, Rep. 76 Stettin (neu) No. 61, p. 34.
4. The Regional Court President for Schneidemühl to the Higher Regional Court President for Stettin, 28 September 1943, in: LAG, Rep. 76 Stettin (neu) No. 61, p. 1. The Regional Court President for Köslin to the Higher Regional Court President for Stettin, 24 September 1943, in: ibid., p. 2.
5. Higher Regional Court President for Stettin to Reich Justice Ministry ("RJM"), 21 February 1944, in: GStA PK, XV. HA Rep. 75a OLG Stettin No. 620, p. 61.
6. The relocation protocols can be found in as much detail as possible in: LAG, Rep. 76 Stettin (neu) No. 61, pp. 177–250.
7. The details of this move are recorded in: LAG, Rep. 75 No. 85.
8. The extent of the destruction can be seen from a letter from the Manager of the Local Court for Stettin to the Regional Court President for Stettin, 17 August 1944, in: LAG, Rep. 76 Stettin (neu) No. 129, p. 132, and from a note by the Higher Regional Court President on this, ibid., p. 134. In summary, see the situation report from the General Prosecutor's Office Stettin to the RJM, 29 September 1944, in: BA, R 3001 No. 23386, p. 64.
9. All information from the situation report of the General Prosecutor's Office Stettin, 10 February 1945; daily report of the General Prosecutor's Office Stettin, 14 February 1945; situation report of the Higher Regional Court President for Stettin, 21 February 1945, all in: BA, R 3001 No. 23386, pp. 74 et seq.
10. A *Rundverfügung* (or "RV," i.e., a circular addressed to subordinate authorities), 13 September 1939, in: BA, R 3001 No. 22489, pp. 134 et seq.
11. For the Higher Regional Court for Cologne note, see Regional Court President for Trier to the Higher Regional Court President for Cologne, 10 October 1939, in: the LAV NRW-R, Ger. Rep. 11 No. 1660, pp. 219–224. For the Higher Regional Court for Zweibrücken note, see for example RV of the Higher Regional Court President for Jena, 20 September 1939, in: the HStAW, Thüringisches OLG Jena No. 780, p. 4.
12. Letter of the Higher Regional Court President for Cologne, 14 September 1939, in: LAV NRW-R, Ger. Rep. 11 No. 1660, pp. 192 et seq.
13. Report of the supervising judge, Saarburg Local Court, 15 September 1939, in: ibid., pp. 201–206.
14. Auxiliary measures: Letter RJM to the Plenipotentiary General for the Reich Administration, 16 September 1939; Responsibilities: RV RJM, 8 September 1939, both cited in: LAV NRW-R, Ger. Rep. 11 No. 1660, pp. 216 and 188.
15. See the order of the Plenipotentiary General for the Reich Administration, 7 September 1939, cited hereafter: GStA PK, XV HA Rep. 76 Stargard No. 675, pp. 189 et seq.
16. All from the situation reports of the Higher Regional Court President for Zweibrücken, 8 January, 15 July, 1 and 16 September 1940 (BA, R 3001 No. 23389, pp. 4 et seq., 24 et seq.).
17. Situation report of the Higher Regional Court President for Zweibrücken, 28 November 1944, and Zweibrücken General Prosecutor, 14 February 1945, both in: BA, R 3001 No. 23389, pp. 118 et seq. and 122 et seq. (quote from 118).

18. Führer decrees of 13 July and 20 September 1944, in: Moll, pp. 426–428, 456 et seq. For Cologne *Allgemeinverfügung* (or "AV," a "general order" addressed to a wider audience) of the Higher Regional Court President of 5 September 1944, in: LAV NRW-R, Ger. Rep. 255 No. 553, p. 195.
19. Express letter from the Plenipotentiary General for the Reich Administration, 18 September 1944, hereafter: GStA PK, XV HA Rep. 76 Stargard No. 675, pp. 187–189.
20. RJM, Richtlinien für Maßnahmen bei Justizbehörden in Operations- und Kampfgebieten, 15 September 1944, in: BA, R 3001 No. 24698, pp. 13 et seq., as a "Secret of the Reich" (or *Geheime Reichssache*) addressed to the Higher Regional Court Presidents for Düsseldorf, Karlsruhe, Kattowitz, Cologne, Königsberg, Posen and Zweibrücken.
21. Situation report Higher Regional Court President for Zweibrücken, 28 November 1944, in: BA, R 3001 No. 23389, p. 118.
22. Situation report of the General Prosecutor's Office in Cologne (currently Eitorf), 30 January 1945, in: BA, R 3001 No. 23374, p. 161.
23. Higher Regional Court President for Cologne (currently Eitorf) note, 1 February 1945, in: LAV NRW-R, Ger. Rep. 255 No. 202, p. 129; also in the overview RJM (undated), in: BA, R 3001 No. 24698, p. 36. For the Lorraine courts see the report by the Higher Regional Court Zweibrücken note, 10 November 1944, in: BA, R 3001 No. 25017, pp. 52–57, 53 et seq.).
24. Memo Higher Regional Court President for Cologne (currently Eitorf), 1 February 1945, in: LAV NRW-R, Ger. Rep. 255 No. 202, p. 129, p. 106.
25. Situation report Higher Regional Court President for Cologne (currently Eitorf), 1 December 1944, in: BA, R 3001 No. 23374, pp. 155 et seq.; memo Higher Regional Court President for Cologne (currently Eitorf), 1 February 1945, in: LAV NRW-R, Ger. Rep. 255 No. 202, p. 129.
26. Management report Higher Regional Court President for Cologne (currently Eitorf), 1 December 1944, in: BA, R 3001 No. 23374, p. 154. The accounting office and Oberjustizkasse were moved to neighboring Hennef. A civil law branch office was also opened in Wiehl in December. See also Manthe, *Richter in der nationalsozialistischen Kriegsgesellschaft*, 121 et seq.
27. Schiller, *Oberlandesgericht Karlsruhe*, 233–241.
28. Situation reports Higher Regional Court President for Königsberg, 11 October and 24 November 1944, in: BA, R 3001 No. 23375, pp. 261, 270; see also the minutes of the meeting of 14 October 1944, ibid., No. 24051 (unpaginated). The district courts of Memel, Tilsit, and Zichenau were closed down.
29. See RJM, Richtlinien für Maßnahmen bei Justizbehörden in Operations- und Kampfgebieten, 15 September 1944, in: BA, R 3001 No. 24698, pp. 13 et seq.
30. Danzig General Prosecutor to all prisons, 9 September 1944, in: BA, R 3001 No. 23360, pp. 128–132. See also Becker, *Mitstreiter im Volkstumskampf*, 252 et seq., and Kershaw, *The End*.
31. RJM memo on call to Higher Regional Court President for Königsberg, 14 October 1944, in: BA, R 3001 No. 24698, p. 15.
32. Travel report MD Dr. Vollmer/Fechner, 8 December 1944, in: BA, R 3001 No. 25017, p. 49.
33. Circular decree of 23 November 1944, in: Ministerialblatt des Reichs- und Pr. Ministeriums des Innern, Ausgabe A No. 49 Jahrgang 1944, 1165 and 1166.
34. These formulations from: Report of the Breslau General Prosecutor's Office, 25 January 1945, (ibid., unpaginated); Report of the Kattowitz General Prosecutor's Office, 1 February 1945; Memorandum on the call of the General Prosecutor's Office

Danzig to the RJM, 2 February 1945, all in: BA, R 3001 No. 24051 (unpaginated); also report of the General Prosecutor Stettin, 10 February 1945, in: BA, R 3001 No. 23386, p. 74.

35. Situation report Higher Regional Court President for Zweibrücken to RJM, 28 November 1944, in: BA, R 3001 No. 23389, pp. 118–121.
36. Documented in various reports from December 1944/January 1945, in: LAV NRW-R, Ger. Rep. 288 No. 517, pp. 2, 8, 28 et seq., 71, 101 et seq., 116. On file backups in the Cologne area, see Herbers, *Organisationen im Krieg*, 307–309.
37. The entire process is documented in: LAV NRW-R, Ger. Rep. 288 No. 517, pp. 14, 19 et seq., 23 et seq., 28, 36, 42–44, 48 et seq., 53, 60, 69, 87, 102a, 123, from which all quotations are taken. On the occupation of Bitburg, see Henke, *Die amerikanische Besetzung Deutschlands*, 344.
38. RJM, Richtlinien für Maßnahmen bei Justizbehörden in Operations- und Kampfgebieten, 15 September 1944, in: BA, R 3001 No. 24698, pp. 13 et seq.
39. Situation report of the General Prosecutor's Office Danzig, 4 October 1944, in: BA, R 3001 No. 23360, pp. 143 et seq. For similar evacuation measures in Posen, see the report of the General Prosecutor's Office, 5 October 1944, in: BA, R 3001 No. 23383, p. 141a.
40. Situation report General Prosecutor's Office Danzig, 5 December 1944, in: BA, R 3001 No. 23360, pp. 145 et seq.
41. In detail: GStA, XV. HA Rep. 75a OLG Stettin, No. 619, citation of p. 2. See also the situation reports of the Higher Regional Court President for Königsberg, 11 and 30 October as well as 24 November 1944, in: BA, R 3001 No. 23375, pp. 261 et seq., 270, 273 et seq.
42. See the corresponding instructions of the Regional Court President for Stargard, 25 January 1945, in: LAG, Rep. 75 No. 30, p. 114.
43. In addition, there were 30 typewriters, 28 telephones and a radio set; see the list of salvaged property Local Court and Regional Court for Köslin, 17 February 1945, in: LAG, Rep. 75 No. 148, p. 62.
44. Letter from the Chief District Judge for Kolberg (currently Stralsund) to the Regional Court President for Köslin (Greifswald), 16 April 1945, in: LAG, Rep. 75 No. 148, p. 116.
45. Supervising Judge of the Local Court for Bublitz to the Higher Regional Court President for Stettin, 26 January 1945, in: LAG, Rep. 76 No. 133, p. 33.
46. All from the RJM notes on calls from First General Prosecutor Büttner (Königsberg), 25, 26 and 28 January 1945, in: BA, R 3001 No. 24698, pp. 18 et seq.
47. Situation report of the Higher Regional Court President for Danzig, 16 February 1945, in: BA, R 3001 No. 23360, p. 157.
48. Regional Court President for Neisse to the Higher Regional Court President for Kattowitz, 9 February 1945, in: BA, R 3001 No. 20243, p. 132.
49. Situation report of the Higher Regional Court President for Leitmeritz, 15 February 1945, in: BA, R 3001 No. 23376, p. 148.
50. AV RJM, 29 November 1944 (cited hereafter as the HStAS), EA 4/001 Bü 665, Vorgang 67.
51. General Plenipotentiary of the Reich Administration to the Supreme Reich Authorities, 1 February 1945, in: BA, R 3001 No. 24435, p. 127, which also contains the letters of 23 and 29 January.
52. RV RJM, 7 February 1945, in: BA, R 3001 No. 8463/24 (unpaginated).
53. Party Chancellery, Order No. 45, 1 February 1945, cited here according to HStAS, EA 4/001 Bü 669, Vorgang 11.

54. Here according to the letter from the Reich Defense Commissioner for Danzig-West Prussia, 11 February 1945, as an appendix in the situation report of the Higher Regional Court President for Danzig, 16 February 1945, in: BA, R 3001 No. 23360, p. 160.
55. AV of the Higher Regional Court President for Breslau (currently Görlitz), 5 February 1945, in: BA, R 3001 No. 22730, p. 2.
56. Situation report of the Higher Regional Court President for Danzig, 31 January 1945, in: BA, R 3001 No. 23360, pp. 154–156.
57. Situation report of the Higher Regional Court President for Cologne (currently Eitorf), 1 December 1944, in: BA, R 3001 No. 23374, p. 158.
58. Higher Regional Court President for Karlsruhe to the Higher Regional Court President for Stuttgart, 11 January 1945, in: HStAS, EA 4/001 Bü 656, Vorgang 95.
59. The central office was set up on 12 December 1944, and dissolved again in March after the RJM intervened (AV of the Higher Regional Court President for Karlsruhe, 9 March 1945, in: StAF), C 20/1 No. 899).
60. Regional Court President for Memel to the Higher Regional Court President for Danzig, 15 February 1945, in: BA, R 3001 No. 23360, pp. 161 et seq.
61. RJM memo on call to General Prosecutor's Office Stettin, 6 February 1945, in: BA, R 3001 No. 24052, p. 35.
62. See the detailed report of the Regional Court President for Stargard (currently Demmin) to the Higher Regional Court President for Stettin (Greifswald), 23 March 1945, in: LAG, Rep. 75 No. 386, pp. 2 et seq., as well as the daily report of the General Prosecutor's Office Stettin of 14 February 1945, memorandum on this in: BA, R 3001 No. 23386, p. 78.
63. RJM memo on call to General Prosecutor's Office Königsberg, 27 January 1945, in: BA, R 3001 No. 24051 (unpaginated).
64. Order of the General Prosecutor's Office Königsberg dated 19 July 1944, here according to: LAV NRW-R, Ger. Rep. 255 No. 214, pp. 8 et seq.
65. RJM to the Higher Regional Court Presidents for Düsseldorf, Karlsruhe, Kattowitz, Königsberg, Posen, and Zweibrücken, 15 September 1944, in: BA, R 3001 No. 24698, p. 12. For the time before that, see the order of the General Prosecutor's Office Cologne to the Senior Public Prosecutors for Koblenz and Trier dated 2 September 1944, both in: LAV NRW-R, Ger. Rep. 255 No. 214, pp. 8 et seq.; see also the report of the Higher Regional Court President for Cologne to RJM, 1 December 1944, in: LAV NRW-R, Ger. Rep. 181 No. 193. Manthe, *Richter in der nationalsozialistischen Kriegsgesellschaft*, 127 mentions a corresponding appointment in Bonn.
66. RJM memo, 2 November 1944, in: BA, R 3001 No. 25017, pp. 61 et seq.
67. Higher Regional Court President for Breslau (currently Görlitz) to RJM, 7 February 1945, in: BA, R 3001 No. 22730, p. 5.
68. Situation report of the Higher Regional Court President for Danzig, 16 February 1945, in: BA, R 3001 No. 23360, pp. 157–159.
69. Higher Regional Court President for Stettin to the Regional Court President for Stolp, call of 2 February 1945, note about it in: LAG, Rep. 76 Stettin (neu) No. 359, p. 151.
70. Regional Court President for Thorn (currently Stettin) to the Higher Regional Court President for Danzig, 7 February 1945, in: LAG, Rep. 75 No. 15, pp. 15–18.
71. Regional Court Manager for Oppeln to the Higher Regional Court President for Kattowitz, 29 January 1945, in: BA, R 3001 No. 22730, pp. 11 et seq.
72. Situation report of the Higher Regional Court President for Breslau (currently Görlitz), 16 February 1945, in: BA, R 3001 No. 23358, pp. 87 et seq.

73. Higher Regional Court President for Breslau (currently Görlitz) to RJM, 7 February 1945, in: BA, R 3001 No. 22730, p. 5.
74. Regional Court President for Neisse to the Higher Regional Court President for Kattowitz (currently Neisse), 9 February 1945, in: BA, R 3001 No. 20243, p. 132.
75. The Chief District Judge for Kolberg (currently Stralsund) to the Regional Court President for Köslin (Greifswald), 16 April 1945, in: LAG, Rep. 75 No. 148, p. 116.
76. Local Judge for Belgard (currently Stralsund) to OLGP Stettin (Greifswald), 20 March 1945, in: LAG, Rep. 76 No. 148, Bl. 67.
77. Regional Court President for Hannover to the Higher Regional Court President for Celle, 5 April 1945, in: LAH, Nds. 710 Acc. 124/87 No. 133, pp. 14–16.
78. Report to the Local Court President for Dresden, 28 August 1945, in: HStAD, 11380 No. 249, pp. 40–42.
79. A good 450 files were therefore preserved. The Chief District Judge for Schwäbisch Gmünd to the Higher Regional Court President for Stuttgart, 9 April 1945, in: HStAS, EA 4/001 Bü 110, Vorgang 1, where further file burnings are also described.
80. See the report from the General Prosecutor's Office Stettin to the RJM, 10 February 1945, in: BA, R 3001 No. 23386, p. 74.
81. Report of the Higher Regional Court President for Kattowitz (currently Neisse) to RJM, 16 February 1945, in: BA, R 3001 No. 22730, p. 14. See also the report of the Regional Court President for Neisse to the Higher Regional Court President for Kattowitz, 9 February 1945, in: BA, R 3001 No. 20243, p. 132.
82. Judicial Inspector Bendsburg to the Higher Regional Court President for Kattowitz (currently Dresden), reproduced in his report to RJM, 16 February 1945, in: BA, R 3001 No. 22730, p. 16. Cf. Fulbrook, *A Small Town*.
83. Regional Court President for Thorn (currently Stettin) to the Higher Regional Court President for Danzig, 7 February 1945, in: LAG, Rep. 75 No. 15, pp. 15–18.
84. RV RJM, 19 February 1945, in: BA, R 3001 No. 22730, p. 20. On the end of secret protection RV RJM, 13 February 1945, here quoted from HStAS, EA 4/001 Bü 654, p. 5.
85. This goes back to a letter from Wilhelm Stuckart dated 7 February 1945, which was forwarded via the Reich Defense Commissioner in Pomerania and the President of the Higher Regional Court in Stettin and finally reached its destination on 19 March, here according to LAG, Rep. 75 No. 148, p. 7.
86. RJM to head of department, early February 1945, in: BA, R 3001 No. 22730, p. 1.
87. RV RJM, 20 February 1945, in: BA, R 3001 No. 8463/24 (unpaginated).
88. Last letter from Hans Heinrich Lammers dated 23 February 1945, forwarded on 5 March in an RV RJM, in: BA, R 3001 No. 22489, p. 92.
89. BA, R 3001 No. 24698, pp. 36 et seq. A single latecomer recorded the transfer of Local Court for Wegberg to Mönchen-Gladbach, presumably as a result of the attacks on Wegberg on 25 February 1945.
90. Justice Administration of the Soviet Occupation Zone (Deutsche Justiz-Verwaltung) memo, 13 March 1946, in: BA, DP 1 No. 563 (unpaginated).
91. Erdsiek, "Chronik der Rechtsentwicklung," 18, 19, with reference to the Higher Regional Court of Karlsruhe.
92. Note Higher Regional Court for Stettin, undated (after 20 February 1945), in: LAG, Rep. 75 No. 133, p. 28. The Higher Regional Court for Königsberg still had an interim station in Stettin-Altdamm; this results from a message from the Local Court for Ludwigslust to RJM, 27 February 1945, in: BA, R 3001 No. 22730, p. 21.
93. RJM memo, 19 February 1945, in: BA, R 3001 no. 22741, p. 6. The stopover in Frankfurt an der Oder is documented in a memo from RJM, 28 January 1945, in: BA,

R 3001 no. 24698, p. 21, and a report from the President of the Court of Appeal to RJM, end of February 1945, in: BA, R 3001 no. 22730, p. 18. The final destination Weißenfels is documented in a letter from the General Prosecutor's Office Posen (currently Weißenfels) dated 28 March 1945, in: HStAD, 11091 No. 19, p. 29.

94. RJM memo on call to the Higher Regional Court President for Kattowitz, 29 January 1945, in: BA, R 3001 No. 24698, p. 23; RJM memo on call to General Prosecutor's Office Kattowitz, 30 and 31 January 1945, both in: BA, R 3001 No. 24051 (unpaginated); General Prosecutor's Office Kattowitz (currently Radebeul) to RJM, in: BA, R 3001 No. 24052, p. 106. Gera is documented in the "Verzeichnis der Verwaltungsstäbe für Justizbehörden aus Freimachungsgebieten" (BA, R 3001 No. 22741, p. 5), which, however, is limited to Danzig, Kattowitz, Königsberg, and Posen.
95. RJM memo, 29 January 1945, in: BA, R 3001 No. 24051 (unpaginated). The station in Krummhübel (the cash register went to Naumburg) can be seen in the letter from the Regional Court President for Görlitz to the Department of Justice of Sachsen, 14 April 1947, in: BA, DP 1 No. 563 (unpaginated).
96. Diary for judicial administration matters Freiberg District Court, 20 March 1945, in: HStAD, 11031 No. 210, file 486.
97. However, he was no longer active in Bayreuth. See on this (and only on this) Koch, Volksgerichtshof, 503.
98. Already in the spring of 1944, see the RV RJM of 30 March 1944 (here according to LAG, Rep. 76 Stettin [new] No. 487, p. 103) and of 18 July 1944 (here according to LAH, Hann. 173 Acc. 123/87 No. 179, p. 117). The file transfers are documented in: BA, R 6 No. 390. The fact that action was actually taken in Frankfurt an der Oder is exemplified by a case of the German Court in Shitomir, which continued to enforce sentences on convicts who had meanwhile fled to Hamburg, also from Frankfurt an der Oder. It can be found in BA, R 137 III No. 6.
99. There was a lot of correspondence about this in February 1945, because the Berlin Higher Regional Court (*Kammergericht*) obtained the approval of the RJM, the Gauleiter, the Reichsführer SS and the NSDAP; see BA, R 3001 No. 24698, pp. 27–35. It is not clear whether the court authorities from the East who were relocated to Frankfurt an der Oder went along with this move.
100. Note from the Stettin Higher Regional Court, 13 January 1945, in: LAG, Rep. 75 No. 136, p. 1.
101. Higher Regional Court President for Breslau (currently Görlitz) to the Regional Court President for Schweidnitz (Waldenburg), 6 April 1945, in: BA, R 3001 No. 22730 (unpaginated appendix).
102. See the telegram from Senior Public Prosecutor Hohensalza to RJM, 27 January 1945, in: BA, R 3001 No. 24698, p. 40.
103. Memo from the Stettin Higher Regional Court, 20 February 1945, in: LAG, Rep. 75 No. 133, p. 28; the general prosecutor's offices in Stolp, Köslin, Stargard, and Schneidemühl were given a joint processing office in Greifswald, see General Prosecutor's Office Stettin (currently Greifswald) to RJM, 5 April 1945, in: BA, R 3001 No. 24052, p. 182.
104. Freiberg Regional Court diary for judicial administration matters, 27 April 1945, in: HStAD, 11031 No. 210, file 765. The general prosecutor's office ended up in Schirgiswalde (RV Senior Public Prosecutor Bautzen [currently Schirgiswalde], 28 April 1945, in: StFilaB, 50016 No. 4358, p. 46). It is not clear from the files whether the Teschen Regional Court, which had chosen Bautzen as an alternative location (Regional Court President for Teschen to the Higher Regional Court President for

Kattowitz, 2 February 1945, in: BA, R 3001 No. 20243, p. 127), went along with this move.

105. Local Court for Plauen to State Administration of Saxony Department of Justice, 27 July 1945, in: HStAD, 11380 No. 280, p. 9.
106. The Chief District Judge for Cosel, report dated 7 February 1945, in: BA, R 3001 No. 20243, p. 136.
107. Supervising Judge Pasewalk to the Higher Regional Court President for Stettin (currently Greifswald), 20 April 1945, in: LAG, Rep. 75 No. 133, p. 45, as well as memo from the settlement office of the Higher Regional Court for Stettin, 5 April 1946, in: ibid., p. 44.
108. Local court manager for Kolberg (currently Stralsund) to the Regional Court President for Köslin (currently Greifswald), 16 April 1945, in: LAG, Rep. 75 No. 148, p. 116.
109. Local Judge for Fiddichow to the Regional Court President for Stettin, 18 February 1945, in: LAG, Rep. 76 Stettin (neu) No. 8, p. 254.
110. Local Court for Plauen to State Administration of Saxony Department of Justice, 27 July 1945, in: HStAD, 11380 No. 280, p. 9.
111. Telegram of the Higher Regional Court President for Düsseldorf to RJM, 13 March 1945, in: BA, R 3001 No. 22729, p. 37.
112. Schmidt, "*Todesstrafe*," 212.
113. Recollection report by Werner Kesseböhmer, 1967, in: LAV NRW-R, RWN 139 No. 8, p. 18.
114. Report of the Chief District Judge for Schwäbisch Gmünd to the Higher Regional Court President for Stuttgart, 9 April 1945, in: HStAS, EA 4/001 Bü 110, p. 1.
115. This information is all taken from memos from the Higher Regional Court President for Cologne dated December 1944 and 1 February 1945, in: LAV NRW-R, Ger. Rep. 255 No. 202, p. 106 and 129.
116. Ibid. Also the Regional Court President for Koblenz to the Higher Regional Court President for Cologne (currently Eitorf), 10 March 1945, in: ibid., p. 130.
117. Note from General Prosecutor's Office Cologne, 13 March 1945, in: LAV NRW-R, Ger. Rep. 449 No. 46, p. 160; General Prosecutor's Office Cologne to RJM, 13 March 1945, in: LAV NRW-R, Ger. Rep. 255 No. 533, p. 230; Senior Public Prosecutor Cologne (currently Königswinter) to GStA Cologne (Eitorf), 5 March, 25 March with note dated 15 March 1945, in: LAV NRW-R, Ger. Rep. 449 No. 28, pp. 210 et seq.; memo General Prosecutor's Office Köln (currently Waldbröl), 25 March 1945, in: ibid. (unpaginated).
118. Speech by Thierack at the conference of the Higher Regional Court Presidents in Weimar, 3–4 February 1944, in: HStAW, Thuringian Higher Regional Court for Jena No. 1166, p. 123 (abridged in Schubert, 501).
119. Department head meetings RJM, 11 October 1944 and 31 January 1945, in: BA, R 3001 No. 24688, pp. 44, 49; RV RJM, 12 January 1945, in: BA, R 3001 No. 8463/24 (unpaginated); as well as the work plan in BA, R 3001 No. 25044, p. 124.
120. Head of department meeting RJM, 31 January 1945, in: BA, R 3001 No. 24688, p. 49; RJM to the Higher Regional Court President for Celle, 15 and 16 February 1945, in: LAH, Nds. 710 Acc. 124/87 No. 124, p. 3, 8; letter Amtsrat Becker to Klempke, 4 December 1945, in: BA, DP 1 No. 7347, p. 311.
121. RJM currently Ichtershausen to RJM, 29 March 1945, in: BA, R 3001 No. 24471, pp. 136 et seq. Previously the Higher Regional Court President for Naumburg to the Higher Regional Court President for Jena, 20 March 1945, in: HStAW, Thuringian OLG Jena No. 909, p. 84.

122. Memo of conversation in General Prosecutor's Office Rostock, 10 April 1945, in: LHASH, 5.12-6/4 No. 854 (unpaginated).
123. Higher Regional Court President for Rostock (currently Schwerin) to RJM, 17 March 1945, in: LHAS, 5.12-6/4 No. 856 (unpaginated). A list with six names was also sent by the Local Court for Ludwigslust (27 February 1945, in: BA, R 3001 No. 22730, p. 21), even at the RJM some judicial employees reported, see BA, R 3001 No. 22741.
124. Diary for judicial administration matters Freiberg Regional Court, in: HStAD, 11031 No. 210. A judge from Breslau was assigned to the Plauen Regional Court (StACh, 30096 No. 8844).
125. The lists and the accompanying letter from the Higher Regional Court President for Stettin to RJM, 12 February 1945, can be found in: LAG, Rep. 76 Stettin (neu) No. 124, pp. 1–21 and ibid., Rep. 75 No. 14. The confirmation of receipt for this is in BA, R 3001 No. 25113. The list of personnel from the Stettin district was continued until 24 February 1946 (!) (albeit with a long interruption between 4 April and 16 September 1945).
126. Local court manager for Celle and the court cashier's office for Celle to the Higher Regional Court for Celle, 8 February 1945, in: LAH, Hann. 173 Acc. 123/87 No. 168, pp. 6 et seq.
127. Regional Court President for Cottbus to the Kammergericht President, 13 February 1945, in: BA, R 3001 No. 22730, p. 19.
128. Court cashier's office for Stade to supervising judge for Stade, in: LAH, Hann. 173 Acc. 123/87 No. 168, pp. 9 and 19.
129. Higher Regional Court President for Stettin to RJM, 12 February 1945, in: LAG, Rep. 76 Stettin (neu) No. 124, p. 21.
130. Both cases are documented in: LAG, Rep. 76 Stettin (neu) No. 83.
131. Higher Regional Court President for Stettin (currently Greifswald), 16 March 1945, in: LAG, Rep. 75 No. 148, p. 32.
132. Regional Court President for Greifswald to the Higher Regional Court President for Stettin (currently Greifswald), 9 April 1945, in: LAG, Rep. 76 Greifswald No. 1151, p. 39.
133. Local court manager for Greifswald to the Regional Court President for Greifswald, 16 April 1945, in: LAG, Rep. 76 Greifswald, No. 1081, p. 37.
134. Higher Regional Court President for Breslau (currently Görlitz) to RJM, 7 February 1945, in: BA, R 3001 No. 22730, p. 6.
135. Higher Regional Court President for Rostock (currently Schwerin) to RJM, 17 March 1945, in: LHAS, 5.12-6/4 No. 856 (unpaginated).
136. Regional Court President for Schneidemühl (currently Anklam) to the Higher Regional Court President for Stettin (Greifswald), 15 March 1945, in: LAG, Rep. 75 No. 316, p. 5.
137. Fechner, "Das bürgerliche Recht," 2482.
138. AV "Rechtsangelegenheiten aus Freimachungsgebieten," 21 November 1944, 289 f. Similarly AV RJM, 28 November 1944, in: BA, R 3001 No. 8463/23.
139. Memorandum from Stettin Regional Court, 28 April 1945, Ref. 2^1 R 36/1945, in: LAG, Rep. 76a Stettin No. 1260, p. 11.
140. RJM memo on business trip to Dresden dated 28 February 1945, in: BA, R 3001 No. 23383, p. 144.
141. Regional Court President for Aachen to the Higher Regional Court President for Cologne, January 1945, in: LAV NRW-R, Ger. Rep. 255 No. 326, p. 232.
142. Higher Regional Court President for Cologne to RJM, February 1945, in: LAV NRW-R, Rep. 255 No. 327, p. 131.

143. Regional Court President for Koblenz (currently Dierdorf) to the Higher Regional Court President for Cologne (currently Eitorf), 10 March 1945, in: LAV NRW-R, Ger. Rep. 255 No. 202, p. 130.
144. MM 6: 333.
145. No files seem to have been preserved. But the Justice Ministry of the Soviet Occupation Zone reported after the war that the Breslau courts "continued their activities when the city had already been declared a fortress and was encircled" (5 April 1946, in: BA, DP 1 No. 6349, p. 44). This corresponds to the inquiry of a refugee who was able to state quite precisely that the Regional Court of Breslau had pronounced a divorce decree on 30 March 1945 by the 10th or 11th Civil Chamber, the files of which he was now looking for (HStAD, 11380 No. 204, p. 39).
146. The employees of the court cashier's office are listed in the list LAG, Rep. 76 Stettin (neu) No. 124, p. 6. Further information in the management report the Higher Regional Court President for Rostock, 6 February 1945, in: BA, R 3001 No. 23385, p. 48. The first business distribution plan dates from 9 March, the last from 20 April 1945, both in: LHAS, 5.12-6/4 No. 289 (unpaginated).
147. The documents are preserved in GStA PK, XX. HA Rep. 31 No. 108, 109, 110, 111 and 112. The employees who remained behind in the lost territories also remained entitled to benefits in principle; see the RV RJM, 7 March 1945, in: BA, R 3001 No. 8463/24 (unpaginated). According to this, the benefits could also be paid to relatives, in particular spouses and children.
148. General Prosecutor's Office Stettin to RJM, 5 April 1945, in: BA, R 3001 No. 24052, p. 182.
149. Telegram from General Prosecutor's Office Stettin to RJM, 22 March 1945, in: BA, R 3001 No. 23386, p. 81. See also the descriptions from General Prosecutor's Office Stettin to RJM, 5 April 1945, in: BA, R 3001 No. 24052, p. 179.
150. See the correspondence between the Regional Court President for Greifswald and the Regional Court President for Stettin, 6 April 1945, in: LAG, Rep. 76 Stettin (neu) No. 306, pp. 100 et seq. and ibid., Rep. 76 Greifswald No. 282 (unpaginated).
151. Business distribution plans in: Local Court in LAG, Rep. 76 Stettin (neu) No. 640 (unpaginated); Regional court and Special court in: ibid., Rep. 76 Stettin (neu) No. 146 and 641 (unpaginated); Higher Regional Court and General Prosecutor in: ibid., Rep. 76 Stettin (neu) No. 316, pp. 217 et seq.; ibid. Rep. 75 No. 148, p. 32.
152. Letter from the Regional Court President for Greifswald to the Regional Court President for Stettin, 26 March 1945, in: LAG, Rep. 76 Greifswald No. 1263, pp. 138, 140.
153. These processes from LAG, Rep. 75 No. 135.
154. Only a small number of case files have survived, but see the approximately 1,000 divorce files in LAG, Rep. 76a Stettin, which also contain proceedings from Greifswald. Moreover, see LAG, Rep. 76 Stettin (neu) No. 146, 445, 446, 454, 531, 670, 687, 714, 1257, 1260, 1455.
155. Higher Regional Court President for Stettin (currently Greifswald) to the Regional Court President for Köslin (Greifswald), 3 March 1945, in: LAG, Rep. 75 No. 148, p. 35. The sparse activity of the Köslin court is also documented there.
156. Regional Court President for Stettin (currently Greifswald) to the Higher Regional Court President for Stettin (Greifswald), 7 April 1945, in: LAG, Rep. 75 No. 10, p. 293.
157. See LAG, Rep. 76 Stettin (neu) No. 208.
158. This is the post-war report of a refugee, documented with further reports from those involved at the time in: LAG, Rep. 77 Stralsund No. 1051.

159. Reichsgesetzblatt I, 566, in conjunction with the Implementing Regulation of the Reich Minister of Finance of 7 May 1935, Reichsbesoldungsblatt, 40, from No. 25 of which the above quotations are taken. The cited exception is announced in the AV RJM of 7 August 1943, in: *Deutsche Justiz* 1943, 404, the application of which was expressly confirmed in November 1944 (here according to AV of the Higher Regional Court President for Celle, 28 November 1944, in: LAH, Hann. 173 Acc. 123/87 No. 171, p. 114).
160. LAG, Rep. 75 No. 122, here: p. 5.
161. Ibid. The time limit of twelve months is probably based on an AV of the RJM, 12 July 1944, in: *Deutsche Justiz*, 218; until then, only six months had been possible.
162. LAG, Rep. 76 Stettin (neu) No. 460; disbursement orders dated 10 May 1945 can be found in ibid., Rep. 76 Greifswald No. 950.

Chapter 6

Between the Years

The Suspension of Law in the Summer of 1945

Creatio Ex Nihilo

The beginning had no precedent. "We must begin anew, from the very beginning," postulated the newly founded *Deutsche Rechts-Zeitschrift* (German Legal Journal) in 1946, "there is nothing that can simply be continued."[1] Its very first issue featured a chronicle that attested to the success of the establishment of a new judicial system, stating that it had emerged "basically out of nowhere"[2] while the Württemberg-Hohenzollern Ministry of Justice registered a new beginning "literally out of nowhere" in its retrospective.[3] In 1947, these rhapsodies about nothingness received their own theological consecration. The Cologne Higher Regional Court President described to his minister the state of judicial business after the war, "The places of law were without form, and void, the notary's offices deserted, the lawyers' offices unoccupied."[4] The Brandenburg state administration summarized in its first statement of accounts in 1946: "When the war was over, everything was actually over. … All orderly life was over," and then allowed itself the rhetorical epiphrase: "Chaos."[5]

The yawning emptiness of the beginning, zero hour and day one, made an impression. Years later, in his history of the legal profession, Fritz Ostler gave his account of the postwar period under the heading, "The earth was without form, and void," while the Berlin General Prosecutor, apparently not quite as familiar with the Bible, reworded the first two sentences of the creation story as, "In the beginning, everything was without form and void" and then, following a familiar pattern, described a reconstruction "almost out of nothing."[6] Before the beginning, there was only darkness.

Everyone could see the traces that the darkness had left behind. The earth was without form, but anything but void. In front of the Charlottenburg Local Court, the *Volkssturm* (the German territorial army) had discarded its war equipment: uniforms, bazookas, machine guns, and ammunition lay strewn about, with corpses strewn in between, the stale stench of death in the air. Rubble, dirt, and excrement were everywhere in the courthouse, the windows broken, shelves overturned, the files were thrown into disarray, and the desks ransacked.[7] Judges everywhere were digging through the ruins, removing debris or carrying their belongings to less damaged areas. The President of the Weimar Regional Court ordered his staff to spend two to three hours a day clearing up. To clarify priorities—the court was still closed—he instructed them that "neither a pen nor a typewriter would be touched."[8] Officials in Essen had to open their umbrellas when it rained because of holes in the roof. The bombed-out public prosecutor's office in Paderborn found shelter in the classroom of a suburban school. In Schwaan, Mecklenburg, the local court was allocated four rooms in a hotel, in Neunburg v.W. in Bavaria, they were accommodated in the local judge's official residence, in Königsbrück, Saxony, the office made a meager new start in a café, while in nearby Lausick, they found shelter in the accounting room of the town bank, even though communication with the public was impossible there; the noise of the accounting machines drowned out the legal hearings.[9]

There were no offices, no courtrooms, no gowns, no typewriters, no legal texts, no literature, no tables, no chairs, no telephones, no shelves, no paper, no coal, no electricity, and nothing to eat. Officials received their wages in a currency for which nothing was available to buy. Every unskilled worker who was paid in kind earned more than a judge. An official in Hamburg is said to have rummaged through garbage cans in search of food because, as he argued in his defense, he could not buy food on the black market due to his job.[10] A bailiff in Baden-Baden came up with the idea of participating in the prisoners' rations so that he could receive at least one hot meal in his twelve-hour day.[11] Although judicial employees in many places had been granted food ration coupons for heavy laborers since mid-1946, the corresponding improvement in their nutrition repeatedly failed due to supply difficulties. At the beginning of 1948, the Central Judicial Office noted that the food crisis was causing the judiciary "serious concern," with absences due to illness and overwork increasing alarmingly.[12] The Saxon Ministry of Justice promised "special supplementary rations" to judges and public prosecutors who had distinguished themselves "in hot spots"—meaning proceedings relating to war crimes and white-collar crime.[13] And the Baden Ministry of Justice filed an article from the newspaper *Das Neue Baden*, which, under the heading "Intellectual Workers are Undernourished," made the delicate calculation that "today's rations" were "far below those of the Buchenwald concentration camp, for example."[14]

There was more to do than ever before. Centrifugal forces of society caused judicial statistics to explode at critical points. Criminal law was fueled by the typical crimes of necessity such as theft and receiving stolen goods, compounded by the endemic expansion of the black market, which promised young people in particular a rapid criminal career. The number and nature of civil proceedings also starkly illustrated the disintegration of traditional ties: divorces continued to account for the majority of the core business. This was roughly how one had to imagine the state of nature before Hobbes' Leviathan reared its head. When the Aachen Regional Court President attempted to report these apocalyptic conditions to his superior, he was overcome by a dramatic surge of emotion: "There is no longer a distinction between mine and yours. Stealing is no longer theft but organizing. Everyone is pushing, everyone is grabbing, everyone is taking advantage. Greed, unkindness, hard-heartedness—these are qualities that are brazenly coming to the fore everywhere. Parents deny their children shelter. Children lock out their elderly parents. Humanity is unleashed."[15]

The Fragmentation of Justice

In a certain sense, the law was also unleashed. The time had taken away the political order of space without inscribing a new one in its place. The old leaders were gone. The *Reichsgericht* ("Supreme Court of the Reich") was closed within minutes on 8 October 1945, and released for liquidation. Its judges were imprisoned, where most of them perished miserably. Whatever inventory appeared valuable was placed under the administration of a "Commission for the Preservation of the Assets of the *Reichsgericht*."[16] The Reich Ministry of Justice, scattered across countless alternative quarters, had also been dissolved. In tiny local courts in the countryside, the judicial administration of the Soviet Zone now rummaged through furniture, inventory, the library, and occasionally compromising files. Otto Thierack's badly battered desk stood in an inn in Mittenwalde.[17] The majority of the files—around 25,000 personnel files and 3,000 general files—were discovered by the Americans in Ichtershausen, Thuringia and immediately brought to one of their Ministerial Collecting Centers in Hesse, where they were managed by ministry officials, who had in the meantime been arrested.[18]

The judiciary, lifted from state to Reich level with great pomp and circumstances ten years earlier, was now municipalized at breakneck speed. Eisenhower had already ordered the closure of all courts and schools in his First Proclamation of September 1944 but had explicitly called on the remaining civil servants to return to their offices and serve there. This was a severe blow to legal sensibilities: judicial business had been degraded to an ideologically contaminated public education project, on a par with elementary schools and other educational institutions. There was no longer even a common sentencing formula. *Im Namen des Deutschen Volkes* ("In the name of the German people") had been the preamble to judgments since the transfer of judicial business to the Reich, but the Allies no longer wanted to hear of a German judiciary and now claimed to speak "in the name of the people," "in the name of the law," or "in the name of justice."[19] Who administered this law depended entirely on local coincidences, the ideas of the military government, the initiative of the locals, and the reserves of personnel, buildings, and inventory. A kind of race between the American and Soviet occupying powers appears to have developed to see under whose rule the courts would be operational again most quickly, albeit for very different reasons. In the case of the Russians, whose military administration was only established at the beginning of June 1945, it was probably a lack of planning that gave local initiative astonishing scope for action, while the Americans, on the other hand, overachieved their plans: not only was the establishment of the justice system—as they had announced—tackled "as soon as possible,"[20] but this also enabled them to create a fait accompli in the areas that were to be handed over to the Red Army at a later date.

The lack of thought and ideological overzealousness in the Soviet Zone soon led to a confusing juxtaposition of old and new judicial institutions. District, municipal, and county courts sprang up all over the zone, claiming their place alongside self-proclaimed people's courts, village courts, and peace courts, but also alongside existing local and regional courts. In criminal law, the power to impose punishment ranged from simple fines to the death penalty, while district, municipal, and local courts now fought over matrimonial matters, which had become the practically exclusive field of employment in civil law. Güstrow received its own "Court Constitution for the City and County of Güstrow," which combined the old and new systems into a strange synthesis by establishing a county court and five local courts below it.[21] Stralsund, which was particularly active in this respect, received new procedural rules for criminal matters, juvenile matters, and matrimonial matters, a "People's Tribunal" for particularly serious offenses, and finally a "Police Judge" for minor offenses, while in Weimar a new "Police Court" was primarily tasked with looting. In Zittau, Saxony, a "People's Court" replaced the old district court to resolve seizures and looting, while civil cases had to be brought before a newly appointed "Peace Justice." The local court in Görlitz disappeared into a new "Legal Office," whose jurisdiction was admittedly very limited because a police court for the administration of criminal law, a housing arbitration office for the confiscation of apartments belonging to former party members, and a rent conciliation office also existed in parallel. In Neustrelitz, the new category was simply called "Court," explaining that this *sui generis* institution was now both a local court and a regional court of first instance.[22]

Business Operations at "Zero Hour"

Was this still the old judicial system or already a new one? There was no moment in which all German courts were simultaneously suspended. On the contrary, judicial business in the summer of 1945 was as diverse as it had last been in the Middle Ages. It is known that a few courts were exempted from the universal closure as a kind of legal rescue center. There seems to have been no generally binding or at least comprehensible standards in this regard, certainly not under Soviet administration, but also not under American administration, where the traditional German court system was chosen as a guide. The Kempten Regional Court in the Allgäu and the Local Courts in Neustadt, Perleberg in Brandenburg, Burgstädt in Saxony, and Annaberg in Saxony, about which corresponding reports are circulating,[23] likely only had limited strategic importance in the postwar order. The Greifswald Regional Court, which was the reception center for half a dozen relocated institutions from the East in the final weeks of the war, also appears to have operated almost continuously. On 7 May, there was a hearing with the original staff, and a week later the judicial employees who could still be employed received a certificate stating that they were "employed in the vital operations of the civil court," and therefore the Red Army was asked to "allow them to pass unhindered everywhere." The court resumed its operations in its new form by 26 May.[24] It is not clear from the files whether it was even closed during this time.

But even among the closed institutions, many were surprisingly quick to resume their services. In Aachen, still under American administration and a special case in every respect, court hearings were held under the new order as early as the end of March.[25] The Tuttlingen Local Court reconvened at the end of April, followed by the Deggendorf public prosecutor's office on 12 May. The Local Courts in Plauen and Leipzig opened two days later—under American occupation—and the courts in the Soviet-administered towns of Ueckermünde, Stralsund, and Anklam the following day.[26] On 16 May, business operations began at the Cologne Local Court, followed one day later at the Siegburg Local Court and one day after that at the Zwickau Local and Regional courts, which is also remarkable because the Aue Local Court, less than 30 kilometers away, remained without occupation and therefore still felt committed to National Socialist rule. [27] On 22 May, the Trier Local

Court followed, on the 24th the Jena Local Court, and by the end of the month the Local Courts in Bamberg, Holzminden and Swinemünde were added; the latter, however, only briefly, because Swinemünde and Stettin soon came under Polish administration and the court was therefore relocated to Usedom in October.[28] And finally, in May 1945, 21 local courts in the former center of power also served the new era: due to extensive destruction, each Berlin district received its own court. Long-forgotten institutions such as the Friedenau Local Court or the Weißensee Local Court owe their brief heyday to this emergency period. From the outset, they were intended as a temporary solution, but in return were granted unlimited jurisdiction for all matters, from tenancy law to capital offenses. [29]

The most peculiar account of this interim period, however, comes from a senior judicial inspector from a small town with the illustrious name of Wolkenstein, 30 kilometers southeast of Chemnitz, whose imposing castle housed a small local court. In June 1945, the loyal employee described the events of the last few months to his new superiors: the courthouse had already been well fortified and had also been specially protected against air raids, which, according to all those in the know, he, the officer on duty, had succeeded in doing in an exemplary manner, as after 32 years on site he "had every wish fulfilled by the craftsmen." As a result, there was minimal bomb damage but almost all of the staff were called up to the *Volkssturm* at the end of February, which is why the chief judicial inspector, as the last man standing, did not leave the courthouse during the day or at night from 27 February to 26 May. His zeal found a wide audience. The air-raid shelter could hold 500 people, refugees needed accommodation, and women sought protection. The capable official did everything in his modest power. He even turned down military requests—a last defensive stronghold of the Wehrmacht, a Red Army hospital: "I averted everything." The devoted civil servant was ultimately so closely intertwined with his workplace that not even the Red Army quartering in his wife's private home could deter him from defending his office. He remained in the courthouse and checked everyone who sought entry, but even during this constant duty as door-keeper, he did not forget what his real vocation was: namely, to serve the law and its enforcement. Therefore, his account of his months of self-sacrifice contains the matter-of-fact remark, casually thrown out: "Legal services were not interrupted for a minute."[30]

Allied Interference

The suspension of law following the Allied invasion could have been anything—contemporaries spoke of "theorizing conceptual speculation," the "deepest humiliation of the German people caused by Hitler's leadership," or simply a "great, month-long pause for reflection"[31]—but it certainly did not mark a historical zero point. A court was always operating somewhere, sometimes still operating and sometimes again. "A rational civil service system continues to function flawlessly when the enemy occupies the territory, with only the top brass changing hands, because it is in the vital interest of all those involved, including, above all, the enemy himself, that this should happen," Max Weber predicted in *Wirtschaft und Gesellschaft* (Economy and Society). "The cultivated attitude to obedient submission" to the existing order brings "the disturbed mechanism to 'snap back into place,' so to speak."[32]

This observation, however, could only be partially applied to the German judiciary. Before 1945, their conduct had moved so far away from the rational virtues of the 19th century that no one, least of all the enemy, had any real—or "vital"—interest in their continued activity. In their case, it was not the conditioning of mechanical obedience that denied the new age access to the lower levels of the apparatus, but their long-practiced independence. Only a short time ago, they had listened with rapt attention to the assurances of their National Socialist minister that their direct connection to the Führer ennobled them as civil servants *sui generis*.[33] The German judge was allowed to decide for himself whose orders he would listen to; Hitler had passed this test with flying colors.

But now there were new masters in charge, masters whose orders the German judiciary perceived as presumptuous. Even the *General Instructions for Judges No. 1* contained the open threat that members of the judiciary would be "severely punished" if they attempted to perpetuate National Socialist ideology. The Potsdam Agreement of 2 August 1945 established the principles of democracy, justice, and legality as the guiding principles of the new judicial system, and a wealth of official directives provided further nuance. It was clear to everyone that too little independence was damaging, but too much independence was obviously even more damaging. The mirror-image formula of the military government was: "Maximum control with minimum interference."[34] Regular reports accounting for its own activities and the legal cases it handled were required. The German judiciary was under general suspicion: crimes committed in the concentration camps, war crimes, and all disputes involving a member of the United Nations were initially outside German jurisdiction. All officials could be dismissed at any time; all decisions were subject to Allied control and could be overturned if not approved—the last time the German judiciary had experienced such conditions was under eighteenth-century absolutism.

They suddenly found themselves at the tail end of a long hierarchy. Officials in uniform were instructed to greet officers of the military government appropriately; there was at least the prospect of a reply if they complied.[35] Otherwise, the principle of reciprocity was removed from the official channels. One side dictated, the other obeyed. Complaints were heard everywhere about confiscations issued without regard for political encumbrances. Even when obligated to clean up, it was reported indignantly, a mayor had declared it irrelevant, with the blessing of the French occupying power, "whether a former Party member was 5 percent or 90 percent to blame for today's conditions."[36] The President of the *Kammergericht* (Higher Regional Court of Berlin) was informed in February 1946 that rude letters to the military government could result in future in the dismissal of those responsible.[37] In Detmold, the military administration reduced a list of over 50 civil servants who were permitted to prepare the opening of the court to just four. To eliminate any arrogance from even the chosen few, the order was issued shortly thereafter to remove nameplates from all office rooms.[38] After all, no one was yet on duty there. At Heilbronn Regional Court, all the local courts in the district were instructed to set up a separate room for the representative of the US military government, Major Ritchie, with a secretary, a sign on the door, "a nice desk, a good carpet, and some good wall paintings." According to the new Allied leaders, the lavishly furnished rooms would only be used by "Major Ritchie when he comes there occasionally."[39]

These were all disruptions that a German legal professional could hardly integrate quietly into the usual business processes. The judges reacted angrily. When the German side rejected "distrust and paternalism" and "any influence of unauthorized persons on the judiciary,"[40] this meant not least the military government. In a whole series of publications, the Tübingen *Institut für Besatzungsfragen* (Institute for Occupation Issues) endeavored to draw parallels between the German occupation of other European countries and the Allied occupation of Germany.[41] An internal report by the Celle Higher Regional Court noted that "the deepest wish of all Germans" had been the "restoration of law," but that they were now constantly experiencing arbitrary arrests. Germans know very well how to distinguish between perpetrators and those "who have clean hands and have merely made political errors."[42]

New *Volksjuristen* ("People's Jurists") in the East

The Allies, it should be added, did not know this, and least of all, according to the expert assessment of those involved, did the Russians. They robbed and marauded through the courts. Whenever the Red Army confiscated a court, hardly any report failed to include the indignant remark that "senseless destruction" had been found upon return,[43] with no one making the effort—then actually indicated—to differentiate between "senseless" and "sensible" destruction. The Russians were particularly rigorous in their treatment of party members. As soon as the note "currently unable to carry out official duties" appeared in a judge's schedule,[44] one could guess what had happened. Whether there was a replacement or not was irrelevant. In Pasewalk, the judge was removed from office and replaced by a senior teacher; in Ueckermünde, a commercial clerk acted as judge and an innkeeper as public prosecutor.[45]

The infamous Order No. 49, often issued frantically by telephone or telegram in early September 1945, made this a program.[46] The Soviet Military Administration in Germany (SMAD) demanded with it the dismissal of all party members by 1 October. This removed four-fifths of all judges from office in one fell swoop. Ernst Melsheimer, later the first General Prosecutor of the GDR, paraphrased Soviet policy with the unequivocal equation that they would "rather accept a *Justitium* than the reinstatement of the Party members."[47] The order was not carried out with the same stringency everywhere. In Saxony in particular, attempts were made to keep even incriminated judges in office. But in small local courts, where often only one or two judges were working, it could well happen that all judges were dismissed at the same time, leaving the court an empty shell.[48] In the Freiberg Regional Court district, one judge had to serve three local courts. In Oederan, criminal law was the responsibility of an 80-year-old official who was certified by his own superiors as being hard of hearing and forgetful.[49] Elsewhere, appointments were repeatedly canceled due to staff shortages.[50]

The new legal system only opened up tiny niches for former party members. In Saxony, for example, it was agreed that party members who had remained inconspicuous would be admitted as lawyers only if there was a local need, whereby they were then to be used "preferably to provide free legal advice to the less well-off sections of the population."[51] However, hardly anyone remained in the judiciary—with serious consequences. At the end of 1946, almost 40 percent of judgeships were still vacant, and even this meager figure was only achieved because after the capitulation the overall requirement had been cut by a third. [52]

The renunciation of the old, fully qualified jurists was also a vote in favor of the *Volksjuristen*. The *Volksrichter* ("people's judges") who joined the judiciary in August 1946 to fill the gaps created by denazification and to satisfy the ideological needs of the judicial administration were, in this respect, only the most visible indication of a broader development. "No more gulf between the people and the law!," Eugen Schiffer, the honorable director of the still-new German Central Administration of Justice, was quoted as saying in September 1945. In addition to the demands of the economy, he affirmed, one must also meet "the spiritual needs of the people."[53] "People-oriented justice is the order of the day," was the motto in Thuringia, while the Saxon judicial administration demanded that court decisions be written in a "short, clear, generally understandable, and popular" manner.[54] The new judge was anti-fascist, democratic, empathetic, and full of creative energy and political—even party-political—drive: in Greifswald, it was announced that all judges were "reliable democrats," no one belonged to the NSDAP, all judges were members of the CDU or SPD and active in the trade union, and the rest of the staff were also "all *politically* organized."[55] In Thuringia, it was reported with satisfaction in 1950 that the number of non-party members had "decreased considerably" and was now only a good 15 percent.[56]

When the East officially returned to the old judicial system at the beginning of 1946—often just as hastily as Order No. 49 had previously been issued—a world had already been created that in the West seemed like the twilight of civil society. The motto, proclaimed with aplomb in the Soviet Occupation Zone, that it was better to have no law at all than the old law, could easily be expanded into a doomsday scenario. While little was known in the Western occupation zones about the uneducated swarm of "judges on immediate deployment," "judges on honorary service," and "people's judges," one thing could be said with certainty: they were not fully qualified lawyers in the sense of the traditional court system. The news of this bizarre army of legal workers was chilling, but productive; few things may have fueled the restoration of judicial policy in the West as much as the laboratory of wild experiments that could be marveled at in the East. The political judge, who was promoted there under the keywords of proximity to the people and democracy, was stylized in the West as the red reincarnation of Roland Freisler's people's judges, and *Kader* ("cadre") was merely seen as a more dashing word for what the Nazis called *Gefolgschaftsmitglied* ("retinue member").

Party affiliations or union involvement among judicial personnel were therefore either frowned upon or banned outright in the West. The problem was seen not in the wrong kind of politicization, but in politicization in general. The presidents of the Higher Regional Courts in the British Zone, trembling with anger at their very first meeting in September 1945, discussed a "journeyman bricklayer" who had become the Greifswald Regional Court President—a complete fabrication, as the person in question actually had decades of experience as a lawyer and notary.[57] The Aachen Regional Court President expressed a global political assessment that certainly commanded consensus in the West when he informed his superior—in a report on the situation in *his own* district, mind you: "In East Germany, we are experiencing a development that, in some respects, is even more fundamental than that overcome by the collapse."[58]

Fully Qualified Lawyers in the West

Better old than Bolshevik civil servants: *tertium non datur.* While the ruins were still smoking, the judicial administration in the West was already informing the military government that, given that 80 to 85 percent of the legal profession were former members of the NSDAP, these former members were indispensable for reconstruction.[59] The statistics supported this sober calculation. In 1946, there were twelve judges for 33 local courts in the Koblenz Regional Court district, six out of 44 posts were filled in Bremen, and 136 out of 548 in the entire Düsseldorf Higher Regional Court district.[60] In Tübingen, two public prosecutors had to deal with 4,300 criminal charges.[61] In Aachen, two district administrators shared 5,485 criminal complaints, in Bonn, three judges accounted for 9,663.[62]

The evidence of such figures helped the attribute "nominal" to an unprecedented boom. Party membership was only a reason for dismissal in the case of particularly high judicial offices—president of a regional court or higher regional court, chief public prosecutor or general prosecutor—for all other judicial posts, special involvement in the NSDAP, SA, or SS was required.[63] Party members were therefore generally eligible at the lower working level. This was the major difference between Control Council Law No. 4, which made a professional ban dependent on "active engagement" in the NSDAP, and Soviet Order No. 49, issued just a few weeks earlier, in which membership in itself was sufficient. As the highest jurisdictional authorities remaining in the West were the presidents of the higher regional courts, who were unable to coordinate with each other for a long time and perhaps initially even unwilling to, there were considerable differences on the ground. Nevertheless, the trend is clear: the "untainted Party member" soon appeared alongside the "non-Party member,"[64] the typical special judge was distinguished from the merely nominal special judge,[65] and to blur all criteria, the merely nominal non-Party member was also identified alongside the nominal Party member. As early as the summer of 1945, there was outrage in the British Zone that many judges had not joined the party "because they were either too old, belonged to a lodge, or because of a general lack of interest."[66] The Bonn Regional Court President expanded these base motives to include "refusal of an application for membership, … Freemasonry, Jewish affiliation" and issued the military government a clear warning that "a non-Party member" was "far from being a person of good character."[67]

The Allies' original plans, if there were any, were therefore soon more or less silently scrapped in practice. Even the infamous 50 percent rule of the British Zone, which allowed one incriminated judge into office for every non-incriminated one, received a powerful subsidy boost: younger civil servants, front-line soldiers, and employees of the judicial administration were not included in the calculation.[68] Even after this politicized math, huge gaps remained. They recruited trainee lawyers, pensioners, lay judges, lawyers, and—less willingly—refugees with legal knowledge. At the end of 1945, the military government agreed to the stipulation that anyone who had been rejected should not be "put forward again too soon." The Celle Higher Regional Court President unofficially constructed a kind of grace period from this when he added a handwritten note next to the minutes stating that rejected candidates could be considered again "after 4–5 months."[69] The state was eternal, and therefore its civil servants were also eternal, and they were even more eternal if they simultaneously served the idea of justice, which, properly understood, remained beyond the reach of earthly distortions. The sheer passage of time would shrink even the most committed Nazi to merely nominal size.

Thus, the matrix was created. The institutions occasionally had to remind the Allied military government that they could not do without the expertise of the suspended officials if the apparatus was to eventually snap back into place properly, in the Weberian sense. The judges concerned pushed the nominal—pressure, conformity, career, caution—to the fore and downplayed their inner ties to the now ostracized regime. The personnel situation began to ease from mid-1946, according to most reporters, and the old officials gradually returned. Transfers, secondments, career advancements, and deferrals had given the apparatus as a whole a new configuration. But the components had largely remained the same: of the 9,000 judges and prosecutors serving in the early 1950s, two-thirds had already been in service before 1945. The Düsseldorf Higher Regional Court President summed it up dryly in 1948, "After the personnel reconstruction of the judiciary, the core of the district's civil servants naturally consisted of people who were already part of it before the collapse."[70]

And so the old duty returned to its rightful place in the structure of justice. Just as it had carried the judiciary through the war, it also helped it to rebuild. The individual official was still "chained to his activity with his entire material and ideal existence," as Max Weber had analyzed.[71] In an almost ideal-typical confirmation of this observation, Werner Kesseböhmer attested to his colleagues that they were "inwardly connected to their old workplace in the closest possible way" and therefore saw it as their duty immediately after the capitulation to restore "their workplace with physical labor for the subsequent resumption of official duties."[72] Civil service discipline and habit, the belief in a higher objectivity of the apparatus, and the desire to allow one's own individuality to be absorbed in an impersonal fulfillment of duty were also the supporting pillars for the judiciary after 1945. The success of the reconstruction work was due to the "devotion to duty and total commitment" of the judicial employees, it was reverently stated in North Rhine-Westphalia, followed by the somewhat lame praise that the officials had been "aware of their duties" and had "achieved extraordinary things."[73] In Württemberg-Hohenzollern, the judges were credited with having dealt with legal issues in "quiet, self-denying fulfillment of duty," such as had "hardly ever been imposed on a generation of lawyers with such frequency and difficulty."[74] The term "silent heroism" made the rounds; "the community asserted itself, carried by a selfless, silent heroism of action, with which everyone fulfilled their duty in their place without hope of reward or thanks," enthused a contemporary, visibly moved. There was "a great deed of all classes of the German people" to be appreciated, "a natural fulfillment of duty in the Kantian sense," in short: "a miracle."[75]

But unfortunately, as is so often the case in the history of philosophical practice, as soon as Kant encountered reality, it became quite un-Kantianly banal. The duty at issue here did not open up the expanses of the starry sky, but the usual official channels. First, a smooth path to one's superior had to be re-established. The poetry of the categorical imperative disintegrated into bureaucratic prose. The Kleve Regional Court President rebuilt a completely destroyed court in a completely destroyed town. His report, literarily faithful to the genre of court minutes, listed difficulties and their overcoming without comment—"Preparation of the necessary rooms … crucial. … On April 12, 1946, 8 rooms were ready for occupancy"—without even a word about *how* any of these heroic deeds were accomplished. The highlight of the review was the opening ceremony, which marked the culmination of twelve months of dedicated service: "Guests included … Short speeches were given … Following the opening, a banquet was held on the garden terrace of the Kock Restaurant on Tiergartenstraße. People sat on garden chairs at garden tables. There was pea soup with bacon. The President of the Higher Regional Court, Lingemann, had donated a few bottles of wine."[76] What more could you want? Sitting comfortably on garden chairs at garden tables. The celebration remained subdued, dignified speeches underscored the significance of the occasion, and local celebrities from the legal world, politics, and society enjoyed a down-to-earth snack in a dignified setting: the legal sense of reality had been restored.

Recycling

And with this restored sense of reality, it was also easy to see that the nothingness around which the reports of the new beginning revolved did indeed cast a long shadow. Law never comes from nothing, neither literally nor almost. All law is linked to a previous history, to the socialization of the personnel, to the customs of the form, to common media, authorities, and arguments. Beginning and end were therefore inextricably intertwined, streaks from the vanished world permeating the chaos. The legal scope of possibilities was not always limited to garden furniture and pea soup. But nowhere was it limitless. In Bautzen, the war had damaged the town and the court as badly as in Kleve, but on orders from the Russians, the newly appointed court president was only allowed to rebuild the prison that the military government had confiscated. The main task there was to repair the windows. As there was no new glass, old glass was used. "To repair the broken windowpanes," the official described his efforts, "the large number of Hitler pictures were removed from their frames, and the resulting glass was used for installation."[77] The systemic upheaval forced a very unique change of perspective. Through the glasses through which the Führer had just stared sternly at the administrators of his ever-shrinking empire, the prisoners of the occupying power now stared into the gray everyday life of the postwar period.

Thus, the legal workers gathered the components for the new legal system from the piles of rubble. File numbers, registries, and deed rolls continued where they had left off at the end of the thousand years, and presumably they even had to, if one did not want to sacrifice bureaucratic clarity to cheap political symbolism. Paper, too, remained the same. Everything that could bear letters was written on: memos, pay slips, personnel lists, land register pages, cost statements, inventory lists—the detritus of the old became the basis of the new judicial administration. Swastikas were everywhere. They had to be removed by hand, torn out of robes, scratched off seals, and pasted over on forms. It was not enough to simply cross out the swastikas, it was sternly warned several times, rather, they had to be made "*completely* unrecognizable."[78]

The Nazi habitus, carefully cultivated for twelve years, repeatedly resurfaced. Even the language itself was difficult to correct. Nazi wording was still popular. In Zittau, the KPD (Communist Party) criticized the—relatively lenient—sentence for a Nazi family in September 1945 and had posters put up publicly declaring the sentence contrary to the "healthy public sentiment" ("*dem gesunden Volksempfinden*"). In 1946, the Aachen Regional Court President diagnosed his residents with "mental degeneracy" ("*seelische Entartungserscheinungen*"). On the occasion of the reopening of his office, the Görlitz Regional Court President saw the widespread divorces of hastily concluded wartime marriages as a "cleansing of the body of the people" ("*Bereinigung des Volkskörpers*") that was, in principle, not undesirable. A lawyer in Freiburg wrote to the local court, in keeping with old habit and without comment, that his client had been "killed in the terrorist attack of November 27, 1944" ("*bei dem Terrorangriff vom 27.11.44 gefallen*"). In Stuttgart, statistics were compiled in 1946 that showed that crime was much higher among Poles than among Germans. However, as was conceded in a state of legal sensitivity, there were also reasons for this "that were not generally to blame on the Poles still here." But whether forced labor or civilian labor, the criminological problem remained the same.[79]

Even among the vast number of legal instruments left behind by the "Third Reich," none were *ipso iure* terminated. Laws and regulations remained in effect for the time being. A return to 1933 was impossible for practical reasons; such a break would have annulled all laws, as well as all contracts, marriages, and tax assessments. The Allies repealed a good two dozen of the notorious Nazi laws in 1945—the large majority disappeared behind the blanket clause of "democracy, civilization, and justice,"[80] which, of course, inspired rather than restricted legal creativity. Whether the application of a norm was required or prohibited by the rule of law could hardly be determined conclusively, and this was compounded by the complete confusion between the zones and districts. Nobody really wanted to know what actually constituted "National Socialist" anymore. There was just as much serious discussion about the state sterilization program, the Treachery Act, and the marriage law reformed in 1938 as about the question of whether the abolition of court holidays in 1935 was ideologically sound. Even in Saxony, where it was solemnly announced that the capitulation had extinguished all state authority and "*all law*," the self-created vacuum was immediately bridged with a universal analogy that helped the allegedly extinguished law to regain validity, now no longer "directly," but "correspondingly."[81] In the French Zone, the same conclusion was reached by claiming that all legal acts based on the Enabling Act were null and void, but had, over the course of twelve years, acquired the status of customary law.[82]

Lis Pendens: The Burden of the Past

This was also the verdict on the dregs of the legal system. The majority of administrative acts, penal orders, and civil proceedings, individually applied for and individually tailored, had remained untouched by the turmoil of politics. Once something entered the legal system, it did not simply disappear. As soon as a court decided to open the main proceedings in criminal law (Section 207 of the Code of Criminal Procedure) or served the complaint in civil law (Sections 253, 263 of the Code of Civil Procedure), the matter could no longer be erased without a trace. The dispute then hung in the archive of the law—a metaphor that originally only referred to the state of limbo before the legal decision, but is said to have reflected an actual practice in the early modern period: the files were hung under the ceiling at the court to protect them from mice.[83] It was therefore quite logical that only the court before which a case had been brought could decide on it—after all, that was the only place where the files were hanging. Nothing had changed in this respect, even if it was now not the mice but the passage of time that had gnawed away at the law. The *lis pendens* prevented the proceedings from being consumed by the adversities of the world.

A considerable part of the reconstruction work therefore consisted of concluding old cases. The daily routine of the law crept back into the limelight and began its further legal processing—swiftly in criminal law, because the Allies had set a clear priority in this regard, but somewhat delayed in civil law because the staff shortages there had taken a toll. Werner Kesseböhmer wrote about the new beginning in Hamm: "A multitude of cases left over from the last months of the war and the bombing period, as well as those that had not yet been concluded, were waiting to be dealt with."[84] At the Celle Higher Regional Court, the President counted 465 open appeals; at the Düsseldorf Regional Court, the new President found over 1,000 outstanding divorces and almost 300 pending appeals when he took office; and more than 600 divorces and over 1,000 criminal cases awaited the legal staff in Chemnitz.[85]

Of course, even *lis pendens* offered no protection against all these persecutions. In criminal law, considerable interventions were sometimes necessary—the ban on retroactive effect was restored, *Volksschädlinge* ("public enemies" or literally "public vermins") no longer existed, special courts and the *Volksgericht* had also been abolished.[86] However, the state's right to punish remained intact. The sentences handed down by the defunct institutions or under application of the incriminated laws had not lost their legal force. Even in the Soviet Zone, the radical proposal—presented with unerring catachresis—to "draw a line through these old matters" was rejected: not only would a general amnesty benefit many Nazis, Ernst Melsheimer argued, but above all, in numerous cases "a substantial moral interest" demanded the continuation of the old criminal proceedings.[87] An automatic legal annulment of particularly offensive convictions—for treason, racial defilement, undermining military morale ("*Wehrkraftzersetzung*"), broadcasting crimes—initially only existed in the American Zone, and from mid-1947 also in the British Zone. Furthermore, the healing effect of the legal process was relied upon: the person concerned filed an application, a court reviewed any political hardship, and enforcement was adjusted if necessary.[88] A looter was no longer a *Volksschädling*, but might still be a thief; a regular customer in court no longer had to fear the "healthy public sentiment," but could still be a habitual criminal.

Even if the sentencing courts were now under Polish or Russian administration, their legacies still required processing. Several prisoners from Pomerania were stranded in Bavaria, and the Munich Local Court now had to rule on their petty thefts. As a rule, sentences were suspended on probation.[89] In Hamburg, the court had to rule on a postal worker who had been sentenced to three years in prison by the German court in Warsaw in 1943 for the theft of field mail. In 1948, the Regional Court reduced the sentence by only one year; after all, one had to consider "that the theft of field mail during a war requires severe atonement."[90] Such considerations were frequently heard. It should not be forgotten *ex post* that criminal law of all civilized nations is harsher in war than in peace. The Cologne General Prosecutor's Office complained that the sentences handed down in the postwar period were "extremely lenient"—especially in comparison to those handed down during the war.[91] The Brandenburg judicial administration even felt compelled to appeal to the courts' conscience, stating that their sentencing practices were now so lenient that they hardly conveyed to the public "the necessary sense of the inviolability of certain legal interests."[92] The jurists were still not entirely comfortable with the new world.

Legal Peace

But just as the state's privilege to punish in criminal law had survived the times, so in civil law the desire for conflict between the parties had come through the war unscathed. Broken marriages remained broken. Those seeking a divorce could often hardly wait for some institution—municipal court, local court, county court, regional court—to finally be available again to free them from the marital yoke. Just one example: in Pomerania, a young couple found marital bliss in 1943. The husband went off to war immediately afterwards but returned home unexpectedly from the front in 1944 and told some stories about an alleged convalescence leave, which earned him a death sentence from the state in early 1945 for desertion and a divorce petition from his wife. After capitulation, only the death sentence—which had not yet been carried out—was lifted. The husband was released from prison. The wife insisted that she wanted to be freed as quickly as possible "from the man who had disappointed her so badly and with whom she could never and would never want to continue the marriage." She prevailed. On 9 October 1946, the Greifswald Regional Court dissolved the marriage and found the husband solely responsible, as his lie had made it impossible for the wife "to continue to show him the respect required by the nature of marriage."[93] In retrospect, it was permissible to lie to the Führer, but not to one's own wife.

The side effects of such lawsuits had not lost their legal relevance either. Disputes over household effects, compensation for breach of engagement, and maintenance payments for illegitimate children continued to be pursued under the new system, where possible. Only a few corrections had to be made to the mostly shoddy evidence. In particular, the hereditary-biological expert opinions with which illegitimate children sought to prove their blood ties to a father unwilling to pay were discredited for several years and were not used again by the highest courts until 1952.[94]

Broken contractual relationships were also just as broken as before. Contract takes precedence over law, that is a good liberal tradition, and therefore purchase contracts, work contracts, or tenancy contracts only rarely had to be influenced by the turmoil of politics. Where the outstanding payment of armaments or even their acceptance was at issue, the debtor only very rarely managed to hide behind the legislation of the military government or general good faith. Here, too, the general rule was: a contract is a contract.[95] And anyone who wanted to get rid of their tenant did not simply give up their wish just because the land had been occupied in the meantime. A landlady had been fighting bitterly against her tenant since March 1945 in the Esslingen Local Court. In an epic complaint she accused her tenant of a whole series of outrageous offenses: "Wait, you lowlife, I'll wipe you out in private," he had said, hitting her twice on the head with a "wooden scythe," going on to say that she deserved to be "punched in the face," that she was a "whore" who had already "had it with every guy in town," an accusation that was summed up once again in the insult "regimental whore." Peace in the household was finally restored in 1948 by the long-awaited verdict.[96]

The fullness of life returned. In Duisburg, a dispute arose over the painting *Kürassierpatrouille*, which the defendant had acquired in 1941, although it bore the clearly visible note "not for sale" on the back. In 1944, the case was brought before the regional court, and in 1946 the same court certified the purchaser's good faith and awarded him the painting.[97] In Dresden, a singer from the State Opera returned from Russian captivity in September 1945 and immediately resumed his legal dispute against a pharmacy that had mixed ten times the amount of zinc chloride into his medication instead of two percent. The singer had lost his voice, and the opera dismissed him in 1944, thus not only ending a brilliant career—even the conductor Karl Böhm had supported the lawsuit with a favorable testimonial—but also his annual salary of an astronomical 23,000 Reichsmarks. A final hearing of evidence failed on 20 April 1945, because the expert witness—who could blame him?—had complained of a lack of the "necessary composure and calm." Of course, composure and calm were rare resources even in postwar Dresden, so clarifying the facts of the case remained difficult.

The consequences of the medical malpractice were likely primarily psychological, and the files of almost everyone involved had been burned. It took another three years until the Higher Regional Court awarded the plaintiff almost 44,000 Reichsmarks and a declaration that any further damages were to be borne by the defendant.[98]

In Zwickau, two former housemates were arguing over the costs of a move, which the defendant had agreed to pay. But the plaintiff had moved her residence at the beginning of 1944 for the outrageous sum of 1,600 Reichsmarks, employed two packers for four days, and even insured everything. The defendant wanted to pay at most half. An epic hearing dragged on into April 1945, and an expert opinion attempted to clarify the reasonableness of packing costs and tips. The decisive opinion of *Reichsverkehrsgruppe Spedition und Lagerei* (Reich Transport Group Freight Forwarding and Warehousing) was lost in the air war. Things did not resume until September 1945, but then they were just as lively as before: haulage contractors appeared as witnesses, manuals provided information on usual transport costs, the postal service repeatedly caused difficulties, and on 16 June 1949, a record that precisely reflected world history stated, "The motions made in the oral hearing on July 12, 1944 will be repeated due to a change of judge"—there had indeed been a change of judge since 1944. A judgment in favor of the plaintiff followed in 1951, then a dismissed appeal a year later, and finally—legal peace.[99]

Judicial Syllogism

And why not? "War" is not a legal argument, and neither is "peace." The law is tied to the political order, to the orders, decrees, ordinances, and laws that the political arena separates out, and yet "politics" is not a quantifiable currency in legal discourse. What happens in world history, no matter how drastic, must first be translated into legal vocabulary to be heard in the world of law. Herbert Ruscheweyh, President of the Hanseatic Higher Regional Court in Hamburg, expressed this strange regularity in 1947 as follows: "Since the occupying power did not allow a revolution, the German jurist logically had to recognize the continuity of the law, even with regard to individual legal and administrative acts from the past National Socialist era."[100] The time between the years—does it still belong to the old year or already to the new? Sometimes one way and sometimes the other, and before the introduction of the Gregorian calendar, both. The earth may have been without form and void, but the legal master narrative was still intact: Revolution 0, continuity 1.

Notes

1. Preface, in: *Deutsche Rechts-Zeitschrift* 1 (1946), 1. Similarly, Schmid, *Justiz in der Bundesrepublik*, 12; Hassemer, "Strafrechtswissenschaft," 259.
2. Erdsiek, "Chronik," 18, 19. Similarly, the Higher Regional Court President for Düsseldorf to the Department of Justice (*Ministerium der Justiz* or "JM") of North Rhein-Westphalia (or "NRW"), 19 November 1947, in: LAV NRW-R, RWN 139 No. 11, p. 11; Regional Court President for Aachen to the Higher Regional Court President for Cologne, 20 January 1947, in: LAV NRW-R, Ger. Rep. 255 No. 176, p. 58).
3. Final report of the Ministry of Justice of Württemberg-Hohenzollern, 1952, in: StAS, Wü 2 T 1 No. 456/4, p. 14.
4. Higher Regional Court President for Cologne to JM NRW, 15 November 1947, in: LAV NRW-R, Ger. Rep. 255 No. 84, p. 116; similarly, memorial report by Werner Kesseböhmer, 1967, in: LAV NRW-R, RWN 139 No. 8, p. 5; Kewer, "Aus der Geschichte," 107.
5. Rechenschaftsbericht 1946, quoted from Benjamin (ed.), *Zur Geschichte der Rechtspflege*, 44; Hoeniger, "Justiz in Brandenburg," 192.
6. Ostler, *Die deutschen Rechtsanwälte*, 307; Günther, "Kammergericht soll bleiben," 71.
7. All this according to Scholz, *Berlin und seine Justiz*, 13.
8. Regional Court President for Weimar to the American military government, 19 April 1945, in: HStAW, LG Weimar No. 135, p. 1.
9. Essen and Paderborn: memorial report by Werner Kesseböhmer, 1967, in: LAV NRW-R, RWN 139 No. 8, p. 73; Schwaan: President District Court Güstrow to Mayor for Güstrow, 16 June 1945, in: LHAS 5.12-6/5 No. 181, p. 5; Neunburg: Local Court for Neunburg v.W. to the Regional Court President for Amberg, 12 September 1945, in: the StAA, StA Amberg No. 172, p. 35; Königsbrück: Mayor for Königsbrück to the regional judicial authority (LV Sachsen Abt. Justiz), 4 April 1946, in HStAD 11380 No. 199 (unpaginated); Lausick: Mayor of Lausick to the Local Court for Borna, 30 August 1945, in: HStAD, 11380 No. 221, p. 2.
10. See Wrobel, *Verurteilt zur Demokratie*, 131. Also noteworthy is the communication from the Regional Court President for Bonn to the Higher Regional Court President for Köln, 29 January 1947, in: LAV NRW-R, Ger. Rep. 255 No. 176, p. 63, which warns that the black market threatens to morally corrupt the "formerly so inviolably clean civil service" and to "balkanize the entire public life."
11. Bailiff Bender to the Local Court for Baden-Baden, 15 March 1947, in: the StAF, C 20/1 No. 158, p. 130
12. Zentral-Justizamt, Protokoll der Justizministerkonferenz, 5 February 1948, in: LAV NRW-R, NW 189 No. 1142, p. 1. Similarly, Report on the rebuilding of the judiciary's personnel in the Higher Regional Court for Düsseldorf note, 3 November 1948, in: LAV NRW-R, RWN 139 No. 11, p. 7; Freiherr von Hodenberg, "Der Aufbau der Rechtspflege," 138. On the whole: Busam, *Kriegsfolgenbewältigung*, 61–64.
13. A *Rundverfügung* or "RV," i.e., a circular issued by a ministry, addressed to subordinate authorities, MdJ Saxony, 3 February 1949, in: StACh, 30096 No. 8844, p. 189.
14. *Das Neue Baden*, 27 February 1948, here according to StAF, C 20/1 No. 157, p. 71. Further references in Biess, *Republik der Angst*, 73.
15. Regional Court President for Aachen to the Higher Regional Court President for Cologne, 20 January 1947, in: LAV NRW-R, Ger. Rep. 255 No. 176, p. 58.

16. See Glöckner, "Die Auflösung des Reichsgerichts," 421–456. The quoted report can be found in BA, DP 1 No. 29, p. 29.
17. The travel reports can be found in BA, DP 1 No. 5603, No. 7347.
18. One of the conscripts reported to a former comrade-in-arms, half bitter and half astonished: "So we were able to celebrate an unexpected reunion with our files" (letter from Amtsrat Becker to Klempke, 4 December 1945, in: BA, DP 1 No. 7347, p. 311). The collection was dissolved at the end of 1946: a large part moved to the *Document Center* in Berlin, while smaller holdings were transferred to the Federal Archives in Koblenz from 1952.
19. General Instructions No. 2; *Allgemeinverfügung* (or "AV," a "general order" addressed to a wider audience), Chef der Justizverwaltung (Head of the Judicial Administration), 20 October 1945, in: StAF, C 20/1 No. 230, p. 2; RV LV Sachsen Abt. Justiz No. 25, 25 September 1945, in: BA, DP 1 No. 6370.
20. Thus, the Handbook for Military Government, quoted from Gerhardt, *Soziologie der Stunde Null*, 338 footnote 109.
21. On 4 June 1945, see LHAS 5.12-6/5 No. 181, pp. 1 et seq.
22. Stralsund: Decisions of June/July 1945, in: LAG, Rep. 77 Stralsund No. 1034, pp. 1, 15; No. 825, pp. 1, 12, 40; Weimar: Announcement, end of April 1945, in: HStAW, Regional Court for Thüringen No. 136, p. 13; Order of the mayor of Zittau, 20 July 1945, in: StA Dresden, 11380 No. 221 (unpaginated); Stadt Görlitz, Rechtsamt an LV Sachen Abt. Justiz, 28 August 1945, in: HStAD, 11380 No. 257 (unpaginated); Gericht Neustrelitz an Ministerpräsidium, Abteilung Justiz, 24 October 1945, in: LHAS, 6.16-6 No. 59.
23. Kempten: Raim, *Justiz zwischen Diktatur und Demokratie*, 76; Neustadt: above chapter 5; Perleberg: Pohl, *Justiz in Brandenburg 1945–1955*, 16 footnote 29; Burgstädt (limited to voluntary jurisdiction): LV Sachsen, Abt. Justiz, Bericht, 20 June 1945, in: HStAD, 11380 No. 285, p. 1; Annaberg: reports in HStAD, 11380 No. 237, p. 3 (14 June 1945) and No. 285, p. 13 (undated).
24. Head of Greifswald Municipal Court to Greifswald Mayor, 28 May 1945, in: LAG, Rep. 76 Greifswald No. 352, p. 4. The appointment in the old occupation: LAG, O 6/1945, in: ibid., Rep. 76 Greifswald No. 2114.
25. Local Court of Aachen, note dated 1 October 1962.
26. Tuttlingen: Final report of the Ministry of Justice Württemberg-Hohenzollern, 1952, in: StAS, Wü 2 T 1 No. 456/4, p. 13; Deggendorf: Raim, op. cit., 76. Plauen: Report Local Court for Plauen, 14 May 1945, in: HStAD, 11380 No. 280, pp. 1–3; Leipzig: Local Court President for Leipzig to LV Sachsen Abt. Justiz, 27 August 1945, in: HStAD, 11380 No. 264 (unpaginated). Ueckermünde: District Court Ueckermünde to President Mecklenburg-Vorpommern Dept. of Justice, 19 August 1945, in: LHAS 6.16-6 No. 202 (unpaginated). Stralsund: Stralsund District Court to President Mecklenburg-Vorpommern Dept. of Justice, 15 August 1945, in: LAG, Rep. 77 Stralsund No. 804, p. 23; Stralsund, in: ibid., No. 1039, p. 4. Anklam: Anklam District Court to President Mecklenburg-Vorpommern Dept. of Justice, 16 August 1945, in: LHAS 6.16-6 No. 202 (unpaginated).
27. On Cologne and Siegburg, Higher Regional Court President for Cologne to JM NRW, 1 April 1947, in: LAV NRW-R, NW 189 No. 1181, pp. 29, 31; Zwickau: Local Court for Zwickau to LV Sachsen Abt. Justiz, 31 July 1945, in: StACh, 30145 AG Zwickau Nachtrag 353, p. 98. See also the judgment of the Local Court for Aue of 23 May 1945, in: ibid, 30100 AG Aue Nachtrag 112, and the report of the Local Court for Aue to LV Sachsen Abt. Justiz, 27 July 1945, in: HStAD, 11380 No. 238, unpaginated.

28. Trier: Kann, "Geschichte des Landgerichtsbezirks Trier," 158 et seq. Jena: Minutes of the meeting between the Higher Regional Court of Jena and the Military Government, in: HStAW, OLG Erfurt No. 7, p. 13, Bamberg (28 May): Raim, op. cit. 75 et seq.; Holzminden: Freiherr von Hodenberg, "Der Aufbau der Rechtspflege," 124. The—handwritten—list in LAH, Nds. 710 Acc. 124/87 No. 53, p. 34, notes 3 August as the opening date for Holzminden. Swinemünde (30 May): Usedom District Court to President Mecklenburg-Vorpommern Dept. of Justice, 16 August 1945, in: LHAS 6.16-6 No. 202 (unpaginated) and No. 203/2.
29. Order of the City Commandant of Berlin, 25 May 1945, in: Dokumente, No. 13; RV des Stadtpräsidenten Berlin, June 1945, in: BA, DP 1 No. 9, p. 1; Berger, "Aus der ersten Zeit," 267 et seq.; Scholz, op. cit., 6–15.
30. Chief judicial inspector Wolkenstein, undated (probably 13 June 1945), in: HStAD, 11380 No. 237, pp. 6 et seq. The local court was a branch of the Local Court for Annaberg.
31. Speculation: Kesseböhmer, Erinnerungsbericht, 1967, in: LAV NRW-R, RWN 139 No. 8, p. 14; Humiliation: Schorn, *Festgabe*, 135; Reflection: Roemer, "Wiederaufbau des Rechts," 93.
32. Weber, *Wirtschaft und Gesellschaft*, 669.
33. See, for example, Thierack, speech at the meeting of the Higher Regional Court Presidents and General Prosecutors in Kochem, 23–25 May 1944, in: HStAW, Thüringisches OLG Jena No. 1166, p. 139 (Schubert, 544 et seq.).
34. Directive of the American military administration, quoted from Görtemaker/Safferling, *Die Akte Rosenburg*, 74 footnote 168.
35. RV *Badische Landesdirektion für Justiz* (the Baden Regional Directorate for Justice), 10 August 1946, in: StAF, C 20/1 No. 151, p. 16. Similarly, RV of the Higher Regional Court President for Hamm, 8 August 1945, in: LAV NRW-OL, D 20 B No. 2571, p. 44; Werner Baerns, Interview mit Joachim Wenzlau, 16 May 1973 (PA Wenzlau, Abt. Interviews).
36. Letter from the mayor of Rastatt, 3 April 1946, in: StAF, C 20/1 No. 154, p. 26. The obligation to work goes back to Control Council Order No. 3 of 17 January 1946. On the confiscations, see, for example, Badisches JM to President of the Baden State Administration, 26 August 1946, in: StAF, C 20/1 No. 161, p. 4; Regional Court President for Detmold to Military Government, 31 May 1945, in: LAV NRW-OL, D 20 B No. 2232, p. 305.
37. Cf. Scholz, op. cit. 76 f.
38. Correspondence between the Military Government/Regional Court President for Detmold, 12, 14, 16 and 21 June 1945, in: LAV NRW-OL, D 20 B No. 2232, files 326 and 330; Regional Court President for Detmold to the Local Court for Lemgo and Bad Salzuflen, 6 August 1945, in: LAV NRW-OL, D 20 B No. 2571, p. 36.
39. RV Regional Court President for Heilbronn, 20 June 1945, in: StAL, FL 300/2 I Zugang 1995/81 Bü 37, p. 3.
40. Mistrust: Final report of the Ministry of Justice Württemberg-Hohenzollern, 1952, in: StAS, Wü 2 T 1 No. 456/4, p. 9; Influence: LGP Aachen an OLGP Köln, 20 August 1946, in: LAV NRW-R, Ger. Rep. 255 No. 176, p. 36.
41. See Maier/von Schmoller, *Besatzungsregime*, esp. 21–32; Hetzel, *Militärgerichtsbarkeit*; Röhreke, *Besatzungsgewalt*; Breuning, *Gerichtsbarkeit*, esp. 101–121; Moritz, *Gerichtsbarkeit*; ibid, *Gerichtsbarkeit. Historische Entwicklung*.
42. Regional Court President for Celle (Gerhard Erdsiek), note January 1946, in: LAH, Nds. 710 Acc. 124/87 No. 10, p. 7.

43. For example, Local Court for Zella-Mehlis to the Higher Regional Court President for Gera, 28 August 1945, in: HStAW, OLG Erfurt No. 7, pp. 3 et seq.; Scholz, op. cit., 5.
44. For example: Communication from Greifswald Municipal Court to the Mecklenburg-Western Pomerania State Administration, Justice Department, 28 July 1945, in: LAG, Rep. 76 Greifswald No. 352, p. 18. The person concerned soon returned there, however.
45. Pasewalk: Regional Court President for Stettin (currently Greifswald) to the Higher Regional Court President for Stettin (Greifswald), 25 May 1945, in: LAG, Rep. 76 Stettin (new) No. 165, p. 118; Kreisgericht Ueckermünde to Ministerpräsident Mecklenburg-Vorpommern, Hauptabteilung Justiz, 19 August 1945, in: LHAS, 6.16-6 No. 202 (unpaginated).
46. Reprinted in: Documents, No. 48.
47. Minutes of the State Conference of the Administration of Justice of 1–2 November 1946, in: HStAW, Land Thüringen—Ministerium der Justiz No. 55, p. 40.
48. For example, at the Annaberg Local Court, where the two judges were dismissed on 28 September (Regional Court President for Chemnitz to LV Sachsen Abt. Justiz, 2 October 1945, in: HStAD, 11380 [unpaginated]), or at the Anklam, Hagenow, Penkun, Ueckermünde, and Usedom Local Courts (Bartusel, "*Generalstaatsanwalt*," 104 footnote 209).
49. Regional Court President for Freiberg to LV Sachsen Abt. Justiz, 9 April 1946, in: HStAD, 11380 No. 69 (unpaginated).
50. For the fall of 1945, see for example the Plauen District Court proceedings in StACh, 30096 No. 2168, 2209.
51. LV Sachsen Abt. Justiz to the Soviet Military Administration in Saxony ("SMAS"), 8 January 1947, in: HStAD, 11380 No. 59, p. 142.
52. Overview of appointments, as of 1 October 1946, in: BA, DP 1 No. 883, p. 7.
53. *Tägliche Rundschau*, 20 September 1945, here according to LAG, Rep. 77 Stralsund No. 812, p. 2. More detailed Schiffer, *Die deutsche Justiz*.
54. President of Thuringia, Circular 37/46, here according to AV of the Higher Regional Court for Jena, 21 February 1946, in: HStAW, OLG Erfurt No. 9, p. 8; LV Sachsen Abt. Justiz, RV No. 137, here in: StACh, 30145 No. 5513, p. 77.
55. Head of Greifswald Municipal Court to Greifswald Soviet Intelligence Office, 17 December 1945, in: LAG, Rep. 76 Greifswald No. 352, p. 99.
56. MdJ Thüringen, Fünf Jahre Aufbau der Justiz in Thüringen, in: HStAW, MdJ No. 34, p. 12.
57. The person concerned, Paul Andrich, was a fully qualified jurist, had been an advocate since 1914 and a notary in Greifswald since 1920 (personnel files of Paul Andrich, in: BA, R 3001 No. 50299; curriculum vitae also in LAG, Rep. 76 Greifswald No. 352, p. 57).
58. Regional Court President for Aachen to the Higher Regional Court President for Cologne, 20 August 1946, in: LAV NRW-R, Ger. Rep. 255 No. 176, p. 35.
59. See, for example, the Regional Court President for Bonn to Oberpräsident Bonn, 30 May 1945, in: LAV NRW-R, Ger. Rep. 255 No. 202, p. 180. Werner Kesseböhmer described the first talks with the military government in the same way (memoir, 1967, in: LAV NRW-R, RWN 139 No. 8, pp. 35 et seq.).
60. Koblenz: Erdsiek, "Chronik," 20; Bremen: Wrobel, *Verurteilt zur Demokratie*, 130. Report on the personnel reconstruction of the judiciary in the Higher Regional Court District of Düsseldorf, 3 November 1948, in: LAV NRW-R, RWN 139 No. 11, p. 3. Further figures, all of which speak a similar language: Minutes of a meeting

of the Regional Court President in the Higher Regional Court District of Celle, 2 October 1946, in: LAV NRW-OL, D 20 B No. 2002, p. 389; General Prosecutor Cologne to JM NRW, 20 November 1947, in: LAV NRW-R, Ger. Rep. 255 No. 84, pp. 169 f.; Regional Court President for Cologne to the Higher Regional Court President for Cologne, 7 August 1946, in: LAV NRW-R, Ger. Rep. 255 No. 176, p. 42.

61. Final report of the Ministry of Justice of Württemberg-Hohenzollern, 1952, in: StAS, Wü 2 T 1 No. 456/4, p. 15.
62. General Prosecutor Cologne to JM NRW, 20 November 1947, in: LAV NRW-R, Ger. Rep. 255 No. 84, pp. 169, 172, 174.
63. Control Council Directive No. 24, 12 January 1946, Art. 10 No. 88, in: Abl. KR, 228. Its implementation is confirmed, for example, by the memoirs of Werner Kesseböhmer, 1967, in: LAV NRW-R, RWN 139 No. 8, p. 54. It is all the more astonishing that Rottleuthner, *Karrieren und Kontinuitäten*, 73–78, has proven particularly high continuities for the higher posts.
64. Thus in the memoir of the President of the Senate at the Higher Regional Court of Cologne, Floß, 1968, in: LAV NRW-R, RWN 139 No. 5, p. 82.
65. See minutes of the meeting between the judicial administration of the French Zone and the military government, 11 May 1946, in: StAF, C 20/1 No. 274.
66. Higher Regional Court President for Celle at a meeting of the Higher Regional Court Presidents for Hamburg, Celle, Braunschweig, Oldenburg, 27 September 1945, in: LAH, Nds. 710 Acc. 124/87 No. 47, pp. 1 et seq.
67. Regional Court President for Bonn to Military Government, 22 June 1945, in: LAV NRW-R, Ger. Rep. 255 No. 202, p. 192. Further evidence in Busam, *Kriegsfolgenbewältigung*, 49 et seq.; Biess, *Republik der Angst*, 78 et seq.
68. See, for example, the Higher Regional Court President for Celle to Military Government, 15 January 1946, in: LAV NRW-R, Ger. Rep. 86 No. 169.
69. Minutes and memo of 24 October 1945 can be found in: LAH, Nds. 710 Acc. 124/87 No. 47, pp. 47 et seq., 57 et seq.
70. Bericht über den personellen Wiederaufbau der Justiz im OLGB Düsseldorf, 3 November 1948, in: LAV NRW-R, RWN 139 No. 11, p. 6. Statistical data in Rottleuthner, *Karrieren und Kontinuitäten*, 58 et seq. Of course, one should not lightly assume that two former party members are twice as bad as one. In this respect, the talk of "renazification" is misleading.
71. Weber, *Wirtschaft und Gesellschaft*, 669.
72. Recollection report by Werner Kesseböhmer, 1967, in: LAV NRW-R, RWN 139 No. 8, p. 16.
73. The Higher Regional Court President for Düsseldorf to JM NRW, 19 November 1947, in: LAV NRW-R, RWN 139 No. 11, p. 16. Similarly, Freiherr von Hodenberg, "Der Aufbau der Rechtspflege," 139, who reports how all employees "honestly and faithfully did their duty."
74. Final report of the Ministry of Justice of Württemberg-Hohenzollern, 1952, in: StAS, Wü 2 T 1 No. 456/4, p. 21).
75. von Löwenstein/Zühlsdorff, *Deutschlands Schicksale*, 24.
76. Memoirs of the then Regional Court President for Kleve, 26 June 1967, in: LAV NRW-R, RWN 139 No. 6, p. 50.
77. Provisional Board of Directors of the Local Court for Bautzen to LV Sachsen Abt. Justiz, 25 July 1945, in: HStAD, 11380 No. 241, pp. 3 et seq.

78. Here: Oberpostdirektion Schwerin to President Mecklenburg-Vorpommern, 29 January 1946, in: LHAS, 5.12-6/5 No. 198 (unpaginated). For numerous examples, see Wrobel, *Verurteilt zur Demokratie*, 128.
79. Popular sentiment: BA, DP 1 No. 8, p. 102; Entartung: Regional Court President for Aachen, Lagebericht, 20 August 1946, in: LAV NRW-R, Ger. Rep. 255 No. 176, p. 25; Volkskörper: Regional Court President for Görlitz to LV Sachsen Abt. Justiz, 6 April 1946, in: HStAD, 11380 No. 69 (unpaginated); terror attack: Local Court for Freiburg, 3 C 20/1944, written statement of 20 April 1948, in: StAF, E 159/1 Paket 22 No. 443, p. 97; statistics: correspondence between the Ministry of Justice of Württemberg and the Military Government, 13 June/18 July 1946, in: HStAS, EA 4/001 Bü 104, Vorgang 16.
80. Here: Control Council Proclamation No. 3, 20 October 1945 (Abl. KR, 22).
81. See consultation between the Saxony Justice Administration and the Justice Ministry of the Soviet Occupation Zone, 19–25 September 1945, in: BA, DP 1 No. 8, p. 13.
82. Higher Regional Court for Tübingen, judgment of 17 April 1947, in: *Deutsche Rechts-Zeitschrift* 1947, 141–143.
83. See Vismann, *Akten*, 177.
84. Memoirs of Werner Kesseböhmer, 1967, in: LAV NRW-R, RWN 139 No. 8, p. 70. Similarly, the Higher Regional Court President for Düsseldorf to JM NRW, 19 November 1947, in: LAV NRW-R, RWN 139 No. 11, p. 21.
85. Correspondence between the Military Government and the Higher Regional Court President for Celle, April 1945, in: LAH, Nds. 710 Acc. 124/87 No. 84, pp. 7 et seq.; Regional Court President to the Higher Regional Court President for Düsseldorf, 14 November 1945, in: LAV NRW-R, Ger. Rep. 142 No. 210, p. 60; Regional Court President for Chemnitz to LV Sachsen Abt. Justiz, 4 October 1945, in: HStAD, 11380 No. 245 (unpaginated).
86. Control Council Law No. 1, 20 September 1945 (OJ KR, 6). Similarly, Eisenhower's Proclamation No. 1, 18 September 1944 (in: Sammlung; SHAEF); Law No. 1; Control Council Proclamation No. 3, 20 October 1945, including instructions on enforcement (OJ KR, 22).
87. Minutes of the state conference of 3 May 1946, in: BA, DP 1 No. 7163/1, pp. 31–38, 34.
88. A complete overview of the relevant provisions in the western zones can be found in the memorandum of the Federal Ministry for Justice, 20 February 1952, in: BAK, B 141 No. 1800, pp. 114–116. Supplements on the Soviet Zone in Kluckhohn, "Chronik," 183.
89. Local Court for Stolp 4 Ds 217/1943 and 4 Ds 336/1943, both in: GStA PK, XV. HA Rep. 77 AG Stolp No. 1521 and 1522, also StA Reichenberg, 5 K Ls 6/1944, in: BA, R 137 II No. 71.
90. The entire case can be found in BA, R 137 I No. 142.
91. General Prosecutor Cologne to JM NRW, 20 November 1947, in: LAV NRW-R, Ger. Rep. 255 No. 84, p. 173.
92. Quarterly report of the Brandenburg Justice Department, 15 July 1946, quoted from Pohl, *Justiz in Brandenburg 1945–1955*, 64.
93. Regional Court Greifswald, R 31/1945, judgment of 22 August 1946, in: LAG, Rep. 76 Greifswald No. 4178.
94. See Bedau, *Entnazifizierung*, 246–264 and Grieß, *Im Namen des Rechts*, 263–268.
95. Numerous references to case law and literature in Busam, *Kriegsfolgenbewältigung*, 109–121.
96. Local Court for Esslingen, C 17–18/1945, in: StAL, FL 300/10 II No. 639.

97. Regional Court for Duisburg 3 O 31/1944, judgment of 8 October 1946, in: LAV NRW-R, Ger. Rep. 3 No. 247.
98. Higher Regional Court for Dresden, 5 U 170/1944, in: HStAD, 11030 No. 133.
99. Local Court for Zwickau, 15 C 269/1944, in: StACh, 30145 No. 5654.
100. Ruscheweyh, "Entwicklung," 1947, 51. Similarly for the judiciary, Bosch, *Zivilgerichtsbarkeit*, 7.

Chapter 7

Winding Up

The War and Its Long End

Self-Delusion: The Justitium of 1945

On 9 May 1945, shortly after eight o'clock in the evening, the Wehrmacht declared the end of its military campaign. "Since midnight, the guns have been silent on the fronts," announced a final Wehrmacht report, adding that the "almost six-year, honorable struggle" was over.[1] The unconditional surrender, signed in Reims early in the morning on 7 May, took effect at 11.01 p.m. on 8 May. Until then, war had been the vanishing point of all state action. Now peace became the problem. What the war had failed to achieve, only the end of war achieved: the suspension of law. Not everywhere, and certainly not everywhere at the same time, but where the Allied troops had pacified the country, one of their first official acts was to close the courts. The war, after all the only legally regulated condition for a *Justitium*, had not been enough to bring about a suspension of law, but its end had. The legal world was upside down.

Adolf Baumbach's bold proclamation, first uttered in 1936, that even the simultaneous "death of all judges" would not bring about a suspension of law,[2] was now put to a distressing test. Not that all judges were dead, that was far from the case. However, it could not be overlooked that the doctrine of the Code of Civil Procedure had been conceived for times of peace, when legal creativity had been able to indulge its fascination for extreme cases so freely because it was certain that they would never occur. Everyone knew that all judges would never die at the same time. But no one knew what to do now that they had survived cryonics. Because the Allies had not occupied the entire country in one fell swoop, it was not possible to make universally valid statements. For the district of the Karlsruhe Higher Regional Court alone, a chronological overview revealed that the end of the war had dragged on for several weeks, and even for this dating, individual municipalities that the Allies had only reached in June had to be disregarded.[3] Moreover, the occupation of a town, as was known, said nothing about the occupation of the court there, because the authorities had often been relocated. It was therefore unknown when the suspension began and when it ended. Literarily, Sleeping Beauty did not know how long her sleep had lasted.

There was no clarification in sight. In some cases, the usual makeshift solution was offered—rejecting any generalization and instead declaring the specifics of the individual case to be inescapable. The Cologne Higher Regional Court, for example, in whose district countless court displacements had taken place, wanted to assume for the benefit of the population that the first relocation of an authority had already established a *Justitium*, whereby it was then "clear" that its exact duration could only be determined "on a case-by-case basis."[4] The Hamm Higher Regional Court appealed to the right brain of its subordinates and advised that one should "not be narrow-minded" when examining individual hardships.[5]

In view of the total defeat, however, this total dilatory approach was an imposition even for the most hardened dogmatists. The judicial administrations soon issued decrees to establish something like legal time zones beyond individual cases. In the British-occupied zone, the presidents of the higher regional courts announced the suspension of law, at least in their own districts.[6] Under the French, where the reopening of the courts had only begun in October, a zone-wide decree was issued that generally limited the suspension of law to the period from 1 April to 20 October 1945.[7] In the Soviet Occupation Zone, Order No. 49 of the Soviet Military Administration (SMAD), which ordered the reorganization of the judicial system by 1 October, allowed for the reverse conclusion that the law had been suspended until 30 September.[8]

But such constructions had a high price and offered little benefit. Administratively, suspending the law was only possible since the so-called Protection Ordinance of 4 December 1943,[9] which, in the service of total war, delegated to the administration a competence that had previously been left to the judiciary. The determinations of the beginning and end of the *Justitium*, made after the Allied invasion, repeated this completely unacceptable encroachment on the autonomy of the courts. The only gain was actually in terms of calculating the statute of limitations. But there was little to be gained in this respect: in all matters relating to the statute of limitations, a universal suspension had been in effect since 1944, which was maintained in all zones until the end of 1946, and in the western zones even well beyond that.[10]

What shone through here was, above all, legal illusion. The *Justitium* was answering a question that nobody had asked. Fearing the incompleteness of their world, the jurists created a file card even for nothingness. And that is why even the *Reichsgericht* ("Supreme Court of the Reich") had something to say about this matter. On 18 April 1945, the Americans occupied Leipzig and closed the court—supposedly temporarily. Two days later, President Erwin Bumke left office by suicide. On 14 May, the Leipzig Local Court was reopened under the commitment to democracy and the rule of law.[11] All of this was also followed closely at the *Reichsgericht*. On 17 May, its presidium, now represented by Eugen Kolb, added a memorandum for the files, which reached the official conclusion "that the conditions for a suspension of law have been met."[12] Even one's own death certificate needs an acknowledgement of receipt, and before the *Reichsgericht* settled into its new normality, it barricaded its gates with the solid fittings of a semantic paradox.

Banning the War From the Law

This set the tone. The past could not simply rest, but at the same time, it eluded legal resolution. On the path from war to peace, the law sputtered again and again. Time could be frozen with a suspension of law, but only legal time, not universal time. Only in a Grimm Brothers' fairy tale would the flies remain and the roast continue to sizzle in the fire uninterrupted after a hundred years. Legal time, on the other hand, now had to find its way in a new world. This new normality was obviously no longer the old one; what was needed at first, therefore, were landmarks, reference points, to somehow relate the old and the new normal to each other. With their efforts to ensure an orderly resolution of the war, however pointless it might be in individual cases, the jurists created a kind of narrative framework that reconstructed even the most radical transposition according to the rules of classical harmony.

This applied to all legal fields. If the war truly was the father of all things, then there were now many things that had lost their father, that had been abandoned by the *Weltgeist* and were now waiting to be freed from their masterless existence by a new era. The end of the war not only rendered the courts unemployed but had also deprived numerous laws and ordinances of their *raison d'*être. Until 1945, laws and regulations had repeatedly been issued that expressly suspended, relaxed, or tightened individual provisions and legal consequences "for the duration of the war," both on a large and small scale. Even in quite inconspicuous ordinances such as the new regulation about international health insurance or the demurrage charge for inland waterway shipping,[13] the war was not merely a matter of bureaucratic resource allocation, but also a national hardship and a national sanctuary. This became even clearer in other regulations. Church holidays were moved to Sundays to increase the labor effort for final victory, authorities could prohibit civilian traffic so that the last of the fuel could be used for the war effort, prison sentences during the war were not taken into account in the execution.[14] Some regulations provided for their automatic termination as soon as the war was over, others promised an explicit repeal, and still others did not even mention the possibility that they might be valid at some point during peacetime. Systematic overviews of judicial administrations ultimately counted no fewer than 122 laws and regulations in which the war was explicitly declared the time horizon of a legal norm.[15] The first thing to be banned from the legal system was therefore the war itself. In the words of the President of the Cologne Higher Regional Court, it was necessary to "replace the emergency law created during the war … with normal regulations."[16]

This was a challenging undertaking. For the legal world, only the fighting had ceased. The war, on the other hand, needed a peace treaty, a legal conclusion that also ended its existence in a legal sense. Unilaterally declaring the unconditional surrender to be the official end of the war was out of the question without the agreement of the victorious powers. Nothing was to be expected in this regard until the summer of 1946. The military governments made it clear on several occasions that they would reject any general definition of the end of the war as an act of state arrogance. In the French Zone, the German judicial administration was forced to revise its presumptuous determination of the end of the war as 8 May and to declare the war as yet unfinished.[17] The British military government was quoted as confirming that "His Majesty is still at war with Germany;" any practice to the contrary was to be stopped, and in particular all proceedings in which a judicial interpretation declared the war to be over were to be "struck down or suspended."[18] They went even further in the American Zone. The military government rejected a draft decree that merely affirmed the continuation of the war, because even this purely declaratory proclamation encroached on the powers of the Allies. The result was a law that declared "the temporary non-occurrence of the legal consequences linked to the concept of the end of the war."[19] Nothing could be said about the war, so a description of its shadow had to suffice.

Admittedly, this rhetorical tension had fatal consequences for the 122 legal regulations, whose validity was expressly linked to the duration of the war. The state of exception for which they were intended was threatened with legal perpetuation for constitutional reasons.

To overcome this dilemma, the legal practitioners' differentiation capabilities devised a whole series of ways to secretly transfer the matter of end of the war to a German interpretation. The situation was most dramatic in the law on missing persons. Missing soldiers were to be declared dead by default one year after the end of the war, which is why an uncontrolled end to the war would have put thousands of prisoners of war at risk of "civilian execution," as observers at the time drastically commented. Ordinances were issued everywhere to avoid this—*contra legem*—which made the start of the one-year period dependent on special regulations of the judicial administration, i.e., again starting with the casting of shadows: whether the war was still ongoing was something only others could say, and whether this had legal consequences was left to the lawyers.[20] In private law, the autonomy of the contracting parties helped, supported in an emergency by the venerable phrase *falsa demonstratio non nocet.* Even the term "the end of the war" was ultimately a matter of interpretation, and it was easily conceivable that contracting parties had spoken of the "end of the war" but had not actually meant the "end of the war" at all. Particularly in leasehold law, where the war had provided the automatic extension of all fixed-term land leases during its duration,[21] the actual end of the war was thus declared to be a matter of individual cases.

The Allies' harsh rhetoric therefore had no real impact. German jurists worked painstakingly to digest the end of the war. At the end of 1945, the Hamm Higher Regional Court ruled—against the instructions of its own military government—that in terms of leasehold matters, the war had ended on 8 May 1945. The lease regulations were themselves measures taken on the occasion of the "total war,"[22] and when they referred to the end of the war, this actually meant the end of the total war, which, as a propaganda stunt by Goebbels, certainly did not require a legal conclusion. The Celle Higher Regional Court took the opposite view: precisely because the war had resulted in a total collapse, its end could not simply be implicitly read into the end of hostilities but required a proper peace treaty.[23] The Oldenburg Regional Court supplemented this view with considerations of *ratio legis*—the supply situation had "deteriorated considerably" since the capitulation, and therefore the existing lease agreements had to remain untouched for the time being—but itself disavowed this essentially understandable consideration by insisting, in open contradiction to its own decision, that the end of the war could not be determined by a court, but required a uniform regulation by the legislature. To conclude the legal hell ride, it cited not the relevant directives of the British Military Government as justification, but rather a commentary published in 1944 in the *Deutsche Justiz* by the then-responsible official, Josef Altstötter.[24] And when the military government abandoned its rigid stance in September

1946 and expressly granted the judiciary the right to decide on the end of the war itself, the Hamm Higher Regional Court also ended its special approach and now declared that the war was not yet over in view of the general supply situation.[25]

Total war was thus followed by the total fragmentation of the end of the war. War in the sense of international law was different from war in the legal sense, and this in turn was different from war in contract law, in all conceivable variations. Talk of the unity of the legal order, a popular all-purpose legal weapon at all times, was silenced by *telos* and party will, two even more popular all-purpose weapons. The Cologne Higher Regional Court became a stronghold of decisionism on this issue. In a judgment of 8 July 1948, it began by stating that there was "no uniform concept of 'end of the war'." Instead, the relevant circumstances in each individual case had to be determined through interpretation. And this was not all: "There are no rules of interpretation for this."[26] This was now a universally applicable blank check, interpretation without a goal or path, legal action without *telos* and without method—the concept of the end of the war, of all things, brought a belated victory to judicial self-empowerment.

Old New World

This could easily be applied to other areas. Even more numerous than the explicit references to the war, which could somehow be grasped hermeneutically, were the laws with a tacit connection to the war. All the emergency regulations aimed at simplifying judicial business, for example, were implicitly linked to the state of war. University studies had become shorter, examinations easier, and the hurdles on the way to becoming a judge lower. The war authorized courts to postpone legal cases for a lack of wartime importance, and notaries to use a colored printing stamp and a seal without a name instead of the embossed stamp.

The hermeneutic pruning of these special provisions was less problematic insofar as it could be semantically decoupled from the end of the war. Where there was no explicit mention of the war, there was no need to explicitly refer to the end of the war. However, this did not make things any easier. When it came to war, one might think of Carl von Clausewitz or Heinrich von Treitschke; war could be a symbol for scarcity and material hardship, but also for ideological fanaticism, and because scarcity and hardship continued, it was impossible to tell from the countless wartime measures whether they had lost their justification with the end of the military conflict. The strict rationing rules, for example, which had even been publishable by criminal law, had not lost their necessity—quite the contrary. In Greifswald in 1946, a public prosecutor noted, "If a food quota system had not been necessary during the war, it certainly would be now."[27] The "urgency of war" was certainly no longer a suitable filter for processing court applications, but it was equally clear that the shortage of personnel had worsened since 1943 and that the Allies must have had a vague notion of a now decisive "peacetime importance" in mind with their regularly repeated warnings to accept a total loss of civil law in favor of criminal prosecution. The same applied to the one-man composition of many tribunals, which had only become standard procedure during the war, but which could hardly be abandoned now.

The Ludwigsburg Local Court came up with the rather naive suggestion that all regulations that described themselves as "war measures" should no longer be applied, while all others should. The Ministry immediately rejected the suggestion; after all, the titles of laws had often enough simply followed chance, in addition to propagandistic purposes, something they could not rely on.[28] The most detailed statement came from Adolf Schönke, a veteran SA soldier and passionate proceduralist in all areas of law. In August 1945, he presented an expert opinion on the continued validity of wartime procedural law, which was read in all occupation zones, but still did not have much to offer in terms of content.[29] Schönke claimed in general terms that the simplifications had "in part already become irrelevant," which was obviously of little use as long as it was not possible to specify which subject matter was actually at issue. Furthermore, Schönke's approach to the matter was severely under-examined: that superfluous laws could simply repeal or correct themselves had never been argued before in the study of legal sources, not to mention legislative powers and questions of legitimacy.

In this constellation, a genuine legal liberation remained impossible.[30] Just how difficult it was to differentiate between the war as a cause and the war as an intention was demonstrated in a nutshell by the Second War Measures Ordinance of September 1944. The war appeared in many different forms within it as a justification for deep cuts in the judicial system, but also as a central argument for legal protection for broad groups of people. On the one hand, there was Section 7, for example, which had largely abolished the obligation to have a lawyer out of consideration for the general hardship, an option that was now no less necessary than before the capitulation. On the other hand, however, there was a provision such as Section 69, which set a deadline for the higher regional courts within which all pending appeals were to be decided or declared closed. Subsequently, appeals were to be abolished, the higher regional courts were to disappear, and the *Reichsgericht* would remain as the sole appellate instance. The ordinary legal process had been reduced to a torso, and it was not even clear which of the amputations had achieved the force of law. Although the

Reich Ministry of Justice had announced on 1 March 1945 that it would extend the relevant deadline to 30 June 1945, the promised publication in the *Deutsche Justiz* never materialized.

What to do? After a brief consolidation phase, the consensus was that Section 69 should be declared generally inapplicable because its sole purpose—to reduce personnel costs in favor of total war—was obsolete.[31] All appeals were to be considered pending and would have to be decided on the merits as soon as the appeal procedure was available again. But even this achieved little. There was no jurisdiction for the appeals that were still pending before the now incapacitated *Reichsgericht* and, moreover, the war had turned the situation on its head. The higher regional courts, essentially moribund, were now more powerful than ever before in their history, while the *Reichsgericht*, which had sought to elevate the National Socialist martial law to an all-powerful oracle, had effectively disappeared. The levels below had also been thoroughly shaken up. The Cologne Higher Regional Court refused to consider appeals of local court decisions because, according to the old-new court system, the regional courts were responsible for these appeals. However, the regional courts initially refused because such a change of jurisdiction would be contrary to the old-new Code of Civil Procedure.[32] Some suggested establishing a retrial for proceedings already declared closed, but others rejected this proposal due to the already heavy overload of the courts. The Kiel Higher Regional Court President reported that there was no need for such considerations in view of the almost 20 relevant proceedings, while the Aachen Regional Court President could only add that he was completely unaware of the War Measures Ordinance in question, as he had not received the *Reichsgesetzblatt* (Reich Law Gazette) since the evacuation of Aachen.[33]

This was another case in which legal activity and political necessity were by no means aligned. The legal professionals were continuing a systemic narrative that no longer had an audience. At that time, only the *Reichsgericht* kept statistics on the number of appeals, but it was impossible to inquire there, as the court no longer had any public presence after its closure. In August 1945, the court itself mentioned to the German judicial administration that "around 700 civil cases, 80 criminal cases, and 23 labor cases" were still pending. This was probably intended as proof of its own indispensability—it was still expected to be reopened[34]—but in reality, it meant that each higher regional court had a maximum of three dozen cases. Of these, in turn, it could be assumed that a large portion had been resolved due to the war situation, while for the rest, it was difficult even to access the Leipzig files. It was apparently not until the end of 1947 that the Leipzig Local Court, which was responsible for winding up the *Reichsgericht*, issued corresponding rules of procedure. [35]

The lawyers therefore were dealing with a tempest in a teapot, solving a problem that the war itself had already solved. In the end, all that remained of the *Reichsgericht* was its spirit; it found loyal servants in Karlsruhe at the *Bundesgerichtshof*. The enormous library, on the other hand, fell into the hands of the Supreme Court of the GDR. As far as we know, it was hardly ever used.

Settlement Offices

In the transformation from wartime to peacetime normality, lawyers repeatedly succumbed to autosuggestion. They regulated things that could not be regulated. The norms themselves were, in this respect, the most rewarding object. Wartime measures could be abolished or, if they could still be used as peacetime measures, made permanent. But the battlefields were conspicuously full of other relics of the law, with institutions, files, actors, and procedures. This material foundation was far too cumbersome for a transition to peacetime. The legal settlement of the war resembled a large-scale attempt to analyze long-melted snow for its height, consistency, and layering.

Hundreds of courts, for example, had disappeared. In 1944, there had been 34 higher regional courts, a good 200 regional courts, and over 2,000 local courts.[36] Now, eight higher regional courts in the east were under Russian, Polish, or Czechoslovakian administration. Another four were in a country that was no longer called Ostmark but Austria, and even cities like Darmstadt or Kassel were practically excluded from getting their higher regional courts back. No one felt truly responsible for Austria, but on the other side of the Oder and Neisse rivers alone there were six higher regional courts, over 50 regional courts, and almost 550 local courts that had ceased operations.

Only three of them received their own settlement office. The Kattowitz Higher Regional Court, whose administrative staff had worked their way to Gera via Neisse, Ottmachau, Dresden, and Radebeul, continued to operate there briefly after the capitulation until the SMAD prohibited any further activity at the end of July.[37] The Weißenfels Local Court, which administered the meager remains of the Posen Higher Regional Court, closed in the fall of 1945.[38] Neither court seems to have achieved more than an initial sorting of its own files; long lists provided information about the evacuated property brought with them, the administration of which was now the responsibility of other institutions. The work was only somewhat more successful in Greifswald: the Stettin Regional Court and Higher Regional Court had moved there in March 1945 and remained after the capitulation until they were officially dissolved on 30 June.[39] When a report about a break-in in the court cellar was still being addressed to the Stettin Higher Regional Court at the beginning of August, the Greifswald City Court reacted with noticeable anger and instructed the President of the Higher Regional Court—who no longer existed—to no longer accept any correspondence and to forward all mail directly. By express order of the Minister of Justice, all judicial matters in the district were to be handled exclusively by the City Court.[40]

Now all that remained was self-administration. The once stately Stettin Higher Regional Court, housed in the palace of the old Dukes of Pomerania until 1944, shrank to one measly room and now operated under the name "Regional Court Building Room 14 (formerly Stettin Higher Regional Court)."[41] A lone senior judicial inspector continued to operate the asylum, originally conceived as a reception center, more or less privately as a settlement office. The matter was too insignificant for the military government to intervene. The Stettin inventory had long since been transferred to other authorities, three typewriters from the Higher Regional Court were transferred to the Greifswald Local Court, and furniture, office equipment, and the library were taken over in Pölitz.[42] The Greifswald Regional Court President attested to the dedicated administrator's "fairly considerable amount of work," which took up four to five hours of his time every day.[43] But this was probably primarily due to salary-related reasons. In November 1946, an advertisement appeared in several judicial journals in the western zones, informing people about the work of the settlement office: it was primarily concerned with personnel matters and also tried to keep up to date with the fate of former employees of the Higher Regional Court. Obviously, however, the whole thing remained a poorly resourced leisure project. It concluded with the note, "As the processing office is run on a voluntary basis, please enclose your return postage with all correspondence."[44]

And the successes were as modest as the resources. The settlement office remained active until 1948. During this time, a dozen or so inquiries from all zones were received asking for case files—mainly from divorce proceedings—along with an equal number of letters requesting personal files, insurance cards, examination records, certificates, and the like.[45] In addition, the list of "repatriated staff members from the East" was continued, on which arriving refugees and their whereabouts had been recorded since February 1945. Here, too, the paper was out of step with the world. Most of those who were now called "resettlers" had no interest in their settlement. Of the thousands of judicial employees who must have been affected, only 35 found their way to the Greifswald settlement office after the end of the war. Almost without exception, their subsequent fate remained unknown in Greifswald.[46]

Wastepaper

The circumstances in Greifswald were favorable in that the Stettin staff had fled along with their files and could now take care of their proper disposal themselves. Elsewhere, judicial supplies were usually left behind after the war. There was paper lying around everywhere that no longer belonged to anyone. Court files from the areas beyond the Oder and Neisse rivers, from Alsace-Lorraine, Luxembourg, or the Sudetenland had made it to all occupation zones in large numbers, some through the planned relocation of entire inventories toward the end of the war, and many more through the confusion of the times. Most of these were individual case files in which a distant court, for example, had been asked to question a witness and had not been able to return the files after completion. The operation had been disrupted at a point where the rules of procedure did not provide for an interruption. The paper posed an intrusive question to its finders: Who will continue to process the files?

In the Soviet Occupation Zone, the first state administrations began to sift through files from across the Oder-Neisse line as early as the fall of 1945.[47] After all, they knew about the administrative staffs of the various higher regional courts that had perished in the final months of the war somewhere in the territory of what was now the Soviet Occupation Zone. The following year, the headquarters in Berlin took up the issue and requested systematic overviews from all parts of the country in order to consolidate the files in a kind of general settlement office. The aim was continued use, not waste. The *Deutsche Justiz-Verwaltung* (or "DJV," the "Justice Administration of the Soviet Occupation Zone") reported that they were constantly confronted with inquiries from judicial staff, which is why they urgently needed to collect the existing documents "in order to have them on hand when processing personnel matters and continuing to pay salaries."[48] And so, little by little, lists and registers, inventories and found objects trickled in from all the provinces: a wagonload of files from Kattowitz turned up in Ronneburg, Thuringia, as well as boxes of ink, paper, and other exhibits from the Silesian judicial administration.[49] There were 1,147 wills from East Prussia at Parchim Local Court, 1,652 wills from Pomerania at Demmin Local Court, even more wills in Schwerin, as well as 19 heavy boxes from Danzig Higher Regional Court, salary documents from Königsberg, and a good 200 construction drawings of court buildings.[50] There were 1,118 wills at Grimma Local Court; 21 personnel forms, 16 passbooks, and four wills at Oelsnitz Local Court; 1,000 personal forms from Breslau Higher Regional Court at Grossenhain Local Court; 38 criminal cases at the Gera Public Prosecutor's Office; a matrimonial case at Radebeul Local Court; a defamation suit at Lissa

Local Court;[51] plus thousands of land registers everywhere, as well as mortgage deeds, salary records, and administrative cases.

Things were similar in the West. In June 1946, the first inventory lists were compiled in the British Zone, soon followed by documents and valuables, until the Cologne Higher Regional Court President issued a blanket order to simply collect "all files, items belonging to the judiciary, personnel records, and the like" and then "initiate the reprocessing of the matters."[52] The valuable materials were to be returned to the judicial system. But here, too, it was chance that filled the lists. In the district of the Braunschweig Higher Regional Court, five legal aid cases from East Prussia, Posen, and Silesia were found. In Flensburg, dozens of volumes of cooperative, model, company, commercial, and association registers from the Zoppot Local Court were discovered, as well as two wills from Wollin, which had been taken by a court employee on the run. Hamm contributed 24 marginalia, Düsseldorf five, Hamburg 17, Kiel 12.[53] Only one item was actually worth mentioning, which—quite symptomatically—was due to an error on the part of the Reichsbahn, which in March 1945 had accidentally diverted a freight wagon 500 kilometers beyond its intended destination, which is why in the tranquil town of Uslar they were now sitting on about 2,000 personnel files from Stettin, almost 100 personnel files from Königsberg, an entire will file, administrative files, land register tables, twelve typewriters and the criminal record from Stargard, a total of almost 20 cubic meters of files, plus the bedding of the Stettin judicial employees.[54]

This trove was the decisive argument for collecting all the legacies of former German courts at the neighboring Hanover Local Court. After the founding of the two German states, relics from all over Germany, including Berlin, were brought there. There were still hopes of legal recycling. The Berlin Regional Court sent its files with the assessment that they were "important documentary material for the public seeking legal advice among the 10 million exiles expelled from the East."[55] Key parties repeatedly reiterated that the files were being collected because they expected "later used and application."[56]

To the extent that the collected piles of paper contained internal judicial administration proceedings, this expectation may have been unnecessary, but not entirely unrealistic. In principle, salary and personnel documents had lost none of their legal value, and the almost completely preserved criminal records still proved to be useful.[57] The rest, on the other hand, was almost without exception wastepaper. The wills had lost heirs and testators. Land registers and mortgage deeds documented a special kind of legal doctrine, namely, a land law whose foundation had been destroyed by the war. But the idea that a normal business transaction could come to an abnormal end had to be suppressed with all one's might. The devotion with which some here, too, endeavored to extract the usable parts from the fragments of the fallen Reich is most impressively demonstrated by a treasure that the Landeszentralbank Hamburg presented to the collection point at the end of 1948. Until now, a "large box" from the Stettin Higher Judicial Treasury had been kept in its own vaults; "the contents," they solemnly announced, "are empty file covers."[58]

Legal Transfer from the Lost Territories

And then there were the individual cases. Their fate was tied to the file collections in East and West but was discussed independently of them. The countless lawsuits, motions, and charges that had remained unresolved at the end of the war now found themselves in a peculiar state of limbo. They hung in places that had disappeared from the scene for the foreseeable future, yet nevertheless exerted a kind of double blocking effect from their grave: it was not allowed to simply take the cases into one's own jurisdiction so long as there was still a court with jurisdiction, and for the same reason it was not allowed to simply discard them. To rule out the possibility of diverging decisions on the same matter, the institution of *lis pendens* required that a legal dispute be resolved by the court in which it had been initiated. A case remained chained to its court until judgment. Anyone who was sued even though the dispute had already been heard by another court could therefore defend themselves with the so-called "plea of *lis pendens*," which meant that the action was already denied admissibility without its merits even being considered.[59]

This difficulty had already arisen with the cession of territories after the First World War. Overcoming it unilaterally by law was considered an encroachment on the sovereign acts of the now foreign institutions and thus a violation of international law, which is why numerous, sometimes shockingly detailed, international treaties were concluded at the time. Of course, the situation after 1945 was much more complex. German courts had operated in various forms on half the continent. In the East, the German Reich had annexed the Sudetenland, Danzig, the Polish Corridor, and the Memel Region, only to lose them again. The same applied in the West to the East Belgian territories around Eupen and Malmedy. German courts had been active in Alsace-Lorraine, Luxembourg, and the region around Maribor, known as "Lower Styria," even though they were not on German soil. And then there were the peculiar "German Courts" that had been set up in the Netherlands, the Protectorate of Bohemia and Moravia, the General Government and the former Reich Commissariats of Ostland and Ukraine, branches of a special judiciary for the German nationals working there, whom no one wanted to subject to the dregs of the local legal system. For a proper legal solution, peace treaties would have had to be concluded with the Netherlands, Luxembourg, Belgium, France, Yugoslavia, Czechoslovakia, Poland, and the Soviet Union. Afterward, and if possible by mutual agreement, they needed to address the questions of who should continue the German proceedings, who would be responsible for enforcing of earlier judgments, where information from German registers could be obtained and, in general, who would be allowed to claim the legacies of the Greater German judicial administration, which were often founded on the basest fantasies of the master race. This was a hopeless and, moreover, politically rather embarrassing undertaking.

The search for a possible way out of this legal quandary began immediately after the capitulation. Several higher regional court districts issued the first regulations to create new jurisdictions for the most urgent matters—estates and guardianships in absentia—starting in October 1945, followed in 1946 by local transfer regulations for criminal cases from Wehrmacht and special courts.[60] The greatest creativity was demonstrated in the Soviet Zone, whereby far the most refugees were stranded in the months following the end of the war. In some countries, it was proposed to exclude the defense of *lis pendens*.[61] The DJV gave the rather un-legal advice to the *Kammergericht* (Higher Regional Court of Berlin) to simply declare a new court to have jurisdiction, while the Berlin-Mitte Local Court was told that it should" not be too narrow-minded" when interpreting the relevant rules.[62]

In May 1946, a conference of Soviet-occupied countries addressed the problem and came to an agreement surprisingly quickly. Although it had been possible to loosen the shackles of *lis pendens* without legislation, a DJV decree now received a majority, which allowed the interrupted proceedings to continue at the defendant's current place of residence.[63] It was not even known how many cases were actually involved. According to the judicial administration files, there were probably no more than a few dozen.[64] The SMAD, however, was told something completely different. In a discussion, the DJV pointed out that it was receiving "almost daily inquiries" about the possibility of continuing old cases, which is why there was an "extremely urgent interest" in a legal regulation, a claim whose dramatic tone was further intensified after months of waiting for approval from the military administration: the number of relevant cases was "extraordinarily large," the inquiries were "accumulating more and more" and, in general, it was unacceptable for resettlers to have "the misery of being without rights in addition to their misery of being refugees."[65]

Nevertheless, the SMAD was reluctant to grant approval, as always without giving any reasons. Perhaps it sensed interference in internal affairs in the administration of the estate over territories that were now largely under Soviet administration, or perhaps it was just its notorious staff shortage that caused the review of the two-page document to take months. In the end, it refused to approve the provisions for reopening cases that had already been concluded but was otherwise conciliatory and even gave the friendly suggestion not to issue a regulation, but instead an "order" to the state administrations to expedite further proceedings. On 8 May 1947, the new regulations were published under the clunky title *Order on Jurisdiction in Judicial Proceedings and Their Transfer.*[66]

The jurists of the Soviet Occupation Zone had a grasp of political reality that was unclouded by sentimentality. It was generally considered impossible that the eastern territories could ever return to German administration. Section 2 of the new order stated quite explicitly that the affected courts had "ceased to be under German jurisdiction" after 8 May. The legal illusions, however, were of almost bourgeois proportions. The lamented lack of rights of the refugees seems to have been primarily motivated by the fear of a gap in the figurative stamp collection of socialist jurists. There is not a single case published in which the order was decisive; even the Supreme Court was apparently never involved.

Comparative Law

The arrangement had a visible impact only in the West. The problem was also known there, but it had been assessed completely differently. At the beginning of 1947, a rather lackluster draft of a regulation was written in Karlsruhe, which primarily dealt with old cases from Alsace-Lorraine, while at the same time the Hamburg Central Justice Office focused on the lost eastern territories.[67] This was followed by an expert opinion from the American Zone, which arrived at a wholly divergent interpretation than the lawyers in the Soviet Occupation Zone, even regarding the historical starting point. According to this opinion, the loss of rights was simply a hardship of the war; refugees could be expected to make a fresh start, and therefore they might also have to "rebuild their legal case."[68] The expert supplemented this consideration with three main arguments. First, an international treaty was needed, at least with regard to the eastern territories, to avoid interference with the sovereign rights of the victorious powers through a simple law. Second, a statutory provision must under no circumstances create the impression that the political reorganization was somehow to be recognized and, as the expert put it, "legally clear the field." Third, transitional provisions were superfluous, as the defense of *lis pendens* presupposed the possibility of bringing the pending dispute to a conclusion, which was clearly not the case in the lost territories.[69]

What had been presented in the Soviet Occupation Zone as a compelling imperative of justice was seen in the West as a political impossibility and legal activism. Practice confirmed this assessment. In Rhineland-Palatinate, only one case had been heard of to date in which *lis pendens* had become a point of dispute, no case at all was filed in Württemberg-Hohenzollern, and in Munich two appeals concerning properties from the East had been dismissed because the basis of the transaction had ceased to exist.[70] In June 1947, the Hamburg Regional Court issued a ruling that was warmly welcomed in the legal literature. It rejected the defense of *lis pendens* if the files of the previous legal dispute were inaccessible, thus allowing a refugee to file a new lawsuit in the same matter at their new place of residence.[71] Judicial pragmatism had thus delivered the desired result even without a legal basis.

However, with the ruling from Hamburg, the Legal Affairs Committee in the American Zone also received news that a corresponding legal regulation had already been passed in the East. Even in Poland, the fate of the former German court proceedings had now been addressed.[72] The procedural settlement of the lost territory of the Reich had thus become a systemic issue. There was no turning back for the Western legal experts. When, after a few weeks, the East German *Order on Jurisdiction in Judicial Proceedings* of 8 May 1947 was finally in hand—the Polish decree remained unattainable for the time being—the bourgeois judicial administration was politically dismayed at the prospect of "a provisional measure being turned into a definitive one," as the Central Judicial Office commented angrily.[73] From a legal point of view, on the other hand, they indulged in cool derision. The colleagues in the eastern zone, it was noted with obvious satisfaction, had forgotten the foreclosure proceedings, the public notice proceedings, the entire law of associations, and, in commercial law, the "functions of a non-registry nature assigned to the registry court." Instead, they had newly regulated certain activities of the guardianship court, even though these would be based on the current place of residence anyway, meaning that a substitute jurisdiction would not have had to be created in the first place.[74]

These naive legal blunders from the Soviet Zone were enough for the West to revise its own starting point and make the legal survival of the interrupted legal acts a touchstone of its own professional honor. The Central Judicial Office painstakingly compiled a twelve-page overview, which presumably listed in full the matters in which the refugees from the lost territories might require substitute jurisdiction for the Code of Civil Procedure, Voluntary Jurisdiction, German Civil Code, Commercial Code, Stock Corporation Act, Marriage Act, Bankruptcy Code, and some ancillary laws: declaration of death, requisition of a ship owner, judicial annulment of child adoption, marriage exemptions, substitute liquidators for a foundation, appointment of supervisory board members—now it was really clear where the war had rendered the legal process ineffective.[75]

For the time being, however, the political fear of inadvertently submitting any kind of incidental declaration of renunciation with regard to the territories in question remained greater than the legal pride. And so, all that remained for this activity—the usefulness of which had been doubtful from the outset—was to work on an exhibit for the legal cabinet of curiosities. Consultation followed draft, and draft followed consultation. At the end of January 1948, the responsible official announced that "the passage of time alone" would soon render a law superfluous, and in September the Hessian Minister of Justice commented grumpily that the proposed law would have been necessary "even two years ago" but was now no longer.[76]

In 1949, the *Grundgesetz* ("Basic Law") placed the matter under federal jurisdiction. After the Federal Ministry of Justice had received a total of eight inquiries regarding the whereabouts of courts from the eastern territories by July 1950, it felt compelled to inquire with the federal states about the need for legal regulation.[77] The federal states pondered this serious question—which they had already answered several times in the previous years—for a year and a half, only to respond with a bored shrug of the shoulders: the law was not necessary, but they would not oppose it if it were to be implemented. Revision, interdepartmental coordination, and editorial finalization ate up another year and a half until, on 18 July 1952, the Bundestag and Bundesrat finally approved the technically flawless *Act to Supplement Jurisdictions in the Fields of Civil Law, Commercial Law, and Criminal Law*, which attempted to legally smooth over the geopolitical upheavals of the Second World War in 24 paragraphs without acknowledging them. Once again, the war was declared over without ending it. The camouflage for this political schizophrenia was: "Courts where German jurisdiction is no longer exercised." The most unspectacular reorganization imaginable, a reference to the "currently applicable regulations," which generally meant that the defendant's new place of residence was decisive.[78]

The result was a law that no one had originally wanted and that no one needed anymore. The legal press largely ignored it, apart from a few tired comments, ranging up to the spiteful observation that the new regulation was nothing more than an "embarrassment law."[79] Only the *Neue Juristische Wochenschrift* was unexpectedly euphoric. Its author was a representative from the Federal Ministry of Justice and very likely the author of the statute itself, who hailed his own legal masterpiece and let the world know that a "minimum level of legal protection required by the rule of law" had finally been achieved, allowing those affected to defend themselves against impairments "caused by the breach of procedural continuity resulting from the end of the war."[80] The historical starting point thus reversed. Under no circumstances should the misery of refugees be allowed to lead to a loss of rights, whereby the author had inadvertently adopted the line that the Eastern DJV had represented to the SMAD six years earlier. Now the West had also completed its figurative stamp collection.

Not much more happened. In criminal law, the law led to a handful of retrials against judgments of former special courts whose seat had been in what is now the Eastern zone; not a single case was transferred from across the Oder-Neisse border. In civil law, the yield was similarly low. In 1956, a legal shyster conjured up the law to withdraw the appeal that his client had filed in 1944 against a divorce judgment by the Breslau Regional Court, thus making the divorce retroactively final, so to speak. In view of the ten years of harmonious marriage that had passed since then, the Federal Court of Justice dismissed the request as an abuse of law.[81] Bankruptcy proceedings from Königsberg were continued in Berlin—although the situation was not regulated, the Federal Court of Justice felt called upon to fill in the gaps due to the explicitly fragmentary nature of the law.[82]

Although honest on all sides, the effort was thus only moderately successful overall. The efforts to portion the end of the war and its consequences into digestible legal morsels only achieved legal reality in a few cases. Inquiries about the fate of legal cases from Außig and Tilsit, Crossen and Bunzlau, Breslau, Goldap, Kolberg, Memel, Neumarkt, Lyck, Königsberg, Oels, and all the other places that now had different names were rejected with regret,[83] until at some point it was possible to hide behind a legal solution, which everyone knew would not help with the loss of the files. The normality of business often remained a fiction that was elaborately constructed, yet nevertheless easy to see through.

Drawing a Line

Many legal matters had lost touch with reality. There was a lack of files, parties, and interest. An alimony case from Königsberg, which could not be returned in March 1945 due to the interrupted postal connection, resurfaced in Hanover. In 1947, enquiries were made to the Celle Higher Regional Court as to where the Königsberg Local Court had relocated, which was then referred to Schwerin. The Schwerin Regional Court knew nothing of the matter. The case was closed on 3 May 1947.[84] In Dresden, the local court struggled to clarify a child support case. It had last met on 30 April 1945. When the alleged father returned from captivity as a prisoner of war, it was supposed to continue, but all attempts to recover the files failed. In the end, nothing happened.[85] In Freiburg, the local court, again in a child support case, made numerous efforts to reconstruct the destroyed files. After inquiries to the lawyer involved, the youth welfare office, the registry office, the guardian, and the university hospital had proved unsuccessful, the local court had to write to the plaintiff to say that restoration was impossible and that it would be advisable to bring a new lawsuit. [86]

A lawyer in Plauen for the defendant, the plaintiff's divorced husband, turned to the regional court on 25 November 1946, saying that he needed the files because all of his own papers had been burned. At the same time, he reminded the court of the facts of the case and the steps that now had to be taken: "This is about the return of furniture. After the defendant returned from Russian captivity on 1 October 1946, the legal dispute must be restarted." Once the captivity is over, justice must continue. No one offered anything more than this appeal to a supposed inevitability.[87] In Celle, a lawyer who found himself confronted with an old case from 1942 in 1950 could only state on record that his office had been completely bombed out in 1943, that he no longer had any documents, had no recollection of the facts of the case, did not know whether he had represented the plaintiff or the defendant, and also had no addresses to contact any of the parties. The case did not recover from so much accumulated futility.[88] In Hamburg, an insurance company that had fled Stettin continued to work on the investigation of a botched salvage operation in the Stettin harbor. The file had arrived in Hamburg in November 1944 so that a witness could be heard there; a year later, the insurance company made several attempts to locate the remaining witnesses, even writing to the Stettin Local Court—without success. In 1948, a final effort was made to continue the proceedings in Flensburg. After several resubmissions, the registry of the Hamburg Local Court finally received the long-awaited instruction in 1950: "File it."[89]

File it. This soon became the formula for salvation for the large paper collections in East and West. Despite all efforts, the files and the legal situation had rarely reconciled. Whatever normative significance the files may have had they quickly lost and became history. On 30 October 1952, the Federal Archives, newly established in Koblenz, contacted the central collection point in Hanover and expressed an urgent interest in the files under the heading "Refugee Documents." Due to the presumed complete loss of comparable material, these files could "claim a very special historical and legal value for themselves" and were therefore "of outstanding archival value." The Federal Archives would now be responsible.[90] What the collection point in Hanover had so diligently compiled was then sent to Koblenz. Now, at last, the long-awaited new cycle of utilization was finally opened. However, the readership of the files no longer consisted of lawyers, but of historians. Today, not even the court itself remembers that the office in Hanover ever existed.

And finally, the normative framework for the transfer of rights from the lost territories, which had been so painstakingly constructed over the years, was also dismantled. The useless existence of the Jurisdiction Supplement Act lasted until 2006, when large parts of the Act fell victim to the attempt to purge the legal system of superfluous legal norms. In principle, no one disputed the fact that the Supplementary Jurisdiction Act could be repealed without loss. However, no one was yet fully confident of the peace. To be on the safe side, the criminal law reinstatement provisions were left in force—who knew whether some old man might discover an unjustly punished youthful sin in his life? With regard to the replacement of destroyed or lost documents, the tried-and-tested legal situation was also retained; a burned certificate of inheritance from Königsberg can therefore still hope for legal goodwill today.

The bottom line, however, was satisfaction. The explanatory memorandum to the law stated that since the fall of the Berlin Wall at the latest, the expectation was justified that "all conceivable continuations of proceedings have now been actually and legally concluded."[91] Who—other than the federal government itself—would disagree with this? On 24 April 2006, the *First Act on the Restructuring of Federal Law within the Jurisdiction of the Federal Minister of Justice* came into force[92]—the procedural death certificate for the war, so to speak. With this, there was nothing left to be settled. Now the war was truly over.

Notes

1. Wehrmacht report, 9 May 1945, in: Schramm, 1281 et seq.
2. Baumbauch, *Zivilprozessordnung*, 1936, § 245.
3. Letter from the Württemberg-Baden Ministry of Justice, 19 January 1946, in: GLAK, Bestand 537 Zugang 1985-37 No. 485, Vorgang 1. On the "long end of the war 1944/45," see Henke, "Deutschland—Zweierlei Kriegsende," 337–354.
4. Higher Regional Court President for Cologne to the Higher Regional Court President for Hamburg, 8 July 1946, in: LAV NRW-R, Ger. Rep. 255 No. 202, p. 241.
5. *Allgemeinverfügung* (or "AV," a "general order" addressed to a wider audience of the Higher Regional Court President for Hamm, 6 December 1945, in: *Juristische Blätter WL* 1945, 39.
6. Second meeting of the Higher Regional Court Presidents of the British Zone (Hamburg, Celle, Braunschweig, Oldenburg), 24 October 1945, in: LAH, Nds. 710 Acc. 124/87 No. 47, p. 59.
7. AV of the head of the German judicial administration in the French Zone in Baden, 31 October 1945, in: StAF, C 20/1 No. 354, p. 1 (Abl. B, 1946, 4).
8. Baumbach, *Zivilprozessordnung*, 1950, § 245 note 2.
9. Art. 7, Reichsgesetzblatt I, 666–668.

10. See in general: Busam, *Kriegsfolgenbewältigung*, 107 et seq.
11. Local Court President for Leipzig to State Administration of Saxony Department of Justice, 27 August 1945, in: HStAD, 11380 No. 264 (unpaginated). The first judges were sworn in there on 4 May.
12. President of the Supreme Court of the Reich, 17 May 1945, quoted from Glöckner, "Die Auflösung des Reichsgerichts," 440.
13. Insurance: Reichsgesetzblatt 1939 I, 2175 et seq.; shipping: Reichsgesetzblatt 1942 I, 620.
14. Public holidays: Reichsgesetzblatt 1941 I, 662; fuel: Reichsgesetzblatt 1944 I, 173 et seq.; custodial sentences: Reichsgesetzblatt 1940 I, 877.
15. First systematic overview: Memo from the Legal Subcommittee of the British Zone, 17 June 1946, in: BAK, Z 21 No. 44, pp. 26–30; a second one dated 9 July 1947 was probably prepared by the Central Justice Office, here according to: StAF, C 20/1 No. 882 (unpaginated).
16. Higher Regional Court President for Cologne, Rechtsentwicklung im OLGB Köln nach dem Zusammenbruch des Deutschen Reiches, 12 November 1947, in: LAV NRW-R, Ger. Rep. 255 No. 84, p. 90.
17. See AV Bad. Ministry of Justice, 25 April 1946 (StAF, C 20/1 No. 354, p. 7) on the one hand and AV, 5 October 1946 (ibid., p. 50) on the other.
18. Higher Regional Court President for Düsseldorf to the Central Legal Office, 18 June 1946, in: BAK, Z 21 No. 44, p. 49.
19. First note Ministry of Justice (*Ministerium der Justiz* or "JM" or "MdJ") for Württemberg-Baden, undated (probably June 1946), in: HStAS, EA 4/001 Bü 662, Vorgang 198/47. The law of 10 September 1947, in: GVBl. H 1947, 79 (same wording in: RegBl. WB 1947, 96).
20. The references are found in Bedau, *Entnazifizierung*, 348 et seq.; for the Soviet Occupation Zone, see the references in Zimmerreimer, "Fragen des Verschollenheitsrechts," 58–61. The "civilian execution" is feared by Rademacher, "Kriegsverschollenheit," 258; the Missing Persons Act of 4 July 1939 can be found in Reichsgesetzblatt I, 1186–1192.
21. Ordinance of 11 October 1944, in: Reichsgesetzblatt I, 245 et seq.
22. Announcement Higher Regional Court President for Hamm, JBl. WL 1945, 27.
23. Higher Regional Court for Celle, decision of 31 May 1946, in: *Süddeutsche Juristen-Zeitung* 1946, 177 et seq.
24. This refers to Altstötter, "Vereinfachung," 285–288 and 293–295. The judgment of the Oldenburg Regional Court of 31 May 1946 can be found in JBl. AOO 1946, 78 et seq.
25. Higher Regional Court for Hamm, decision of 16 May 1947, in: JMBl. NRW 1947, 32–35. Likewise, Higher Regional Court for Düsseldorf, decision of 18 August 1947, in: JMBl. NRW 1947, 72–76. The letter from the British Military Government is printed, for example, in JBl. B 1946, 145 et seq. A different approach was taken in the French Zone. The end of the war had not yet arrived, it was decidedly declared, only to subsequently create some special termination rights for contracts that could not be terminated due to the war (meeting of the judicial administrations of the French Zone, 3–4 September 1946, in: StAF, C 20/1 No. 354, pp. 44 et seq.).
26. Higher Regional Court for Cologne, judgment of 8 July 1948, in: ZJBl. 1948, 254 et seq.
27. Criminal case Js 154/46, counter-declaration of 16 April 1946, in: LAG, Rep. 76 Greifswald No. 1573, p. 15.

28. Chief District Judge for Ludwigsburg to JM Württemberg-Baden, 6 November 1945, in: HStAS, EA 4/001 Bü 656, Vorgang 185/3.
29. The expert opinion had been commissioned by the French judicial administration (StAF, C 20/1 No. 432, p. 1). For the other western zones, see for example LAH, Hann. 173 Acc. 123/87 No. 2, pp. 77 et seq. and HStAS, EA 4/001 Bü 263, for the Soviet Occupation Zone LAG, Rep. 76 Greifswald No. 1573, 5 et seq.
30. Overview in Stein/Jonas, *Zivilprozessordnung*, Introduction A, § 7.
31. See on the whole: Erlass JM Württemberg-Baden, 30 November 1945, in: HStAS, EA 4/001 Bü 656, Vorgang 185/2; for Württemberg-Hohenzollern see StAS, Wü 25 T 1 No. 559, Vorgang 1; Meeting Protocol of the Higher Regional Court Presidents of the British Zone, 13–15 May 1946, in: LAH, Nds. 710 Acc. 124/87 No. 47, pp. 237 et seq.; Expert opinion of the Legal Subcommittee of the British Zone, 15 June 1946, in: LAH, Hann. 173 Acc. 123/87 No. 73, pp. 60–63; Baden Higher Regional Court for Freiburg, judgment of 5 June 1946, in: Deutsche Rechts-Zeitschrift 1946, 29; Schuler, "Rechtmittel," 34.
32. Correspondence between the Higher Regional Court President for Cologneand the Higher Regional Court for Cologne, 5 June, 17 July and 28 September 1946, in: LAV NRW-R, Ger. Rep. 255 No. 237, pp. 84 et seq., 87 et seq., 91.
33. Reopening: Regional Court President for Cologne to the Higher Regional Court President for Cologne, 1 December 1945, in: LAV NRW-R, Ger. Rep. 255 No. 237, p. 98. In contrast: Regional Court President for Stuttgart, 10 September 1945, in: HStAS, EA 4/001 Bü 43, pp. 55 et seq.; Minutes of the meeting between the judicial administration of the French Zone and the military government, 3–4 September 1946, in: StAF, C 20/1 No. 275; Higher Regional Court President for Kiel to the Higher Regional Court President for Cologne, 10 November 1945, in: LAV NRW-R, Ger. Rep. 255 No. 237, p. 95; Regional Court President for Aachen to the Higher Regional Court President for Cologne, 22 November 1945, and reply letter, in: LAV NRW-R, Ger. Rep. 255 No. 237, pp. 99 et seq.
34. *Reichsgericht* to DJV, 21 August 1945, in: BA, DP 1 No. 29, p. 19. The hopes for a reopening were entirely in line with Law No. 2. See Glöckner, "Die Auflösung des Reichsgerichts."
35. This can be seen in the letter from the Regional Court President for Leipzig to the State Administration of Saxony, MdJ, 7 October 1947 (HStAD, 11380 No. 59, p. 23).
36. See *Reichsjustizkalender* (last 1941) and *Gerichtsorganisation* (1944).
37. Administrative Staff of the Higher Regional Court for Kattowitz to MdJ Thuringia, 22 August 1945, in: HStAW, Higher Regional Court for Erfurt No. 95, p. 124.
38. Local Court for Weißenfels to Provincial Government of Saxony-Anhalt, 24 April 1947, in: BA, DP 1 No. 563, Lagereinheit 1, unpaginated.
39. Note from the Greifswald Municipal Court, July 1945, in: LAG, Rep. 76 Greifswald No. 352, p. 26. Some minor administrative matters from June 1945 can be found in: ibid., Rep. 76 Stettin (new) Nos. 165 and 321.
40. Head of Greifswald City Court to the Higher Regional Court President for Stettin, 9 August 1945, in: LAG, Rep. 75 No. 134, p. 6.
41. Settlement office to the Local Court for Rostock, 20 December 1945, in: LAG, Rep. 75 No. 135, p. 7. Likewise, letter to the Local Court for Demmin, 12 January 1946, in: ibid., Rep. 75 No. 133, p. 36.
42. Memo from Greifswald Regional Court, 10 January 1946, in: LAG, Rep. 75 No. 134 (unpaginated); Pölitz District Court to Greifswald City Court, 19 September 1945, in: Rep. 76 Greifswald No. 352 (unpaginated).

43. Report Regional Court President for Greifswald to DJV, 20 May 1946 (BA, DP 1 No. 563, unpaginated).
44. Here according to JBl. B 1946, 163 (15 November 1946).
45. All in: LAG, Rep. 76 Greifswald No. 4176 (without reply letter), ibid., No. 3990 (there occasionally with replies) and ibid., Rep. 75 No. 133.
46. See the list in LAG, Rep. 75 No. 14, which ends with the serial number 321 on 24 February 1946.
47. See, for example, the Saxony Judicial Administration's *Rundverfügung* (or "RV," i.e., a circular addressed to subordinate authorities) No. 29 of September 1945, which aims to record files of Silesian provenance (BA, DP 1 No. 6370).
48. Initial registration began in March 1946, and on 14 February 1947 the DJV sent a letter to all ministries of justice (BA, DP 1 No. 563, unpaginated).
49. More details on this can be found above in Chapter 6, footnotes 137–139.
50. Mecklenburg-Vorpommern state government to DJV, 7 and 27 January 1947, 20 January and 9 November 1948, all in: BA, DP 1 No. 563 (unpaginated). Further deliveries from the 1950s in BA, DP 1 No. 344.
51. Grimma: MdJ Sachsen to MdJ GDR, 3 February 1950, in: BA, DP 1 No. 535, p. 1; Oelsnitz: Regional Court for Plauen to the Saxony Department of Justice, 2 October 1945, in: HStAD, 11380 No. 98 (unpaginated); Großenhain: Regional Court for Desden to LV for the Saxony Department of Justice, 18 September 1945, in: ibid. (unpaginated); Gera: Public Prosecutor for Gera to the General Prosecutor's Office for Gera, 19 May 1947, in: HStAW, OLG Erfurt No. 95, p. 49; Radebeul (and much more: BA, DP 1 No. 616; Lissa: Provincial Government of Sachsen-Anhalt to the DJV, 10 June 1947, in: BA, DP 1 No. 563 Lagereinheit 1 (unpaginated).
52. Higher Regional Court President for Cologne to the Higher Regional Court President of the British Zone, 27 July 1946, in: BAK, Z 21 No. 260, p. 2. Also, minutes of the meeting of the Higher Regional Court Presidents of the British Zone in Bad Pyrmont, 15/16 August 1946, in: LAH, Hann. 173 Acc. 123/87 No. 151, p. 64.
53. The entire collection process of the British Zone is recorded in BAK, Z 21 No. 260, sheets 5–61.
54. The case had already come to light before the capitulation, see General Prosecutor's Office Stettin (currently Greifswald) to the Reich Ministry of Justice (or "RJM"), 5 April 1945, in: BA, R 3001 No. 24052, p. 181. January 1946 can be found in LAH, Nds. 710 Acc. 124/87 No. 135, p. 9. For the contents, see the directories of the Higher Regional Court for Celle of 20 February 1953, in: LAH, Hann. 173 Acc. 123/87 No. 159, p. 312, and ibid, No. 51, pp. 388–402 (undated).
55. Regional Court President for Berlin to the Central Legal Office for the British Zone, 12 April 1949, in: BAK, Z 21 No. 260, p. 97 and letter from the Magistrate of Greater Berlin dated 20 June 1949 and 10 September 1949, in: ibid., p. 99, 105.
56. Minister of Justice of Lower Saxony to the other West German Ministers of Justice, 28 June 1949, in: BAK, Z 21 No. 260, p. 102. See also AV of the Central Legal Office for the British Zone, 28 February 1949, in: ZJBl. 1949, 47 f. and the corresponding note, 23 April 1948, in: BAK, Z 21 No. 260, p. 74, also the minutes of the conference of the Ministers of Justice on 29/30 April 1948 (ibid., p. 75).
57. The fate of the East Prussian criminal records, which a judicial employee had brought to Mecklenburg in January 1945, is particularly worth mentioning. See the report of the Local Court Judge for Königsberg, 30 January 1945, in: LAG, Rep. 75 No. 136, before p. 1 and the letter from the Court Assistant from Königsberg to DJV, 23 September 1945, in: BA, DP 1 No. 352, p. 15.

58. Landeszentralbank Hamburg to Central Legal Office for the British Zone, undated copy, in: BAK, Z 21 No. 260, p. 82.
59. See §§ 263, 274 Code of Civil Procedure. For more information: Stein/Jonas, *Zivilprozeßordnung*, § 263 note III; Schönke, *Zivilprozeßrecht*, § 48 III.
60. The individual references are listed in § 22 ZustErgG, 7 August 1952, in: Reichsgesetzblatt I, 410; see also Regulation on the transfer of criminal proceedings in the event of courts being abolished, 4 December 1946, in: VOBl. BZ 1947, 8 et seq.
61. For example, President of Mecklenburg-Western Pomerania, Department of Justice Administration, to DJV, 22 April 1946, in: BA, DP 1 No. 7163/1, p. 10.
62. The correspondence between the DJV and the Local Court for Berlin-Mitte, January 1947, in: BA, DP 1 No. 528, pp. 7–9. Incidentally, the *Kammergericht* did not consider the solution according to § 36 ZPO "even with the freest possible interpretation" because the courts concerned were not prevented in an individual case, but no longer existed as such (ibid., p. 13).
63. The minutes of the state conference of 3 May 1946 can be found in BA, DP 1 No. 7163/1, pp. 31–38.
64. Inquiries about the fate of defunct court authorities are collected for the DJV in: BA, DP 1 No. 528 and 529. For Saxony, see HStAD, 11380 No. 199, 205, 377, where the whereabouts of personnel files, savings bank books, etc. were also frequently inquired about.
65. Note, DJV, 22 October 1946, in: BA, DP 1 No. 7163/1, p. 40, then DJV to SMAD, 8 February 1947, in: BA, DP 1 No. 7163/1, p. 45.
66. Anordnung über die Zuständigkeit in gerichtlichen Verfahren und ihre Überleitung, in: ZVBl., 15 et seq.
67. Previously, Higher Regional Court President for Cologne, draft of a regulation on *lis pendens*, September 1946, in: LAV NRW-R, Ger. The—very brief—Karlsruhe draft was sent to the Central Legal Office on 28 March 1947, where they referred to their own considerations with regard to the eastern territories (HStAS, EA 4/001 Bü 696, files 11 and 15; parallel records in BA K, Z 21 No. 406, 407, 408). Previously already the Higher Regional Court President for Cologne, draft of a regulation on *lis pendens*, September 1946, in: LAV NRW-R, Ger. Rep. 255 No. 237, p. 179.
68. Expert opinion of the Legal Committee of the Council of States of the American Zone, 28 May 1947, in: HStAS, EA 4/001 Bü 696, Vorgang 16.
69. Ibid.
70. JM Rheinland-Pfalz, 10 May 1947, in: HStAS, EA 4/001 Bü 696, Vorgang 17 Anlage 4; Landesdirektion der Justiz Württemberg-Hohenzollern, 17 April 1947, in: ibid., Vorgang 21 Anlage 1; letter from Higher Regional Court President Munich to Bavarian MdJ, 21 October 1947, in: ibid., Vorgang 40 Anlage 3. Similar figures from the Higher Regional Court for the district of Cologne, September 1946—January 1947, in: LAV NRW-R, Ger. Rep. 255 No. 237, pp. 175 et seq., 191 et seq.
71. Regional Court for Hamburg, judgment of 12 December 1946, in: Süddeutsche Juristen-Zeitung 1947, 271 et seq. At its very next meeting, the Legal Committee stated that "in what is probably general court practice," the plea of *lis pendens* was declared irrelevant if it was impossible to continue the legal dispute at the court of origin (minutes, 25 July 1947, in: HStAS, EA 4/001 Bü 696, file 23). Reports from practice confirm this; see for example the descriptions of the Regional Court President for Cologne to the Higher Regional Court President for Cologne, January 7, 1947, in: LAV NRW-R, Ger. Rep. 255 No. 237, pp. 194–196, or the reports from the Higher Regional Court for Celle note, in: LAH, Hann. 173 Acc. 123/87 No. 73, pp. 80–92.

In agreement: Riezler, "Fragen des interzonalen Zivilprozeßrechts," esp. 238 et seq.; von Köller, "Ersatzzuständigkeiten," 450–452.

72. Minutes of the Legal Committee of the Council of States of the American Zone, 25 June 1947, in: HStAS, EA 4/001 Bü 696, Vorgang 22. The Polish regulation probably refers to the Decree o mocy obowiązującej orzeczeń sądowych, wydanych w okresie okupacji niemieckiej na terenie Rzeczypospolitej Polskiej, 6 June 1945 (DU No. 25, Poz. 151, amended on 11 April 1947), amended on 11 April 1947 (DU No. 32, Poz. 144), which dealt with the legal force of German court judgments from the occupation period.
73. President of the Central Legal Office to the Ministry of Justice of Württemberg-Baden, 18 July 1947, in: HStAS, EA 4/001 Bü 696, file 28.
74. President of the Central Legal Office to the Ministry of Justice of Württemberg-Baden, 18 July 1947, in: HStAS, EA 4/001 Bü 696, Vorgang 28 (somewhat more reserved, ZJBl. 1947, 46).
75. File note, 26 June 1947, in: BA K, Z 21 No. 406, pp. 25–32.
76. "Passage of time": minutes of the conference of justice ministers, 26–28 January, 1948, in: HStAS, EA 4/001 Bü 696, Vorgang 51; "years": letter Hesse MdJ, 14 September 1948, in: HStAS, EA 4/001 Bü 696, Vorgang 67; The objections are summarized in a memo from the Central Legal Office dated 16 September 1948, in: BA K, Z 21 No. 406, 147–150.
77. Overview in: BA K, B 141 No. 1799, pp. 72 f.; minutes of the conference of justice ministers, 23–24 October, 1950, in: ibid., p. 92; this shows that many more inquiries were received regarding estates and guardianships in absentia. For the Central Legal Office, see the list in BAK, Z 21 No. 407 and 408 (probably two cases in total).
78. Gesetz zur Ergänzung von Zuständigkeiten auf den Gebieten des Bürgerlichen Rechts, des Handelsrechts und des Strafrechts (Zuständigkeitsergänzungsgesetz), 7 August 1952, in: Bundesgesetzblatt I, 407–410. The legislative process at federal level is documented in BAK, B 141 No. 1799–1801.
79. See: Wieczorek, *Zivilprozeßordnung* 1/II, § 245 B III; "embarrassment law": Karl, "Sitzverlegung," 317.
80. Mundt, "Zuständigkeitsergänzungsgesetz," 1279–1281.
81. Bundesgerichtshof, judgment of 10 March 1956, in: BGHZ 20, 198–209. The few other references are documented in NJW-Fundheft Zivilrecht, 1956–1958.
82. Federal Court of Justice, decision of 17 October 1952, in: Entscheidungen des Bundesgerichtshofs in Zivilsachen 7, 307–311.
83. These examples are all from BA, DP 1 No. 528 and 529.
84. Local Court for Königsberg, 12 C 358/1944, in: GStA PK, XX. HA Rep. 38a No. 24.
85. Higher Regional Court for Dresden 5/10 U 145/1943, in: HStAD, 11045 No. 221.
86. Local Court for Freiburg 2 C 53/1944, in: StAF, E 159/1 Paket 20 No. 402.
87. Regional Court for Plauen, 3 O 11/1943, in: StACh, 30096 No. 1736.
88. Higher Regional Court for Celle, 3 U 147/1950, in: LAH, Nds. 720 Acc. 53/61 No. 1.
89. The case is now in GStA PK, XV. HA, Rep. 76 No. 702—presumably arranged by the Hanover Collection Agency.
90. Federal Archives to the Local Court President for Hanover, 30 October 1952, in: LAH, Hann. 173 Acc. 123/87 No. 159, p. 308.
91. Bundestags-Drucksache 16/47, 59.
92. Bundesgesetzblatt I, 866–893.

Epilogue

The Dream of Real Life

Fantasies of Omnipotence

The suspension of law is a legal plant that sprouts in the dark. "Should, as the consequence of war, the court cease its activities, the proceedings shall be interrupted for the duration of this situation," has been the mindlessly repeated legal definition of the judiciary for a good 150 years. If the courts are not working, then they are no longer working, a solemnly proclaimed self-evident fact with which lawyers like to philosophically elevate their own existence. Here, in the penumbra of the legal ecotone, many famous sayings have been unearthed. The most reliable producer in this respect was the borderline jurist Carl Schmitt. In his metaphysical frenzy, he poured out a whole cornucopia of dark wisdom about the inadequacy of the law: "The normal proves nothing, the exception proves everything." Only the suspension of law reveals sovereignty, and only the state of exception allows the "absolute purity" of decision and unleashes "the force of real life."[1] The state of exception, transcendent of all place and time, was elevated from a once pathological finding to the rank of a kind of universal legal formula.

For the time being, Giorgio Agamben has taken the last dip in this pool of emotion. In his explorations through the history of humankind, he suddenly came across the *Justitium*, in which he believes he has found the historical reassurance for Carl Schmitt's apodictic sayings. The ancient *Justitium*, according to Agamben in his *State of Exception*, published in 2004, is in fact the "archetype of the modern *Ausnahmezustand*."[2] In times of extreme internal or external danger—war or civil war—ancient Rome preferred to suspend all law rather than violate it in individual cases. The suspension of justice was in reality a suspension of law in general, "a zone of absolute indeterminacy between anomie and law, in which the sphere of creatures and the juridical order are caught up in a single catastrophe." Big words. The primal grammar of the state of exception revolves around a vacuum, a moment that is uncontaminated by any legal agenda and therefore allows for a truly political act. And because since Carl Schmitt there has been an unspoken obligation to describe such places of longing as melodramatically as possible, Agamben sees through the prism of *Justitium* nothing other than "life itself."

In the historiographical derivation of all these pious reflections, Agamben has uncovered only a meager footnote. His sole source is Adolph Nissen, a criminal law professor from Straßburg, who made a foray into civil law in 1877 and put forward similar theses in a peculiar treatise on *Justitium*. For a short time, the scholarly literature granted Nissen the polite status of an outsider's view, before this reprieve was exhausted and his colleague's civilist poaching was concealed behind embarrassing silence.[3] One hundred years later, Agamben came along, triumphantly proclaimed his literary discovery and declared the oft-refuted outsider a prophet.

The true prophet eluded him. Heinrich van Huyssen, a shifty diplomat from Essen, happened to be in Speyer in 1689 when the French arrived and destroyed the *Reichskammergericht* ("Imperial Chamber Court"). For some, it was an act of war, for others, a doctoral thesis: *De Justitio. Vom Stillstand des Gerichts*,[4] was the title of Huyssen's dissertation, with which he brought the enforced suspension of law to its legal application, a meticulous list of every problem that could ever have arisen in a universal history of *Justitium*: war, plague, famine, fire—with and without fault—poisoned air, storms, earthquakes, floods, whether wills could be validly drawn up, who owed default interest for what period, whether there were special termination rights for leases, which court employees were to be remunerated how, etc. and so on. Long, often agonizingly detailed distinctions about every conceivable aspect that could require legal attention if law was suspended. In this legal vacuum, things are apparently more legalistic than almost anywhere else in the world.

Nissen does not mention Huyssen, nor does Agamben. Instead, they traipse through the history of the world like tourists. Without realizing it, Agamben sinks a good 400 years into the black hole of "life itself," during which time work is done on the legal embalming of the state of exception. Agamben has thus also missed the peculiar way in which life itself breaks through when entrusted to the intercession of lawyers. With Huyssen, a representative of the intellectual featherweight, proclaimed the age of legal grandeur, an impostor who only needed his doctorate for the button placket of his diplomatic suits and therefore—*noblesse oblige*—did not write his dissertation himself.

Huyssen enrolled in Strasbourg on 15 February 1689, when the siege of Speyer was still in full swing. Fourteen weeks later, with the ruins of the *Reichskammergericht* still smoking, he finished his 95 pages of densely printed Latin.[5] An inexperienced amateur researcher producing a print-ready page every day for three months? Huyssen's money needed intellect. The war granted him the help of Johann Deckher, a lawyer from the *Reichskammergericht* and excellent writer, who had fled Speyer before the destruction and was now left with nothing in Strasbourg. In retrospect, Huyssen freely admitted that from Deckher he had "learned a lot through many conversations."[6] You can guess the rest. The rich Huyssen demoted the poor Deckher to his personal scribe. Huyssen later boasted that he had even been offered a professorship for his masterpiece. He declined, instead traveling carefree through Europe and becoming propaganda chief for the Russian Tsar in 1702. Deckher stayed behind and died in Strasbourg in 1694.

At the beginning of the modern *Justitium*, there was indeed a catastrophe in the creaturely sphere, but one quite different from what Schmitt, Agamben, and their ilk could ever have dreamed of. The first report of a lawless vacuum was bought by a vanity-seeking careerist from a refugee in need; sovereign is who decides on the state of exception.

Normality as Strategy

The lawless vacuum is a lawless dream. Heinrich van Huyssen would prove himself right: before the law is swept away by a state of exception, the pension entitlements of public officials must be examined. In the centuries after Huyssen, there was therefore no room for the ravings of political romanticism. Even when the realities of the world came close to the facts of a *Justitium*, the law kept any hint of anomie at bay. Even under the greatest pressure, it was far removed from the sterility of a normatively emptied state of exception.

The *Justitium* only became a serious threat in the late phase of the Second World War. People were prepared for it. After 1939, a separate military procedural code was created which, by making extensive use of the experiences from the First World War, was intended to free up as much personnel as possible for the front, while avoiding a suspension of law at all costs. The plan succeeded. The operational capability of the judiciary remained intact until the fall of the "Third Reich." Despite all the bureaucratic adversities—without files, without staff, without buildings, and ultimately even beyond the traditional court locations—the judiciary retained the ability to tailor right and wrong to individual cases. This required an administrative effort that exceeded the norm in every respect. The rule of law came under increasing pressure due to the reduction in jurisdiction, exemptions for politically sensitive areas, protective custody, and revision of judgments. But where the judiciary was still active, it was also able to draw on a large part of its traditional arsenal of actions, with which in principle any disturbance from the environment could be legally operationalized.

This was an attractive proposition for everyone involved: the everyday, routine, and uniform nature of legal administration offered both legal professionals and their audience the reassuring illusion of undisturbed normality. The world was not yet out of joint, the courts had letters and seals, and even the most servile subordination still remained a form of order. The formal language and vocabulary of civil society remained applicable. Court personnel were given the opportunity to escape conscription by being particularly active. The economy, always dependent on predictable and binding decisions, could continue to rely on the judiciary to resolve blockages in its cycle. Citizens, in turn, could indulge in the idea of an untroubled everyday life, a paper refuge whose clean black and white became all the more appealing the more confusing and dirtier the rest of the world became. The country might be in ruins, but court hearings were taking place, and if an army of elegantly dressed constables, clerks, registrars, record keepers, and judges were actually on hand to handle one's affairs, then things could not be so bad in the rest of the world.

And last but not least, the regime benefited from the legal normality that was repeatedly flaunted. Even the totalitarian state depended on stabilization measures that it could not guarantee itself. Without the normative state, the prerogative state would have neither functioned nor found acceptance. Without the ordinary, even the horrific would have remained formless. Only between the psychosocial supports of the law could the ideological state of exception unfold at all—in an orderly fashion, so to speak. In the fields of normality, the regime offered its citizens options for action whose integrative power ensured identification with the state far beyond these fields. The form of law, however insignificant the content conveyed might have been in individual cases, was a playground for cognitive dissonance, an invitation to live in empty rhetoric. This was not suitable for a government program. But it was the prerequisite for any government program. For all its contempt for the sluggishness of the normative state, even in its wildest activities the prerogative state remained dependent on the predictable order of the normative state. Even in the notorious political criminal law, pockets of normality persisted, and even for industrial mass murder, the normal services of the judiciary were useful. Land registers were also created for the concentration camps.

Civilization or Perversion

These mechanisms had not lost their value after 1945. Where the war had severed the legal lines of conversation, they were now resumed. Forms continued to be filled out, case numbers updated, trials continued. The social services of everyday life continued to provide comfort. Through the *Justitium*, the most diverse layers of time could be connected, while everything that separated these layers was degraded to mere interim period, a blending mechanism that can be interpreted technically as a kind of legal cryonics and literarily as a self-imposed Sleeping Beauty slumber. At some point, things will move on; and if they are completely different from before, then they will still be normal. Even the first codifications of the modern era saw the conflict between the suspension of law and the progression of world time. In the Prussian Land Law of 1620, there is a sentence that describes the legal serenity in dealing with life and death with baroque wisdom: "But when the war/and the dying cease,/time resumes its course."[7]

Court records, such as those at the center of this study, are therefore at odds with the times. They document a diachronic legal transfer through which the normality of the "Third Reich" was transformed into the normality of the postwar period: experiences, expectations, claims, dreams, brought together behind a file cover to which German legal zoology has given the name *Blattsammlungshülle* ("leaf collection cover"). In criminal law it is red, in civil law it is green—but a green with a lot of dull gray mixed in, because behind the cover, alongside hopes for a better future, the abysses of the present are hidden. Chronology compresses together what should not be happening at the same time. "Not everyone is here in the same now. They are only there on the outside, by the fact that they can be seen today. But they are not yet living with the others at the same time," wrote Ernst Bloch in 1932.[8] In September 1945, a refugee from Hirschberg in Silesia wrote angrily to the Saxon Ministry of Justice. His marriage was supposed to have been dissolved in the regional court on 17 April 1945, but that this had not happened because of the enemy occupation. His wife was still in Hirschberg, and he now absolutely had to be divorced, "because I am a single man, I cannot exist so," which is why he asked that "a way be shown to me in which I can be freed from this uncertainty and ambiguity."[9]

In Ellwangen, a plaintiff sought relief from a dry rot fungus. A settlement agreement failed on 7 April 1945—a death march from the Hessental and Kochendorf concentration camps was passing through the town—but the fungus continued to grow unabated, and after several expert opinions and written statements, the plaintiff wrote angrily on 20 May 1947 that the dry rot was "slowly growing into a catastrophe" and had to be removed at all costs. After several on-site meetings with architects and engineers, expert opinions, and interviews with all residents since 1900, a settlement was reached in October 1949.[10]

In Esslingen, the catastrophe was the neighbor. Since 1938, a landlord had been arguing bitterly with a tenant whose untidiness, uncleanliness, and unruly children were disturbing the peace of the house. In 1943 the case went to court, in 1948 the plaintiff returned from an internment camp and found that the conditions were still as filthy as before, but that the defendant was now also receiving visits from gentlemen. On 31 May 1949, already visibly resigned, he had his lawyer present the argument: "This fight has been going on for 10 years." But it was no use. The male visitors did stop, but the landlord lost the case in 1950. After two more years of witness statements, accusations, and evidence, the Stuttgart Regional Court could only conclude "that the parties are hostile to one another to such an extent that peaceful coexistence appears impossible in the future."[11]

To each citizen his own war: the law created the opportunity to counter a collective state of exception with an individual state of normality, to dissociate oneself from the frailty of the world and to bring the reality experienced back into line. The normality created in this way is sometimes cheerful, sometimes exhilarating, sometimes grim, sometimes gloomy. It is never dispensable. Normality can never be eliminated without replacement. The postwar period was not the "Third Reich," and the new normality was not the old one. But the normality of law secured identity in this difference. The *Justitium* offers a stage on which to conduct a monologue, on the normal and the abnormal, in total war and in total defeat. And apparently this murmur of voices does not cease even when the content being discussed can no longer hope to resonate. The chatter of the law, however, does not bury "life itself;" it *is* life itself in all its splendor: rent disputes, insults, physical assaults, divorces, belligerence and vanity, resentment and subservience, envy and servility, the same excrements of social interaction over and over again—bureaucratically treated, legally catalogued, and finally filed away in the archive of law. To return to the quote from Hans Magnus Enzensberger: "Normality is a defensive force, but it is incapable of resignation."[12]

The anomic space is therefore a figment of the imagination, a philosophical will-o'-the-wisp. The *Justitium* is not a lawless rudiment, but on the contrary the moment of the greatest normative condensation, a potentiated normality, so to speak. Without the assistance of the law, man is in danger of losing his humanity; only with the assistance of the law does the raw flesh of the world become the noble word. The *Justitium* counters the impending natural state with an unconditional *praesumptio aeternitatis*, a postponement into eternity.

But the flesh is still there. The banality of legal service unfolded in the midst of the German collective frenzy, alongside concentration camps, death marches, but also alongside the bombing war, *Volkssturm*, occupation, and flight. The old conundrum of simultaneity: everyone fights for themselves, unable or unwilling to synchronize their own horizons of experience with that of others. Violence was omnipresent, and yet, time and again, people stubbornly referred to the tenuous power of paper. The normal did not lose its appeal even under completely abnormal circumstances. Is this the pinnacle of civilization or its ultimate perversion?

Paper World

It begins with the paper, and it ends with the paper. In the paper world of law, even memory finds grace. Looking back, the law presents the image of a frozen stream, so generously concealing the disruptions and caesuras of time that even a completely new normality looks like a continuation of the old. There could be no such thing as a "zero hour." Paper was not tolerant enough: the appropriate forms for a true new beginning were lacking. What should they have looked like? Blank, no columns to fill in, no questions to answer, history-less, timeless, unstandardized, and unpunched, without any trace of the past and without any trace of this lack of a past. Presumably, just blank white paper.

Notes

1. Schmitt, *Political Theology*, 13–21.
2. Agamben, *State of Exception*, from which the following quotations are taken. Agamben's preoccupation with the Justitium may have been prompted by the description in Livy (4, 31, 9) that in the Justitium "omnia castris quam urbi similiora."
3. Nissen, *Das Justitium*. For an overview, see Kunkel/Wittmann, *Staatsordnung und Staatspraxis*, 226.
4. Huyssen, *Justitio*. The fundamental discoveries about Huyssen (in particular the discovery of his self-biography) are due to the work of Petschauer; see "In Search of Competent Aides," 481–502. Most recently, Korzun, *Heinrich van Huyssen*.
5. The title page of the dissertation invited to the disputation on 23 May 1689, to enroll Knod, *Die alten Matrikeln*, vol. 3, 540.
6. Van Huyssens Selbstbiographie, 18 (PA Petschauer, Huyssiana II).

7. Landrecht 1620, Book 3, Titulus IV, Art. On the problem, see also Huyssen, *Justitio*, Caput I, §§ 18, 23, Caput II, §§ 20–24; similarly, Wolde, *De eo quod justum est*, Caput II, §§ 17–20.
8. Bloch, "Ungleichzeitigkeit," 104.
9. Letter from Meißen, 20 September 1945, in: HStAD, 11380 No. 377, p. 11.
10. District Court Ellwangen 3 O/1945, in: StAL, E 341 IV Zugang vom 28.12.1979 B 27 Nr. 3. The death march is documented in Blatman, Die Todesmärsche 1944/45, 119 et seq.
11. Local Court for Esslingen C 115/1944 and Local Court for Stuttgart, 8/1 S 120/1949, both in: StAL, F 264 II No. 1471. Local Court for Stuttgart, 8/1 S 120/1949, judgment of 14 September 1950, in: ibid.
12. Enzensberger, "Normalität," 224.

Bibliography

Unpublished Sources

Archives marked with an asterisk* were consulted online.

Archiwum Państwowe w Katowicach* (APK)

133	Wyższy Sąd Krajowy, Katowice (Oberlandesgericht Kattowitz)

Archiwum Państwowe w Katowicach Oddział w Bielsku-Białej (APBB)

362	Akta miasta Oświęcimia (Gemeinderat Auschwitz)
554	Sąd Obwodowy w Oświęcimiu (Amtsgericht Auschwitz)
908	Dyrekcja Dóbr Żywieckich w Żywcu (Amt des Gutes Saybusch in Saybusch)

Archiwum Państwowe w Poznaniu* (APP)

299	Reichsstatthalter im Reichsgau Wartheland—Posen

Archiwum Państwowe w Szczecinie* (APS)

141	Wyższy Sąd Krajowy w Szczecinie (Oberlandesgericht Stettin)

Archiwum Państwowe we Wrocławiu* (APW)

257	Wyższy Sąd Krajowy we Wrocławiu (Oberlandesgericht Breslau)

Bundesarchiv Bayreuth (BA)

Ost-Dok. 13	Deutsche Verwaltung in den annektierten und okkupierten Gebieten Polens, des Baltikums und der Sowjetunion 1939–1945

Bundesarchiv Berlin (BA)

DP 1	Ministerium der Justiz, Deutsche Justizverwaltung (DJV)/MdJ
R 6	Reichsminister für die besetzten Ostgebiete
R 43 I	Akten der Reichskanzlei*
R 137	Justizbehörden außerhalb des Gebietes der Bundesrepublik
R 187	Sammlung Schumacher
R 3001	Reichsjustizministerium

Bundesarchiv Koblenz (BAK)

B 120	Institut für Besatzungsfragen
B 141	Bundesministerium der Justiz
Z 21	Zentral-Justizamt für die Britische Zone

Bundesarchiv Reinickendorf (BA [PA])
Werner Günther
Dr. Hans Keutgen
Dr. Franz Langer

Generallandesarchiv Karlsruhe (GLAK)

537 Zugang 1985-37	Justizministerium Württemberg-Baden, Nebenstelle Karlsruhe

Geheimes Staatsarchiv Preußischer Kulturbesitz (GStA PK)

I. HA Rep. 84a	Justizministerium
XV. HA Rep. 76	Landgericht Stargard
XV. HA Rep. 77	Amtsgericht Stolp
XV. HA Rep. 75a	Oberlandesgericht Stettin
XVII. HA Rep. 222a	Oberlandesgericht Breslau
XVII. HA Rep. 223a	Landgericht Oppeln
XVII. HA Rep. 223b	Amtsgerichte
XX. HA Rep. 31	Oberlandesgericht Königsberg
XX. HA Rep. 38a	Amtsgericht Königsberg

Hauptstaatsarchiv Dresden (HStAD)

11380	Landesregierung Sachsen, Ministerium der Justiz
11031	Landgericht Freiberg
11045	Amtsgericht Dresden
11091	Amtsgericht Riesa

Hauptstaatsarchiv Stuttgart (HStAS)

EA 4/001	Justizministerium Württemberg-Baden

Hauptstaatsarchiv Weimar (HStAW)
Land Thüringen—Ministerium der Justiz
Oberlandesgericht Erfurt
Thüringisches Oberlandesgericht Jena
Landgericht Weimar

Het Utrechts Archief* (HUA)
1221-1-1974 Burgerlijke Stand van de gemeenten in de provincie Utrecht

Landesarchiv Greifswald (LAG)

Rep. 75	Oberlandesgericht Stettin
Rep. 76 Greifswald	Landgericht Greifswald
Rep. 76 Köslin	Landgericht Köslin
Rep. 76 Stettin (neu)	Landgericht Stettin
Rep. 76a Stettin	Landgericht Stettin Ehesachen
Rep. 77 Stralsund	Amtsgericht Stralsund

Landesarchiv Hannover (LAH)

Nds. 700	Ministerium der Justiz
Hann. 173	Oberlandesgericht Celle
Nds. 710	Oberlandesgericht Celle
Nds. 720	Landgericht Hannover
Hann. 172	Amtsgericht Hannover
Nds. 725	Amtsgericht Hannover

Landesarchiv Nordrhein-Westfalen, Abteilung Ostwestfalen-Lippe (f NRW-OL)

D 20 B	Landgericht Detmold

Landesarchiv Nordrhein-Westfalen, Abteilung Rheinland (LAV NRW-R)

NW 174	Justizministerium
NW 189	
NW 1213	
BR-Pe	Personalakten
NW-Pe	
Ger. Rep. 86	Oberlandesgericht und Generalstaatsanwaltschaft Düsseldorf
Ger. Rep. 142	
Ger. Rep. 203	
Ger. Rep. 11	Oberlandesgericht und Generalstaatsanwaltschaft Köln
Ger. Rep. 255	
Ger. Rep. 449	
Ger. Rep. 563	
Ger. Rep. 113	Staatsanwaltschaft Aachen—Sondergericht Aachen
Ger. Rep. 3	Landgericht und Staatsanwaltschaft Duisburg
Ger. Rep. 308	Landgericht Essen
Ger. Rep. 28	Landgericht Köln
Ger. Rep. 198	Landgericht und Staatsanwaltschaft Krefeld
NW 1037	Der Sonderbeauftragte für die Entnazifizierung im Lande NRW
NW 1048	
NW1049	
NW 1079	
RWN 139	Sammlung Hüttenberger zu Politik und Verwaltung in NRW nach 1945

Landeshauptarchiv Schwerin (LHAS)

6.16-6	Ministerpräsidium, Hauptabteilung Justiz
5.12-6/4	Oberlandesgericht und Generalstaatsanwaltschaft Rostock
5.12-6/5	Landgericht Güstrow
5.12-6/6	Landgericht Rostock

Oberlandesgericht Köln (Archiv OLG Köln)
Personalakte des Referendars Hans Keutgen
Personalakte über den Vorsitzenden Richter am LG Dr. Hans Keutgen
Ersatz-Personalakte des LG über Dr. Hans Keutgen
Ersatz-Personalakte des OLG betreffend Dr. Hans Keutgen

Privatarchiv Peter Petschauer (PA Petschauer)
Huyssiana II: Selbstbiographie

Privatarchiv Joachim Wenzlau (PA Wenzlau)
Interviews
Korrespondenzen

Profit Over Life* (POL)
Akten der Nürnberger Prozesse, Fall VI

Stadtarchiv Aachen
KKG, Abitur 1932, Klasse OI b.

Staatsarchiv Amberg (StAA)
Staatsanwaltschaft Amberg

Staatsarchiv Bamberg (StAB)
K 100 Oberlandesgericht Bamberg

Staatsarchiv Chemnitz (StACh)
30095 Landgericht Chemnitz
30096 Landgericht Plauen
30100 Amtsgericht Aue
30145 Amtsgericht Zwickau

Staatsarchiv Coburg (StACo)
Spruchkammer Hof/Stadt

Staatsarchiv in Eupen (StAE)
X 49 Amtsgericht Malmedy

Staatsarchiv Freiburg (StAF)
C 20/1 Badisches Ministerium der Justiz
E 159/1 Amtsgericht Freiburg

Staatsarchiv Ludwigsburg (StAL)
E 315 Landgericht Stuttgart
E 341 IV Landgericht Ellwangen
EL 300 V Oberlandesgericht Stuttgart
F 254 II Amtsgericht Besigheim
F 264 II Amtsgericht Esslingen
F 276 III Amtsgericht Kirchheim unter Teck
FL 300/2 I Amtsgericht Backnang
FL 300/10 II Amtsgericht Esslingen

Staatsarchiv Marburg (StAM)
263 Oberlandesgericht Kassel

Staatsarchiv Sigmaringen (StAS)
Wü 2 T 1 Staatskanzlei Württemberg-Hohenzollern
Wü 25 T 1 Justizministerium Württemberg-Hohenzollern

Staatsfilialarchiv Bautzen (StFilaB)
50016 Amtshauptmannschaft Zittau

Technische Universität Berlin, Zentrum für Antisemitismusforschung (TUB ZfA)
Akten der Nürnberger Prozesse, Fall VI

Unternehmensarchiv der BASF (UA BASF)
PB 4/898 Auschwitz/Buna IV

Historisches Archiv der Universität Köln (UA Köln)
Zugang 42 Rechtswissenschaftliche Fakultät, Dekanat
Zugang 600 Matrikelkartei I
Zugang 489 Matrikelkartei II
Zugang 604 Universitätskasse und Quästur

Yad Vashem Archives* (YVA)
O.51 Nazi documentation
O.2 Wiener Library Collection

Official Collections and Source Editions

ABl. B: Amtsblatt der Landesverwaltung Baden, Französisches Besatzungsgebiet, ed. von der Landesregierung Baden. Freiburg: Poppen & Ortmann, 1946–1947.

ABl. Kattowitz: Amtsblatt der Regierung in Kattowitz, 1939–1945.

ABl. KR: Official Gazette of the Control Council for Germany [...]. Berlin: Allied Secretariat, 1945–1948.

AGO: Allgemeine Gerichtsordnung für die Preussischen Staaten. Berlin: Decker, 1795.

General Instructions: Allgemeine Anweisungen für *Richter No. 2 der Militärregierung D*eutschland. Wiesbaden: Carl Ritter & Co, [1946].

ALR: Allgemeines Landrecht für die Preussischen Staaten. Berlin: Decker, 1794.

BPO Sachsen 1860: Entwurf einer bürgerlichen Prozeß-Ordnung für das Königreich Sachsen. Dresden: Heinrich, 1860.

CCM: Des Corpus Constitutionum Marchicarum Anderer Theil [...] Erste Abtheilung. Berlin: Buchladen des Waysenhauses, 1737.

CIF: Corpus Iuris Fridericianum. Berlin: Verlag der Königlichen Akademie der Wissenschaften, 1781.

Cohn: Cohn, Willy. Kein Recht, nirgends. Tagebuch vom Untergang des Breslauer Judentums 1933–1941, vol. 1, ed. Norbert Conrads. Köln: Böhlau, 2006.

Corpus iuris canonici: Friedberg, Emil and Emil Ludwig Richter, eds. Corpus Iuris Canonici, vol. 2. Leipzig: Tauchnitz, 1881.

Corpus iuris: Mommsen, Theodor and Paul Krüger, eds. *Corpus iuris civilis*, 10th edn. Berlin: Weidmann, 1905/1929.

CPO Bosnien 1883: *Civil-Proceß-Ordnung für Bosnien und Hercegovina*. Wien: Hof- und Staatsdruckerei, 1883.

CPO Siebenbürgen 1852: *Provisorische Civil-Proceß-Ordnung für das Großfürstenthum Siebenbürgen und die damit vereinigten Theile mit Einführungsverordnung*. Wien: Hof- und Staatsdruckerei, 1852.

DJ: *Deutsche Justiz. Rechtspflege und Rechtspolitik. Amtliches Blatt der deutschen Rechtspflege*, Reichsminister der Justiz. Berlin: R. v. Decker, 1933–1945.

Dokumente: Ministerium für Auswärtige Angelegenheiten der DDR, ed. *Um ein antifaschistisch-demokratisches Deutschland. Dokumente aus den Jahren 1945–1959*. Berlin: Staatsverlag, 1968.

DU: *Dziennik Ustaw (polnisches Gesetzblatt).*

EKO: *Entscheidungen des Königlichen Obertribunals*, ed. im amtlichen Auftrag von [wechselnden Herausgebern]. Berlin: Heymanns/Dümmler, 1837–1879.

Entwurf 1848: Koch, Friedrich Christian. *Entwurf einer Civil-Prozeß-Ordnung für den preußischen Staat, mit den Motiven, nebst einem Anhange, welcher einen Vorschlag über die Einrichtung des Gerichtskostenwesens und einen Gesetzentwurf über die Gerichtsgebühren enthält*. Berlin: Trautwein, 1848.

Entwurf PO Preußen 1864: *Entwurf einer Prozeß-Ordnung in bürgerlichen Rechtsstreitigkeiten für den Preußischen Staat*. Berlin: R. von Decker, 1864.

Frei: Frei, Norbert, Thomas Grotum, Jan Parcer, Sybille Steinbacher and Bernd C. Wagner, eds. *Standort- und Kommandanturbefehle des Konzentrationslagers Auschwitz 1940–1945*. München: K.G. Saur, 2000.

Gerichtsorganisation 1944: *Gerichtsorganisation des Deutschen Reiches*. Berlin: Beamtenpresse, 1944.

Gritzbach: Göring, Hermann. *Reden und Aufsätze*, ed. Erich Gritzbach. München: Franz Eher, 3rd edn. 1939.

Gruner: Gruner, Wolf and Götz Aly, eds. *Die Verfolgung und Ermordung der europäischen Juden durch das nationalsozialistische Deutschland 1933–1945*, vol. 1. Deutsches Reich 1933–1937. München: Oldenbourg, 2008.

GVBl. H: *Gesetz- und Verordnungsblatt für das Land Hessen*, ed. Hessischen Staatskanzlei. Wiesbaden: Wiesbadener Kurier, 1947.

GVBl. HH: *Hamburgisches Gesetz- und Verordnungsblatt*, ed. Senat der Freien und Hansestadt Hamburg. Hamburg: Lütcke & Wulff, 1945.

Hahn: Hahn, Carl, ed. *Die gesammten Materialien zur Civilprozeßordnung und dem Einführungsgesetz zu derselben vom 30. Januar 1877*. Berlin: R. v. Decker, 1880.

Handbuch der Justizverwaltung: *Handbuch der Justizverwaltung. Bearbeitet im Büro des Reichsjustizministeriums*. Berlin: R. v. Decker, 1942.

Handbuch der Justiz: *Handbuch der Justiz*, ed. Deutschen Richterbund. Hamburg: R. v. Decker, 1953.

Hartmann: *Adolf Hitler, Reden, Schriften, Anordnungen. Februar 1925 bis Januar 1933*. vol. 3, part 3, ed. Christian Hartmann. München: K.G. Saur, 1994.

HRPfl.: *Hannoversche Rechtspflege. Verordnungen und Mitteilungen für den Oberlandesgerichtsbezirk Celle*, ed. Justizverwaltung des Oberlandesgerichts Celle.

IMT: International Military Tribunal, ed. *Der Prozess gegen die Hauptkriegsverbrecher vor dem Internationalen Militärgerichtshof. Nürnberg, 14. November 1945–1. Oktober 1946*. Nürnberg: Internationaler Militär-Gerichtshof, 1947–1949.

JBl. AOO: Justiz-Blatt für Aurich, Oldenburg und Osnabrück, ed. Oberlandesgericht in Oldenburg. Oldenburg: Ad. Littmann Buchdruckerei, 1945–1947.

JBl. B: *Justizblatt für den Oberlandesgerichtsbezirk Braunschweig*, ed. Verwaltung des Oberlandesgerichts Braunschweig. Braunschweig: Limbach, 1946–1947.

JBl. Köln: *Justizblatt für den Oberlandesgerichtsbezirk Köln*, ed. Oberlandesgerichtspräsidenten in Köln. Moers: Brendow, 1946–1947.

JBl. WL: *Justiz-Blatt für Westfalen und Lippe*, ed. Verwaltung des Oberlandesgerichts Hamm. Hamm: Griebsch 1945–1946.

JMBl. NRW: *Justizministerialblatt für das Land Nordrhein-Westfalen*, ed. Justizministerium Nordrhein-Westfalen. Moers: Brendow, 1947.

Juristentag 1947: *Konstanzer Juristentag (Sträter): Konstanzer Juristentag (2.–5. Juni 1947)*, ed. Militärregierung des Französischen Besatzungsgebietes in Deutschland. Generaljustizdirektion. Tübingen: J.C.B. Mohr (Paul Siebeck), 1947.

Kästner: Kästner, Erich. *Das Blaue Buch. Geheimes Kriegstagebuch 1941–1945*, ed. Sven Hanuschek. Zürich: Atrium, n.d.

Klemperer: Klemperer, Victor. *Tagebücher 1942*, ed. Walter Nowojoski. Berlin: Aufbau, 1995.

Landrecht 1620: *Allgemeines Land-Recht des Hertzogthumbs Preussen*. Rostock: Augustin Ferber, 1620.

Landrecht 1685: *Churfürstlich Brandenburgisches Revidirtes Landrecht des Hertzogthumbs Preussen*. Königsberg: Friedrich Reusner, 1685.

Landrecht 1721: *Verbessertes Land-Recht des Königreichs Preussen*. Königsberg: Reussner, 1721.

Matthäus: Matthäus, Jürgen, ed. *Jewish Responses to Persecution*, vol. 3. 1941–1942. Lanham: AltaMira, 2013.

Meldungen: Heinz Boberach, ed. Meldungen aus dem Reich 1938–1945. Herrsching: Pawlak, 1984.

Moll: Moll, Martin, ed. *"Führer-Erlasse" 1939–1945*. Stuttgart: Franz Steiner, 1993.

Motive BPO Sachsen 1860: Marschner, Gustav, ed. *Motiven [sic!] zu dem Entwurfe einer bürgerlichen Prozeß-Ordnung für das Königreich Sachsen*, 1860.

Motive: *Motive zu dem Entwurfe eines Bürgerlichen Gesetzbuches für das Deutsche Reich.* Berlin: Guttentag, 1888–1896.

NCC: *Novum Corpus Constitutionum Prussico-Brandenburgensium Praecipue Marchicarum [...] 1753–1822.* From vol. 3, Berlin: Decker; from vol. 5, Berlin: Kunst.

NMT: Nuernberg Military Tribunals, ed. Trials of War Criminals Before the Nuernberg Military Tribunals Under Control Council Law N. 10. Washington: Government Printing Office, 1949–1953.

OMGUS: Karl Heinz Roth, ed. *OMGUS, Ermittlungen gegen die I.G. Farbenindustrie AG—September 1945.* Nördlingen: Greno, 1986.

PreußGS: *Gesetzsammlung für die Königlichen Preußischen Staaten [...].* Berlin: Decker.

Preußischer Terminkalender: *Preußischer Terminkalender für das Jahr 1933. Zum Gebrauch für Justizbeamte,* bearbeitet im Büro des Preußischen Justizministeriums. Parts 1 and 2. Berlin: R. v. Decker, 1932.

Project 1766: *Project des Codicis Fridericiani Marchici.* Königsberg: Johann Jacob Kanter, 1766.

Protokolle CPO NDB: *Protokolle der Ausarbeitung des Entwurfs einer Civilprozeßordnung für die Staaten des Norddeutschen Bundes.* Berlin: R. v. Decker, 1868.

RegBl. T: *Regierungsblatt für das Land Thüringen.* Part 1: *Gesetzsammlung.* Weimar: Landesverlag Thüringen, 1945–1949.

RegBl. WB: *Regierungsblatt der Regierung Württemberg-Baden.* Stuttgart: Staatsministerium, 1946–1952.

Reichsjustizkalender: *Kalender für Reichs-Justizbeamte,* part 2. Berlin: R. v. Decker, 1941.

RGBl.: *Reichsgesetzblatt,* part 1, ed. Reichsministerium des Innern. Berlin: Reichsverlagsamt, 1922–1945.

Richterbriefe: Boberach, Heinz, ed. *Richterbriefe. Dokumente zur Beeinflussung der deutschen Rechtsprechung 1942–1944.* Boppard am Rhein: Harald Boldt, 1975.

Rogall: Rogall, Joachim, ed. *Die Räumung des "Reichsgaus Wartheland" vom 16. bis 26. Januar 1945 im Spiegel amtlicher Berichte.* Sigmaringen: Jan Thorbecke, 1993.

Sammlung: *Sammlung der Gesetze, Verordnungen, Anweisungen und Anordnungen der Militärregierung Deutschland.* Krefeld: Verlag Albert Höntges: 1950.

Schoenberger: Schoenberger, Gerhard, ed. *Wir haben es gesehen. Augenzeugenberichte über Terror und Judenverfolgung im Dritten Reich.* Hamburg: Rütten & Loening, 1962.

Schramm: Schramm, Percy E., ed. *Kriegstagebuch des Oberkommandos der Wehrmacht,* vol. 8: 1944–1945, part 2 (1961). Herrsching: Manfred Pawlak, 1982.

Schubert: Werner Schubert, ed. *Reichsjustizministerium und die höheren Justizbehörden in der NS-Zeit (1935–1944). Protokolle und Mitschriften der Arbeitstagungen der Reichsjustizminister mit den Präsidenten der Oberlandesgerichte, des Volksgerichtshofs, des Reichsgerichts sowie mit den Generalstaatsanwälten.* Frankfurt am Main: Peter Lang, 2015.

Schwarzbuch: Comité des Délégations Juives, ed. *Das Schwarzbuch. Tatsachen und Dokumente. Die Lage der Juden in Deutschland 1933.* Paris, 1934. Neudruck Berlin: Ullstein, 1983.

SHAEF: Supreme Headquarters Allied Expeditionary Force (Office of the Chief of Staff), *Handbook for Military Government in Germany Prior to Defeat or Surrender.* N.p., 1945.

Tausk: Tausk, Walter. *Breslauer Tagebuch 1933–1940,* ed. Ryszard Kincel. Berlin: Rütten & Loening, 1988.

VOBl. BZ: *Verordnungsblatt für die Britische Zone. Amtliches Organ zur Verkündung von Rechtsverordnungen der Zentralverwaltungen,* ed. Zentral-Justizamt für die Britische Zone. Hamburg: Girardet & Co., 1947–1949.

VOBl. MB: *Verordnungsblatt der Provinzialverwaltung Mark Brandenburg.* Potsdam: Steiner, 1945–1946.

Wolan: Wolan, Hubert. "Świdnickie procesy narodowosocjalistycznych bojówkarzy (1929–1930)," in: *Studia Śląskie* 30 (1976), 341–362.
ZJBl. BZ: *Zentral-Justizblatt für die Britische Zone*, ed. Zentral-Justizamt für die Britische Zone. Hamburg: Rechts- und staatswissenschaftlicher Verlag, 1947–1949.
ZVBl.: *Zentralverordnungsblatt. Amtliches Organ der Deutschen Wirtschaftskommission und ihrer Hauptverwaltungen, sowie der Deutschen Verwaltungen für Inneres, Justiz und Volksbildung*, ed. von der Deutschen Justizverwaltung der sowjetischen Besatzungszone in Deutschland. Berlin: Zentralverlag, 1947–1949.

Newspaper Articles

Anonymous. "Plädoyer gegen die Todesstrafe. Landgerichtsdirektor Dr. Keutgen sprach im Roten Hörsaal—Referat und persönliche Meinung—Eindeutige Stellungnahme gegen die Todesstrafe," in: *Aachener Nachrichten*, 11 March 1959.
Anonymous. "Silberjubiläum. Dr. Keutgen 25 Jahre beim Landgericht," in: *Aachener Zeitung*, 1 February 1961.
Anonymous. "25 Jahre bei der Justiz," in: *Aachener Nachrichten*, 1 February 1961.
Anonymous. "25 Jahre bei der Justiz," in: *Aachener Volkszeitung*, 1 February 1961.
Anonymous. "Plädoyer für die Justiz. Landgerichtsdirektor Dr. Keutgen sprach über ein aktuelles Thema," in: *Aachener Nachrichten*, 21 April 1964.
Anonymous. "Dr. Hans Keutgen wird Zivilrichter," in: *Aachener Volkszeitung*, 1 December 1964.
Anonymous. "Keine Strafprozesse mehr," in: *Aachener Nachrichten*, 1 December 1964.
Anonymous. "Wechsel beim Landgericht," in: *Aachener Zeitung*, 1 December 1964.
Anonymous. "Dr. Hans Keutgen: Steckbrief eines Richters," in: *Aachener Zeitung*, 5 December 1964.
Anonymous. "Dr. Hans Keutgen. Seit 25 Jahren Presse-Dezernent. Ein Mittler zwischen Justiz und Journalismus," in: *Aachener Nachrichten*, 10 July 1971.
Anonymous. "Dr. Hans Keutgen ein Freund der Presse auch von 'Amts wegen'," in: *Aachener Volkszeitung*, 10 July 1971.
Anonymous. "Dr. Keutgen. Einmaliges Jubiläum," in: *Aachener Zeitung*, 12 July 1971.
Anonymous. "Hans Keutgen ist tot. Ehemaliger Landgerichtsdirektor wurde 86," in: *Aachener Zeitung*, 11 February 1999.

Bibliography

Adler, Hans. *Der verwaltete Mensch. Studien zur Deportation der Juden aus Deutschland.* Tübingen: J.C.B. Mohr (Paul Siebeck), 1973.
Adorno, Theodor W., Max Horkheimer and Eugen Kogon. "Die verwaltete Welt oder: Die Krisis des Individuums" (1950), in: Max Horkheimer, *Gesammelte Schriften*, vol. 13: *Nachgelassene Schriften 1949–1972*, ed. Gunzelin Schmid Noerr. Frankfurt am Main: Fischer, 1989, 121–142.
Agamben, Giorgio. *Homo sacer. Die souveräne Macht und das nackte Leben.* Frankfurt am Main: Suhrkamp, 2002.
———. *State of Exception.* Chicago: Chicago University Press, 2005.

Altstötter, Josef. "Die volksgenössische Rechtspflege im totalen Krieg. Zur Zweiten Kriegsmaßnahmenverordnung vom 27. September 1944 (RGBl. I S. 299)," in: *Deutsche Justiz* 1944, 253–262.

———. "Vereinfachung des Agrarrechts im totalen Kriege," in: *Deutsche Justiz* 1944, 285–288 and 293–295.

Amos, Heike. *Justizverwaltung in der SBZ/DDR. Personalpolitik 1945 bis Anfang der 50er Jahre*. Köln: Böhlau, 1996.

Anders, Freia. *Strafjustiz im Sudetengau 1938–1945*. München: Oldenbourg, 2008.

Anders, Helmut. "Die Demokratisierung der Justiz beim Aufbau der antifaschistisch-demokratischen Ordnung 1945–1949," in: *Jahrbuch für Geschichte*, 1973, 385–438.

Angermund, Ralph. "Die geprellten 'Richterkönige'. Zum Niedergang der Justiz im NS-Staat," in: Hans Mommsen and Susanne Willems, eds., *Herrschaftsalltag im Dritten Reich. Studien und Texte*. Düsseldorf: Schwann, 1988, 304–373.

———. *Deutsche Richterschaft 1919–1945. Krisenerfahrung, Illusion, politische Rechtsprechung*. Frankfurt am Main: Fischer, 1990.

Anonymous. "Auschwitz," in: *Allgemeine deutsche Real-Encyklopädie für die gebildeten Stände. Conversations-Lexikon*, vol. 2. Leipzig: F.A. Brockhaus, 11th edn. 1864.

Anonymous. "Dorf=Buch," in: Johann Georg Krünitz, *Oekonomische Encyklopädie*. vol. 7, 2nd edn. 1784.

Anonymous. "Flur," in: Johann Georg Krünitz, *Oekonomische Encyklopädie*. vol. 14, 2nd ed. 1786.

Anonymous. "Grundlinien der Entwicklung des deutschen Zivilrechts seit dem Zusammenbruch," in: *Archiv für civilistische Praxis* 1948, 52–59.

Anonymous. "Der Juristentag in Konstanz," in: *Deutsche Rechts-Zeitschrift* 1947, 231–234.

Anonymous. "Justitium (antiquar.)," in: Ludwig Julius Friedrich Höpfner, *Deutsche Encyclopädie oder Allgemeines Real-Wörterbuch aller Künste [...]*. vol. 18, 1794.

Anonymous. "Vermeidet Rechtsstreit! Haltet Rechtsfrieden," in: *Deutsches Recht*, 1943: 259.

Applebaum, Anne. *Der Eiserne Vorhang. Die Unterdrückung Osteuropas 1944–1956*. München: Siedler, 2013.

Arendes, Cord, Edgar Wolfrum and Jörg Zedler, eds. *Terror nach Innen. Verbrechen am Ende des Zweiten Weltkrieges*. Göttingen: Wallstein, 2006.

Arendt, Hannah. *Eichmann in Jerusalem. Ein Bericht von der Banalität des Bösen* (1963). München: Piper, 4th edn. 1976.

Asaria, Zvi. *Die Juden in Köln von den ältesten Zeiten bis zur Gegenwart*. Köln: Bachem, 1959.

Ascher, Abraham. *A Community under Siege. The Jews of Breslau under Nazism*. Stanford: SUP, 2007.

Augsberg, Steffen. "Denken vom Ausnahmezustand her," in: Felix Arndt et al., eds., *Freiheit—Sicherheit—Öffentlichkeit*. Baden-Baden: Nomos, 2009, 17–39.

Ausschuß für Deutsche Einheit, ed. *Hitlers Sonderrichter—Stützen der Adenauer-Regierung*. Berlin: n.p., October 1957.

———. *Wir klagen an. 800 Nazi-Blutrichter—Stützen des Adenauer-Regimes*. Berlin: n.p., February 1959.

Bach, Adolf. *Deutsche Volkskunde. Ihre Wege, Ergebnisse und Aufgaben. Eine Einführung*. Leipzig: S. Hirzel, 1937.

Bade, Claudia, Lars Skowronski and Michael Viebig, eds. *NS-Militärjustiz im Zweiten Weltkrieg. Disziplinierungs- und Repressionsinstrument in europäischer Dimension*. Göttingen: Vandenhoeck & Ruprecht, 2015.

Baedeker, Karl. *Das Generalgouvernement. Reisehandbuch*. Leipzig: Baedeker, 1943.

Bahlcke, Joachim and Roland Gehrke, eds. *Institutionen der Geschichtspflege und Geschichtsforschung in Schlesien. Von der Aufklärung bis zum Ersten Weltkrieg.* Köln: Böhlau, 2017.

Bajohr, Frank and Christoph Strupp, eds. *Fremde Blicke auf das 'Dritte Reich'. Berichte ausländischer Diplomaten über Herrschaft und Gesellschaft in Deutschland 1933–1945.* Göttingen: Wallstein, 2011.

Ball, Wolfgang. "Sondergerichte im Oberlandesgerichtsbezirk Zweibrücken," in: Sven Paulsen, ed., *175 Jahre pfälzisches Oberlandesgericht. 1915 Appellationshof, Oberlandesgericht 1990.* Neustadt: Meininger, 1990, 227–255.

Bär, Fred. "Die Berliner Justiz in der Besatzungszeit am Beispiel der Ziviljustiz am Amtsgericht Berlin-Mitte," in: Rainer Schröder, ed., *Zivilrechtskultur der DDR vol. 1.* Berlin: Duncker & Humblot, 1999, 31–87.

Barkai, Avraham. *"Wehr Dich!." Der Centralverein deutscher Staatsbürger jüdischen Glaubens (C. V.) 1893–1938.* München: C.H. Beck, 2002.

Bartels, Gundolf. "Zivilrechtsprechung in Oldenburg 1933–1945. Dargestellt vor allem am Beispiel des Ehe- und Familienrechts," in: Eberhard Stalljohann, ed., *175 Jahre Oberlandesgericht Oldenburg. Festschrift.* Köln: Carl Heymanns, 1989, 253–288.

Bartusel, Rolf. *"Der Generalstaatsanwalt braucht durchaus kein Jurist zu sein." Die Transformation des Rechtswesens in Mecklenburg-Vorpommern, 1945–1952.* Münster: Rhema, 2008.

Bast, Jürgen. *Totalitärer Pluralismus. Zu Franz L. Neumanns Analysen der politischen und rechtlichen Struktur der NS-Herrschaft.* Tübingen: Mohr Siebeck, 1999.

Bästlein, Klaus. "Zur 'Rechts'-Praxis des Schleswig-Holsteinischen Sondergerichts 1937–1945," in: Heribert Ostendorf, ed., *Strafverfolgung und Strafverzicht. Festschrift zum 125jährigen Bestehen der Staatsanwaltschaft Schleswig-Holstein.* Köln: Carl Heymanns, 1992, 93–185.

Baumbach, Adolf. *Die Kriegsvorschriften zum Prozeß- und Kostenrecht.* München: C.H. Beck, 1939.

———. *Zivilprozeßordnung.* München: C.H. Beck, 11th edn. 1936; 19th edn. 1950; 78th edn. 2018.

Baumgarten, Arthur. "Über die Rechtspflege in der Ostzone," in: *Neue Justiz,* 1949, 274–276.

Becker. "Volkstümliche Fassung von Anklagen und Urteilssprüchen," in: *Deutsche Justiz,* 1943, 512.

Becker, Maximilian. *Mitstreiter im Volkstumskampf. Deutsche Justiz in den eingegliederten Ostgebieten.* München: De Gruyter Oldenbourg, 2014.

Beckmann, Rainer. "Rechtsgrundlagen zur Aufhebung nationalsozialistischen Unrechts in der Strafrechtspflege," in: *JuristenZeitung* 1997, 922–930.

Bedau, Maren. *Entnazifizierung des Zivilrechts. Die Fortgeltung von NS-Zivilrechtsnormen im Spiegel juristischer Zeitschriften aus den Jahren 1945 bis 1949.* Berlin: BWV, 2004.

Bednarek, Andreas. *Gerichtsbauten in Schlesien 1815 bis 1945. Preußische Justizarchitektur zwischen Klassizismus und Moderne.* Görlitz: Oettel, 2013.

Benjamin, Hilde, ed. *Zur Geschichte der Rechtspflege der DDR 1945–1949.* Berlin: Staatsverlag, 1976.

Benjamin, Walter. "Über den Begriff der Geschichte, VIII," in: *Gesammelte Werke. vol. I/2,* ed. Hermann Schweppenhäuser and Rolf Tiedemann. Frankfurt am Main: Suhrkamp, 1991, 690–708.

Benz, Wolfgang. "Von der Entrechtung zur Verfolgung und Vernichtung. Jüdische Juristen unter dem nationalsozialistischen Regime," in: Helmut Heinrichs, Harald Franzki,

Klaus Schmalz and Michael Stolleis, eds., *Deutsche Juristen jüdischer Herkunft*. München: Beck, 1993, 813–852.

Beradt, Martin. *Der deutsche Richter*. Frankfurt am Main: Rütten & Loening, 1930.

Bergemann, Hans and Simone Ladwig-Winters. *Richter und Staatsanwälte jüdischer Herkunft in Preußen im Nationalsozialismus*. Köln: Bundesanzeiger, 2004.

Bertrand, Nicolas. *L'enfer réglementé. Le régime de détention dans les camps de con-centration*. Paris: Perrin, 2015.

Biermann, Gottlieb. *Zur Geschichte der Herzogthümer Zator und Auschwitz*. Wien: Gerold, 1863.

Biess, Frank. *Republik der Angst. Eine andere Geschichte der Bundesrepublik*. Reinbek: Rowohlt, 2019.

Billen, A. ed. *Bericht über das Schuljahr … am Kaiser-Karl-Gymnasium*, Aachen: n.p., 1926–1931.

Birmanns, Martin. "Die Aachener Justiz im Zeitalter des Nationalsozialismus," in: *Zeitschrift des Aachener Geschichtsvereins* 101 (1997/98), 209–262.

Blank, Ralf. "Kriegsalltag und Luftkrieg an der 'Heimatfront'," in: Ralf Blank, ed., *Die Deutsche Kriegsgesellschaft 1939 bis 1945. vol. 1: Politisierung, Vernichtung, Überleben*. München: Deutsche Verlags-Anstalt, 2004, 357–461.

———. "Die Kriegsendphase an Rhein und Ruhr 1944/45," in: Bernd-A. Rusinek, ed., *Kriegsende 1945. Verbrechen, Katastrophen, Befreiungen in nationaler und internationaler Perspektive*. Göttingen: Wallstein, 2004, 88–124.

Blaschke, Annette. *Zwischen "Dorfgemeinschaft" und "Volksgemeinschaft." Landbevölkerung und ländliche Lebenswelten im Nationalsozialismus*. Paderborn: Ferdinand Schöningh, 2018.

Blatman, Daniel. *Die Todesmärsche 1944/45. Das letzte Kapitel des nationalsozialistischen Massenmords*. Reinbek: Rowohlt, 2011.

Bloch, Ernst. "Ungleichzeitigkeit und Pflicht zu ihrer Dialektik" (1932), in: ibid., *Erbschaft dieser Zeit*. Frankfurt am Main: Suhrkamp, 1962, 104–126.

Bohne, Gotthold. "Kriminalpolitik und Eugenik," in: *Deutsche Juristen-Zeitung* 34 (1939), 17–27.

Boor, Hans Otto de. *Zur Reform des Zivilprozesses. Vom Sinn staatlicher und ständischer Gerichtsbarkeit. Antrittsvorlesung, gehalten vor der Leipziger Juristenfakultät*. Leipzig: Weicher, 1938.

Bosch, Friedrich Wilhelm. *Zur gegenwärtigen Lage der Zivilgerichtsbarkeit. Betrachtungen im Hinblick auf die Neuordnung Deutschlands und den Erlaß eines Besatzungsstatuts*. Schorndorf: Verlag für Personenstandswesen und Standesamtsbedarf, 1948.

Boss, Sonja. *Unverdienter Ruhestand. Die personalpolitische Bereinigung belasteter NS-Juristen in der westdeutschen Justiz*. Berlin: BWV, 2009.

Bracht, Fritz. *Die heimgekehrten Gebiete in Oberschlesien*, in: Otto H. Spatz, ed., *Wiedergewonnenes deutsches Land*. München: J.F. Lehmanns, 2nd edn. 1943.

Brand, Arthur and Leo Schnitzler. D*ie Grundbuchsachen in der gerichtlichen Praxis*. Berlin: Springer, 6th edn. 1936.

Braun, Hans, Uta Gerhardt and Everhardt Holtmann, eds. *Die lange Stunde Null. Gelenkter sozialer Wandel in Westdeutschland nach 1945*. Baden-Baden: Nomos, 2007.

Bräutigam, Otto. *So hat es sich zugetragen … Ein Leben als Soldat und Diplomat*. Würzburg: Holzner, 1968.

Breithaupt. "Die Feststellung erloschener Rechte in den eingegliederten Ostgebieten," in: *Deutsche Justiz* 1942, 251–256.

Breuning, Heinz. "Die Beschränkung der deutschen Gerichtsbarkeit durch die Besatzungsmächte." Ph.D. diss, Tübingen, 1952.

Broszat, Martin. "Siegerjustiz oder strafrechtliche 'Selbstreinigung'. Aspekte der Vergangenheitsbewältigung der deutschen Justiz während der Besatzungszeit 1945–1949," in: *Vierteljahreshefte für Zeitgeschichte* 29 (1981), 477–544.

Broszat, Martin, Klaus-Dietmar Henke and Hans Woller, eds. *Von Stalingrad zur Währungsreform*. München: Oldenbourg, 1989.

Browning, Christopher. *Ordinary Men: Reserve Police Battalion 101 and the Final Solution in Poland*. New York: HarperCollins, 1993.

Brunswig, Hans. *Feuersturm über Hamburg. Die Luftangriffe auf Hamburg im Zweiten Weltkrieg und ihre Folgen*. Stuttgart: Motorbuch-Verlag, 10th edn. 1994.

Buchholz, Karl. "Zur Ostrechtspflegeverordnung," in: *Deutsches Recht*, 1941, 2476–2481.

Buchwald, Friedrich. *Gerechtes Recht*. Weimar: Hermann Böhlau, 1947.

Bull, Hans-Joachim. "Die volkstümliche Urteilsformel," in: *Deutsche Justiz* 1943, 162–164.

Buruma, Ian. "Year Zero. A History of 1945." London: Atlantic, 2013.

Busam, Katharina. *Kriegsfolgenbewältigung in der Rechtsprechung. Der Umgang mit kriegsbedingt veränderten Umständen in der Zivilrechtsjudikatur des Landgerichts Bonn nach dem Zweiten Weltkrieg*. Tübingen: Mohr Siebeck, 2017.

Caplan, Jane. *"Jetzt judenfrei." Writing tourism in Nazi-occupied Poland*. London: German Historical Institute, 2013.

Christoffel, Edgar. *Krieg am Westwall 1944/45. Das Grenzland im Westen zwischen Aachen und Saarbrücken in den letzten Kriegsmonaten*. Trier: Akademische Buchhandlung Interbook, 1989.

Cicero. *Die politischen Reden*, ed. Manfred Fuhrmann, vol. 3. Darmstadt: WBG, 1993.

Claproth, Justus. *Einleitung in den ordentlichen bürgerlichen Proceß. Zum Gebrauche der practischen Vorlesungen. Erster Teil*. Göttingen: Vandenhoeck, 2nd edn. 1786; 3rd edn. 1795; 4th edn. 1816.

Coulon, Karl-Albert. "Nationalsozialistische Volkstumspolitik," in: *Deutsches Recht*, 1941, 2468–2471.

Dahrendorf, Ralf. *Gesellschaft und Demokratie in Deutschland*. München: Piper, 1965.

Dauer, Friederike. *Die Bibliothek des Reichsgerichts*. Graz: Wolfgang Neugebauer, 2013.

Dean, Martin. "The role of law in the seizure of Jewish property in Nazi-occupied Eastern Europe," in: Johannes Bähr and Ralf Banken, eds., *Das Europa des "Dritten Reiches." Recht, Wirtschaft, Besatzung*. Frankfurt am Main: Klostermann, 2005, 81–103.

Deist, Wilhelm. "'Blitzkrieg' or Total War? War Preparations in Nazi Germany," in: Roger Chickering and Stig Förster, ed., *The Shadows of Total War. Europe, East Asia, and the United States 1919–1939*. Cambridge: CUP, 2003, 271–283.

Deuerlein, Ernst. "Frankreichs Obstruktion deutscher Zivilverwaltungen 1945," in: *Politische Studien* 1971, 466–491.

Döblin, Alfred. *Schicksalsreise. Bericht und Bekenntnis. Flucht und Exil 1940–1948*. Frankfurt am Main: Joseph Knecht, 1949.

Donnison, Frank and Siegfried Vernon. *Civil Affairs and Military Government. North-West Europe 1944–1946*. London: Her Majesty's Stationary Office, 1961.

Dörner, Bernward. "Justiz und Judenmord. Zur Unterdrückung von Äußerungen über den Genozid an den europäischen Juden durch die deutsche Justiz," in: *Jahrbuch für Antisemitismusforschung* 4 (1995), 226–253.

———. *"Heimtücke": das Gesetz als Waffe. Kontrolle, Abschreckung und Verfolgung in Deutschland 1933–1945*. Paderborn: Schöningh, 1998.

———. "Justizterror bei weitgehender Wahrung der Form. 'Politische Delikte' vor deutschen Sondergerichten zur Sicherung des NS-Regimes," in: Justizministerium des Landes Nordrhein-Westfalen, ed., " … *eifrigster Diener und Schützer des Rechts, des nationalsozialistischen Rechts ..." Nationalsozialistische Sondergerichtsbarkeit.* Düsseldorf: Justizministerium des Landes NRW, 2007, 9–32.

Dreyer, Martin. *Die zivilgerichtliche Rechtsprechung des Oberlandesgerichts Düsseldorf in der nationalsozialistischen Zeit.* Göttingen: Vandenhoeck & Ruprecht, 2004.

Dülfer, Jost. "Frieden nach dem Zweiten Weltkrieg? Der Friedensschluß im Zeichen des Kalten Krieges," in: Bernd Wegner, ed., *Wie Kriege enden. Wege zum Frieden von der Antike bis zur Gegenwart.* Paderborn: Schöningh, 2002, 213–237.

Echternkamp, Jörn. "Im Kampf an der inneren und äußeren Front. Grundzüge der deutschen Gesellschaft im Zweiten Weltkrieg," in: ibid., ed., *Die Deutsche Kriegsgesellschaft 1939 bis 1945. Vol. 1: Politisierung, Vernichtung, Überleben.* München: Deutsche Verlags-Anstalt, 2004, 1–92.

Eckert, Astrid M. *Kampf um die Akten. Die Westalliierten und die Rückgabe von deutschem Archivgut nach dem Zweiten Weltkrieg.* Stuttgart: Franz Steiner, 2004.

Enke, Paul. "Die Rechtspflege im Volkstumskampf," in: *Deutsches Recht,* 1941, 2489–2491.

Enzensberger, Hans Magnus. "Zur Verteidigung der Normalität" (1982), in: ibid., *Politische Brosamen.* Frankfurt am Main: Suhrkamp, 1985, 207–224.

Erdsiek, Gerhard. "Chronik der Rechtsentwicklung," in: *Deutsche Rechts-Zeitschrift* 1946, 18–26.

Erker, Paul. "Revolution des Dorfes? Ländliche Bevölkerung zwischen Flüchtlingsstrom und landwirtschaftlichem Strukturwandel," in: Martin Broszat, Klaus-Dietmar Henke and Hans Woller, eds., *Von Stalingrad zur Währungsreform.* München: Oldenbourg, 1989, 367–425.

Ernst, Waltraud, ed. *Histories of the Normal and the Abnormal. Social and Cultural Histories of Norms and Normativity.* London: Routledge, 2006.

Eschrich, Wilhelm. *Beamtenrecht.* Berlin: Deutscher Rechtsverlag, 2. Auflage 1944.

Etzel, Matthias. *Die Aufhebung von nationalsozialistischen Gesetzen durch den Alliierten Kontrollrat (1945–1948).* Tübingen: Mohr Siebeck, 1992.

Evans, Richard. *The Third Reich at War.* London: Penguin, 2008.

Fechner, Fritz. "Gerichtsverfassung und Verfahren in bürgerlichen Rechtssachen nach den Verordnungen vom 1. September 1939," in: *Deutsches Recht,* 1939, 1732–1378.

———. "Das bürgerliche Recht in den eingegliederten Ostgebieten. Zu den Verordnungen vom 25. Sept. 1941 (RGBl. I, 597, 599)," in: *Deutsches Recht,* 1941, 2481–2488.

Fechner, Max, ed. *Beiträge zur Demokratisierung der Justiz.* Berlin: Dietz, 1948.

Festus, Sextus Pompeius. *De verborum significatione,* part 1, ed. Emil Thewrewk de Ponoir. Budapest: Budapestini Sumptibus academiae litterarum Hungaricae, 1889.

Finger, Jürgen, Sven Keller and Andreas Wirsching, eds. *Vom Recht zur Geschichte. Akten aus NS-Prozessen als Quellen der Zeitgeschichte.* Göttingen: Vandenhoeck & Ruprecht, 2009.

Foitzik, Jan. *Sowjetische Militäradministration in Deutschland (SMAD) 1945–1949. Struktur und Funktion.* Berlin: Akademie-Verlag, 1999.

Foljanty, Lena. *Recht oder Gesetz. Juristische Identität und Autorität in den Naturrechtsdebatten der Nachkriegszeit.* Tübingen: Mohr Siebeck, 2013.

Fraenkel, Ernst. *Der Doppelstaat. Recht und Justiz im 'Dritten Reich'* (1941). Frankfurt am Main: Fischer, 1984.

Frasch, Werner. *Kirchheim unter Teck. Aus Geschichte und Gegenwart einer Stadt und ihrer Bewohner.* Kirchheim unter Teck: Teckbote, 1985.

Frei, Norbert. *Vergangenheitspolitik. Die Anfänge der Bundesrepublik und die NS-Vergangenheit.* München: C.H. Beck, 1996.

———. *1945 und wir. Das Dritte Reich im Bewußtsein der Deutschen.* München: C.H. Beck, 2005.

Frevert, Ute. "Soldaten, Staatsbürger. Überlegungen zur historischen Konstruktion von Männlichkeit," in: Thomas Kühne, ed., *Männergeschichte—Geschlechtergeschichte. Männlichkeit im Wandel der Moderne*. Frankfurt am Main: Campus, 1996, 69–87.

Friedla, Katharina. *Juden in Breslau/Wroclaw 1933–1949*. Köln: Böhlau, 2015.

Froböß, Hellmut. "Zwei Jahre Justiz im Warthegau," in: *Deutsches Recht*, 1941, 2465 f.

Fulbrook, Mary. *A Small Town Near Auschwitz. Ordinary Nazis and the Holocaust*. Oxford: Oxford University Press, 2012.

Gaab, Jeffrey S. *Justice Delayed. The Restoration of Justice in Bavaria under American Occupation, 1945–1949*. New York: Peter Lang, 1999.

Gagern, von. "Ursachen und Auswirkungen der Verordnung über die Abwicklung der Forderungen und Schulden polnischer Vermögen vom 15. August 1941 (RGBl. I, 516)," in: *Deutsches Recht*, 1941, 2505–2509.

Gaupp, Ludwig, Friedrich Stein and Martin Jonas. *Kommentar zur Zivilprozeßordnung. Erster Band*. Tübingen: J.C.B. Mohr (Paul Siebeck), 1934.

Gebhardt, Cord. *Der Fall des Erzberger-Mörders Heinrich Tillessen. Ein Beitrag zur Justizgeschichte nach 1945*. Tübingen: Mohr Siebeck, 1995.

Gellius, Aulus. *Noctes Atticae*, ed. Carl Hosius. Vol 3. Leipzig: Teubner, 1903.

Gephart, Werner. "Versteinerte Rechtskultur. Zur kultursoziologischen Analyse von Gerichtsbauten," in: Heinz Mohnhaupt and Dieter Simon, eds., *Vorträge zur Justizforschung* 1. Frankfurt am Main: Klostermann, 1992, 401–431.

Gerhardt, Ute. *Soziologie der Stunde. Null*. Frankfurt am Main: Suhrkamp, 2005.

Geyer, Michael. "Krieg als Gesellschaftspolitik. Anmerkungen zu neueren Arbeiten über das Dritte Reich im Zweiten Weltkrieg," in: *Archiv für Sozialgeschichte* 26 (1986), 557–601.

Gimbel, John. *Amerikanische Besatzungspolitik in Deutschland 1945–1949*. Frankfurt am Main: Fischer, 1971.

Glöckner, Hans-Peter. "Die Auflösung des Reichsgerichts im Spiegel der archivalischen Überlieferung," in: FS Bernhard Diestelkamp, 1994, 421–456.

Godau-Schüttke, Klaus-Detlev. *Ich habe nur dem Recht gedient. Die "Renazifizierung" der Schleswig-Holsteinischen Justiz nach 1945*. Baden-Baden: Nomos, 1993.

Golden, Gregory. *Crisis Management During the Roman Republic. The Role of Political Institutions*. Cambridge: CUP, 2013.

Göppinger, Horst. *Die Verfolgung der Juristen jüdischer Abstammung durch den Nationalsozialismus*. Villingen: Ring-Verlag, 1963; München: C.H. Beck, 2nd edn., 1990.

Göring, Hermann. *Die Rechtssicherheit als Grundlage der Volksgemeinschaft*. Hamburg: Hanseatische Verlagsanstalt, 1935.

Görtemaker, Manfred. "In eigener Sache. Das BMJ und seine Beiträge zur Aufarbeitung der NS-Vergangenheit," in: Manfred Görtemaker and Christoph Safferling, ed., *Die Rosenburg. Das Bundesministerium der Justiz und die NS-Vergangenheit—eine Bestandsaufnahme*. Göttingen: Vandenhoeck & Ruprecht, 2013, 17–42.

Görtemaker, Manfred and Christoph Safferling, eds. *Die Akte Rosenburg. Das Bundesministerium der Justiz und die NS-Zeit*. München: C.H. Beck, 2016.

Greiser, Arthur. *Der Aufbau im Osten*. Jena: Gustav Fischer, 1942.

Grieß, Martin. *"Im Namen des Rechts." Der Oberste Gerichtshof für die Britische Zone als Höchstgericht in Zivilsachen zwischen Tradition und Neuordnung*. Tübingen: Mohr Siebeck, 2015.

Grohnert, Reinhard. *Die Entnazifizierung in Baden 1945–1949. Konzeptionen und Praxis der "Epuration" am Beispiel eines Landes der französischen Besatzungszone*. Stuttgart: Kohlhammer, 1991.

Groß, Joachim. *Die deutsche Justiz unter französischer Besatzung 1945–1949. Der Einfluss der französischen Militärregierung auf die Wiedererrichtung der deutschen Justiz in der französischen Besatzungszone*. Baden-Baden: Nomos, 2006.

Gross, Raphael. "Guilt, Shame, Anger, Indignation: Nazi Law and Nazi Morals," in: Alan E. Steinweis and Robert D. Rachlin, eds., *The Law in Nazi Germany. Ideology, Opportunism, and the Perversion of Justice*. New York: Berghahn, 2013, 89–103.

Gruchmann, Lothar. *Justiz im Dritten Reich 1933–1940. Anpassung und Unterwerfung in der Ära Gürtner*. München: Oldenbourg, 3rd edn. 2001.

———. "'Generalangriff gegen die Justiz'? Der Reichstagsbeschluß vom 26. April 1942 und seine Bedeutung für die Maßregelung der deutschen Richter durch Hitler," in: *Vierteljahreshefte für Zeitgeschichte* 2003, 509–520.

Grunsky, Wolfgang. "Gesetzesauslegung durch die Zivilgerichte im Dritten Reich," in: *Kritische Justiz* 1969, 146–162.

Günther, Hans. "'Kammergericht soll bleiben'—'ok'," in: *Deutsche Richterzeitung*, 1968, 71–76.

Haffner, Sebastian. *Geschichte eines Deutschen. Die Erinnerungen 1914–1933*. Stuttgart: DVA, 2002.

Hampe, Erich. *Der Zivile Luftschutz im Zweiten Weltkrieg. Dokumentation und Erfahrungsberichte über Aufbau und Einsatz*. Frankfurt am Main: Bernard & Graefe Verlag für Wehrwesen, 1963.

Hansen, Reimer. *Das Ende des Dritten Reiches. Die deutsche Kapitulation 1945*. Stuttgart: Klett, 1966.

Hartig, Georg Ludwig. *Anweisungen zur Holzzucht für Förster*. Marburg: Neue akademische Buchhandlung, 1791.

Hassemer, Winfried. "Strafrechtswissenschaft in der Bundesrepublik Deutschland," in: Dieter Simon, ed., *Rechtswissenschaft in der Bonner Republik. Studien zur Wissenschaftsgeschichte der Jurisprudenz*. Frankfurt am Main: Suhrkamp, 1994, 259–310.

Haun, Oscar. *Die Behandlung von Forderungen und Schulden aus der Zeit vor dem 8. Mai 1945*. München: Biederstein, 1947.

Hayes, Peter. "Die IG Farben und die Zwangsarbeit von KZ-Häftlingen im Werk Auschwitz," in: Hermann Kaienburg, ed., *Konzentrationslager und deutsche Wirtschaft 1939–1945*. Opladen: Leske + Budrich, 1996, 129–148.

———. *Industry and Ideology. IG Farben in the Nazi Era*. Cambridge: CUP, 2nd edn. 2001.

Hedemann, Justus Wilhelm. *Grundbuchrecht*. Berlin: Spaeth & Linde, 1936.

———. "Der Krieg und das bürgerliche Rechtsleben," in: *Deutsche Justiz*, 1939, 1516–1523.

Heidegger, Martin. "25 Jahre nach unserem Abiturium, 26./27. Mai 1934," in: ibid., *Gesamtausgabe. Band 16: Reden und andere Zeugnisse eines Lebensweges*. Frankfurt am Main: Klostermann, 2000, 279–284.

Heilbronn, Wolfgang. "Der Aufbau der nordrhein-westfälischen Justiz in der Zeit von 1945 bis 1948/9," in: Justizministerium NRW, ed., *Juristische Zeitgeschichte*. Vol. 5. *50 Jahre Justiz in Nordrhein-Westfalen*. Düsseldorf: Justizministerium des Landes NordrheinWestfalen, 1996, 1–60.

Heller, Hermann. *Staatslehre*, ed. Gerhart Niemeyer. Leiden: A.W. Sijthoff's Uitgeversmaatschappij N.V., 1934.

Hellpach, Willy. *Einführung in die Völkerpsychologie*. Stuttgart: Ferdinand Enke, 2nd edn. 1944.

Henke, Klaus-Dietmar. *Die amerikanische Besetzung Deutschlands*. München: Oldenbourg, 1995.

———. *Deutschland—"Zweierlei Kriegsende,"* in: Ulrich Herbert and Axel Schildt, eds., *Kriegsende in Europa. Vom Beginn des deutschen Machtzerfalls bis zur Stabilisierung der Nachkriegsordnung 1944–1948*. Essen: Klartext, 1998, 337–354.

Herbers, Matthias. *Organisationen im Krieg. Die Justizverwaltung im Oberlandesgerichtsbezirk Köln 1939–1945*. Tübingen: Mohr Siebeck, 2012.

Herbert, Ulrich. *Best. Biographische Studien über Radikalismus, Weltanschauung und Vernunft 1903–1989*. Bonn: Dietz, 1996.

Herbst, Ludolf. *Das nationalsozialistische Deutschland 1933–1945*. Frankfurt am Main: Suhrkamp, 1996.

Hermsen, Ernst. "Zum Geleit!," in: *Justiz-Blatt für Westfalen und Lippe* 1, 24 August 1945, 1.

Hetzel, Alfred. "Die Militärgerichtsbarkeit der Besatzungsmächte in Deutschland." Ph.D. diss., Tübingen, 1948.

Heym, Stefan. *Schwarzenberg*. München: Bertelsmann, 1984.

Hoeniger, Walther. "Justiz in Brandenburg—ein Rückblick," in: *Neue Justiz* 1949, 192 f.

Iluk, Łukasz. "Das deutsche Amtsgericht in Saybusch und seine Urteile aus den Jahren 1939–1945," in: Hans-Werner Retterath, ed., *Germanisierung im besetzten Ostoberschlesien während des Zweiten Weltkriegs*. Münster: Waxmann, 2018, 199–221.

Jähner, Harald. *Wolfszeit. Deutschland und die Deutschen 1945–1955*. Berlin: Rowohlt, 2019.

Jellinek, Georg. *Allgemeine Staatslehre*, ed. Walter Jellinek. Berlin: Häring, 3rd edn. 1914.

Jersak, Tobias. "Entscheidungen zu Mord und Lüge. Die deutsche Kriegsgesellschaft und der Holocaust," in: Jörn Echternkamp, ed., *Die Deutsche Kriegsgesellschaft 1939 bis 1945. Vol. 1: Politisierung, Vernichtung, Überleben*. München: Deutsche Verlags-Anstalt, 2004, 273–355.

Johe, Werner. *Die gleichgeschaltete Justiz. Organisation des Rechtswesens und Politisierung der Rechtsprechung 1933–1945 dargestellt am Beispiel des Oberlandesgerichtsbezirks Hamburg*. Frankfurt am Main: Europäische Verlagsanstalt, 1967.

Jonas, Martin. *Kommentar zur Zivilprozeßordnung*. Tübingen: Mohr Siebeck, 15th edn., 1934. 16th edn. 1943.

Kaiser, Anna-Bettina. *Ausnahmeverfassungsrecht*. Tübingen: Mohr Siebeck, 2020.

Kann, Heinz Peter. "Geschichte des Landgerichtsbezirks Trier," in: Ministerium der Justiz, ed., *50 Jahre Oberlandesgericht und Generalstaatsanwaltschaft Koblenz*. Frankfurt am Main: Peter Lang, 1996, 145–161.

Kant, Immanuel. "Metaphysische Anfangsgründe der Rechtslehre" (1797), in: *Kants Werke. Akademie-Textausgabe VI*. Berlin: Reimer, 1907 (tr. Paul Guyer, ed. Allen W. Wood, The Cambridge Edition of the Works of Immanuel Kant).

Karl, Fritz. "Zur Sitzverlegung deutscher juristischer Personen des privaten Rechts nach dem 8. Mai 1945," in: *Archiv für civilistische Praxis* 159 (1960/61), 293–319.

Keller, Sven. *Volksgemeinschaft am Ende. Gesellschaft und Gewalt 1944/45*. München: Oldenbourg, 2013.

Kempowski, Walter. *Das Echolot. Abgesang '45. Ein kollektives Tagebuch*. München: Albrecht Knaus, 2005.

Kermann, Joachim. "Das Oberlandesgericht Zweibrücken und der Aufbau einer deutschen Justizverwaltung in Lothringen 1940/41," in: Sven Paulsen, ed., *175 Jahre pfälzisches Oberlandesgericht. 1915 Appellationshof, Oberlandesgericht 1990*. Neustadt: Meininger, 1990, 207–226.

Kern, Eduard. "Die Stunde der Justiz," in: *Deutsche Rechts-Zeitschrift* 1947, 105–107.

Kershaw, Ian. *The End. Hitler's Germany 1944/45*. London: Allen Lane, 2011.

Kesseböhmer, Werner. "Aus den Jahren des Wiederaufbaus," in: Verein für Rechtsgeschichte im Gebiet des Oberlandesgerichts Hamm, ed., *Festschrift zum 150jährigen Bestehen des Oberlandesgerichts Hamm*. Hamm: Verein für Rechtsgeschichte im Gebiet des Oberlandesgerichts Hamm. Hamm: Griebsch, 1970, 133–147.

Kessler, Wolfgang. "Das 'befreite Schlesien'. Der Regierungsbezirk Kattowitz 1939–1945 in der deutschen Wahrnehmung," in: Hans-Werner Retterath, ed., *Germanisierung im besetzten Ostoberschlesien während des Zweiten Weltkriegs*. Münster: Waxmann, 2018, 17–54.

Keutgen, Hans. "Private und öffentliche Sühne im Strafrecht." Ph.D. diss., Köln, 1936.

———. "Kritische Betrachtung des Besonderen Teils des Entwurfs eines Strafgesetzbuchs (E 1960)," in: Bundeskriminalamt, ed., *Strafrechtspflege und Strafrechtsreform. Arbeitstagung im Bundeskriminalamt Wiesbaden vom 20. März bis 25. März 1961 über Strafrechtspflege und Strafrechtsreform*. Wiesbaden: BKA, 1961, 47–61.

Kewer, L. "Aus der Geschichte des Oberlandesgerichts Hamm," in: Verein für Rechtsgeschichte im Gebiet des Oberlandesgerichts Hamm, ed., *Rechtspflege zwischen Rhein und Weser. Festschrift zum 150jährigen Bestehen des Oberlandesgerichts Hamm*. Hamm: Griebsch, 1970, 43–130.

Kißener, Michael. *Zwischen Diktatur und Demokratie. Badische Richter 1919–1952*. Konstanz: UVK, 2003.

Klautke, Egbert. *The Mind of the Nation. "Völkerpsychologie" in Germany, 1951–1955*. New York: Berghahn, 2013.

Klee, Hans-Joachim. *Die bürgerliche Rechtspflege in den eingegliederten Ostgebieten und die Behandlung ehemaligen polnischen Vermögens*. Berlin: R. v. Decker, 1942.

Kleßmann, Christopher. "Kriegsende—Dimensionen, Erinnerungen, Verdrängungen," in: Bernd-A. Rusinek, ed., *Kriegsende 1945. Verbrechen, Katastrophen, Befreiungen in nationaler und internationaler Perspektive*. Göttingen: Wallstein, 2004, 211–218.

Kluckhohn, "Chronik der Rechtsentwicklung," in: *Deutsche Rechts-Zeitschrift* 1946, 178–183.

Knod, Gustav C. *Die alten Matrikeln der Universität Straßburg 1621–1793*. Vol. 3. Straßburg: J.H. Heitz, 1897.

Koch, Hannsjoachim W. *Volksgerichtshof. Politische Justiz im 3. Reich*. München: Universitas, 1988.

Köller, Jürgen von. "Der Begriff Kriegsende in Gesetzen und Verordnungen," in: *ZJBl. BZ* 1947, 75–77.

———. "Ersatzzuständigkeiten in Zivilsachen," in: *Monatsschrift für Deutsches Recht*, 1948, 450–452.

Koppel, Wolfgang. *Justiz im Zwielicht: Dokumentation. NS-Urteile, Personalakten, Katalog beschuldigter Juristen*. Karlsruhe: Koppel, 1963.

Korzun, Svetlana. *Heinrich van Huyssen (1666–1739). Prinzenerzieher, Diplomat und Publizist in den Diensten Zar Peters I., des Großen*. Wiesbaden: Harrassowitz, 2013.

Kroll, Kurt and Arthur Christiansen, eds. *Kriegssachschädenrecht. Sammlung sämtlicher Gesetze, Verordnungen, Erlasse sowie der Beschlüsse des Reichskriegsschädenamts und der Mitteilungen des Präsidenten des Reichsverwaltungsgerichts (Reichskriegsschädenamt) mit Ausnahme der Schäden der Seeschiffahrt und der Schäden außerhalb des Reichsgebiets*. Hamburg: Hanseatische Verlagsanstalt, 1945.

Kühl, Stefan. *Ganz normale Organisationen. Zur Soziologie des Holocaust*. Berlin: Suhrkamp, 2014.

Kühne, Thomas. *The Rise and Fall of Comradeship. Hitler's Soldiers, Male Bonding and Mass Violence in the Twentieth Century*. Cambridge: CUP, 2017.

Kunkel, Wolfgang and Roland Wittmann. *Staatsordnung und Staatspraxis der römischen Republik, Zweiter Abschnitt.* München: C.H. Beck, 1995.

Lang, Dieter. "Die Justiz in der Stunde Null," in: Andreas Roth, ed., *125 Jahre Amtsgerichte im heutigen Rheinland-Pfalz.* München: Luchterhand, 2004, 37–43.

Lange, Richard. "Zu neuen Ufern im Strafrecht," in: *Neue Justiz* 1947, 8.

Langer, Franz. "Die Untervollmacht." Ph.D. diss., Breslau, 1928.

Latour, Conrad F. and Thilo Vogelsang. *Okkupation und Wiederaufbau. Die Tätigkeit der Militärregierung in der amerikanischen Besatzungszone Deutschlands 1944–1947.* Stuttgart: DVA, 1973.

Lenz, Hubert. *Der Schluss-Strich? Gedanken zur Entnazisierung.* Köln: Epoche, 1948.

Lingemann, "Zur 'Erbschaft des Reichsgerichts'," in: *Deutsche Rechts-Zeitschrift* 3 (1948), 426 f.

Link, Jürgen. *Normalismus und Antagonismus in der Postmoderne. Krise, New Normal, Populismus.* Göttingen: Vandenhoeck & Ruprecht, 2018.

Litchfield, Edward H., ed. *Governing Postwar Germany.* Ithaca: Cornell University Press, 1953.

Livius, *Ab urbe condita,* ed. Wilhelm Weissenborn and Hermann Johannes Müller. Leipzig: Teubner, 1897–1900.

Loose, Ingo. "Die Enteignung der Juden im besetzten Polen 1939–1945," in: Katharina Stengel, ed., *Vor der Vernichtung. Die staatliche Enteignung der Juden im Nationalsozialismus.* Frankfurt am Main: Campus, 2007, 283–307.

Lorenz, Thomas. "Die Deutsche Zentralverwaltung der Justiz (DJV) und die SMAD in der sowjetischen Besatzungszone 1945–49," in: Hubert Rottleuthner, ed., *Steuerung der Justiz in der DDR. Einflußnahme der Politik auf Richter, Staatsanwälte und Rechtsanwälte.* Köln: Bundesanzeiger, 1994, 135–165.

Lowe, Keith. *Der wilde Kontinent. Europa in den Jahren der Anarchie 1943–1950.* Stuttgart: Klett-Cotta, 2014.

Löwenstein, Hubertus von and Volkmar Zühlsdorff. *Deutschlands Schicksale 1945–1957.* Bonn: Athenäum, 1957.

Ludyga, Hannes. *Das Oberlandesgericht München zwischen 1933 und 1945.* Berlin: Metropol, 2012.

Luhmann, Niklas. *Rechtssoziologie.* Opladen: Westdeutscher Verlag, 3rd edn. 1987.

———. *Das Recht der Gesellschaft.* Frankfurt am Main: Suhrkamp, 1993.

———. *Die Gesellschaft der Gesellschaft.* Frankfurt am Main: Suhrkamp, 1997.

———. "Gerechtigkeit in den Rechtssystemen der modernen Gesellschaft" (1973), in: ibid., *Ausdifferenzierung des Rechts.* Frankfurt am Main: Suhrkamp, 2nd edn. 1999, 374–418.

———. "Weltzeit und Systemgeschichte. Über Beziehungen zwischen Zeithorizonten und sozialen Strukturen sozialer Systeme" (1975), in: ibid., *Soziologische Aufklärung 2. Aufsätze zur Theorie der Gesellschaft.* Wiesbaden: VS, 2005, 103–133.

Maier, Hedwig and Gustav von Schmoller. *Das Besatzungsregime in den drei westlichen Besatzungszonen. Eine kritische Untersuchung der Praxis der Besatzungsmächte in den Jahren 1945–1948. Erster Teil: Die Beschränkungen der staatlichen Hoheitsgewalt und der Grundrechte.* Tübingen: Deutsches Büro für Friedensfragen, 1948.

Majer, Diemut. *'Fremdvölkische' im Dritten Reich. Ein Beitrag zur nationalsozialistischen Rechtssetzung und Rechtspraxis in Verwaltung und Justiz unter besonderer Berücksichtigung der eingegliederten Ostgebiete.* Boppard: Harald Boldt, 1981.

———. *Grundlagen des nationalsozialistischen Rechtssystems. Führerprinzip, Sonderrecht, Einheitspartei.* Stuttgart: Kohlhammer, 1987.

Manthe, Barbara. *Richter in der nationalsozialistischen Kriegsgesellschaft. Beruflicher und privater Alltag von Richtern des Oberlandesgerichtsbezirks Köln, 1939–1945*. Tübingen: Mohr Siebeck, 2013.

Markovits, Inga. *Diener zweier Herren. DDR-Juristen zwischen Recht und Macht*. Berlin: Christoph Links Verlag, 2020.

Marxen, Klaus. *Das Volk und sein Gerichtshof. Eine Studie zum nationalsozialistischen Volksgerichtshof*. Frankfurt am Main: Klostermann, 1994.

Marxen, Klaus and Holger Schlüter. *Terror und "Normalität." Urteile des nationalsozialistischen Volksgerichtshofs 1934–1945*. Eine Dokumentation. Düsseldorf: JM NRW, 2004.

Maurer, Trude. "Vom Alltag in den Ausnahmezustand: Juden in der Weimarer Republik und im Nationalsozialismus 1918–1945," in: Marion Kaplan, ed., *Geschichte des jüdischen Alltags in Deutschland. Vom 17. Jahrhundert bis 1945*. München: C.H. Beck, 2003, 388–410.

Meinck, Jürgen. "Justiz und Justizfunktion im Dritten Reich," in: *Zeitschrift für Neuere Rechtsgeschichte*, 1981, 28–39.

Meiß, Wilhelm. "Pachtnotrecht und Kriegsende," in: *Süddeutsche Juristenzeitung* 1946, 172–174.

Melsheimer, Ernst. "Zu einer neuen Justiz," in: *Neue Justiz*, 1947, 26.

———. "Kriegslieferungsverträge sind nichtig!," in: *Neue Justiz*, 1948, 11–13.

———. "Vom politischen und unpolitischen Richter," in: *Neue Justiz*, 1950, 70–73.

Meyer, Georg. *Lehrbuch des deutschen Staatsrechts*, ed. Gerhard Anschütz. München: Duncker & Humblot, 7th edn. 1919.

Meynen, Johann. *Das Gesetz über Umzugskostenvergütung der Beamten vom 3. Mai 1935 mit Durchführungsverordnung einschl. der Bestimmungen über Trennungsentschädigung und Beschäftigungsvergütung und Sondervorschriften*. Berlin: Bath, 4th edn. 1937.

Mommsen, Hans. *Beamtentum im Dritten Reich. Mit ausgewählten Quellen zur nationalsozialistischen Beamtenpolitik*. Stuttgart: Deutsche Verlags-Anstalt, 1966.

Mommsen, Theodor. *Römisches Staatsrecht. Vol. 1*. Leipzig: S. Hirzel, 2nd edn. 1876.

Morin, Edgar. *Das Jahr Null. Ein Franzose sieht Deutschland*. Berlin: Volk und Welt, 1948.

Moritz, Günther. *Gerichtsbarkeit in den von Deutschland besetzten Gebieten* 1939–1945. Tübingen: Institut für Besatzungsfragen, 1955.

———. *Die Gerichtsbarkeit in besetzten Gebieten. Historische Entwicklung und völkerrechtliche Würdigung*. Tübingen: Institut für Besatzungsfragen, 1959.

Morris, Douglas G. "Discrimination, Degradation, Defiance. Jewish Lawyers under Nazism," in: Alan E. Steinweis and Robert D. Rachlin, ed., *The Law in Nazi Germany. Ideology, Opportunism, and the Perversion of Justice*. New York: Berghahn, 2013, 105–135.

Mühlmann, Wilhelm. *Die Völker der Erde*. Berlin: Deutscher Verlag, 1944.

Müller, Rolf-Dieter, ed. *Der Zusammenbruch des Deutschen Reiches*. München: Deutsche Verlags-Anstalt, 2008.

Mundt, J. "Das Zuständigkeitsergänzungsgesetz vom 7. August 1952," in: *Neue Juristische Wochenschrift* 1952, 1279–1281.

Naimark, Norman M. *Die Russen in Deutschland. Die sowjetische Besatzungszone 1945 bis 1949*. Berlin: Propyläen, 1997.

Niermann, Hans-Eckhard. *Die Durchsetzung politischer und politisierter Strafjustiz im Dritten Reich. Ihre Entwicklung aufgezeigt am Beispiel des OLG-Bezirks Hamm*. Düsseldorf: Justizministerium des Landes NRW, 1995.

Niethammer, Lutz. *Die Mitläufer-Fabrik. Die Entnazifizierung am Beispiel Bayerns*. Berlin: Colloquium, 1982.

Nissen, Adolph. *Das Justitium. Eine Studie aus der römischen Rechtsgeschichte*. Leipzig: J.M. Gebhardt, 1877.

Olechowski, Thomas. "Auflassung," in: *Handwörterbuch zur Rechtsgeschichte* 1 (2008), Sp. 339–342.

Ostler, Fritz. *Die deutschen Rechtsanwälte, 1871–1971*. Essen: Ellinghaus & Co., 1971.

Payk, Ernst. *Die Geschichte der 206. Infanterie-Division 1939–1944*. Bad Nauheim: Hans-Henning Podzun, 1952.

Petschauer, Peter. "In Search of Competent Aides: Heinrich van Huyssen and Peter the Great," in: *Jahrbücher für Geschichte Osteuropas* 26 (1978), 481–502.

Pohl, Dieter. *Justiz in Brandenburg 1945–1955. Gleichschaltung und Anpassung*. München: Oldenbourg, 2001.

Pungs, Wilhelm, Karl Buchholz and Joseph Wolany. *Die Ost-Rechtspflege-Verordnung und Erste Ost-Rechtspflege-Durchführungsverordnung*. Berlin: Walter de Gruyter, 1943.

Raape, Leo. *Deutsches internationales Privatrecht. Anwendung fremden Rechts. Ein Grundriß*. Berlin: Franz Vahlen, 2nd edn. 1945.

Radbruch, Gustav. "Gesetzliches Unrecht und übergesetzliches Recht," in: *Süddeutsche Juristenzeitung* 1946, 105–108.

Rademacher, H. "Die Kriegsverschollenheit," in: *Neue Juristische Wochenschrift* 1948, 258–260.

Raim, Edith. *Justiz zwischen Diktatur und Demokratie. Wiederaufbau und Ahndung von NS-Verbrechen in Westdeutschland 1945–1949*. München: Oldenbourg, 2013.

Rass, Christoph, René Rohrkamp and Peter M. Quadflieg. *Gerhard Graf von Schwerin und das Kriegsende in Aachen. Ereignis, Mythos, Analyse*. Aachen: N.p. 2007.

Reichardt, Sven and Wolfgang Seibel, eds. *Der prekäre Staat. Herrschen und Verwalten im Nationalsozialismus*. Frankfurt am Main: Campus, 2011.

Reuß, Ernst. *Berliner Justizgeschichte. Eine rechtstatsächliche Untersuchung zum strafrechtlichen Justizalltag von 1945–1952, dargestellt anhand der Strafgerichtsbarkeit des Amtsgerichts Berlin-Mitte*. Berlin: Nomos, 2000.

Reuß, Wilhelm. *Kriegsschäden-Recht*. Stuttgart: Forkel, 1944.

Riezler, Erwin. "Fragen des interzonalen Zivilprozeßrechts," in: *Süddeutsche Juristenzeitung* 1947, 233–240.

Roemer, Walter. "Wiederaufbau des Rechts—Ein Rückblick," in: *Süddeutsche Juristenzeitung* 1947, 93–101.

Röhreke, Heinrich. "Die Besatzungsgewalt auf dem Gebiete der Rechtspflege." Ph.D. diss., Tübingen, 1950.

Roth, Karl Heinz. "I.G. Auschwitz. Normalität oder Anomalie eines kapitalistischen Entwicklungssprungs?," in: *1999. Zeitschrift für Sozialgeschichte des 20. und 21. Jahrhunderts*, 1989(4): 11–28.

Rottleuthner, Hubert. *Karrieren und Kontinuitäten deutscher Justizjuristen vor und nach 1945*. Berlin: BWV, 2010.

Rückert, Joachim. "Die Beseitigung des Deutschen Reiches—die geschichtliche und rechtsgeschichtliche Dimension einer Schwebelage" (2006), in: ibid., *Abschiede vom Unrecht. Zur Rechtsgeschichte nach 1945*. Tübingen: Mohr Siebeck, 2015, 166–194.

Ruscheweyh, Herbert. "Die Entwicklung der hanseatischen Justiz nach der Kapitulation bis zur Errichtung des Zentral-Justizamtes," in: *FS Kiesselbach*, 1947, 37–71.

Rusinek, Bernd-A. *Gesellschaft in der Katastrophe. Terror, Illegalität, Widerstand. Köln 1944/45*. Essen: Klartext, 1989.

Rüthers, Bernd. *Die unbegrenzte Auslegung. Zum Wandel der Privatrechtsordnung im Nationalsozialismus*. Tübingen: Mohr Siebeck, 1968.

Salmasius, Claudius. *De modo usurarum liber*. Leiden: Ex Officina Elseviriorum, 1639.

San Nicolò, Mariano and Artur Steinwenter, eds. *Festschrift für Leopold Wenger. Zu seinem 70. Geburtstag dargebracht von Freunden, Fachgenossen und Schülern. Zweiter Band.* München: C.H. Beck, 1945.

Schädler, Sarah. *'Justizkrise' und „Justizreform" im Nationalsozialismus. Das Reichsjustizministerium unter Reichsjustizminister Otto Thierack (1942–1945).* Tübingen: Mohr Siebeck, 2009.

Schiffer, Eugen. *Die deutsche Justiz. Grundzüge einer durchgreifenden Reform.* München: Biederstein, 2nd ed. 1949.

Schiller, Christof. *Das Oberlandesgericht Karlsruhe im Dritten Reich.* Berlin: Duncker & Humblot, 1997.

Schlegelberger, Franz. "Kriegs-Zivilrecht, einst und jetzt." Eine Übersicht, in: *Deutsche Justiz* 1939, 1881 f.

Schmaltz, Florian. "Die IG Farbenindustrie und der Ausbau des Konzentrationslagers Auschwitz 1941–1942," in: *Sozial Geschichte*, 21 (2006): 33–67.

Schmid, Richard. *Justiz in der Bundesrepublik.* Pfullingen: Neske, 1967.

Schmidt, Herbert. '*Beabsichtige ich, die Todesstrafe zu beantragen'. Die nationalsozialistische Sondergerichtsbarkeit im Oberlandesgerichtsbezirk Düsseldorf 1933–1945.* Essen: Klartext, 1998.

Schmitt, Carl. *Politische Theologie. Vier Kapitel zur Lehre von der Souveränität* (1922). Berlin: Duncker & Humblot, 8th edn. 2004.

———. *Die geistesgeschichtliche Lage des heutigen Parlamentarismus.* Berlin: Duncker & Humblot, 1923.

Schmoller, Gustav von. *Das Wirtschaftsrecht in Böhmen und Mähren. Eine Einführung in die Rechtsgrundlagen und Methoden der Wirtschaftslenkung im Bereich der gewerblichen Wirtschaft.* Brünn, München and Wien: Rudolf von Rohrer, 1945.

Schneider, Herbert. "Erfahrungen mit dem Kriegsverfahrensrecht," in: *Deutsches Recht*, 1940, 1688–1690.

———. "Die Kriegsmaßnahmenverordnung," in: *Deutsches Recht*, 1943, 778–780.

Schneider, Ute. "Der deutsche Einheitsjurist in der frühen DDR. Elitenbildung beim Aufbau der DDR-Justiz," in: *Archiv für Sozialgeschichte* 39 (1999), 235–264.

Scholz, Franz. *Die Rechtssicherheit.* Berlin: Walter de Gruyter, 1955.

———. *Ein Leben für die Gerechtigkeit. Erinnerungen.* Berlin: Walter de Gruyter, 1955.

Scholz, Friedrich. *Berlin und seine Justiz. Geschichte des Kammergerichtsbezirks 1945–1980.* Berlin: Walter de Gruyter, 1982.

Schönke, Adolf. *Das Zivilprozeßrecht des Krieges. Insbesondere VereinfachungsVO., SchutzVO., ZahlungsfristVO.* Berlin: R. v. Decker, 1940.

———. *Zivilprozeßrecht.* Berlin: R. v. Decker, 2nd ed. 1943.

Schorn, Hubert. *Festgabe zur Wiederkehr des Tages des 100jährigen Bestehens des Landgerichts Bonn. Zur Geschichte des Landgerichts in Bonn.* Bonn: Soennecken, 1950.

———. *Der Richter im Dritten Reich.* Frankfurt am Main: Klostermann, 1959.

Schröder, Rainer. *'… aber im Zivilrecht sind die Richter standhaft geblieben!' Die Urteile des OLG Celle aus dem Dritten Reich.* Baden-Baden: Nomos, 1988.

Schuler. "Die bei der Besetzung anhängigen Rechtsmittel in Zivilsachen," in: *Süddeutsche Juristenzeitung*, 1946, 34.

Schwab, Dieter. "Entwicklungen im Familienrecht vor und nach 1945," in: Manfred Görtemaker and Christoph Safferling, eds., *Die Rosenburg. Das Bundesministerium der Justiz und die NS-Vergangenheit—eine Bestandsaufnahme.* Göttingen: Vandenhoeck & Ruprecht, 2013, 296–326.

Seibel, Wolfgang. *Verwaltung verstehen. Eine theoriegeschichtliche Einführung.* Berlin: Suhrkamp 2016.

Setkiewicz, Piotr. "Ausgewählte Probleme aus der Geschichte des IG Werkes Auschwitz," in: *Hefte von Auschwitz* 22 (2002), 7–147.

———. *The Histories of Auschwitz IG Farben Werk Camps 1941–1945*. Oświęcim: Auschwitz-Birkenau State Museum, 2008.

Siemens, Daniel. *Stormtroopers. A New History of Hitler's Brownshirts*. New Haven: Yale University Press, 2017.

Simon, Dieter. "Vorurteile und Werturteile in der rechtshistorischen Forschung zum Nationalsozialismus," in: Michael Stolleis, ed., *NS-Recht in historischer Perspektive*. München: Oldenbourg, 1981, 33–52.

———. "Waren die NS-Richter 'unabhängige Richter' im Sinne des § 1 GVG?," in: Bernhard Diestelkamp and Michael Stolleis, eds., *Justizalltag im Dritten Reich*. Frankfurt am Main: Fischer, 1988, 11–25.

Stackelberg, Curt Freiherr von. *Das bürgerliche Kriegsrecht einschließlich der kriegsrechtlichen Bestimmungen des Handels- und Verfahrensrechts*. Bad Oeynhausen: August Lutzeyer, 1940.

Staud, Eberhard. "Die bürgerliche Rechtspflege in Kriegszeiten," in: *Deutsche Justiz*, 1939, 1481–1484.

———. "Kriegsmaßnahmenverordnung und Zivilprozeß," in: *Deutsche Justiz*, 1943, 273–275.

———. "Die Schutzverordnung vom 4. Dezember 1943," in: *Deutsche Justiz*, 1944, 49 f.

Steidle, "Der Plan für den Aufbau des Rechtspflegewesens in der Amerikanischen Zone," in: *Süddeutsche Juristenzeitung*, 1946, 13–15.

Stein, Friedrich and Martin Jonas. *Kommentar zur Zivilprozessordnung*. Tübingen: Mohr Siebeck, 17th edn. 1949.

Steinbacher, Sybille. *'Musterstadt' Auschwitz. Germanisierungspolitik und Judenmord in Ostoberschlesien*. München: K.G. Saur, 2000.

Stephenson, Jill. *Hitler's Home Front. Württemberg under the Nazis*. London: Hambledon, 2006.

Stolleis, Michael. *Gemeinwohlformeln im nationalsozialistischen Recht*. Berlin: J. Schweitzer, 1974.

———. "Rechtsordnung und Justizpolitik 1945–1949" (1982), in: ibid., *Recht im Unrecht. Studien zur Rechtsgeschichte des Nationalsozialismus. Mit einem neuen Nachwort*. Frankfurt am Main: Suhrkamp, 2nd edn. 2005, 247–274.

———. "Vorurteile und Werturteile der rechtshistorischen Forschung zum Nationalsozialismus" (1982), in: ibid., 36–56.

———. Recht im Unrecht," in: ibid., 7–35.

———. "Nachwort," in: ibid., 335–342.

Stuckart, Wilhelm. "Führung und Verwaltung im Kriege," in: *Jahrbuch der Akademie für Deutsches Recht*, 1939, 1–20.

———. *Führung und Verwaltung im Kriege*. Berlin: Spaeth & Linde, 1941.

Sueton. *De Vita Caesarum VII*, ed. Maximilian Ihm. Leipzig: Teubner, 1907.

Süß, Dietmar. *Tod aus der Luft. Kriegsgesellschaft und Luftkrieg in Deutschland und England*. München: Siedler, 2011.

Szanajda, Andrew. *The Restoration of Justice in Postwar Hesse 1945–1949*. Lanham: Lexington, 2007.

Tacitus. *Annales*, ed. Ludwig Maenner (1923). Berlin: de Gruyter, 2014.

Taylor, Frederick. *Zwischen Krieg und Frieden. Die Besetzung und Entnazifizierung Deutschlands 1944–1946*. Berlin: Bloomsbury, 2011.

Tessin, Georg. *Verbände und Truppen der deutschen Wehrmacht und Waffen-SS im Zweiten Weltkrieg 1939–1945. Sechster Band: Die Landstreitkräfte 71–130; Achter Band: Die Landstreitkräfte 201–280*. Osnabrück: Biblio, 1972 f.

Thiele, Gerhard. "Die Bestrafung des Treibers beim Jagdvergehen des § 292 StGB." Ph.D. diss., Breslau, 1928.

Thierack, Otto. "Sammlung der Kräfte!," in: *Deutsche Justiz*, 1943, 65 f.

———. "Deutsche Rechtswahrer! Meine Mitarbeiter!," in: *Deutsche Justiz*, 1944, 1.

———. "Deutsche Rechtswahrer! Meine Mitarbeiter!," in: *Deutsche Justiz*, 1945, 1.

Thiessen, Jan. "Wirtschaftsrecht und Wirtschaftsrechtler im Schatten der NS-Vergangenheit," in: Manfred Görtemaker and Christoph Safferling, eds., *Die Rosenburg. Das Bundesministerium der Justiz und die NS-Vergangenheit—eine Bestandsaufnahme*. Göttingen: Vandenhoeck & Ruprecht, 2013, 204–295.

Thompson, Dominik A. *Krieg ohne Schaden. Vertragsstreitigkeiten und Haftpflichtprozesse im Kontext von Kriegswirtschaft und Amtshaftungskonjunktur ausgehend von der Rechtsprechung des Landgerichts Bonn während des Zweiten Weltkriegs (1939–1945)*. Tübingen: Mohr Siebeck, 2015.

Thüsing, Andreas. *Demokratischer Neubeginn? Aufbau, Organisation und Transformation des Sächsischen Justizministeriums 1945–49*. Dresden: Hannah-Arendt-Institut für Totalitarismusforschung, 2003.

Ullrich, Volker. *Acht Tage im Mai. Die letzte Woche des Dritten Reiches*. München: C.H. Beck, 2020.

Van Huyssen, Heinrich. *De Justitio. Vom Stillstand des Gerichts*. Argentorati: Johann Friedrich Spoor, 1689.

Versnel, Hendrik Simon. "Destruction, *devotio* and despair in a situation of anomy: the mourning for Germanicus in triple perspective," in: Ugo Bianchi et al., eds., *Perennitas. Studi in onore di Angelo Brelich*. Rom: Edizioni dell'Ateneo, 1980, 541–618.

Virailly, Michael. *Die internationale Verwaltung Deutschlands vom 8. Mai 1945 bis 24. April 1947*. Baden-Baden: Régie autonome des publications officielles, 1948.

Vismann, Cornelia. *Akten. Medientechnik und Recht*. Frankfurt am Main: Fischer, 2000.

Vogel. "Bemerkungen zur KriegsmaßnahmenVO und zur KriegsbeschwerdeVO," in: *Deutsche Notarzeitschrift*, 1943, 187–190.

Vollnhals, Clemens, ed. *Entnazifizierung. Politische Säuberung und Rehabilitierung in den vier Besatzungszonen 1945–1949*. München: dtv, 1991.

Von Gruenewaldt, Arthur. *Die Richterschaft des Oberlandesgerichts Frankfurt am Main in der Zeit des Nationalsozialismus. Die Personalpolitik und Personalentwicklung*. Tübingen: Mohr Siebeck, 2015.

Von Hodenberg, Freiherr. "Der Aufbau der Rechtspflege nach der Niederlage von 1945," in: *250 Jahre Oberlandesgericht Celle. 1711–1961*. Celle: Pohl, 1961, 121–153.

Vurgun, Oskar. *Die Staatsanwaltschaft beim Sondergericht Aachen*. Berlin: Duncker & Humblot, 2017.

Wagner, Albrecht. *Die Umgestaltung der Gerichtsverfassung und des Verfahrens- und Richterrechts im nationalsozialistischen Staat*. Stuttgart, 1968.

Wagner, Bernd C. *IG Auschwitz. Zwangsarbeit und Vernichtung von Häftlingen des Lagers Monowitz 1941–1945*. München: K.G. Saur, 2000.

Wagner, Walter. *Der Volksgerichtshof im nationalsozialistischen Staat (1974)*. München: Oldenbourg, 2001.

Waibel, Dieter. *Von der wohlwollenden Despotie zur Herrschaft des Rechts. Entwicklungsstufen der amerikanischen Besatzung Deutschlands. 1944–1949*. Tübingen: J.C.B. Mohr (Paul Siebeck), 1996.

Walk, Joseph. *Kurzbiographien zur Geschichte der Juden 1918–1945*. München: K.G. Saur, 1988.

Walk, Joseph, ed. *Das Sonderrecht für die Juden im NS-Staat*. Heidelberg: C.F. Müller, 2nd edn. 1996.

Weber, Hellmuth von. Die Bedeutung der "Allgemeinen Anweisung an Richter" No. 1, in: *Süddeutsche Juristenzeitung* 1946, 238–240.

Weber, Max. *Wirtschaft und Gesellschaft*. Tübingen: J.C.B. Mohr (Paul Siebeck), 1922.

Weber, Petra. *Justiz und Diktatur. Justizverwaltung und politische Strafjustiz in Thüringen 1945–61*. München: Oldenbourg, 2000.

Weber, Wilhelm. *Der Einfluß des Krieges und der Kriegsfolgen auf die privaten Rechtsverhältnisse*. Heidelberg: Lambert Schneider, 1947.

Weinkauff, Hermann. *Die deutsche Justiz und der Nationalsozialismus*. Stuttgart: Deutsche Verlagsanstalt, 1968.

Weinke, Annette. *Die Verfolgung von NS-Tätern im geteilten Deutschland. Vergangenheitsbewältigungen 1949–1969 oder: eine deutsch-deutsche Beziehungsgeschichte im Kalten Krieg*. Padenborn: Schöningh, 2002.

Welsh, Helga A. *Revolutionärer Wandel auf Befehl? Entnazifizierungs- und Personalpolitik in Thüringen und Sachsen (1945–1948)*. München: Oldenbourg, 1989.

Welzel, Hans. *Naturalismus und Wertphilosophie im Strafrecht. Untersuchungen über die ideologischen Grundlagen der Strafrechtswissenschaft*. Mannheim: Deutsches Druck- und Verlagshaus, 1935.

———. *Naturrecht und materiale Gerechtigkeit. Prolegomena zu einer Rechtsphilosophie*. Göttingen: Vandenhoeck & Ruprecht, 1951, 4th edn. 1962.

Welzer, Harald. *Täter. Wie aus ganz normalen Menschen Massenmörder werden*. Frankfurt am Main: Fischer, 2005.

Wentker, Hermann, ed. *Volksrichter in der SBZ/DDR 1945 bis 1952*. München: Oldenbourg, 1997.

———. *Justiz in der SBZ/DDR 1945–1953. Transformation und Rolle ihrer zentralen Institutionen*. München: Oldenbourg, 2001.

Wenzlau, Joachim Reinhold. *Der Wiederaufbau der Justiz in Nordwestdeutschland 1945 bis 1949*. Königstein: Athenäum, 1979.

Werle, Gerhard. *Justiz-Strafrecht und polizeiliche Verbrechensbekämpfung im Dritten Reich*. Berlin: Walter de Gruyter, 1989.

Werner, Stefan. *Wirtschaftsordnung und Wirtschaftsstrafrecht im Nationalsozialismus*. Frankfurt am Main: Peter Lang, 1991.

White, Joseph Robert. "IG Auschwitz. The Primacy of Racial Politics." Ph.D. diss., Nebraska, 2000.

Wieczorek, Bernhard. *Zivilprozeßordnung und Nebengesetze auf Grund der Rechtsprechung kommentiert*. Vol. 1. Berlin: Walter de Gruyter, 1957; 2nd edn. 1976.

Wildt, Michael. "Die politische Ordnung der Volksgemeinschaft. Ernst Fraenkels Doppelstaat neu betrachtet" (2003), in: ibid., *Die Ambivalenz des Volkes. Der Nationalsozialismus als Gesellschaftsgeschichte*. Berlin: Suhrkamp, 2019, 261–278.

———. "'Wir wollen in unserer Stadt keine Juden sehen'. Antisemitismus und Volksgemeinschaft in der deutschen Provinz" (2004), in: ibid., 117–134.

———. *Volksgemeinschaft als Selbstermächtigung. Gewalt gegen Juden in der deutschen Provinz 1919 bis 1939*. Hamburg: Hamburger Edition, 2007.

Wirsich, K. "Die siedlungspolitische Bedeutung der Schuldenabwicklung in den eingegliederten Ostgebieten," in: *Deutsche Justiz*, 1942, 373–376.

Wittreck, Fabian. *Die Verwaltung der Dritten Gewalt*. Tübingen: Mohr Siebeck, 2006.

Wolany, Joseph. "Das Zwangsvollstreckungsrecht in den eingegliederten Ostgebieten auf Grund der verschiedenen Beschlagnahmen," in: *Deutsches Recht*, 1941, 2494–2500.

———. "Geltung und Geltungsbereich des deutschen Zivilrechts in den eingegliederten Ostgebieten." Ph.D. diss., Posen, 1942.

Wolde, Caspar. *Dissertatio juris publici: De eo quod justum est durande justitio*. Halle: Christoph Andrea Zeitler, 1705.

Wolf, Gerhard. *Ideologie und Herrschaftsrationalität. Nationalsozialistische Germanisierungspolitik in Polen*. Hamburg: Hamburger Edition, 2012.

Wrobel, Hans. *Verurteilt zur Demokratie. Justiz und Justizpolitik in Deutschland 1945–1949*. Heidelberg: Decker & Müller, 1989.

Zechner, Johannes. *Der deutsche Wald. Eine Ideengeschichte*. Darmstadt: Philipp von Zabern, 2016.

Zink, Harold. *The United States in Germany 1944–1955*. Princeton: Van Nostrand, 1957.

Index

www.ingramcontent.com/pod-product-compliance
Ingram Content Group UK Ltd.
Pitfield, Milton Keynes, MK11 3LW, UK
UKHW021837150926
8656IPUK00004B/28

9 781836 956266